- You can return this item to any Bournemouth library but not all libraries are open every day.

- Items must be returned on or before the due date. Please note that you will be charged for items returned late.

- Items may be renewed unless requested by another customer.

- Renewals can be made in any library, by telephone, email or online via the website. Your membership card number and PIN will be required.

- Please look after this item - you may be charged for any damage.

Bournemouth
Libraries

www.bournemouth.gov.uk/libraries

Contents

CREATAS IMAGES / GETTY IMAGES ©

VENETIAN HARBOUR, RETHYMNO P107

ALAN BENSON / GETTY IMAGES ©

DAKOS P43

Contents

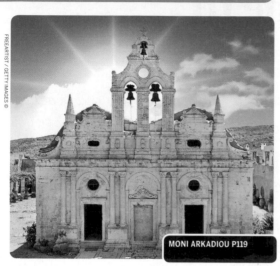

FREEARTIST / GETTY IMAGES ©

MONI ARKADIOU P119

Welcome to Crete

Crete is a tapestry of splendid beaches, ancient treasures, and landscapes encompassing vibrant cities and dreamy villages, where locals share their traditions, cuisine and generous spirit.

Bewitching Scenery

There's something undeniably artistic in the way the Cretan landscape unfolds, from the sun-drenched beaches in the north to the rugged canyons spilling out at the cliff-lined southern coast. In between, valleys cradle moody villages, and round-shouldered hills rise to snow-dabbed mountains. Take it all in on a driving tour, trek through Europe's longest gorge, hike to the cave where Zeus was born or cycle among orchards on the Lasithi Plateau. Leave time to plant your footprints on a sandy beach, and boat, kayak or snorkel in the crystalline waters.

Rich Historical Tapestry

Crete's natural beauty is equalled only by the richness of its history. The island is the birthplace of the first advanced society on European soil, the Minoans, who ruled some 4000 years ago. Evocative vestiges include the famous Palace of Knossos. At the crossroads of three continents, Crete has been coveted and occupied by consecutive invaders. History imbues Hania and Rethymno, where labyrinthine lanes – laid out by the Venetians – are lorded over by mighty fortresses, and restored Renaissance mansions rub rafters with Turkish mosques. The Byzantine influence stands in magnificent frescoed churches and monasteries.

Bountiful Cuisine

If you're a foodie, you will be in heaven in Crete, where 'locavore' is not a trend but a way of life. Rural tavernas often produce their own meat, cheese, olive oil, *raki* and wine, and catch their own seafood. Follow a gourmet trail across the landscape and you'll delight in distinctive herbs and greens gathered from each hillside, cheeses made fresh with unique village- or household-specific recipes, and honey flavoured by mountain herbs. The Cretan diet is among the healthiest in the world. Pair your meal with excellent local wine, and cap it off with a fiery shot of *raki*.

Village Culture

Crete's spirited people champion their unique culture and customs, and time-honoured traditions remain a dynamic part of the island's soul. Look for musicians striking up a free-form jam on local instruments, like the stringed *lyra*, or wedding celebrants weaving their time-honoured traditional regional dances. Meeting regular folk gossiping in *kafeneia* (coffee houses), preparing their Easter feast, tending to their sheep or celebrating during the island's many festivals is what makes a visit to Crete so special.

Why I Love Crete

By Alexis Averbuck, Author

It's said in Greece that Crete could be its own country. Not only is that absolutely true, but the more I travel its seashores and explore its mountain villages, and see how proud and true Cretans are to their ways of life, the more I see why it stands apart, a rich, intriguing land. Crete offers the chance to luxuriate on pink-sand beaches, then zip inland to mountain-rimmed gorges and quiet villages where locals are happy to jaw with a foreign visitor. Crete feels huge. Is that its heart or its landscape? I'd say both.

For more about our authors, see page 288.

Crete

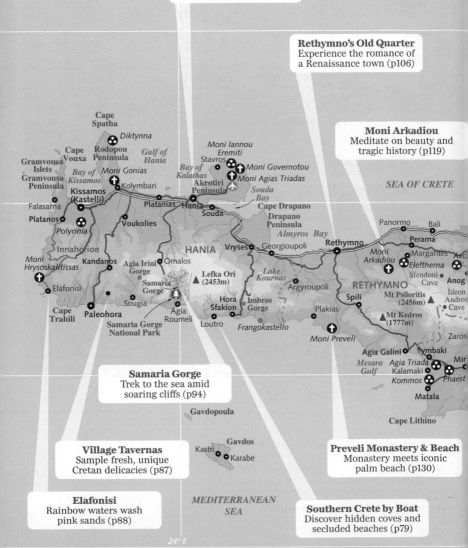

MEDITERRANEAN SEA

Hania's Old Town
Stroll the charming Venetian harbour (p56)

Rethymno's Old Quarter
Experience the romance of a Renaissance town (p106)

Moni Arkadiou
Meditate on beauty and tragic history (p119)

SEA OF CRETE

Cape Spatha
Diktynna
Cape Vouxa
Rodopou Peninsula
Gulf of Hania
Moni Iannou Eremiti
Stavros
Moni Governotou
Gramvousa Islets
Bay of Kissamos
Moni Gonias
Bay of Kalathas
Moni Agias Triadas
Gramvousa Peninsula
Kolymbari
Akrotiri Peninsula
Souda Bay
Falasarna
Kissamos (Kastelli)
Platanias
Hania
Cape Drapano
Panormo
Bali
Platanos
Souda
Drapano Peninsula
Perama
Polyrinia
Voukolies
Almyros Bay
Rethymno
Margarites
Axo
Innahorion
HANIA
Vryses
Georgioupoli
Moni Arkadiou
Eleftherna
Moni Hrysoskalitissas
Kandanos
Agia Irini Gorge
Omalos
Lefka Ori (2453m)
Lake Kournas
Sfendoni Cave
Anog
Elafonisi
Samaria Gorge
Argyroupoli
RETHYMNO
Mt Psiloritis (2456m)
Ideon Andro
Cave
Sougia
Hora Sfakion
Imbros Gorge
Spili
Cape Trahili
Paleohora
Samaria Gorge National Park
Agia Roumeli
Loutro
Frangokastello
Plakias
Mt Kedros (1777m)
Zaros
Moni Preveli
Agia Galini
Tymbaki
Mir
Mesara Gulf
Agia Triada
Kalamaki
Phaest
Kommos
Matala
Cape Lithino

Samaria Gorge
Trek to the sea amid soaring cliffs (p94)

Gavdopoula

Village Tavernas
Sample fresh, unique Cretan delicacies (p87)

Gavdos
Kastri
Karabe

Preveli Monastery & Beach
Monastery meets iconic palm beach (p130)

Elafonisi
Rainbow waters wash pink sands (p88)

MEDITERRANEAN SEA

Southern Crete by Boat
Discover hidden coves and secluded beaches (p79)

24° E

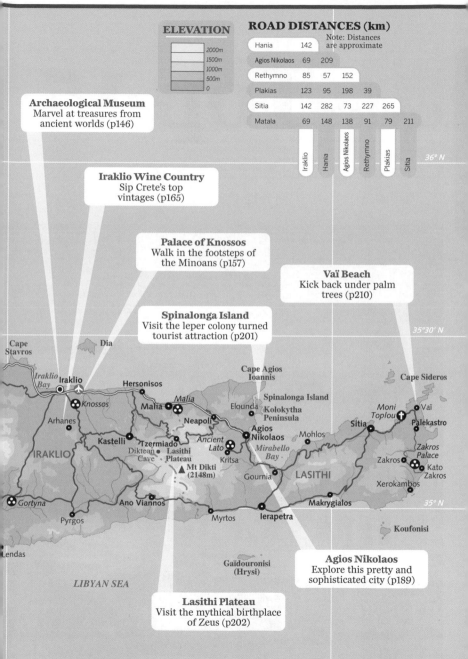

ELEVATION

2000m
1500m
1000m
500m
0

ROAD DISTANCES (km)

Note: Distances are approximate

	Iraklio	Hania	Agios Nikolaos	Rethymno	Plakias	Sitia
Hania	142					
Agios Nikolaos	69	209				
Rethymno	85	57	152			
Plakias	123	95	198	39		
Sitia	142	282	73	227	265	
Matala	69	148	138	91	79	211

Archaeological Museum
Marvel at treasures from ancient worlds (p146)

Iraklio Wine Country
Sip Crete's top vintages (p165)

Palace of Knossos
Walk in the footsteps of the Minoans (p157)

Vaï Beach
Kick back under palm trees (p210)

Spinalonga Island
Visit the leper colony turned tourist attraction (p201)

Agios Nikolaos
Explore this pretty and sophisticated city (p189)

Lasithi Plateau
Visit the mythical birthplace of Zeus (p202)

36° N

35°30' N

35° N

34°30' N

25°E

26° E

Cape Stavros

Iraklio Bay • Iraklio

Dia

Hersonisos

Malia

Malia

Neapoli

Cape Agios Ioannis

Spinalonga Island

Elounda • Kolokytha Peninsula

Agios Nikolaos

Mirabello Bay

Mohlos

Moni Toplou ✝

Vaï

Cape Sideros

Sitia

Palekastro

Knossos

Arhanes

Kastelli

Tzermiado •

Dikteon Cave •

Lasithi Plateau

Ancient Lato

Kritsa

IRAKLIO

▲ Mt Dikti (2148m)

LASITHI

Gournia

Zakros ◦

Zakros Palace

Kato Zakros

Xerokambos

Gortyna

Ano Viannos

Myrtos

Ierapetra

Makrygialos

Pyrgos

Koufonisi

Lendas

LIBYAN SEA

Gaïdouronisi (Hrysi)

Crete's Top 15

Hania's Old Town

1 You will be enthralled by Hania's old town (p56). At its romantic and captivating Venetian harbour, pastel-coloured historic townhouses rim the waterfront promenade, where tourists and locals stroll, gossip and people-watch as the sparkling sea swirls between a peachy portside mosque, cream-stone lighthouse and the imposing Firkas Fortress. In the winding old streets radiating out from the quay, you'll find minarets, boutique hotels and some of the island's best dining options. The Splantzia quarter offers cool, leafy cafes and shops filled with handmade and hard-to-find traditional goods.

Elafonisi

2 It's the beach everyone promises to see while in Crete, though not everyone manages to fulfil the promise, hidden as it is deep in the wild southwest of the island, beyond the craggy mountains and little villages. Elafonisi (p88) is a long, sandy stretch renowned for its sparkling, clear turquoise waters and pink-and-cream sands. It gets busy in high summer, but in autumn, when most visitors disappear, it is heavenly. Wade out to Elafonisi's tiny tidal island and feel the warm southern winds… bliss.

JON ARNOLD IMAGES / GETTY IMAGES ©

PIOTRWZK / SHUTTERSTOCK ©

Palace of Knossos

3 Rub shoulders with the ghosts of the Minoans, a Bronze Age people who attained an astonishingly high level of civilisation and ruled large parts of the Aegean from their capital in Knossos (p157) some 4000 years ago. Until the site's excavation in the early 20th century, a wealth of frescoes, sculptures, jewellery, seals and other remnants lay buried under the Cretan soil. Despite a controversial partial reconstruction, Knossos remains one of the most important archaeological sites in the Mediterranean and is Crete's most-visited tourist attraction. Top: Throne Room (p161)

Heraklion Archaeological Museum

4 A treasure trove spanning thousands of years, this museum (p146) opens a fascinating window onto the ancient world. Prime billing goes to the world's largest and finest Minoan collection, and with its recently renovated building and grounds, it's become a superbly curated feast of priceless artefacts from other periods as well. A visit will deeply enrich your understanding of Knossos and the other famous archaeological sites on the island. If you see only one museum in Crete, make it this one.

Southern Crete by Boat

5 This is for escapists, beach lovers and adventurers – and it's so easy! Large sections of southern Crete's mountainous coast are accessible only by boat, and a frequent ferry service allows you to access remarkable sites, such as the glittering jewel of Loutro (p79), tucked between secluded beaches, and laid-back Sougia, with its friendly folk and fresh seafood. The beginning and end of the voyage – Paleohora and Hora Sfakion – represent two of the most iconic (and affordable) towns in Crete, full of rugged individuals and live Cretan music.
Top: Loutro (p79)

Samaria Gorge

6 The gaping gorge of Samaria (p94), starting at Omalos and running down through an ancient riverbed to the Libyan Sea, is the most-trod canyon in Crete – and with good reason. The magnificent gorge is home to varied wildlife, soaring birds of prey and a dazzling array of wildflowers in spring. It's a full day's walk (about six hours down), and you'll have to start early, but the scenery is worth it. To get more solitude, try lesser-known gorges such as Agia Irini, Imbros and Aradena, running roughly parallel to Samaria.

WALTER BIBIKOW / GETTY IMAGES ©

Rethymno's Old Quarter

7 Traffic fades to a quiet hum in the lanes of this historic old quarter (p106) with its charismatic Renaissance-era Venetian buildings sprinkled with exotic features from the Turkish period. Embark on an aimless wander and you'll find wonderful surprises: a romantic flower-filled courtyard, perhaps, or an idyllic plaza, a cafe in an Ottoman bathhouse or a Venetian mansion turned boutique hotel. Don't miss a spin around the massive fortress and cap your old-quarter exploration with dinner in one of the many excellent restaurants.

Spinalonga Island

8 Fast becoming one of Greece's most iconic sights, this one-time leper colony has shot to stardom, thanks to the bestselling romantic novel *The Island,* by British writer Victoria Hislop. The book was adapted as a Greek television series (*To Nisi*) that has won critical acclaim for its atmospheric take on Spinalonga's powerful history. You may have to share the experience with fellow admirers, but Spinalonga (p201), with its ruins of Venetian fortifications and reconstructed buildings of the period described in the novel, is both moving and inspiring.

Agios Nikolaos

9 Agios Nikolaos (p189) is well established as one of the loveliest towns in Crete. The setting on the Gulf of Mirabello – the Venetians' 'beautiful view' – is a winner, and the town's pleasing layout around a small harbour and circular lake adds to the appeal. You can relax by day in the lakeside cafes and then enjoy the nighttime scene when an influx of visitors from nearby resorts mixes happily with modish young locals in the harbourside bars.

Preveli Monastery & Beach

10 Get high on the knockout views from this 17th-century monastery (p130) in its lofty eyrie above the Libyan Sea, then descend down to Preveli Beach, whose rare grove of palm trees makes it one of Crete's most celebrated sandy strips. There's fantastic swimming, but in peak season you won't be alone. The monastery itself has repeatedly entered the tomes of history, the last time during WWII when the local abbot facilitated the evacuation of 5000 Allied soldiers trapped in Crete during the Nazi occupation.

Iraklio Wine Country

11 South of the urban sprawl of Iraklio lies sylvan hillsides quilted with olive groves and vineyards and dotted with villages whose pride and joy is their local vintage. About 70% of Crete's excellent wine comes from the Iraklio Wine Country (p165). A relatively relaxed and old-world region, the wine country is based around the gateway villages of Arhanes, also home to crumbling Minoan ruins, and Dafne, which share two dozen wineries between them. The region is particularly lively in the autumn, when the grapes are harvested.

Below: winemaker in Dafnes (p163)

Vaï Beach

12 This is where Crete takes on the feel of the South Seas with this exotic beach of golden sand backed by a deep forest of palm trees. Vaï (p210) means 'palm frond' in the local dialect and the palms are said to have sprouted from date stones cast off by Roman soldiers or pirates. Vaï is a popular place, of course, but on the quieter edges of summer it's a pleasure, and during busy times just follow your nose to either end of the beach for less-crowded options.

ABB PHOTO / SHUTTERSTOCK ©

STEFAN LAWS / GETTY IMAGES ©

Moni Arkadiou

13 Moni Arkadiou (p119) offers one of those particularly moving experiences: a combination of beauty and tragedy. The 16th-century church and cloister enclosed by stone walls on a rolling high plain south of Rethymno appear lovely, pastoral. But the monastery was also the site of one of Crete's great tragedies. In 1866, 2000 Turkish soldiers surrounded hundreds of Cretan men, women and children here, who set off their gunpowder, killing all but one small girl, rather than surrender. The monastery remains a place of quiet contemplation, and is particularly striking in soft evening light.

Lasithi Plateau

14 Getting to the Lasithi Plateau (p202) can feel like a Jack-and-the-Beanstalk-style trip as the main access routes climb relentlessly from sea level through ever-steepening bends on scenic roads. The plateau bursts dramatically into view, when you see that the green expanse before you is surrounded by soaring mountains. The fairytale theme continues at famous Dikteon Cave, the mythical birthplace of Zeus and a cathedral-like cavernous space full of fantastical limestone features. Zeus may be long gone, but the Olympian spirit lingers on.

Top right: Dikteon Cave (p204)

Village Tavernas

15 A paramount highlight of Cretan travel is its delicious and distinctive cuisine. Make time to stop at village tavernas where you'll frequently find yourself presented with a wholesome feast at surprisingly reasonable prices, and with great pride. Don't be surprised if you're offered a complimentary sweet and *raki* at meal's end. One sure-fire spot for top Cretan treats is To Skolio (p87), in the hills near Paleohora, where local produce is crafted into inventive small dishes, and served with views of the Libyan Sea.

Need to Know

For more information, see Survival Guide (p253)

Currency
Euro (€)

Language
Greek

Visas
Generally not required for stays up to 90 days (or at all for EU nationals). Some nationalities need a Schengen Visa – check with the Greek embassy.

Money
ATMs widely available in cities, towns and larger villages. Visa and MasterCard accepted in cities and tourist centres, not in villages.

Mobile Phones
Local SIM cards can be used in European and Australian phones. Most other phones can be set to roaming. US/Canadian phones need to have a dual- or tri-band system.

Time
Eastern Europe Time (GMT/UTC plus two hours)

When to Go

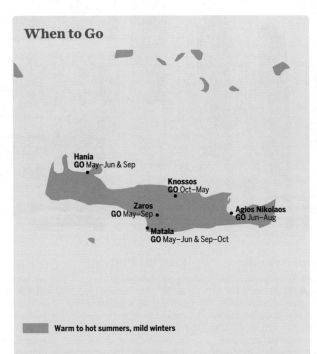

Hania
GO May–Jun & Sep

Knossos
GO Oct–May

Zaros
GO May–Sep

Agios Nikolaos
GO Jun–Aug

Matala
GO May–Jun & Sep–Oct

Warm to hot summers, mild winters

High Season (Jul & Aug)
➡ Queues at big sights, heavy traffic, busy beaches.

➡ Prices for lodgings are at their peak.

➡ *Meltemi* (dry) winds can make sandy beaches unpleasant.

➡ Hot days, but balmy evenings and warm sea for swimming.

Shoulder (Apr–Jun & Sep–Oct)
➡ Best time for hiking and outdoor activities.

➡ Moderate temperatures, smaller crowds.

➡ Wildflowers in springtime, grape harvest in autumn.

➡ Lower rates and wide availability for lodgings.

Low Season (Nov–Mar)
➡ Sights, attractions and restaurants scale back their hours; beach resorts close down.

➡ No crowds at major sights.

➡ Locals have the most time to sit and chat.

➡ Highest chance of rain.

Useful Websites

Visit Greece (www.visitgreece. gr) Greece's official tourism portal.

Explore Crete (www.explore crete.com) Good general travel site.

Interkriti (www.interkriti.org) Comprehensive guide to the island.

Lonely Planet (www.lonely planet.com/crete) Destination information, hotel bookings, traveller forum and more.

OpenSeas (www.openseas.gr) Ferry timetables.

Crete Region (www.crete-region .gr) Official government site.

Important Numbers

To call any regular number in Greece, dial the full 10-digit number.

Greece country code	☏30
International access code	☏00
Ambulance	☏166
Police/tourist police	☏100/171
Roadside assistance (ELPA)	☏104

Exchange Rates

Australia	A$1	€0.63
Canada	C$1	€0.67
Japan	¥100	€0.74
NZ	NZ$1	€0.56
UK	UK£1	€1.37
US	US$1	€0.88

For current exchange rates see www.xe.com.

Daily Costs

**Budget:
Less than €60**

➡ Hostel, camping or domatia: €10–25

➡ Picnic or meal at basic taverna: €20

➡ Bus from Hania to Elafonisi: €10

**Midrange:
€60–150**

➡ Apartment or double room in hotel: €35–80

➡ Meal at nice taverna with wine: €30–40

➡ Hire car per day: €35

**Top End:
More than €150**

➡ Double room in boutique hotel or beach resort: from €120

➡ High-end tavernas and gourmet restaurants in prime locations: €50–100

➡ Activities like diving and boat hire: €80–150

Opening Hours

Opening hours vary throughout the year. The following are high-season opening hours; hours decrease significantly in the shoulder and low seasons, when many places shut completely.

Banks 8am–2.30pm Monday–Thursday, to 2pm Friday

Bars 8pm–late

Cafes 9am–midnight

Clubs 10pm–late

Post Offices 7.30am–2pm Monday–Friday (rural); 7.30am–8pm Monday–Friday, 7.30am–2pm Saturday (urban)

Restaurants 11am–3pm & 7pm–1am

Shops 9am–2pm Monday–Saturday and 5.30–8.30pm or 9pm Tuesday, Thursday and Friday; all day in summer in resorts

Arriving in Crete

Nikos Kazantzakis International Airport (Iraklio; p262) Bus 1 (€1.10) serves the city centre every five minutes (6.15am to midnight, in summer). Taxis cost €12 to €15. Car hire at the airport.

Hania Airport Ioannis Daskalogiannis (p262) Buses serve central Hania up to 27 times daily (€2.30, 30 minutes). Taxis cost €20 (plus €2 per bag).

Sitia Airport (p262) No airport bus; taxis cost about €6.

Iraklio Ferry Port Walkable 500m to the east of the old harbour. Taxis cost about €10. The main bus station is just opposite the main entrance to the port.

Hania Ferry Port Hania buses (€1.50) meet each boat, as do buses to Rethymno. Taxis to Hania cost about €9.

Kissamos Ferry Port In summer a bus (€1.50) to town meets ferries; taxis cost around €5.

Getting Around

Car Best for keeping your own pace and visiting regions with minimal bus service. Hire cars in towns and resorts. Drive on the right. Away from main highways, roads are paved but often narrow and winding; some unpaved roads require 4WD. Locals pass boldly and straddle the shoulder if going slow, so others can pass.

Bus Service is widespread in summer and between major towns, but it's nonexistent to many small villages and some beaches, and much reduced in winter. Schedules: Western Crete (www.bus-service-crete -ktel.com) and Central & Eastern Crete (www.ktelherlas.gr).

For much more on **getting around**, see p264

First Time Crete

For more information, see Survival Guide (p253)

Checklist

➡ Ensure your passport is valid for at least six months after your arrival date.

➡ Make bookings for accommodation and travel.

➡ Check airline baggage restrictions, especially for regional flights.

➡ Inform your credit/debit card company of your travel plans.

➡ Organise travel insurance.

➡ Check if you'll be able to use your mobile (cell) phone.

What to Pack

➡ Hat, sunglasses, sunscreen

➡ Money belt

➡ Driver's licence/ international driver's licence

➡ Phrasebook

➡ Diving qualifications

➡ Phone for local SIM & charger

➡ Mainland European power adapter

➡ Lock/padlock

➡ Seasickness remedies

➡ Mosquito repellent

➡ A hollow leg – for all that *raki*

Top Tips for Your Trip

➡ If at all possible, visit in the shoulder seasons – late spring or early autumn. The weather is softer and the crowds are slim.

➡ Be sure to visit a few out-of-the-way villages where you can still find full-on, un-self-conscious traditional culture. The best way to do this is to rent a car, buy a good map, and explore. Stop for lunch, check out the local shops and test out your Greek.

➡ Visit at least one local *kafeneio* (coffee house), one seafood taverna on the waterfront, and one traditional live-music venue. This is where you'll experience Cretan culture at its most potent.

What to Wear

Crete is casual. Locals wear simple but respectfully covered-up clothes. In summer, the heat will make you want to run naked; instead bring quick-drying tops and cool dresses. Bars or fashionable restaurants require more effort – the scene is stylish rather than dressy. Don't wear swimsuits into shops and tavernas without a cover-up. Cretans take their churches seriously: don't go inside wearing hats, tank tops, short shorts or miniskirts. Sturdy walking shoes are a must for treks. Cretans will not go nude on beaches; you'll see some Europeans do it, but it pays to be respectful of locals and therefore discreet.

Sleeping

Reserving your accommodation out of season is important, as in some locations many hotels close for months on end. In high season it's equally essential as hotels can be fully booked well in advance.

➡ **Hotels** Classed from A through E, with A being five-star resort-style hotels and E having shared bathrooms and questionable hot water.

➡ **Domatia & studios** The Cretan equivalent of the British B&B, minus the breakfast. Nowadays, many are purpose-built with fully equipped kitchens.

➡ **Campgrounds** Several around the island; often include hot showers, minimarkets, restaurants and swimming pools.

Money

Cash is king in Crete. Most large towns have ATMs but they can be out of order for days at a time. It's therefore wise (and necessary) to carry extra cash in a safe place like a money belt. You can usually use debit and credit cards (Visa and MasterCard) in cities and large resorts, but check. They are rarely accepted in small villages. American Express and Diners Club are accepted in larger tourist areas but unheard of elsewhere. (Note: card companies often put an automatic block on cards after the first withdrawal/charge abroad as an antifraud mechanism. To avoid this happening, inform your bank of your travel plans.) **For more information, see p258.**

Bargaining

Bargaining is acceptable in flea markets and markets, but elsewhere you are expected to pay the stated price.

Tipping

➡ **Restaurants** Usually service is included, but a small tip is customary if service was good. Round up the bill or leave 10%.

➡ **Taxis** Round up the fare by a couple of euros. There's a small fee for handling bags; this is an official charge, not a tip.

➡ **Bellhops** Bellhops in hotels or stewards on ferries expect a small gratuity of €1 to €3.

Language

Tourism is big business in Crete and being good business people, many Cretans have learned the tools of the trade – English. In cities and popular resorts, you can get by with less than a smattering of Greek; in smaller villages or out-of-the-way spots, a few phrases in Greek will go a long way. Wherever you are, Cretans will hugely appreciate your efforts to speak their language.

For more on language, see p269.

Etiquette

➡ **Eating & dining** Meals are commonly laid in the middle of the table and shared. Always accept an offer of a drink as it's a show of goodwill (unless it's an unwanted advance). Don't insist on paying if invited out; it insults your hosts. In restaurants, the pace of service might feel slow; dining is a drawn-out experience in Crete and it's impolite to rush waitstaff.

➡ **Photography** If a sign says no photography, honour it. This goes for camera-phones and tablets, too. In churches, avoid using a flash or photographing the main altar, monks or nuns, which is considered taboo. At archaeological sites, you may be stopped from using a tripod, which marks you as a professional and thereby requires special permissions.

➡ **Places of worship** If you plan to visit churches, carry a shawl or long sleeves and a long skirt or trousers to cover up in a show of respect.

➡ **Body language** If you feel you're not getting a straight answer, you might need literacy in Cretan body language. 'Yes' is a swing of the head and 'no' is a curt raising of the head or eyebrows, often accompanied by a 'ts' click-of-the-tongue sound.

Eating

Like much of Europe, the Cretans dine late and many restaurants don't open their doors for dinner until after 7pm. You will only need reservations in the most popular restaurants and these can usually be made a day in advance.

➡ **Taverna** Informal and often specialising in seafood, chargrilled meat or traditional homestyle baked dishes.

➡ **Estiatorio** More formal restaurant serving similar fare to tavernas or international cuisine.

➡ **Mezedhopoleio** Serves mezedhes (small dishes, like tapas); an *ouzerie* is similar but serves a round of ouzo with a round of mezedhes.

➡ **Kafeneio** One of Greece's oldest traditions, serving coffee, spirits and little else. Traditionally a male domain.

If You Like...

Beaches & Islets

Balos Go tropical on this incredibly photogenic lagoon-like sandy beach. (p99)

Elafonisi Pink sands and warm waters extending across shallow isles make this Crete's most magical beach. (p88)

Gavdos Island The southernmost spot in Europe gives a sense of happy isolation outside busy August. (p89)

Vaï Watch out for falling dates as you revel in Europe's largest natural palm forest. (p210)

Preveli Beach Crete's 'other' famous palm beach at the confluence of river and sea amid cave-combed cliffs. (p130)

Falasarna Take in splendid sunsets and waves on this long, sandy ribbon. (p97)

Agios Pavlos For crowd-free tanning, head to the sand dunes spilling into this isolated southern-coast beach. (p131)

Spinalonga Island Absorb the island's poignant, powerful history, even among summertime crowds. (p201)

Enchanting Villages

Hora Sfakion This whimsical southern port boasts larger-than-life characters and a long, colourful history. (p77)

Argyroupoli Devour trout while surrounded by rushing natural springs in this ancient mountain village. (p117)

Mohlos Minoan antiquity meets seashore vibes and some of Crete's best tavernas. (p204)

Kritsa In the heart of the mountains, Kritsa offers fine craftwork and an atmospheric old town. (p197)

Myrthios See if you can spot Africa from this whitewashed village high above the Libyan Sea. (p129)

Amari In the heart of pastoral Amari Valley, and dotted with Byzantine churches. (p120)

Theriso Recharge your batteries at this historically significant mountain village in thick forest south of Hania. (p91)

Food & Drink

Iraklio Wine Country Sample fine vintages on a tasting tour of Crete's largest wine-growing region. (p165)

Agreco Farm Visit a showcase of traditional, organic farming at this enchantingly located farm. (p107)

Maroulas Cretan hillsides are redolent with sage, thyme and other herbs. Learn their medicinal purposes at a herb shop in Maroulas. (p114)

Thalassino Ageri Watch the sun set while dining on Crete's most expertly prepared seafood. (p66)

Taverna Iliomanolis The village taverna, one of the delights of travelling through Crete, is a must. (p128)

Brink's Brewery The only brewery in Crete, and a good one at that. (p127)

Outdoor Adventures

Mt Psiloritis For the ultimate fitness fix, climb Crete's highest peak and escape the summer heat. (p125)

Lasithi Plateau Strap on your helmet and cycle among orchards, fields and windmills. (p202)

Kapetaniana Fire up the adrenalin as you rock climb around the cliffs and clefts with expert guides. (p181)

Palekastro Catch Crete's wildest winds at Kouremenos Beach, the island's top windsurfing venue. (p211)

Aradena Gorge Trek to the Libyan Sea through this serene and spectacular cousin of Samaria Gorge. (p79)

Falasarna Crash headlong into the breakers rolling in from the open Med at this pristine beach. (p97)

Museums

Heraklion Archaeological Museum A must for every visitor to Crete: the island's top collection of Minoan and other artefacts. (p146)

Nikos Kazantzakis Museum Discover what the famous Cretan writer was up to when not writing *Zorba the Greek*. (p166)

Lychnostatis Museum Time travel to a traditional Cretan village. (p183)

Museum of Cretan Ethnology Fascinating immersion into centuries of Cretan daily life. (p176)

Ierapetra Archaeological Museum Marvel at a marble Persephone and abstract images on ancient coffins. (p215)

Art & Archaeology

Knossos Crete's marquee Minoan site; ideally paired with Heraklion Archaeological Museum. (p157)

Malia Spectacular Minoan palace complex on the northern coast, with excavations still ongoing. (p185)

Kato Zakros Hike the Valley of the Dead along ancient burial sites to reach the ruins of Minoan Zakros Palace. (p211)

Polyrrinia This Dorian stronghold offers spectacular sea and mountain views from its Acropolis. (p101)

Late Minoan Cemetery of Armeni Beautiful oak forest with 231 tombs carved into the rock between 1300 and 1150 BC. (p125)

Phaestos Second most important Minoan complex after Knossos, with awe-inspiring panoramas of Messara Plain and Mt Psiloritis. (p172)

PLAN YOUR TRIP IF YOU LIKE...

Top: Nikos Kazantzakis Museum (p166), Myrtia
Bottom: Mohlos (p204)

Month by Month

January

Winter is the time
when Cretans have the
island pretty much to
themselves. Views of the
snow-capped mountains
are tremendous, but cold
and windy weather makes
this a good month for
museums and churches.

New Year's Day (Feast of St Basil)

A day of gift-giving, singing, dancing, feasting and
the slicing of the *vasilopita*
(golden glazed cake). The
person who gets the piece of
cake with the hidden coin is
promised a lucky year.

Epiphany (Blessing of the Waters)

The day of Christ's baptism
by St John, 6 January, is
celebrated by seas, lakes
and rivers being blessed by
a priest who then tosses a
cross into the water. The
brave soul who retrieves it
can expect a year of good
luck.

February

Carnival

Pre-Lent is celebrated with
three weeks of dancing,
masquerade balls, games
and treasure hunts, cul-
minating in a grand street
parade on the last Sunday.
The biggest party is in
Rethymno.

Shrove Monday

On the first day of Lent
(referred to as Kathara
Deftera or Clean Monday),
people take to the hills
throughout Greece to enjoy
picnicking and kite-flying.

March

Winter will soon be a
distant memory as days
get longer and sunny
days more frequent. No
swimming yet, but a great
chance to see the sights
without the crowds.

Independence Day

It's a double whammy on
25 March: military parades
and dancing commemorate
the beginning of the 1821
War of Independence, while
the Feast of the Annun-
ciation celebrates the day
when Mary discovered she
was pregnant.

April

A painter's palette of
wildflowers blankets the
island as locals prepare for
the big Easter feast, giving
you a chance to experience
Cretan hospitality at its
finest.

Orthodox Easter

This is the most important
religious holiday in Greece.
Endeavour to attend some
of the Orthodox Easter
services, which include a
candlelit procession on
Good Friday evening and
fireworks at midnight on
Easter Saturday. Sunday,
feast on roast lamb. It's
often not the same date as
Catholic Easter.

May

Sunny weather and
moderate temperatures
make May the perfect

month for walking, cycling and island explorations. The countryside is redolent with thyme, sage and other aromatic herbs.

✈ May Day

There's a mass exodus to the countryside on 1 May. During picnic excursions, wildflowers are gathered and made into wreaths to decorate houses. Since this is also International Labour Day, the bigger cities stage demonstrations.

✈ Battle of Crete Anniversary

This epic battle and the Cretan resistance are commemorated during the last week of May with ceremonies, re-enactments, athletic events and folk dancing. The biggest celebrations are in Hania and Rethymno.

June

The start of summer, so time to head for the beaches before they get crowded. Gourmands rejoice in the bounty of fresh, local produce in the markets.

✈ Navy Week

Navy Week honours Crete's relationship with the sea with music, dancing, swimming and sailing. Held in late June, celebrations are especially big in Souda, near Hania.

July

Peak season starts, so you'd better be the gregarious type. Definitely

prebook if you're coast-bound or else escape the heat by heading for the hills and traditional villages. Strong winds are common.

☆ Renaissance Festival

Top international talent descends upon Rethymno for two weeks of theatre, dance and music from the Renaissance period (www.rfr.gr).

☆ Iraklio Summer Festival

Renowned local and international performers (from the Bolshoi Ballet to the Vienna State Opera) come to this high-calibre festival of dance, music, theatre and cinema, held from July to mid-September.

August

It's hot, hot, hot! The height of the festival season spills over from July when the sea is at its balmiest and ripe melons, figs, peaches and cherries jam-pack markets. It's still windy.

✈ Feast of the Assumption

The day Mary ascended to heaven, 15 August, is a major celebration that sees everyone on the move back to their villages for family reunions. Expect curtailed services and heavy traffic.

October

Autumn is a fabulous time weatherwise, but with hardly any crowds. Winds

die down and the harvest of sun-plump grapes kicks into high gear. Also a good time for exploring Crete's natural beauty on foot.

✈ Ohi Day

A simple 'no' (*ohi* in Greek) was Prime Minister Ioannis Metaxas' famous response when Mussolini demanded free passage through Greece for his troops on 28 October 1940. The date is now a national holiday with remembrance services, parades, feasting and dance.

November

Tourist resorts all but shut down in early November as the weather gets cooler and more unpredictable. The air is clear and mountains start receiving a dusting of snow. In the villages, the *raki* distilling season peaks.

✈ Moni Arkadiou Anniversary

Patriotism kicks into high gear from 7 to 9 November during the anniversary of the explosion at Moni Arkadiou, a key holiday in Crete. (p119)

December

✈ Christmas

Although not as important as Easter, Christmas is still celebrated with religious services and feasting. Western European influences include trees, decorations and gift-giving.

Plan Your Trip
Itineraries

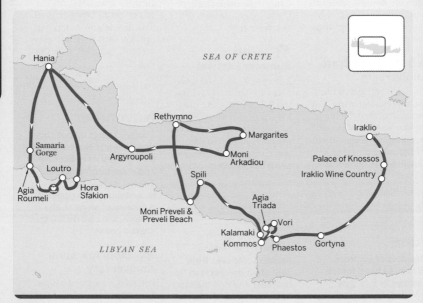

Essential Crete

Bookended by two of Crete's great cities, this route is a roller-coaster ride through the natural wonders of mountain and sea, and several of Crete's most famous historical treasures. You'll also get to soak up Venetian architecture, and feast on both mountain-village and seafront cuisine.

Start in bustling **Iraklio**, checking out the superb museums and soaking up its cafe culture, before heading to the **Palace of Knossos** where the mysterious Minoans ruled about 4000 years ago. Spend a day

enjoying the fruits of the **Iraklio Wine Country**, where 70% of Crete's wine is produced, and which is dotted with wineries. Next, stake out a base near Matala to combine trips to **Gortyna**, the former capital of Roman Crete, as well as the grand Minoan palaces of **Phaestos** and **Agia Triada**. The outstanding Cretan cultural museum at **Vori** and swimming at wide, sandy **Kommos** and **Kalamaki** beaches round out the area's offerings.

Travelling west, lunch in the quaint village of **Spili**, home to several excellent tavernas creating traditional Cretan cuisine. Then drive (or hike the Kourtaliotiko

Venetian lighthouse (p56), Hania

Gorge) to **Moni Preveli**, a working monastery on a hill with sweeping views of the Libyan Sea, and picture-postcard **Preveli Beach** down below. Start week two by heading north to soulful **Rethymno**, where you can spend two days wandering the maze of Venetian lanes and another exploring the countryside, perhaps steering towards the pottery village of **Margarites**, the peaceful **Moni Arkadiou**, site of momentous historical events, or the cool natural spring oasis at the mountain village of **Argyroupoli**.

For a taste of the west stay in **Hania**, a lively modern city wrapped around a romantic Venetian harbour and atmosphere-laden pedestrianised quarters. When you've had your fill of this historic beauty, take the early bus to **Samaria Gorge** and trek one of Europe's most famous canyons to the beachfront terminus at the small hamlet of **Agia Roumeli**. Stay over or catch a boat to **Loutro**, to spend the night in this quaint harbour accessible only on foot or by boat.

Next morning, take the boat to **Hora Sfakion** where you can have a seafood lunch and the local cheese-stuffed-crêpe speciality, and then loop back to Hania.

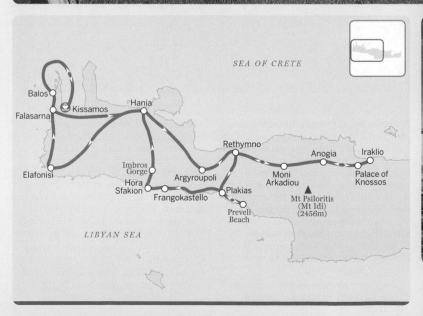

Central to West Crete

10 DAYS

This trip presents you with the mother lode of soul-stirring attractions, including the unspoiled southern coast, higgledy-piggledy mountain villages, Crete's best beaches, and spirit-lifting culture in Crete's two most attractive towns, Rethymno and Hania.

Kick off your trip in **Iraklio**, taking in the Archaeological Museum and imposing fortress, and swinging out to the **Palace of Knossos**, before steering west to quaint **Anogia**, where ancient traditions and Cretan music thrive at the foot of Mt Psiloritis. Continue west via the pottery village of Margarites to **Moni Arkadiou**, the site of one of the bloodiest moments in Crete's struggle for independence from the Turks. Spend the next day in stately **Rethymno**, taking your sweet time ambling around its bewitching mix of Turkish and Venetian buildings.

From Rethymno push on to the southern coast, where the lively beach town of **Plakias** makes an ideal base for exploring nearby secluded beaches, including palm-studded **Preveli Beach**, stunningly located at the mouth of a rugged gorge.Heading west, make a pit stop at the seaside fortress of **Frangokastello** before zipping over to **Hora Sfakion**, where you can hop on a boat to explore the remote villages along this beautiful stretch of coast for a day (or two!). Continue north from Hora Sfakion towards the Lefka Ori (White Mountains) and make time for a hike through spectacular **Imbros Gorge**. Continue to the northern coast and linger a night or two in **Hania**, with its beautiful harbour, grand fortress and ambience-packed old town.

From here you can explore the far western reaches of Crete. Take the circular route southwest via Kolymbari and the Innahorion villages to the westernmost tip of the island at **Elafonisi**, which beckons with pink-shimmering sandy beaches. Pushing back north via the coastal road, continue the beach theme at broad **Falasarna** with its rolling waves, or detour to the Gramvousa Peninsula's spectacular lagoon-like beach at **Balos**, which you'll most likely access by day-boat from **Kissamos**.

Returning back to Iraklio via Hania, consider making a quick detour to the springs of **Argyroupoli** before taking the coastal road east of Rethymno via peaceful Panormo and busy Bali.

Top: Plakias (p127)
Bottom: Balos beach (p99)

1 WEEK Around Iraklio

Iraklio is a big, busy city, but it can be a useful base from which to access many of Crete's most famous sights, even without your own vehicle. Or if you have wheels and your budget allows, stay in Arhanes in the nearby Iraklio Wine Country, to make these looping day trips.

Crete's largest city, **Iraklio** offers top-notch museums, a Venetian fortress, a colourful street market, lively nightlife and excellent dining. While there, make sure you visit the beautifully renovated and curated Heraklion Archaeological Museum so that you'll be prepared for Crete's grandest Minoan palace. Drive or hop on a bus for the quick ride to the world-famous **Palace of Knossos** for a full-scale introduction to Minoan society, partially reconstructed.

On another day, apply what you've learned on a visit to the **Palace of Malia**, another Minoan site, and some people's favourite, with sweeping sea views. You can then explore small mountain villages by zigzagging through tiny Krasí to **Kerá**, which is home to the revered Panagia Kardiotissa monastery, with its 14th-century frescoes and holy icon. Nearby Sfendile was controversially inundated by the creation of a dam.

If you have your own wheels, designate a driver and spend a day sampling the local vintages of the **Iraklio Wine Country**, which is dotted with wineries and tasting rooms. Plan to stop at the Nikos Kazantzakis Museum in **Myrtia** and the moody Minoan vestiges in **Arhanes**, which also has great traditional tavernas – perfect for a lunch break. Or sample the tipple around Dafnes, the other main hub of the wine country.

Take a scenic drive to the rustic mountain village of **Zaros**, at the foot of Mt Psiloritis. Leave time to hike nearby trails, explore Byzantine churches and dine on fresh trout. If you're thirsty for a beach day instead of a hike, continue a bit further along to beautiful sands at Kommos or **Kalamaki Beach**. And if you have time to sleep over, the next day you can explore quaint villages Sivas and **Kamilari**, Minoan ruins at **Phaestos**, and Roman ones at **Gortyna**, before looping north again.

Top: Palace of Malia (p185)
Bottom: Palace of Knossos (p157)

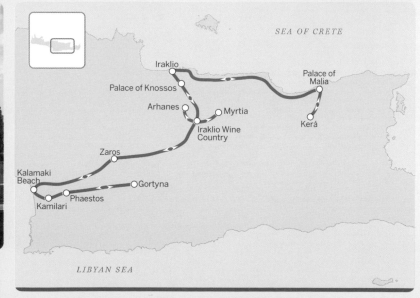

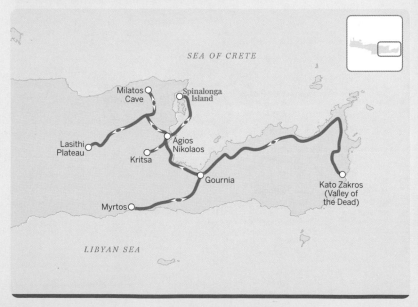

ABBPHOTO / GETTY IMAGES ©

1 WEEK Eastern Crete

There's a world of discoveries awaiting in eastern Crete, from the inviting town of Agios Nikolaos to some of the island's most beautiful churches and moodily historic sights. Arm yourself with some curiosity and a good map, and the week will fly by with no two days spent the same way.

Make your base at charming **Agios Nikolaos**, arrayed beautifully along both the sea and an interior lake. You'll have to tear yourself away from its bustling cafes and delicious waterfront eateries in order to take in the gorgeous mountain scenery on the **Lasithi Plateau**, high on the upper decks of the Dikti Mountains, where wind power once drove the sails of thousands of windmills. Plan a day of walks or cycling, and visit Zeus' birthplace in the Dikteon Cave, to earn your meal when you return to the coast.

It's easy to lose yourself along the winding roads north of **Myrtos**, where bare mountains crowned with coxcombs of rock rise from green woods. You can also easily lose a few days along the coast here, soaking up bohemian beach living.

If you're keen on history, plan a day wandering among the fascinating ruins on **Spinalonga Island**, made famous recently by Victoria Hislop's novel, *The Island*. Or, visit **Milatos Cave**, the site of an 1823 massacre of villagers by Turkish besiegers, which today is a serene and absorbing corner of rural Crete.

To satisfy artistic cravings, steer yourself to the Church of Panagia Kera near **Kritsa** for a feast of fabulous 13th-century frescoes, the finest in Crete. Archaeology fans can indulge their passion at the Late Minoan site of **Gournia**, where a full Minoan town is overlooked by a once-great palace.

Outdoors lovers should not miss the walk along the tail-end of the E4 European Path, down the Valley of the Dead, where the awesome landscape overwhelms the human element. You'll pass Minoan cave burials and reach the eastern coast at the ruined Minoan palace of **Kato Zakros (Valley of the Dead)**.

DENISSHUMOV / SHUTTERSTOCK ©

Top: Church of Panagia Kera (p198)
Bottom: Traditional windmills, Lasithi Plateau (p202)

Plan Your Trip
Outdoor Activities

Given Crete's spectrum of terrain, ranging from valleys to gorges, plateaux to rivers, lakes and caves, it's little surprise it should be such a wonderland for the lover of outdoor adventure. Crete also lays claim to some of Greece's finest underwater sites. You'll find a wealth of tour specialists to take you to the best of it all.

Best Outdoor Activities

Best Coastal Hike
Delve into the past among Hellenistic, Roman and Byzantine ruins at Lissos on the 14.5km hike from Paleohora to Sougia (p86).

Best Dive Site
The Messerschmitt WWII wreck (p39) near Malia; ghostly intact and crawling with moray eels.

Best Birdwatching
The marshes, lakes and rivers at Georgioupoli (p73) throng with migrant birds such as kingfishers and egrets.

Best Off-Road Bike Trip
Get high along mountain trails between the Lasithi and Katharo Plateaux.

Best Horse Riding
Exhilarating coastal and inland riding treks around Malia and through the Dikti Mountains.

Best Gorge Walk
Eastern Crete's Zakros Gorge (p213), aka the Valley of the Dead, is only 4km in length, but packs in all that's best in gorge walking.

Planning Your Trip

Get outdoors and active in Crete and you'll experience the rewards of this stunning island beyond the relaxed pleasures of sun and sand. Crete's rugged terrain, soaring mountains, dramatic gorges and wild coastline beyond the resorts make for an adventurer's paradise, and such is the relative ease of access to these splendid wilderness areas that you can sample just about every outdoor activity available through selective day trips.

If you're keen to sample a more edgy and exhilarating take on outdoor sport, opportunities for active and challenging holidays have increased on Crete, with several specialist operators operating on the island. There are excellent horse-riding trails, and more extreme pursuits, including rock climbing, canyoning and bungee jumping, are available with experienced guides and instructors.

Luxuriate on Crete's superb beaches, of course, but take off now and then for memorable experiences on the wild side of this wonderful island.

When to Go

You can follow walking routes on the island's hills and mountains and along the unspoiled coastlines at all times of the year, though, for the higher mountains, experience and full equipment is required during the winter period. While Crete is a veritable paradise for hikers, walking is not much fun between July and August, when the temperature can reach 40°C. Spring and autumn are the best times for great walks and serious hikes through beautiful gorges or along scenic coastal paths and alpine trails, while cycling, even for a day, is a rewarding way to explore Crete's country byways and off-road tracks. For water enthusiasts, the sea has warmed come mid-June, ready for windsurfing and swimming.

Hiking

Crete offers an enormous variety of options for keen hikers and trekkers that pass through remote villages, across plains and into gorges. There are a few detailed English-language guides in publication and local booklets are beginning to appear. Check out www.discoveronfoot.com for some excellent walking guidebooks. Trails are not too well indicated, although places like the Kato Zakros (Valley of the Dead) are now thoroughly and expertly marked. Many visitors may opt for a guided hike or a short off-road stroll, but experienced walkers will find plenty to test and stimulate them.

Walking the Gorges

Crete's numerous gorges attract hikers from all over the world. The walks can be a breathtaking and sometimes hard-going experience. The bonuses include the sheer pleasure of the spectacular surroundings, the aroma of wild herbs and flowers, shaded picnic spots and the potential for spotting wildlife.

Preparation

Most gorge walks require a fairly decent level of fitness. A few require only straightforward walking, although tough footwear and a fair degree of stamina are still needed. Several demand some rock-scrambling experience and agility. The most extreme, such as the mighty Ha Gorge, require serious canyoning and rock-climbing abilities and the services of a competent guide.

Consider what time of year you visit, too. If it's just after the winter there's every chance the river level may still be high, so do a little homework first.

Getting Around

Gorge walking will involve a bit of planning if you have your own transport. You will either have to walk back the same way to pick up your vehicle, or arrange for someone to collect you at the other end. Buses can normally get you to within striking distance of a gorge entrance.

Several companies run walking and hiking tours across Crete, including specialists Happy Walker (p110) and Strata Walking Tours (p38).

Seven of the Best

➡ **Agia Irini Gorge** (p81) A full-day walk best tackled from the village of Agia Irini, north of Sougia. This is a fairly straightforward and rewarding hike with only a few steep sections. The last couple of kilometres to Sougia are unfortunately along the surfaced road.

➡ **Agiofarango** (p180) A popular hike in south-central Crete running from Moni Odigitrias, 24km southwest of Mires. The walk ends at a lovely beach.

➡ **Hohlakies Gorge** Not as well known as its near neighbour at Zakros, this short 3km walk runs from Hohlakies village to the coast. Hikers can walk a further 7km northwards to Palekastro.

➡ **Imbros Gorge** (p75) Perhaps the second most popular gorge walk after Samaria, and a reasonable outing for walkers. It runs from just south of the village of Imbros for 8km to Komitades, near Hora Sfakion.

➡ **Rouvas Gorge** (p168) This short link hike runs from the village of Zaros on the southern slopes of Mt Psiloritis to meet up with the alpine route of the E4 European Path. It's a convenient way to get to and from the trans-Crete hike.

➡ **Valley of the Dead** (p213) A stunning two-hour hike in far-eastern Crete, the conclusion of which is ancient ruins and a turquoise bay. A new cave has also opened nearby. The valley is the last section of the E4 hiking path and runs from Zakros to the palace at Kato Zakros.

➡ **Samaria** (p94) Crete's longest and most famous (and usually very crowded) gorge route.

THE E4 EUROPEAN PATH

The trans-European E4 walking trail starts in Portugal and ends in Crete. In Crete, the trail picks up at the port of Kissamos in the west and ends – after 320km – on the pebbly shore of Kato Zakros in eastern Crete. Enthusiasts planning to tackle the Cretan leg can do it in a minimum of three weeks, allowing for 15km per day, or more comfortably in four weeks allowing for stops and/or shorter hiking trips. You can, of course, tackle only sections of the route if your time is limited or if you just want to walk the most interesting parts. However, you will need to make important decisions early on as the trail splits into two distinct sections through western Crete: the coastal and alpine routes.

Making Your Way

Hikers tackling the E4 trail need to do some planning. While there is nearly always accommodation within the range of a six- to seven-hour daily hike, some of it will need to be arranged beforehand – particularly the mountain refuges, for which you might need to pick up keys.

The E4 trail is marked throughout its length with black and yellow posts and signs, but it's not always well-maintained: paths are overgrown and in many sections signs are hard to find. The three-volume GPS-compatible 1:100.000 scale touring maps by Anavasi (www.anavasi.gr) show the E4 across Crete, but its walking maps cover sections in greater detail (at a scale of 1:25,000) for the Lefka Ori (Sfakia and Pahnes), Samaria Gorge/Sougia, Mt Psiloritis and Zakros-Vaï.

The E4 can be a lonely trail and there is no food (and little water) along most of the route – it is always wise to get local advice before setting off.

Online Resources

Crete Walks (www.crete-walks.com) Info on the best walks to take as well as images and maps.

Completely Crete (www.completely-crete.com/E4-path.html) All things Cretan, from best beaches to culture.

Cycling & Mountain Biking

Get on your bike and take off for freewheeling Crete. Traditional cycling has caught on in a big way on the island, despite the mountainous terrain. While it's possible to cycle from one end of Crete to the other and barely raise a sweat, north–south routes and the southern coast are likely to test your stamina and fortitude. In contrast, the escarpment villages and valleys of the northern coast and the Mesara Plain of the south do allow for some relatively flat cycling experiences on surfaced roads. Crete, of course, is an off-road mountain-biker's dream.

Bike Touring

Plateau tours (especially around the Lasithi Plateau) are big business, with specialist companies transporting bikes up to the plateau to save you the gruelling Tour de France–like haul up from the coast. There are also more extreme biking options and eight-day tours covering more than 650km.

Several companies and small specialist operators offer tours for all levels of experience and fitness:

➡ **Martinbike Crete** (p193) Small specialist operator going strong for 20 years. Based near Agios Nikolaos, it runs one- and five-day trips in the surrounding areas.

➡ **Freak Mountain Bike Centre** (p211) This Palekastro-based operator offers four-day escapes around the surrounding countryside on well-maintained German bikes.

➡ **Hub MTB Adventures** (☑28970 32650; www.mtbhub.gr; V Kornarou 5, 70007; 4hr ride from €60; ☺10am-noon) Operating out of Malia, Hub MTB Adventures covers the whole of Crete. Has one-day tours of the Lasitihi Plateau and two-day coast-to-coast tours.

E4 Walking Trail

SAMARIA GORGE ALTERNATIVE: MT GINGILOS

The Samaria Gorge is something of a must-do for many visitors to Crete, even if 'wild walking' is not their thing. The result is a sometimes less than solitary experience. If you're an experienced mountain walker and fancy an 'up' rather than a 'down' adventure, veer off to the right from Xyloskalo at the entrance to the gorge. This will take you towards the top of the 2080m Mt Gingilos, the mighty peak whose precipitous north face towers over Samaria. Head uphill past the cafe and on to where the surfaced road ends at a lodge-style building and a good path begins.

Tackling the Mountain

It will take about six hours to climb to the summit of Gingilos and back. This is a real mountain trek with some rocky sections. The path throughout the first part of the climb has been greatly improved in recent years and winds delightfully up steep slopes on well-laid stones and stepped sections dotted with shrub and gnarled cypresses. The path then levels off and winds south, passing beneath a fascinating rock arch. The ground for the next few hundred metres can be a touch loose, especially just after the springtime thaw. The path soon leads up to the spring of Linoseli and then zigzags up steep scree to a rocky saddle at 1700m, from where the Trypiti Gorge can be seen running to the south below.

From the saddle the route turns east and climbs steadily through a rocky landscape. There is no well-defined path and care should be taken at the start to stay clear of a steep-sided cavity. Red paint spots and arrows on boulders point the way to the summit. The descent is rocky at first, but should pose no problem for experienced hikers.

Preparation & Safety

Keep an eye on the weather reports: as late as the month of May heavy rain can fall, as was the case in 2015 when several hikers were trapped when the river that flows through the gorge flooded its banks. Reliable mountain footwear and clothing must be worn. Carry plenty of water and some food. You should also carry a compass and think twice about continuing if mist descends. From the saddle to the summit there can be fierce winds and care should be taken. For more information visit www.west-crete.com/gingilos.htm. And remember: you don't have to go all the way...

On Your Own

Independent cyclists coming to Crete with their own bikes are advised to bring sturdy touring bikes with multiple gears. You can hire mountain bikes for about €8 to €20 per day from a range of places around the island.

Canyoning, Climbing & Bungee Jumping

While Crete's mountains may not offer the level of altitude on offer in Austria or Switzerland, its peaks are by no means shrinking violets, with the likes of Mt Thripti (1489m), the Dikti Mountains (2148m), the Idi Mountains (2456m) and the Lefka Ori (White Mountains; 2452m).

Mountaineering Clubs

To tackle Crete's mountains, the island has a number of established mountaineering clubs. Each prefecture has its own club, which maintains the E4 European Path and mountain refuges. They are all members of the association of Greek Mountaineering Clubs (EOS) and organise regular climbing, walking, speleology and skiing excursions around Crete, which visitors are welcome to join.

For decent info on Cretan climbs check out the excellent www.climbincrete.com.

➡ **Greek Mountaineering Association** (p62) Visit the local EOS branch in Hania or check its website to get the scoop on outdoor sports, including serious climbing in the Lefka Ori, mountain refuges and the E4 European Path.

➡ **Mountaineering Club of Iraklio** (☑28102 27609; www.eos-her.gr; Dikeosynis 53, Iraklio;

⊗8.30-10.30pm Mon-Fri) The local Iraklio chapter arranges hiking trips across the island most weekends (trip programs are published on its website). Anyone is welcome to join.

➡ **Mountaineering Club of Rethymno** (☑28310 57766; www.eosrethymnou.gr; Dimokratias 12, Rethymno; ⊗9-11pm Tue) Offers advice on local hikes along with the possibility to join excursions. It's best to make contact via the website.

Canyoning

Canyoning is a developing sport in Crete and should not be confused with gorge walking. Most canyoning routes require serious rock climbing and/or caving experience, including the ability to abseil (rappel) under your own control. Most routes also require swimming ability and experience of constricted water flows. There is no shortage of wild and challenging canyons on the island.

The well-organised **Cretan Canyoning Association** (☑6997090307; www.canyon.gr) has equipped more than 50 gorges in southern Crete with abseil and belay bolt anchors and guide wires. One of the most awe-inspiring is the mighty Ha Gorge near Mt Thripti in eastern Crete. The savage cleft of the gorge splits apart the great curtain wall of the Thripti Mountains in eastern Crete. The gorge is over 1.5km in length and rises in a series of rocky steps between narrow walls over 300m high. Its name is said to derive, not surprisingly, from the Greek word 'to gape', which is what most of us do from the safety of the main road.

The association's website has useful information and a published guide to Crete's canyons. It organises regular excursions and also runs beginners' courses. Canyoning is not a 'thrill-seeker's' day out and you should be certain of your capabilities before getting involved. If you're new to the sport, you should always be accompanied by an experienced canyoning guide.

The multilingual *Canyoning in Crete,* by Yiannis Bromirakis (Road Editions, 2007), covers many of Crete's newly accessible gorges in fine detail with maps and drawings. Check out Cretan Adventures (p151) for well-run, safety-conscious canyoning trips.

Rock Climbing

Rock climbing is on the increase in Crete. Southern Iraklio is one of the most popular areas for climbing, particularly the stunning cliffs around Kapetaniana and Mt Kofinas on the southern flanks of the Asteroussia mountains. The Agiofarango Gorge near Matala is another popular climbing spot, while many new venues are being developed around Crete, including around Samaria, Plakias, Loutro and Malia. The offshoot sport of deep-water soloing – traversing sea cliffs unroped directly above deep water – has potential around Hora Sfakion.

Unless you are experienced, you are advised to contact local organisations before attempting any form of rock climbing. Visit www.climbincrete.com for plenty of information and some entertaining articles, including an account of an early descent of the Ha Gorge.

Rock & Sun (www.rockandsun.com) is the UK's top climbing holiday operator and organises mountaineering holidays in Crete.

MOUNTAINEERING CLUB REFUGES
You must call Rethymno Climbing Association (☑6977915978) to book.

NAME	LOCATION	ALTITUDE	CAPACITY (BEDS)	EOS
Kallergi	Near the Samaria Gorge	1680m	50	Hania
Katsiveli-Svourihtis	Svourihtis foothills	1970m	25	Hania
Limnarkarou	Lasithi Plateau	1350m	15	Lasithi
Prinos	Asites, East Psiloritis	1100m	45	Iraklio
Tavris	Plateau of Askyfou	1200m	42	Hania
Toubotos Prinos	Mt Psiloritis	1500m	28	Rethymno
Volikas	Volikas Keramion	1400m	40	Hania

Bungee Jumping

High above the Aradena Gorge, on the southern coast, is a spectacular bungee-jumping location; it's the highest bungee-jumping bridge in Greece and the second-highest in Europe.

Thrill seekers can jump 138m into the narrow gorge from the bridge that crosses over the canyon. Jumps are held every weekend in July and August by Liquid Bungy (p79). Head to www.bungy.gr for more information.

Golf

Crete has a few nine-hole golf courses, but the island's only 18-hole pro course is the Crete Golf Club (p183) in Hersonisos. This desert-style, par-72 course has been designed to blend in with the environment. The course is quite tough and also has a double-ended driving range, a golf academy and club house. It's not for casual hackers, however.

A nine-hole round in summer costs €50, an 18-hole round €80 (excluding clubs or buggies). At the time of research the course was set to undergo a makeover to bring it up to world standards.

Horse Riding

Several places in Crete offer horse riding and guided trail rides through the countryside.

➡ **Odysseia Stables** (☎28970 51080; www.horseriding.gr) The most impressive operation is Odysseia, above Avdou, at the foot of Mt Dikti. These stables have excellent facilities (including accommodation) and run anything from two-hour beginners' rides to three-day rides on the Lasithi Plateau and weeklong trails through the Dikti Mountains to the southern coast. Typical prices range from €20 for a one-hour beach ride, €35 for a two-hour hack, €65 for a day trip and from €540 for eight-day courses including accommodation and meals. An eight-day trek up to the Lasithi Plateau area costs about €990.

➡ **Zoraida's Horseriding** (☎28250 61745; www.zoraidas-horseriding.com) Located in Georgioupoli. Offers beach and nature trails, including day safaris and a six-day course for advanced riders.

➡ **Melanouri Horse Farm** (p177) Located in Pitsidia, near Matala. Runs rides through the surrounding region.

➡ **Arion Stables** (info@arionstables.com) Running since 2007 this German-Greek operation in Hersonisos is also an animal rescue centre, and offers you the chance to ride horses in wild places as well as on the beach.

OUTDOOR ADVENTURES IN CRETE

The following companies run a range of organised hikes, biking and other outdoor activities in Crete. Guided walks start from €45 per day and €500 per week, including accommodation, transfers and meals.

Cretan Adventures (p151) Organises hiking and trekking tours, mountain biking and other specialist and extreme activities. Highly recommended.

Happy Walker (p110) Runs a range of walks from March to November, including summer walks in the Omalos Plateau and Lefka Ori.

Korifi Tours (p182) Hiking and climbing tours around Kapetaniana, in southern Iraklio. Based in Kapetaniana.

Strata Walking Tours (☎28220 24336; www.stratatours.com) In Kissamos, offering anything from leisurely day trips to seven- to 15-day walking tours to the southern coast.

Trekking Hellas (☎210 331 0323; www.trekking.gr; Gounari 96, Marousi) Organises nature excursions for all ages, be it cycling, walking, rafting or canoeing.

Trekking Plan (p62) This outfit at Agia Marina, located 10km west of Hania, will take you hiking, rock climbing, abseiling (rappelling) and mountain biking in western Crete.

Water Sports

Crete's long northern and southern coasts are boxed off by short east and west shorelines, resulting in a range of sea conditions that lend themselves to all sorts of water sports.

What to Do

You can start with the 'fun sports' on the main organised beaches where everything is on offer, including waterskiing, jet skiing, pedalos, banana boats, and doughnut rides. The most spectacular beachside trip is parasailing, which can be done singly or in tandem.

On Crete's northern coast, you'll find a water-sports centre attached to most luxury hotels, and they are usually open to nonguests.

The more specialised water sports available in Crete include diving and snorkelling, windsurfing, kayaking and sailing. With diving and windsurfing, there are specific areas where ideal conditions prevail and there are numerous commercial operators who organise trips and rent equipment.

Diving & Snorkelling

The sea off much of Crete's coastline is a paradise for snorkelling and diving. There is nothing quite like cruising gently through water that can be as clear as air with visibility at times well over 30m.

For many years there were restrictions on diving anywhere in Greece due to fears of potential damage to ancient undersea ruins and because of the very real problem of theft of ancient artefacts from the seabed. Diving interests and the tourism lobby pushed for a sensible easing of the restrictions and in 2005 the Greek government opened up most Greek waters to recreational diving, with the exception of about 100 important archaeological sites. Some permitted recreational dive sites have ancient walls, fallen columns and large amphorae, the giant urns once used for storing wine, olive oil and grain.

The diving landscape of Crete is superb with a fascinating mix of natural features, rocks, reefs, caverns, cliffs and shining sand. Sea life on view includes the beautiful 'wallpaper' of marine plants, red and green algae, corals, sea anemones and

> ### POSEIDON'S SECRETS: CRETE'S BEST DIVE SITES
>
> **El Greco Cave** Stunning stalactites and stalagmites in a 30m-long underwater cave, home to lobster, moray eel, grouper and tuna. Close to Agia Pelagia.
>
> **Messerschmitt WWII wreck** An upended German aeroplane lies 24m down in fragmented sections, though the cockpit is still intact. Head to Analipsi.
>
> **Mononaftis** Rich in marine life, you'll meet octopus, barracuda, moray eel, scorpionfish and often dolphin and stingray here. Also reef, canyons and underwater grottoes. Find it at Mononaftis Bay near Agia Pelagia. This dive is also suitable for beginners.
>
> **Shrimps Cave** For the more experienced diver, expect to see thousands of shrimp in this stunning cave which plunges 40m. Close to Hersonisos.

sponges that coat undersea rocks and reefs, while the often variegated volcanic rocks of Crete create a kaleidoscope of undersea colour. You stand a good chance of spotting a roll-call of favourite fish and crustaceans including octopus, cuttlefish, squid, sea horses, lobster, moray, scorpionfish, snapper, bream and even stingrays.

The most popular region for diving is Crete's north coast, where accessibility and sea conditions are more favourable, but many diving outfits also operate on south coast sites where there is a distinct upping of the ante on diving's sense of adventure.

Some of the more interesting, easy snorkelling is around the sunken city of Olous near Elounda, which can be accessed from the shore. Bali, Panormo, Ammoudara, Malia, Plakias and Paleohora are popular diving sites.

Several diving centres offer courses from beginners to PADI certification. It's wise to call at least a day in advance to book a dive.

Dive Operators

Crete has many reputable dive operators. A few favourites include **Happy Divers** (☑28410 82546; www.happydivers.gr; dives from €25) at Plaka and Elounda, Pelagos

WATER WISE

The sea can still be a hostile environment even when flat calm and lapping a Greek beach, making all water sports potentially dangerous. The more specialised sports such as diving and kayaking are usually well regulated and clients are accompanied by qualified instructors. You should, however, always check your operators' certification. With beach sports such as parasailing, make sure that whoever is operating the facility has full certification and a good safety record. Ringo rides are best left to capable youngsters with good swimming abilities! Parents should also keep an eye on teenagers when jet skis are up for hire. By law, operators must exercise strict checks on age limits and that the driver is not under the influence of alcohol.

Dive Centre (p189) in Agios Nikolaos, Blue Adventures Diving (p62) in Hania, and Paradise Diving Center (p110) in Rethymno.

Sea Kayaking

Crete's south coast has become increasingly popular for sea-kayaking trips. Between Paleohora and Hora Sfakion, especially, the coast is dramatic and fascinating and there are plenty of places to pull ashore at remote beaches and coves. However, there are not many kayaking operators on Crete and the tendency is for multiday expeditions catering for groups, with accommodation included along the way. It's worth enquiring about day trips, however, and you may even be able to hire a canoe for the day if you have evidence of personal expertise. Some trips combine kayaking with hiking.

Hania Alpine Travel (p62) offers canoeing holidays, for families, groups and individuals. At Plaka, near Elounda, Petros Watersports (p201) rents kayaks by the hour and day.

Windsurfing

Windsurfing, or sailboarding, as the dedicated call it, is one of the most exhilarating of all water sports. A lot of practice and much skill is needed before you get anywhere near the spectacular freestyle and wave jumping of the experts. Still, even in

the early stages of learning this is an exciting sport and enjoying it off the beautiful beaches of Crete is a bonus. Stand up, hang on and fly!

The best windsurfing in Crete is at Kouremenos beach, north of Palekastro in Sitia, where Freak Windsurf (p211) is a key local operator. Kouremenos is affected by the *meltemi,* the summer wind that can blow fiercely throughout the Aegean, and this wind coupled with a local funnelling effect creates some ideal windsurfing conditions. Windsurfing is also good in Almyrida, near Hania.

For more information about windsurfing in Greece check out the **Hellenic Windsurfing Association** (210 323 3696; www.speedslalom.gr; Filellinon 4, Syntagma, Athens).

Sailing & Boat Trips

To sail round Crete on a well-found yacht is a glorious experience, but unless you are an experienced yachting fan with your own boat, the answer is usually a charter trip. Some companies in Crete do offer daily sailing excursions and most commercial tourist offices will have information on sailing.

Amazing Sailing in Crete (p199), in Elounda, takes you to hidden coves and a traditional fishing village. From Agios Nikolaos, General (p189) and Nostos Tours (p189) will both take you to Spinalonga Island.

Plan Your Trip

Eat & Drink Like a Local

Cretan food, which is distinct from Greek food in general, is some of the best to be found in the Mediterranean. This rustic but rich cuisine combines seasonal ingredients and balanced flavours which reflect the bounty of Crete's sun-blessed, fertile land. Across the island, regional variations create a diverse gourmet trail.

Food Experiences

One of the delights of travelling through Crete is coming across a family-run taverna where traditional local dishes are made from ancient recipes but with farm-fresh, home-grown produce, where the wild aromatic greens were picked in the mountains earlier that day, the oil and cheese is homemade, the tender lamb is from a local shepherd and the fish was caught by the owner. Really, that happens.

Meals of a Lifetime

➡ **To Maridaki** (p65) Tender calamari, panna cotta to die for and friendly service to match, in Hania town's cool Splantzia quarter.

➡ **Thalassino Ageri** (p66) Oceanfront seafood meets sunset and romance on the coast just east of Hania.

➡ **To Skolio** (p87) Casual but delicious, with locally sourced produce creatively prepared, and views of the Libyan Sea.

➡ **Castelvecchio** (p114) Sit on the open-air terrace for people-watching paired with rich Cretan specialities created with flair, in Rethymno.

➡ **Vrisi** (p129) In Myrthios, let a parrot serenade you on a secluded patio, while your taste buds tingle with local treats.

The Year in Food

Spring (Mar–May)

Easter feasts feature tender roasted lamb and *kreatotourta* (meat pies), and red-dyed boiled eggs decorate *tsoureki* (brioche-style bread). Spring brings edible wild plants, herbs and artichokes.

Summer (Jun–Aug)

Cheesemaking kicks into high gear. By July, watermelon, peaches and other fruit fill markets; mussel season peaks. August food festivals: Sitia pays homage to the sultana raisin, Tzermiado celebrates the potato, and Arhanes toasts the grape/wine.

Autumn (Sep–Nov)

Grape harvest begins. In October sample sweet chestnuts in Elos, with its quirky Chestnut Festival. *Raki* distilling hits its peak in November with raucous festivals all over, especially in mountain villages.

Winter (Dec–Feb)

Sugar-dusted *kourabiedes* (almond shortcake) and honey-dipped *melomakarona* are top Christmas cookies. The *vasilopita* (New Year's cake) comes with a hidden coin which promises a year of good luck.

CRETAN FOOD & DRINK ONLINE

➜ **Greek Recipe** (www.greek-recipe. com) Popular Greek recipes.

➜ **Gourmed** (www.gourmed.gr) Mediterranean cuisine, with Greek recipes and features.

➜ **All About Greek Wine** (www. allaboutgreekwine.com) Information on Greek wines.

➜ **Wines of Crete** (www.winesof crete.gr) Vintners of Iraklio Wine Country.

➜ **Avli** (p114) One of Rethymno's top tables, Avli never disappoints, perfectly melding the Venetian with the Cretan.

➜ **Zorba's Tavern** (p207) Get a warm welcome with live music and a moustachioed owner, Zorba, at Sitia's most authentic spot.

➜ **Pelagos** (p195) Choose between interior elegance or a garden terrace at Agios Nikolaos' best bet for food to remember.

➜ **Taverna Giorgos** (p202) Live the Greek seafront taverna dream in Plaka, whether supping on wood-fired chops or grilled octopus.

Cheap Treats

➜ **Souvlaki** Greece's favourite fast food, both the *gyros* and skewered meat versions wrapped in pitta bread, with tomato, onion, french fries and lashings of tzatziki.

➜ **Pies** Bakeries make endless variations of *tyropita* (cheese pie) and *spanakopita* (spinach pie) and other pies. *Kalitsounia* (filled pastries) are the Cretan speciality.

➜ **Street food** Includes *koulouria* (fresh pretzel-style bread) and seasonal snacks such as roasted chestnuts or corn.

➜ **Food to go** In a hurry but want a full meal? Tavernas with *mayirefta* (ready-cooked dishes) are the best bet.

Dare to Try

➜ **Ameletita** Literally, 'unspeakables'; fried sheep's testicles.

➜ **Gardhoumia** Stomach and offal wrapped in intestines.

Cooking Courses

Culinary tours and cooking courses are becoming more popular in Crete, and some restaurant owners will give them, if asked.

➜ **Rodialos** (p134) Regularly hosts one- to seven-day cooking seminars in a lovely villa in Panormo, near Rethymno. Mary Frangaki takes participants through the principles of Cretan cooking and the cooking of several courses.

➜ **Enagron** (p122) Outside the village of Axos, Enagron runs cooking workshops and organises seasonal events around the production of cheese, wine and *raki*. The farm setting is lovely and there's accommodation on-site.

➜ **Crete's Culinary Sanctuaries** (www. cookingincrete.com) Greek-American chef and writer Nikki Rose focuses on organic agriculture and traditional approaches to Cretan cuisine with hands-on classes and demonstrations in people's homes, visits to local farmers and producers. Courses are held island-wide.

➜ **Vamos Traditional Village** (p72) Conducts Cretan cooking courses in an olive press, and rents restored stone cottages, east of Hania.

➜ **Katerina** (☑6948325739; mains €5.50-19.50; ⊙lunch & dinner) Pair herb-collecting and cooking lessons with restaurateurs in Myrtos, on the south coast of Lasithi.

➜ **Eleonas Cottages** (p168) Head to Zaros, in central Iraklio province, to stay in traditional and ecofriendly cottages while learning to cook with organic Cretan produce.

Cook It at Home

Leave room in your baggage for local treats (customs and quarantine rules permitting) such as olives and extra virgin olive oil from small, organic producers; aromatic Greek thyme honey; dried oregano, sage, mountain tea or camomile flowers; and dried barley rusks. A jar of fruit preserves or 'spoon sweets' make an easy dessert poured atop Greek yoghurt or ice cream.

➜ *Cretan Cooking* by Maria and Nikos Psilakis is a well-translated version of their popular guide to Cretan cooking. It contains 265 mouth-watering recipes, some fascinating asides on the history of the dishes, and background to the Cretan dietary phenomenon.

➜ *The Glorious Foods of Greece* by award-winning Greek-American food writer Diane Kochilas is a must-have for any serious cook, with a regional exploration of Greek food and a 60-page chapter on Crete.

Local Specialities

The grand Cretan diet evolved from the abundance of local produce, coupled with enormous Cretan ingenuity. You'll find not only all the Greek staples but a wonderful array of Cretan specialities as well as regional variations across the island. While the cuisine has its roots in antiquity, and has been influenced by all the visiting cultures over time, it essentially relies on organically grown, farm-fresh, unadulterated seasonal produce and aromatic herbs as well as free-range meats and locally caught seafood. Cretan olive oil, produced in vast quantities across the island, is among the world's best and is an integral part of cooking and meals.

Cheese & Dairy

Beyond the ubiquitous and delicious fresh feta (in stores, ask for the kind wet from the barrel, not mass-produced), Crete produces its wonderful cheeses primarily from goat's and sheep's milk, or a combination of the two. Many Cretan villages have their own signature cheese.

➡ **Anthotiro** Buttery white cheese that can be soft or hardened when dry.

➡ **Graviera** Nutty, mild gruyère-like hard sheep's-milk cheese, often aged in special mountain caves and stone huts called *mitata*. Delicious eaten with thyme honey.

➡ **Myzithra** Soft, mild ricotta-like cheese produced from whey, which can be eaten soft or hardened for grating; the hardened sour version is *xinomyzithra*. Hania's speciality is *galomyzithra*. Variations abound across the island.

➡ **Pichtogalo Chanion** Hania's thick yoghurt-like sheep's milk or sheep's-and-goat's milk cheese with AOC protection, sometimes used in *bougatsa* pastries.

➡ **Xigala** Creamy cheese from Sitia in eastern Crete with a rich, slightly acidic flavour.

➡ **Yiaourti** Thick, tangy sheep's-milk yoghurt is something to savour, best eaten with honey, walnuts or fruit.

Wild Greens, Vegetables & Salads

Part of the magic of Cretan cuisine are the ingredients gathered from hillsides and around villages. For centuries Cretans have been gathering extremely nutritious *horta* (wild greens) and boiling them for warm salads or cooking them in pies and stews. There are more than 100 edible *horta* on Crete, though even the most knowledgeable might not recognise more than a dozen. The *vlita* (amaranth) variety is the sweetest, while *stamnagathi,* found in the mountains, is considered a delicacy and served boiled as a salad or stewed with meat. Other common *horta* include wild radish, dandelion, nettles and sorrel.

Another Cretan hillside speciality are *askordoulakous* (mountain bulbs), the bulbs of a wild green. They usually come fresh as a salad, dressed with oil and vinegar or lemon, pickled, or stewed with olive oil, vinegar and flour. The plant's tender white blossoms are boiled or incorporated into recipes.

Cretan *paximadia* (rusks), a hangover from times of famine, are made from barley flour or whole wheat and double-baked to produce a hard, dry cracker that can keep, literally, for years. Don't miss the excellent and popular dish called *dakos* (or *koukouvagia* and *kouloukopsomo*), often categorised as a salad on menus, where the rusks are moistened with water or oil and topped with tomato, olive oil and creamy *myzithra*.

Cretan cuisine also shines in such vegetable dishes as *aginara* (artichokes) and tasty *anthoi* (zucchini flowers) stuffed with rice and herbs. Beans and pulses were the foundation of the winter diet, so you will find dishes such as delicious *gigantes* (lima

---

THE HEALTHY CRETAN DIET

Cretan cuisine gained legendary status for its health benefits following scientific studies of the Mediterranean diet in the 1960s that showed Cretans had the lowest levels of heart disease and other chronic illnesses. This was largely attributed to a balanced diet high in fruits, vegetables, pulses, whole grains, virgin olive oil and wine, and few processed foodstuffs. Another important factor may be the *horta* (wild greens) that Cretans gather in the hills (and survived on during wars), which may have protective properties that are not yet fully understood.

beans in tomato and herb sauce). Also look for *fasolakia yiahni* (green bean stew), *yemista* (stuffed tomatoes) and *bamies* (okra). *Melitzana* (aubergines) are also widely used, particularly in dishes such as *briam* (oven-baked vegetable casserole) or wonderful *melidzanosalata* (a smoky garlicky purée).

Seafood

Fish is usually sold by weight in restaurants and it is customary to pick from the selection on display or in the kitchen. Make sure it's weighed (raw) so you don't get a shock when the bill arrives, as fresh fish is not cheap. The choice fish for grilling are *tsipoura* (sea bream), *lavraki* (sea bass) and *fangri* (bream), while smaller fish such as *barbounia* (red mullet) are delicious fried.

Speciality Cretan Dishes

Cretan tavernas usually offer the full range of Greek one-pot stews, casseroles and *mayirefta* (ready-cooked meals) in addition to food cooked to order *(tis oras)* such as grilled meats. The most common *mayirefta* are *mousakas* (baked layers of eggplant or zucchini, minced meat and potatoes topped with cheese sauce), *pastitsio* (layers of buttery macaroni and seasoned minced lamb), *yemista* (stuffed vegetables), *yuvetsi* (a hearty dish of baked meat or poultry in a fresh tomato sauce with *kritharaki*, rice-shaped pasta), *stifadho*, *soutzoukakia* (meat rissoles in tomato sauce) and *hohlioi* (snails). Meat is commonly

baked with potatoes, with lemon and oregano, or braised in tomato-based stews or casseroles *(kokkinisto)*.

But then there are the Cretan specialities that should not be missed. As you travel, you'll see the flocks of lamb and goat that figure so prominently in Cretan mountain cuisine, and Cretans have their own way of barbecuing called *ofto,* in which big chunks of meat are grilled upright around hot coals. In parts of Crete meat is cooked *tsigariasto* (sautéed).

➡ **Arni (lamb) me stamnagathi** In this favourite Cretan speciality, local lamb is cooked to tenderness with a popular wild green called *stamnagathi.* You may also find the dish with *katsiki* goat.

➡ **Boureki** Richly layered cheese and vegetable pie.

➡ **Gamopilafo** This rice dish is offered at traditional Cretan weddings (*gamos* means wedding) and some high-end restaurants. It's a sort of deluxe risotto prepared in a rich meat broth and *stakovoutiro,* a butter created from the creamy skin that forms on the top of boiled fresh goat's milk which is then made into a roux.

➡ **Hirina apakia (pork delicacy)** It takes an involved, multiday process to create this, from marination to smoking over a fire of local herbs. It can also be served cold in thin slices.

➡ **Hohlioi (snails)** Collected after rainfall and prepared in dozens of interesting ways: try *hohlioi bourbouristoi,* simmered in wine or vinegar and rosemary, or snails stewed with *hondros* (cracked wheat). Cretans eat more snails than the French do and even export to France.

CRETAN OLIVE OIL

The Minoans were among the first to grow wealthy on the olive, and Crete remains an important olive-growing area, producing the largest quantity of extra virgin olive oil in Greece. Today, with an estimated 30 million olive trees in Crete, it works out to 62 olive trees for every man, woman and child. More and more organic oil is being produced and at least nine olive regions have gained the EU's Protected Appellation of Origin status.

The best Cretan olive oil is from Kolymbari, west of Hania, and Sitia in the east. Biolea, near Hania, makes superb organic olive oil, as do monasteries – particularly the award-winning olive oil produced at Moni Agia Triadas (p70) near Hania and Moni Toplou (p209), east of Sitia.

The oil that is prized above all others is *agoureleo* (meaning unripe), a thick, green oil pressed from unripe olives.

Greeks are the world's biggest per capita consumers of olive oil; in Crete the annual per person consumption averages 31L.

MEZEDHES

Cretans love to share a range of mezedhes (small dishes), or mezze for short, often making a full meal of them or adding a main or two. You'll find restaurants (*mezedhopoleio, ouzerie, rakadiko*) that serve only mezze, and usually offer *raki* or ouzo to pair with the meal, but you can also make a meal of them at most standard restaurants and tavernas. Think tapas, Greek style!

Common mezedhes are dips such as *taramasalata* (fish roe), tzatziki (yoghurt, cucumber and garlic) and *fava* (split-pea purée). Hot mezedhes include *keftedhes* (small tasty rissoles, often made with minced lamb, pork or veal), *loukaniko* (pork sausages), *saganaki* (skillet-fried cheese) and *apaki* (Cretan cured pork), as well as a full range of bite-sized seafood. Also look for rice-filled dolmadhes (vine leaves), deep-fried zucchini or aubergine slices. If you can't make up your mind, often you can order a *pikilia* (mixed mezedhes plate).

Pick an array, sip your drink, and watch with delight as they arrive at the table in waves.

➡ **Kouneli (rabbit)** Local favourite stewed (*stifado*) with rosemary and *rizmarato* (vinegar).

➡ **Soupies (cuttlefish)** Excellent stewed with wild Cretan fennel.

➡ **Staka** Rich, soft buttery roux somewhere between a cheese, yoghurt and sauce, usually found on menus with goat or pork. It's a rich but delicious dish, with the meat absorbing the flavours of the *staka*. It's also often added to rice *pilafi* (pilaf) to make it creamier.

➡ **Vrasto (mutton or goat stew)** Found in traditional mountain village tavernas.

➡ **Psari (fish)** A staple along the coast and is cooked with minimum fuss – usually grilled whole and drizzled with *ladholemono* (a lemon-and-oil dressing). Also look for *ohtapodi* (octopus), *lakerda* (cured fish), mussel or prawn *saganaki* (usually fried with tomato sauce and cheese), crispy fried *kalamari* (calamari, squid), fried *maridha* (whitebait) and *gavros* (mild anchovy), either marinated, grilled or fried.

Sweet Treats

As well as traditional Greek sweets such as baklava, *loukoumadhes* (ball-shaped doughnuts served with honey and cinnamon), *kataïfi* ('angel hair' pastry; chopped nuts inside shredded pastry soaked in honey), *rizogalo* (rice pudding) and *galaktoboureko* (custard-filled pastry with syrup), Cretans have their own sweet specialities. Also, traditional syrupy fruit preserves (known as spoon sweets) are served as dessert, but are also delicious on yoghurt or ice cream. Some tavernas serve *halva* (wedge of semolina) after a meal.

➡ **Bougatsa** Traditional breakfast food, a pastry stuffed with creamy custard or cheese and sprinkled with powdered sugar.

➡ **Kaltsounia** Cretan stuffed cheese pies start with handmade pastry dough, often formed into tiny cups. Fillings vary by region and household, though they tend towards the sweet, using cheeses, like *myzithra* or *malaka* (but not feta) and honey or spices.

➡ **Sfakianes pittes** From the Sfakia region of Hania, fine pancake-like sweets with a light *myzithra* cheese filling, served with honey. The dough incorporates a dash of *raki*.

➡ **Xerotigana** Deep-fried pastry twirls with honey and nuts.

Wine

Krasi (wine) has been produced in Crete since Minoan times, and Crete's farmers have long made wine for their own consumption. Commercial production, however, did not start until the 1930s and only in 1952 did Minos in Peza become the first winery to bottle wine on Crete.

Today, Crete produces about 20% of Greek wine, most of it through huge co-operatives that aim for higher yields rather than higher quality. Much of that type is blended and sold in bulk, and is usually what you get when you order 'house wine' in restaurants. An ever-growing crop of boutique wineries are overseen by internationally trained winemakers who produce excellent bottled wines. Minos-Miliarakis, Lyrakakis and the Sitia Coop are among those producing Crete's top wines, some of which are exported. Wine tourism, too, is picking up as wineries open visitor centres that double as mini-museums and tasting rooms.

Retsina, white wine flavoured with the resin of pine trees, has taken on an almost folkloric significance with foreigners. An acquired taste, it goes well with strongly flavoured mezedhes and seafood.

Beer

Brink's is the only beer actually produced on Crete; their organic lagers are made at Brink's Brewery (p127), near Rethymno. Other craft beers include Vergina and Hillas lagers from northern Greece, organic Piraiki made in Piraeus, Craft from Athens, and Yellow Donkey from Santorini. Major Greek brands include Mythos, Fix and Alfa.

Coffee & Tea

➡ **Greek coffee** Traditionally brewed in a special copper *briki* (pot) and served in a small cup. Grounds sink to the bottom (don't drink them). It is drunk *glykos* (sweet), *metrios* (medium) and *sketo* (plain; without sugar).

➡ **Frappé** Iced instant-coffee concoction that you see everyone drinking.

➡ **Tsai (tea)** Try camomile or aromatic Cretan *tsai tou vounou* (mountain tea), both nutritious and delicious. Endemic *diktamo* (dittany) tea is known for its medicinal qualities.

How to Eat & Drink

Food and the ritual of dining together play an integral role in Cretan life, whether at home or eating out with family and friends. Cretans will travel far to get to a great restaurant or eat specific food, heading to the mountains for local meat and the sea for fresh fish. Some of the best tavernas are tucked away in unexpected places.

The key to picking a restaurant is to steer away from 'tourist' restaurants and go where locals eat. As a general rule, avoid places on the main tourist drags, especially those with touts outside and big signs with photos of food. Be wary of hotel recommendations, as some have deals with particular restaurants.

CRETAN WINE VARIETALS

Crete has three wine-producing areas. The largest is the Iraklio Wine Country, which makes about 70% of Cretan wine. It produces mostly Kotsifali, Mandilaria and Vilana grapes in two centres; one around Peza/Arhanes south of Iraklio and the other around Dafnes, a bit further west. The smallest wine region is east of here in Lasithi. Vineyards cluster primarily around Sitia and are specialised in Liatiko grapes. In western Crete, the main grape-growing region is west of Hania, where the main varietal cultivated is Romeiko.

➡ **Dafni** Lively with subtle acidity and an aroma resembling laurel, common in Lasithi and Iraklio wine regions.

➡ **Kotsifali** Indigenous red grape with high alcohol content and rich flavour, typical of Iraklio region, often blended with Mandilaria.

➡ **Liatiko** Very old indigenous red variety with complex character, found mainly around Sitia.

➡ **Malvasia** Original Cretan variety, strong flower aroma with notes of muscat, ages well if blended with Kotsifali.

➡ **Mandilaria** Dark-coloured but light-bodied red wine, prevalent around Arhanes and Peza.

➡ **Romeiko** Red grapes mostly grown around Hania and turned into robust red, white and rosé wines.

➡ **Vidiano** White indigenous wine with intensive and complex peach and apricot aromas; often blended with Vilana.

➡ **Vilana** Main white grape of Iraklio growing area; fresh, low-alcohol wine with a delicate aroma evoking apples.

RAKI & OUZO

The Cretan pomace brandy *raki* (also known as *tsikoudia*) is an integral part of local culture. A shot of the fiery brew is offered as a welcome, at the end of a meal and pretty much at any time and on all occasions. Distilled from grape stems and pips left over from the grapes pressed for wine, it is similar to the *tsipouro* found in other parts of Greece, Middle Eastern *arak*, Italian grappa, Irish poteen or Turkish *raki*.

Each October, the *raki* distilling season starts, with distilleries and private stills around the island producing massive quantities. Expect lots of drinking and feasting, and if you pass a village distilling *raki*, you may well get an invitation. Good *raki* has a smooth mellow taste with no noticeable after-burn and shouldn't cause a hangover. It does not incorporate herbs, and is drunk neat. Family-owned distilleries bottle the potent brew in plastic water bottles, sold in groceries, tavernas or by the roadside.

In winter look for warm *rakomelo* – *raki*, honey and cloves.

Ouzo, the famous Greek aniseed spirit, has a more limited following in Crete. It is served neat, with ice and a separate glass of water for dilution (which makes it turn milky white).

Given the long summers and mild winters, alfresco dining is central to the dining experience – with tables set up on pavements, roads, squares and beaches.

When to Eat

Greece doesn't have a big breakfast tradition, unless you count coffee and a cigarette, and maybe a *koulouri, tyropita* or *bougatsa* eaten on the run. You'll find Western-style breakfasts in hotels and tourist areas.

While changes in working hours have affected traditional meal patterns, lunch is still usually the biggest meal of the day, starting after 2pm. Greeks eat dinner late, after sunset in summer. This coincides with shop closing hours, so restaurants often don't fill until after 10pm. Arrive by 9pm to avoid crowds.

Most tavernas open all day, but some upmarket restaurants open for dinner only. Cafes do a roaring trade, particularly after the mid-afternoon siesta.

Where to Eat

Estiatorio Restaurant with upmarket international cuisine or Greek classics in a more formal setting.

Kafeneio Coffee house and cultural institution, largely the domain of men.

Mayireio Restaurant specialising in ready-cooked homestyle one-pot stews, casseroles and baked dishes (known as *mayirefta*).

Mezedhopoleio & ouzerie Serve lots of different mezedhes (shared small dishes), often with ouzo or *raki*.

Rakadiko The Cretan equivalent of an *ouzerie* serves increasingly sophisticated mezedhes with each round of *raki*. Particularly popular in Sitia, Ierapetra and Rethymno.

Taverna Common, casual, family-run (and child-friendly) place. They usually have barrel wine, paper tablecloths and traditional menus. Specialist variations: *psarotaverna* (fish and seafood), and *hasapotaverna* or *psistaria* (chargrilled or spit-roasted meat).

Zaharoplasteio A cross between a patisserie and a cafe (some only do takeaway).

Etiquette & Customs

➤ Try to adapt to local eating times – a restaurant that was empty at 7pm might be heaving with locals at 11pm.

➤ Book for upmarket restaurants, but reservations are unnecessary in most tavernas.

➤ In tavernas, it's totally customary to browse the *mayirefta* behind the counter. Just ask for a look before ordering.

➤ Taverna dress code is generally casual, but in high-end restaurants dress to impress.

➤ Expect a small charge for bread and nibbles served on arrival.

➤ Hospitality is a key element of Cretan culture, from the glass of water on arrival to the customary complimentary fruit or dessert and *raki* served at the end of a meal, when you ask for the bill.

➡ Dining is a drawn-out ritual; if you eat with locals, pace yourself, as there will be plenty more to come.

➡ Service can be slow (and patchy) by Western standards, but there's no rushing you out of there, either.

➡ Tipping is not mandatory but Greeks usually round up on the bill or add around 10% for good service. To split the bill, work it out among your group – Greeks tend to treat the whole table.

➡ Cretans are generous hosts. Don't refuse a coffee or drink – it's a gesture of hospitality and goodwill. If you're invited out, the host normally pays.

➡ If you are invited to someone's home, take a small gift (flowers or sweets) and pace yourself, as you'll be expected to eat everything on your plate.

➡ Smoking is banned in enclosed public spaces, including restaurants and cafes, but you'll see plenty of Cretans flouting the law.

➡ Drinking age is 18. Public drunkenness is uncommon and frowned upon.

Plan Your Trip

Travel with Children

Crete doesn't cater to kids in the obvious ways other countries do; there's often a scant supply of safety ropes in ancient ruins, and a lack of children's menus and the spatial awareness not to smoke in their presence. But what Greeks embed in their children is a strong sense of social inclusion and spirit of adventure, while they will treat your own kids with kindness and genuine warmth. From your children's first bite of calamari to their first snorkel or descent into a cave, Crete is a place they will never forget.

Crete for Kids

Crete has plenty of beaches from which to choose, from sugar-fine sand to pebbles, and hidden coves to public stretches. Add to this coral-blue waters aglimmer with sunken ships to snorkel, and fun boat trips to be had, and you can see that H_2O is going to be a big part of your Cretan adventure. But there are many other attractions that will also light their imaginations, from myriad ruins to creepy caves.

Hiking, Cycling & Horse Riding

Apart from the more strenuous gorge and mountain walks, such as the Samaria Gorge, there are numerous options to suit the family. The same goes for cycling, while most horse-riding outfits are excellent at tailoring sessions to all ages. For more info, see Outdoor Activities (p32).

Museums & Attractions

Head to Iraklio's Natural History Museum (p150), where the Discovery Centre is crammed with interactive features. And the Cretaquarium (p182), where youngsters will love the shark tank, jellyfish tank and hands-on pool.

Best Regions for Kids

Iraklio
Iraklio City has the best kid-friendly museums in Crete.

West & South Hania
The ideal active family area with glorious mountains and 'desert island' beaches.

Rethymno
Youngsters love Rethymno's Venetian fortress and a romp along the lovely promenade.

Eastern Lasithi
The lonely ancient sites of this region will spark young imaginations.

Eating Out

Greek tavernas are particularly kid-friendly. Some dishes that kids might grow to love include *kalamari* (fried squid), *tiropitakia* (cheese parcels in filo pastry), dolmadhes (flavoured rice wrapped in vine leaves) and *saganaki* (fried cheese).

Nuts and dairy find their way into lots of Cretan dishes, so if your kids suffer from any severe allergies, ask someone to write this down clearly in Greek so you can show restaurant staff before you order.

Children's Highlights

Great Beaches

➡ **Elafonisi** (p88) Fun bathing in tiny lagoons amid beautiful surroundings.

➡ **Bali** (p135) A series of accessible coves with all services.

➡ **Kato Gouves** Rock pools and clear water for young explorers.

➡ **Vaï** (p210) Palm tree paradise; quietest outside August.

Outdoor Adventures

➡ **Boat trips** Along Hania's south coast or around Elounda in Lasithi.

➡ **Hiking** Short sections of easy gorges like Zakros (p213) or Agia Irini (p81).

➡ **Horse riding** At Avdou, below the Lasithi Plateau.

SAFETY
• •

Crete is generally a safe pace to travel with children. The largest danger is heatstroke – remember Crete is blessed with a regular breeze so it's easy to become overexposed to the sun without realising it. Be careful, too, at isolated beaches and coves that may have powerful offshore currents. And always be mindful of youngsters at ancient sites, where there might be no safety fences or loose masonry.

There are doctor's surgeries around the island, but for anything serious head to Venizelio hospital (p155) in Iraklio. If hiring a car, check for agencies that have child seats available and fit the seats yourself.

➡ **Caves** Dikteon Cave (p204) on the Lasithi Plateau or Skotino Cave (p183) near Hersonisos.

Interactive Attractions

➡ **Water City** (p182) Enjoy the water fun park at Anopoli, southeast of Iraklio.

➡ **Natural History Museum** (p150) Visit the children's section in Iraklio's imaginative museum.

➡ **Agora** (p67) Browse Hania's daily market.

➡ **Cretaquarium** (p182) Get up close and personal with magical sea creatures near Iraklio.

➡ **Fortezza** (p107) Explore Rethymno's fortress.

Planning

When to Go

For younger kids and toddlers it's worth thinking about visiting in spring, early summer or autumn when the sun is not too strong and temperatures are pleasantly warm. June is probably the earliest your kids can swim in the sea; anytime before and the water is cold.

Accommodation

Big resort-style hotels tend to open later in the year than independent accommodation, even as late as June; however, they are generally more tailored to kids' needs. Many hotels don't charge for young children and will often provide you with a camp bed.

Don't Forget

➡ Sunscreen – and plenty of it!

➡ Travel highchair (either deflatable booster seat or a cloth one that attaches to the back of a chair).

➡ Lightweight pop-up cot for babies.

➡ Medicine, inhalers etc along with prescriptions.

➡ Plastic cups and cutlery for little ones.

➡ Newborn's car seat – unless you have pre-checked with the car rental agency, you'll likely be disappointed.

➡ Portable change mat and hand sanitiser.

➡ For toddlers not yet walking consider bringing a sturdy carrying backpack as strollers are a struggle in villages with steep cobbled streets.

If you come unstuck for baby monitors, car seats, bottle warmers etc, **My Baby In Greece** (www.mybabyingreece.com) rents, sells and will deliver these items across Crete.

Regions at a Glance

The birthplace of Zeus, Crete is a vast and multifaceted island whose sun-blessed landscape is a quilt of soaring mountains, dramatic gorges and stunning beaches.

The northern coast, with its nearly uninterrupted strip of beach resorts, has built-up infrastructure and gets the most visitors.

The rugged interior, by contrast, is largely untouched by mass tourism. A dreamy mosaic of sleepy villages, terraced vineyards and fertile valleys, dotted with Byzantine churches and historic monasteries, the interior invites exploration at a leisurely pace.

Those with a sense of adventure will be enchanted by the largely untamed south, where serpentine roads dead-end in isolated coves and the landscape is sliced by steep gorges where rare plants and animals thrive.

Hania

History
Beaches
Activities

Venetian Chic

The splendid Venetian port of Hania is bursting with colour and the time-tested pomp appropriate to the former maritime empire of Venice. Trace your way down the massive stone walls, past the arsenals and shipyards, and along the historic mansions (now housing stylish hotels), to gaze over the waterfront, drink in hand.

Crystal-Clear Seas

Embraced by the open Mediterranean (next stop, Spain or Africa!), western Crete has pristine, crystal-clear waters, heated to almost tropical temperatures on pink-sand beaches like Elafonisi, Balos and Falasarna.

Ultimate Adventure

The Lefka Ori (White Mountains) south of Hania comprise Crete's wildest terrain, interspersed with deep gorges, labyrinthine caves and raw cliffs. Whether you're after white-knuckle driving, gorge trekking, rock climbing or even (way) off-piste skiing in winter, this is the place to go.

p54

Rethymno

History
Beaches
Scenery

Cross-Cultural Influences

All phases of Cretan history are omnipresent in Rethymno, whose eponymous main town is itself a pretty pastiche of Venetian and Ottoman architecture. Monasteries that stood firm against the Turks and remote mountain villages drenched in age-old traditions will leave you wanting more.

Remote Shores

There's something otherworldly about Rethymno's corrugated southern coast, where craggy inlets embrace perfect little beaches that are often footprint-free. This is the place to dig your toes in the sand and indulge in island dreams.

Jaw-Dropping Views

Lorded over by Crete's highest peak, the often snow-capped Mt Psiloritis, Rethymno will delight shutterbugs with dazzling vistas of dramatic gorges, tranquil valleys and velvety hills blanketed with olive groves, vineyards and wildflowers.

p104

Iraklio

Ancient Sites
Hiking
Kids' Activities

Minoan Marvels

Endowed with the greatest concentration of Minoan ruins, Iraklio is a mecca for archaeology fans. Stand in awe of the achievements of Europe's oldest civilisation when surveying the palaces of Knossos, Malia, Phaestos and Agia Triada, plus scores of minor sites.

Gorge-ous Walks

From the spectacular gorges at Rouvas and Agiofarango to the trails connecting hidden chapels and monasteries around Zaros, and the olive groves and tombs around Kamilari, Iraklio promises top walks.

Childish Delights

Not only do Cretans love kids, in Iraklio they have also come up with myriad ways to entertain them in grand style, be it by letting them frolic at the sea or by taking them to enchanting aquariums, adrenalin-packed water parks, placid playgrounds and hands-on museums.

p143

Lasithi

Ancient Sites
Beaches
Hiking

Moody Minoans

Lasithi may not have the painted and polished ruins of Knossos, but the Minoan sites of Gournia and Kato Zakros evoke a sometimes deeper awareness. Their wild surroundings and the haunting sense of a lost world fire the imagination towards a more personal sense of place, and the past.

Beyond the Main Beach

Although famous venues such as Vaï draw thick summer crowds, Lasithi's beaches are generally free of too much organised lounging. You'll find myriad hidden coves and small sandy bays where you'll luxuriate in blissful isolation, such as Almyros and Xerokambos.

Mountain Highs

Some of Crete's finest mountains dominate the Lasithi skyline. Their airy summits and deep gorges offer superb hiking and trekking, and put you amid the heady scents of wildflowers and aromatic herbs. Hiking the spectacular Valley of the Dead to the sea is one of your options.

p188

On the Road

Hania
p54

Rethymno
p104

Iraklio
p143

Lasithi
p188

Hania

Best Places to Eat

➜ To Maridaki (p65)

➜ Taverna Tamam (p65)

➜ Thalassino Ageri (p66)

➜ Methexis (p86)

➜ To Skolio (p87)

Best Places to Stay

➜ Serenissima (p64)

➜ Milia (p97)

➜ Casa Delfino (p64)

➜ Elia Suites (p63)

➜ Elafonisi Resort (p88)

Why Go?

The west of Crete stands apart in so many ways. A land of giant mountains, grandiose legends and memorials to great battles past, it is presided over by the romantic port city of Hania (Χανιά), once Venice's jewel of a capital and now filled with arty hotels, interesting shops and some of Greece's best eateries. The region also boasts the grandest gorge in Europe, west coast beaches that are among the most beautiful in the world, Europe's southernmost possession (tranquil Gavdos, a remote island nearer to Africa than Greece), and mountain villages hardly affected by modernity. The steep mountains that ripple across the west and into the southern sea guarantee that the region generally remains untouched by the excesses of tourism. From the olive oil to moustachioed elders, if you want to see beautiful and traditional Crete, Hania and the west is definitely the place.

Road Distances (km)

	Omalos	Hora Sfakion	Kissamos	Paleohora
Hora Sfakion	107			
Kissamos	59	106		
Paleohora	56	137	44	
Hania	38	73	38	72

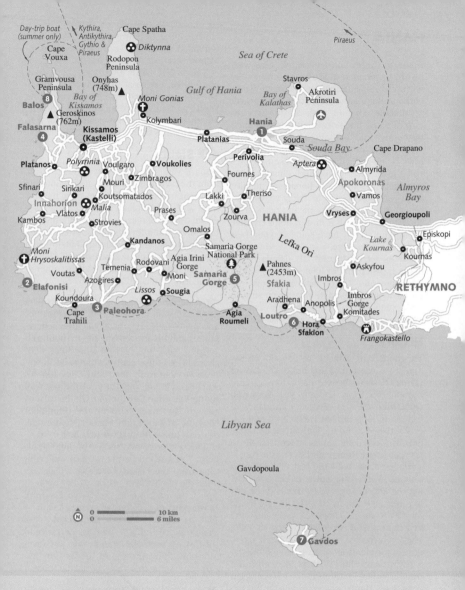

Hania Highlights

① Soak up Hania's splendid **Venetian harbour** (p56).

② Luxuriate on the fine pink-cream sands of **Elafonisi** (p88) in the remote southwest.

③ Enjoy live Cretan music in its natural habitat in laid-back **Paleohora** (p83).

④ Ride the waves at Crete's most entertaining beach, **Falasarna** (p97).

⑤ Hike grand **Samaria Gorge** (p94) to the southern sea, or trek its many neighbouring gorges.

⑥ Go by boat to escape the masses in the sparkling southern hamlet of **Loutro** (p79).

⑦ Get (really) away from it all on the barely populated island of **Gavdos** (p89).

⑧ Swim magical teal lagoons at **Balos** (p99), on the western edge of remote Gramvousa Peninsula.

HANIA XANIA

POP 54,000

Hania is Crete's most evocative city, with its pretty Venetian quarter, criss-crossed by narrow lanes, culminating at a magnificent harbour. Remnants of Venetian and Turkish architecture abound, with old townhouses now restored, transformed into atmospheric restaurants and boutique hotels.

Although all this beauty means the old town is deluged with tourists in summer, it's still a great place to unwind. Plus it's got a university and a modern portion to the city, so in winter it retains its lively charm. Excellent local handicrafts mean there's good shopping, and with a multitude of creative restaurants, you'll have some of your best meals in Greece here.

Crete's second-biggest city, Hania is the major transit point for hikers walking Samaria Gorge, and it's the main transport hub for all western destinations. But be sure to budget enough time to join the sunset promenade around the harbour, and soak it all in.

History

The important Minoan settlement of Kydonia was centred on the hill to the east of Hania's harbour, between Akti Tombazi and Karaoli Dimitriou. Kydonia was destroyed along with the rest of Crete's Minoan civilisation in 1450 BC, but was rebuilt and later flourished as an ancient Greek city-state during Hellenistic times. It continued to prosper under Roman and Byzantine rule.

Hania, along with the rest of Crete, was claimed by the rising power of Venice following the Fourth Crusade (1204), and the city was renamed La Canea. After briefly losing the city to their Genoese rivals in 1266, the Venetians finally wrested it back in 1290. They constructed massive fortifications to protect the city from pirates, making the city a key strategic hub in their Mediterranean trading empire for three-and-a-half centuries.

In 1645 Hania was captured by the Ottoman Empire, after a two-month siege. The Turks made it the seat of the Turkish Pasha until they were forced out finally in 1898. During the Tourkokratia (Turkish occupation of Greece), the city's churches were converted into mosques and the architectural style of the town changed, becoming more oriental, with wooden walls, latticed windows and minarets (two survive today).

When Crete became independent of Turkish rule in 1898, Hania was declared the island's capital by Europe's Great Powers. It remained so until 1971, when the administration was transferred to Iraklio.

The WWII Battle of Crete largely took place along the coast to the west of Hania. The town itself was heavily bombed during WWII, particularly around Ancient Kydonia, but enough of the old town survives for it to be regarded as Crete's most beautiful city.

⊙ Sights

Hania's Venetian quarter begs for a stroll, from the ravishing old harbour back into the shopping streets that arc between the fortress walls. The Splantzia quarter is a wonderful warren of narrow streets with historic buildings, and a few shopping promenades, mostly pedestrianised. Along Chatzimichali Daliani street, you will see one of Hania's two remaining **minarets**, and the other is on nearby Plateia 1821 (Splantzia Sq).

★**Venetian Harbour**   HISTORIC QUARTER

A stroll around the old harbour is a must for any visitor to Hania. Pastel-coloured historic homes and businesses line the harbour, zigzagging back into narrow lanes lined with shops. The entire area is ensconced in impressive **Venetian fortifications**, and it's worth the 1.5km walk around the sea wall to the **Venetian lighthouse**. On the eastern side of the inner harbour the prominent **Mosque of Kioutsouk Hasan** (Mosque of Janissaries) houses regular exhibitions.

The best-preserved section of the massive outer fortifications is the western wall, running from the **Firkas Fortress**, which was once the old Turkish prison, at the western tip of the harbour, to the **Siavo Bastion**. It was part of a defensive system begun in 1538 by engineer Michele Sanmichele, who also designed Iraklio's defences. Entrance to the fortress is via the gates next to the Naval Museum. From the top of the bastion you can enjoy some fine views of the old town.

★**Archaeological Museum**   MUSEUM

(☑28210 90334; Halidon 30; adult/child €3/free; ⊙8am-8pm Mon-Fri, to 3pm Sat & Sun) The setting alone in the beautifully restored 16th-century Venetian Church of San Francisco is reason to visit this fine collection of artefacts from neolithic to Roman times. The museum's Late Minoan sarcophagi catch the eye as much as a large glass case with an entire herd of clay bulls (used to worship Poseidon). Other standouts include three Roman floor mosaics, Hellenistic gold jewellery, clay tablets with Linear A and Linear B script, and a marble sculpture of Roman emperor Hadrian.

Also particularly impressive are the statue of Diana, and in the pretty courtyard, a marble fountain decorated with lions' heads, a vestige of the Venetian tradition. A Turkish fountain is a relic from the building's days as a mosque.

The church itself was a mosque under the Turks, a movie theatre in 1913, and a munitions depot for the Germans during WWII.

If you first visit the city's Byzantine & Post-Byzantine Collection, that box office sells a joint ticket (adult/child €3/free).

★ **Maritime Museum of Crete**   MUSEUM
(☑ 28210 91875; www.mar-mus-crete.gr; Akti Koundourioti; adult/child €3/2; ☉ 9am-5pm Mon-Sat, 10am-6pm Sun, closed Sun Nov-Apr) Part of the hulking Venetian-built Firkas Fortress at the western port entrance, this museum celebrates Crete's nautical tradition with model ships, naval instruments, paintings, photographs, maps and memorabilia. One room is dedicated to historical sea battles while upstairs there's thorough documentation on the WWII-era Battle of Crete. The gate to the fortress itself is open from 8am to 2pm.

★ **Byzantine &**
Post-Byzantine Collection   MUSEUM
(☑ 28210 96046; Theotokopoulou 82; admission €2; ☉ 8am-3pm Tue-Sun) The Byzantine museum is in the impressively restored Venetian Church of San Salvatore. It has a small but fascinating collection of artefacts, icons, jewellery and coins spanning the period from AD 62 to 1913, including a fine segment of a mosaic floor for an early Christian basilica and a prized icon of St George slaying the dragon. The building features a mixed bag of

---

THREE PERFECT DAYS

Day One
Rise early to beat the crowds and contemplate Hania's wonderful **Venetian harbour** (p56) with a coffee at **Pallas** (p65), then stroll out to the **lighthouse** (p56). Or, visit the fascinating **Archaeological Museum** (p56), **Byzantine & Post-Byzantine Collection** (p57) or **Maritime Museum** (p57) by the Venetian **Firkas Fortress** (p56) before enjoying a quick lunch at **To Karnagio** (p65), or in the spiffy Splantzia quarter at **Kouzina EPE** (p65). Then, if you can resist the call of the siesta, take a drive past olive groves to superlative **Falasarna beach** (p97) on the western edge of the island. Circle back for a late dinner at one of Hania town's outstanding eateries, like **To Maridaki** (p65) or **Taverna Tamam** (p65), with wine and grilled octopus under the stars. If you can't make it back, stay at Falasarna or at nearby ecovillage **Milia** (p97).

Day Two
Work off all that excellent Cretan cookery with a full-day trek through **Samaria Gorge** (p94) or shorter **Agia Irini** (p81) or **Imbros** (p75) gorges. Along the way, look out for the elusive *kri-kri* (Crete's shy wild goat) up in the cliffs, and watch the birds of prey circle in the hope of nibbling on a heat-struck hiker. When you emerge at the coast, you can ferry between remote hamlets **Agia Roumeli** (p80), **Sougia** (p81) or **Loutro** (p79), staying the night on the Libyan sea, or boat all the way to **Hora Sfakion** (p77) for a dinner of fresh fish and *sfakies pites* at **Nikos** (p78), the harbour-front taverna, or for the bus back to Hania. Alternatively, catch the boat west to relaxed Paleohora for a dinner of Cretan specialities at **Methexis** (p86), and live music in the bars.

Day Three
Either a long drive from Hania town or a short morning boat trip from **Paleohora** (p83) brings you to gorgeous **Elafonisi** (p88) beach and islet. Use the full day to savour the splendid sands of striated cream, grey and pink tones, and the Libyan Sea's lapping warm waters. Then stay over at **Elafonisi Resort** (p88) to have the place to yourself for a sunset walk across the islet, and do it all over again the next day, or zip back to Hania town for one last extravagant seafood meal at **Thalassino Ageri** (p66).

An alternative to Elafonisi is **Balos** (p99) – a great looping lagoon of teal water and remote adventure – accessible by morning **boat** (p99) from Kissamos (Kastelli). To eat en route, stop at **Gramvousa** (p99) or **Leventis** (p100) for Cretan dishes made with love.

Hania

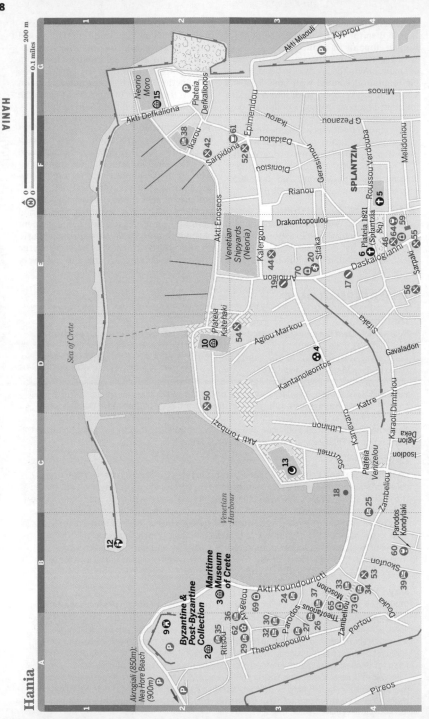

0 0
N
0.1 miles
200 m

Akrogiali (850m);
Nea Hore Beach
(900m)

Sea of Crete

Venetian Harbour

**Byzantine &
Post-Byzantine
Collection**

**Maritime
Museum
of Crete**

Neorio
Moro

Plateia
Defkalionos

Akti Defkaliona

SPLANTZIA

Plateia 1821
(Splantzia
Sq)

Venetian Shipyards
(Neoria)

Plateia
Katehaki

Plateia
Venizelou

Akti Miaouli

Kyprou

Minoos

Melidoniou

Sarpaki

Gavaladon

Karaoli-Dimitriou

Agion Deka

Isodion

Zambeliou

Parodos
Kondylaki

Skouton

Douka

Pireos

Portou

Zambeliou

Theotokopoulou

Theofanous

Parodos
Moschon

Akti Koundourioti

Angelou

Ritsou

Theotokopoulou

Akti Tombazi

Akti Enoseos

Sourmeli

Kanevaro

Katre

Lithinon

Kantanoleontos

Agiou Markou

Arholeon

Kalergon

Daskalogianni

Sifaka

Sitaka

Rianou

Drakontopoulou

Roussou-Verdouba

G Pezanou

Gerasimou

Ikarou

Dionisiou

Epimenidou

Daidalou

Ikarou

Sarpidona

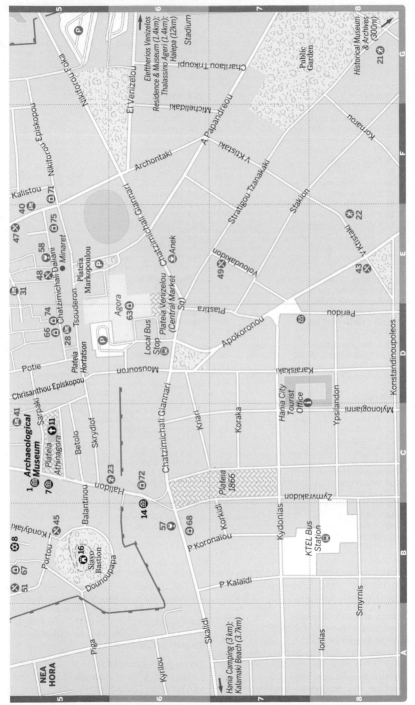

Hania

interesting architectural features from its various occupiers. A joint ticket with the Archaeological Museum costs adult/child €3/free.

Church of Agios Nikolaos   CHURCH
(Plateia 1821; ⊙ 7am-noon & 2-7pm) This church is quite memorably attached to one of Hania's two remaining minarets, and a bell tower rises over its opposite end. The church's foundations were laid in 1205 by Venetians, but Franciscan monks can prob-

ably be credited with the massive structure's curving ceiling and simple stained-glass windows (1320). In 1645 the Ottomans made the church into a mosque, but the Orthodox Church recovered it in 1918. Just across the square you'll find the restored Venetian **Church of San Rocco**.

Etz Hayyim Synagogue   SYNAGOGUE
(☎ 28210 86286; www.etz-hayyim-hania.org; Parodos Kondylaki; ⊙ 10am-6pm Mon-Thu, to 3pm Fri)

Crete's only remaining synagogue (dating from the 15th century) was badly damaged in WWII and reopened in 1999. It sports a *mikve* (ritual bath), tombs of rabbis and a memorial to the local Jews killed by the Nazis. Today it serves a small congregation and is open to visitors. Find it on a small lane accessible only from Kondylaki street.

Greek Orthodox Cathedral CATHEDRAL
(Church of Panagia Trimartyri; Plateia Athinagora) The Greek Orthodox Cathedral Church of Hania is a neoclassical cathedral built to honour the city's patron saint: the Virgin of the Three Martyrs. It is built on the site of a church dating to the 11th century, and during the Turkish rule it was converted into a soap factory. November 21 is the saint's feast day and a city holiday.

Cretan House Folklore Museum MUSEUM
(☑ 28210 90816; Halidon 46b; adult/child €2/free; ⊙ 9am-6pm Mon, Tue, Thu & Fri, to 5pm Wed & Sat, 11am-6pm Sun) Hania's interesting Folklore Museum contains a selection of crafts including weavings with traditional designs, local paintings, as well as several rooms of a traditional Cretan house. Find the entrance inside the courtyard and upstairs.

Historical Museum & Archives MUSEUM
(☑ 28210 52606; www.chaniatourism.com; Ioannou Sfakianaki 20; ⊙ 9am-2pm Mon-Fri) FREE The Historical Museum & Archives of Hania, about a 1.5km walk southeast of the old harbour, traces Crete's war-torn history with a series of exhibits focusing on the struggle against the Turks. There are also displays of the belongings of national hero Eleftherios Venizelos (1864–1936), the Cretan leader and Greek prime minister, plus a folklore collection.

Grand Arsenal HISTORIC BUILDING
(☑ 28210 40101; www.kam-arsenali.gr; Plateia Katehaki) The stunningly restored 16th-century Venetian arsenal is now home to the Centre for Mediterranean Architecture, which hosts regular events and exhibitions.

Permanent Collection of Ancient & Traditional Shipbuilding MUSEUM
(☑ 28210 91875; Neorio Moro, Akti Defkaliona; adult/child €2/1; ⊙ 9am-5pm Mon-Sat, 10am-6pm Sun May-Oct) The *Minoa,* a painstaking replica of a Minoan ship that sailed from Crete to Athens for the 2004 Olympics ceremonies, now permanently docks in a converted Venetian shipyard *(neoria).* Tools used in

---

DON'T MISS

HANIA'S BEST BEACHES

➜ **Elafonisi** (p88) Sublime southwestern beach famed for its pink sands.

➜ **Balos** (p99) Stunningly clear lagoon of translucent blues and greens, on the Gramvousa Peninsula.

➜ **Falasarna** (p97) The best waves in the west slam into this long, sandy beach.

HANIA HANIA

its making and photographs from the epic journey bring to life this amazing feat.

Municipal Art Gallery GALLERY
(☑ 28210 92294; www.pinakothiki-chania.gr; Halidon 98; adult/child €2/free; ⊙ 10am-2pm Tue-Sat & 7-10pm Mon-Sat) Hania's modern three-level art gallery hosts exhibitions of contemporary Greek art.

Eleftherios Venizelos Residence & Museum MUSEUM
(☑ 28210 56008; www.venizelos-foundation.gr; Plateia Helena Venizelou, Halepa; adult/child €3/1; ⊙ 10.30am-1.30pm & 6.30-9.30pm Mon-Fri, 10.30am-1.30pm Sat & Sun mid-Jun–Sep, shorter hours Oct–mid-Jun) Some 2km east of the old town, in the Halepa neighbourhood, the Eleftherios Venizelos Residence & Museum preserves the great statesman's home in splendid fashion, with original furnishings, maps and other information. Hours are reduced in winter.

Ancient Kydonia RUIN
You can see excavations in progress at the site of Ancient Kydonia to the east of the old harbour at the junction of Kanevaro and Kandaloneou. The discovery of clay tablets with Linear B script has led archaeologists to believe that Kydonia was both a Minoan palace site and an important town. Much of Kydonia's ruins lie beneath modern Hania, so excavations have been limited and thus yield fewer finds than at Iraklio-area Minoan sites such as Knossos and Phaestos.

Most of the unearthed artefacts are housed in Hania's Archaeological Museum.

Beaches
The town beach 2km west of the Venetian harbour at **Nea Hora** (Akti Papanikoli) is crowded but generally clean if you need to cool off and get some rays, while that of **Koum Kapi** is less used (and less clean). For better swimming, keep heading west

and you'll come to the beaches (in order) of **Agioi Apostoli, Hrysi Akti** and **Kalamaki** (about 3.5km). There are regular local buses heading there and all the way to **Platanias** and beyond.

🏃 Activities

Most activities from Hania centre around exploring the grand gorges and beaches to the south and southwest.

Greek Mountaineering Association
HIKING, OUTDOORS

(EOS; ☑ 28210 44647; www.eoshanion.gr; Tzanakaki 90, Hania; ☺ 8.30am-6pm) Visit the local EOS branch or check its website to get the scoop on outdoor sports, including serious climbing in the Lefka Ori (White Mountains), mountain refuges and the E4 European Path. EOS also runs regular hiking excursions.

Trekking Plan
HIKING, CYCLING

(☑ 28210 27040, 6932417040; www.cycling. gr; Halidon 85; hiking & cycling per day from €35, climbing per hr €15, private guiding per half-day €100; ☺ 9am-2pm & 6-8.30pm, closed Sun Nov-Apr) Trekking Plan offers hikes to Agia Irini and Imbros gorges, and climbs of Mt Gingilos, as well as canyoning, rappelling, rock climbing, and kayaking and mountain-biking tours. There are ski tours in winter.

Hania Alpine Travel
HIKING

(☑ 28210 50939, 6932252890; www.alpine.gr; Boniali 11-19) Offers tailored hiking, climbing and canoeing holidays, for families, groups and individuals. Based in Hania.

HANIA FOR CHILDREN

If your five-year-old has lost interest in Venetian architecture, head to the **public garden** between Tzanakaki and A Papandreou, where there's a playground and a shady cafe. Eight kilometres south of town the giant water park **Limnoupolis** (☑ 28210 33246; www.limnoupolis.gr; Varypetro; day pass adult/child 3-12 €23/17, afternoon pass €16/13; ☺ 10am-7pm mid-May–Sep) has enough slides and pools to keep kids amused, and cafes and pool bars for adults. Buses leave regularly from the KTEL bus station.

E-Bikes
CYCLING

(☑ 28215 03879; Sifaka 60; regular/electric bike per day €9/15; ☺ 9am-noon & 4-8pm Mon-Sat) Hires street bikes or electrically assisted bikes, in Hania's old town.

Hellas Bikes
CYCLING

(☑ 28210 60858; www.hellasbike.net; Agia Marina; bicycle per day from €13; ☺ 9am-1pm & 5-8.30pm) In Agia Marina, 10km west of Hania, this group hires out bikes and leads half- and full-day bike tours around the region.

Blue Adventures Diving
DIVING

(☑ 28210 40403; www.divingchania.com; Arholeon 11; ☺ Apr-Nov) This established outfit offers a host of dive options, including PADI open-water certification (€450), diving trips around Hania (two dives €90, with gear), and beginner dives. There are also snorkelling trips (€40). It also has a branch at Nea Hora beach.

Chania Diving Center
DIVING

(☑ 28210 09083; www.chaniadiving.gr; Arholeon 1; 2 dives incl gear €85, PADI open-water certification €410) Runs dives around Hania, including PADI courses, dive trips, beginner dives, and snorkelling trips (€45).

👉 Tours

Captain Nick's Glass Bottom Boat
BOAT TOUR

(☑ 28210 86732; www.captainnickchania.com; Hania Harbour; 1/2/3½hr trip €10/20/25) The best bet among Hania's lacklustre day-trip boats, Captain Nick cruises the nearby offshore islands and has snorkelling equipment on board.

Chania Segway Tours
SEGWAY TOUR

(www.chaniasegwaytours.com; 1¼hr tour €39) Segway tours around Hania include the Old City and Harbour tour.

🎉 Festivals & Events

Battle of Crete
CULTURAL

Hania commemorates the WWII Battle of Crete anniversary with athletics competitions, folk dancing and ceremonial events for a week at the end of May.

Summer Festival
PERFORMING ARTS

(www.chania.gr) From June to August the municipality hosts cultural events around the city, including in the public gardens and at the open-air theatre on the outskirts of the city walls (on Kyprou), which has regular music and theatrical performances.

🛏 Sleeping

Hania's Venetian quarter brims with chic boutique hotels and family-run atmospheric pensions in restored Venetian buildings. There are no hostels, but there is a nearby campground. Most hotels have no lift. They tend to be open year-round, and it's a good idea to book ahead for weekends and in summer when there also may be two- or three-day minimum stay requirements.

The western end of the harbour and along Zambeliou is jammed with good places, but it can get noisy and crowded at night, especially along the harbour. You'll find quieter, cheaper rooms around the Splantzia quarter. To get away from the action head up to the Halepa neighbourhood overlooking the water 2.5km east of the old harbour. Hotel complexes with pools start at Nea Hora and run along the beaches west to Platanes and beyond.

Pension Theresa   PENSION €
(☑ 28210 92798; www.pensiontheresa.gr; Angelou 8; r €50-60; 🌢🛜) Part of the Venetian fortifications, this creaky old house with a steep (and narrow!) spiral staircase and antique furniture delivers snug rooms with character aplenty. The location is excellent and views are stunning from the rooftop terrace with communal kitchen stocked with basic breakfast items. They have another annexe as well.

Ifigenia Rooms & Studios   APARTMENT €
(☑ 28210 94357; www.ifigeniastudios.gr; Gamba 23, cnr Parodos Agelou; r €50-110; 🌢@🛜🛗) This network of refurbished houses around the Venetian harbour offers anything from simple rooms to fancy suites with kitchenettes, jacuzzis and views. There are nice touches like elaborate stone-wrought bed frames and neat archways. Some bathrooms are very basic, though. To get a sea view in a standard rooms, expect to pay €15 to €30 more.

Iason Studios   APARTMENT €
(☑ 28210 87102; www.iasonstudios.gr; Agelou 32; d/studio from €50/55; 🌢🛜) Simple, spacious studios in the heart of the old town are run by a friendly proprietress, Despina, who is fluent in English. Some have town-facing balconies.

Camping Hania   CAMPGROUND €
(☑ 28210 31138; www.camping-chania.gr; Agii Apostoli; camp sites per tent/adult/child €4/7/4; ⏰ Apr-Oct; 🅿🛜🏊) Hania's nearest campground is 5km west of town on the beach and has a large swimming pool with separate kids' section. The site is shaded and has a restaurant, bar, minimarket and laundry. There's wi-fi near reception and the bar. Also rents tents, mobile homes and kitchen facilities. Buses heading west from the southeast corner of Plateia 1866 can let you off at the campground.

⭐ Elia Suites   DESIGN HOTEL €€
(☑ 28210 83778; www.eliahotels.gr; Chatzimichali Daliani 57, cnr Gavaladon; d/q €100/140; 🌢🛜🛗) Four spacious, modern and luxurious suites fill this restored townhouse on pedestrianised Daliani, just behind the town market. Rooms were renovated in 2014 with sleek, stylish touches such as slate-coloured bedding and stone bathrooms with enormous walk-in showers. Large flat-screen TVs, firm beds and small balconies round out the offerings. No on-site reception; book ahead. It has other properties around Hania as well.

Splantzia Hotel   BOUTIQUE HOTEL €€
(☑ 28210 45313; www.splanzia.com; Daskalogianni 20; d/tr incl breakfast from €115/130; 🌢@🛜) In the appealing Splantzia quarter, this smart, recently renovated hotel in an Ottoman building has eight stylish rooms, some decorated with four-poster timber beds and drapery. The back rooms overlook a lovely courtyard with bougainvillea that features one of Hania's few remaining Turkish wells. Proprietors are friendly and down to earth.

Palazzo Duca   APARTMENT €€
(☑ 28210 70460; www.palazzoduca.gr; Douka 27-29; d/ste from €80/110; 🌢🛜) This small hotel tucked back into the streets of Hania's old harbour is a reader favourite. It has super-comfy studios and apartments with kitchenettes, some offering port views or small balconies.

Ionas Hotel   HOTEL €€
(☑ 28210 55090; www.ionashotel.com; cnr Sarpaki & Sorvolou; s/d/ste incl breakfast from €95/100/120; 🌢🛜) One of the new breed of boutique hotels in the quieter Splantzia quarter, Ionas is housed in an historic building with contemporary interior design and friendly owners. The nine rooms are kitted out with all mod cons (including a smallish jacuzzi in one) and share a terrace. Original touches include a Venetian archway in the entrance, and walls from the mid-16th century.

Amphora Hotel
HOTEL €€
(📞 28210 93224; www.amphora.gr; Parodos Theotokopoulou 20; s/d/tr from €95/110/115; ❊ 🛜) Most of the elegantly decorated rooms at this immaculately restored Venetian mansion wrap around a courtyard, with a few more in a connected wing. Those on the top floors have harbour views, but front rooms can be very noisy in the summer.

Porto Veneziano
HOTEL €€
(📞 28210 27100; www.portoveneziano.gr; Akti Enoseos & Glafkou; s/d/tr incl breakfast from €80/90/120; ❊ 🛜) Smack on the quieter eastern end of Hania's old harbour, this business-style hotel has unobstructed city or harbour views and clean, comfortable rooms with flat-screen TVs. Some have balconies.

Madonna Studios
APARTMENT €€
(📞 28210 94747; www.madonnastudios.gr; Gamba 33; studio €90-115; ❊ 🛜) This charming small hotel has five attractive and well-appointed studios around a lovely flower-filled courtyard. Rooms are furnished in traditional style and the front top room has a superb balcony, while the courtyard room has the original stone wash trough.

Porto de Colombo
HOTEL, APARTMENT €€
(📞 28210 70945; www.portodelcolombo.gr; Theofanous & Moshon; d/apt incl breakfast from €85/100; ❊ @ 🛜 📶) Once the French embassy and office of Eleftherios Venizelos, this 600-year-old Venetian townhouse is now a charming hotel with 10 well-appointed rooms, the top suites have fine harbour views. The standard rooms can fit up to three (though it's a bit snug), while the three self-catering apartments are more child-friendly.

Vranas Studios
APARTMENT €€
(📞 28210 58618; www.vranas.gr; Agion Deka 10; studio €65-70; ❊ 🛜) In the heart of the old town, this place is on a lively pedestrian street and has spacious, immaculately maintained studios with kitchenettes. All rooms have polished wooden floors, balconies, TVs and telephones. There's a handy internet cafe attached.

Bellmondo
HOTEL €€
(📞 28210 36216; www.belmondohotel.com; Zambeliou 10; s/d/tr incl breakfast from €70/90/105; ❊ 🛜) This hotel has Turkish and Venetian features, including part of an old *hammam* (Turkish baths) in one room, but it's furnished with simple wooden pieces. The nicest rooms have balconies (for about €20 more than the rate) and harbour views.

Nostos Hotel
BOUTIQUE HOTEL €€
(📞 28210 94743; www.nostos-hotel.com; Zambeliou 42-46; s/d/tr/ste incl breakfast from €80/125/160/140; ❊ 🛜) Mixing Venetian style and modern fixtures, this 600-year-old building has been remodelled into 12 decent rooms with fridge, phone and TV. Studios have kitchens. There are good views from the roof garden, and balcony rooms with harbour views.

Pension Lena
PENSION €€
(📞 28210 86860; www.lenachania.gr; Ritsou 5; d €65; ❊ 🛜 📶) Run by the friendly Lena, this pension near Firkas Fortress has tastefully done rooms with an old-world feel and a scattering of antiques, though the front rooms are the most appealing. Lena also offers three independent houses.

★ Serenissima
BOUTIQUE HOTEL €€€
(📞 28210 86386; www.serenissima.gr; Skoufon 4; d/ste from €170/230; ❊ 🛜) The newest entry in Hania's luxury boutique hotel game, Serenissima opened its pearlescent doors in 2015. A spacious townhouse, renovated to impeccable standards, it offers a full-service experience year-round. The minimalist restaurant-bar downstairs is painted in soft peach tones, and rooms have the latest in TV technology, high-end decor and bathroom style.

★ Casa Delfino
BOUTIQUE HOTEL €€€
(📞 28210 87400; www.casadelfino.com; Theofanous 9; r/ste incl breakfast from €190/210; ❊ 🛜) Luxury is taken very seriously at this elegant 17th-century mansion in the Venetian quarter. The 24 suites come in various sizes but all are richly trimmed in bespoke furniture, marble floors and romantic flourishes. Days start with breakfast in the pebble-mosaic courtyard while the Turkish spa and the rooftop terrace are perfect end-of-day unwinding spots.

★ Casa Leone
BOUTIQUE HOTEL €€€
(📞 28210 76762; www.casa-leone.com; Parodos Theotokopoulou 18; d/ste incl breakfast from €135/160; ❊ 🛜) This Venetian residence has been converted into a classy and romantic family-run boutique hotel. The rooms are spacious and well appointed, with balconies overlooking the harbour. There are honeymoon suites, with classic drape-canopy beds and sumptuous curtains. Discounts for prebooking or cash payments.

✗ Eating

Hania has some of the finest restaurants in Crete. As might be expected, most of the prime-position waterfront tavernas are generally mediocre, overpriced and fronted by annoying touts – head for the quieter backstreets for the best food and grog. Chatzimichali Daliani has a particularly lively group of *mezedhopoleia* (restaurants specialising in mezedhes, or small dishes) and *ouzeria* serving small plates and crisp *raki* (distilled spirits), near the corner with Malmou.

★ Bougatsa tou Iordanis   CRETAN €

(☑28210 88855; Apokoronou 24; bougatsa €2.80; ☺8am-2.30pm Mon-Sat, to noon Sun) You haven't lived until you've eaten the *bougatsa* at this little storefront dedicated to the flaky, sweet-cheesy treat. It's cooked fresh in enormous slabs and carved up in front of your eyes. Pair it with a coffee and you're set for the morning. There's nothing else on the menu!

Kouzina EPE   CRETAN €

(☑28210 42391; Daskalogianni 25; mains €4-8; ☺noon-7.30pm Mon-Sat) This cheery lunch spot serves contemporary designer flair from the cement floor, country-white tables and dangling silver origami boats. It's a local favourite away from the crowds, serving blackboard-listed *mayirefta* (ready-cooked meals) that can be inspected in the open kitchen.

Pallas   CAFE €

(Akti Tombazi 15-17; mains €8-16; ☺8am-midnight; ☎) For coffee and breakfast at Hania's old harbour, head to local favourite Pallas, with a 2nd-floor dining room, superb views and a brunch menu to match.

Mesogeiako   MEZEDHES €

(Chatzimichali Daliani 36; mezedhes €3.50-6; ☺6pm-1am) Near the minaret in the Splantzia quarter, this trendy *mezedhopoleio* sits among a group of similarly popular eateries and serves an array of classic and more creative dishes. Try the fried zucchini flowers, aubergines, pork meatballs and its excellent *raki*.

Portes   CRETAN €

(☑28210 76261; Portou 48; mains €7-10; ☺noon-late; ☎) Fine dining without the pretence. Both tourists and neighbourhood denizens give this place top marks for its creative Cretan fare that veers towards modernity without straying from simplicity. You can't go wrong ordering from the specials list.

Glymidakis   BAKERY €

(☑28210 61714; Plateia 1821; baked goods from €1; ☺7am-8pm) Packed with fresh Cretan breads and sweets this bakery gets jammed with locals, too, buying its wares or taking them out to the shaded plaza tables with coffee.

Oasis   FAST FOOD €

(Vouloudakidon 2; souvlaki €2; ☺during shop hours Mon-Sat) Locals swear by the undeniably tasty souvlaki at tiny, old-style Oasis. As elsewhere in western Crete, specify souvlaki 'kalamaki' to get small cubes of meat grilled on a skewer, instead of *gyros* (meat slivers cooked on a vertical rotisserie).

Doloma   TAVERNA €

(☑28213 01008; Kalergon 8; mains €4.50-7; ☺noon-midnight Apr-Oct, shorter hours Nov & Dec, closed Jan-Mar; ☎) This unpretentious restaurant tucked behind the harbour is half-hidden amid vines surrounding the outdoor terrace and parking area. The basic, traditional *mayirefta* are filling, if you can't get in elsewhere.

★ To Maridaki   CRETAN €€

(☑28210 08880; Daskalogianni 33; dishes €7-12; ☺noon-midnight Mon-Sat) This modern seafood *mezedhopoleio* is not to be missed. In a cheerful, bright dining room, happy visitors and locals alike tuck into impeccable local seafood and Cretan specialities. Ingredients are fresh, the fried calamari is to die for, the house white wine is crisp and delicious, and the complimentary panna cotta to finish the meal is transcendent. What's not to love?

★ Taverna Tamam   MEDITERRANEAN €€

(☑28210 96080; Zambeliou 49; mains €7-12; ☺noon-midnight; ☎☑) This excellent, convivial taverna in a converted Turkish bathhouse fills with chatting locals at tables spilling out onto the street. Dishes incorporate Middle Eastern spices, and include tasty soups and a superb selection of vegetarian specialities. Cretan delicacies include tender goat with *staka* (a rich goat's milk sauce).

To Karnagio   CRETAN, SEAFOOD €€

(☑28210 53366; Plateia Katehaki 8; mains €5-18; ☺noon-midnight May-Oct; ☎) This popular place fills outdoor tables on a harbourside plaza next to the Great Arsenal. There's a good range of seafood and classic Cretan dishes, such as octopus *stifadho* (in red tomato and wine sauce) and perfectly flaky *boureki* (stuffed pastry), plus a fine wine list.

Well of the Turk
MIDDLE EASTERN €€

(Pigadi tou Tourkou; ☑ 28210 54547; www.wellof
theturk.com; Sarpaki 1-3; mains €8-15; ☺ dinner
Wed-Mon) In an age-old stone building which
used to house a *hammam,* and flanking a
quiet square, this romantic taverna specialises in richly textured dishes inspired by
North Africa, the Middle East and Turkey,
yet all prepared with the finest Cretan ingredients. The cheesecake with rosewater and
orange makes a great culinary coda.

Apostolis I & II
SEAFOOD €€

(☑ 28210 43470; Akti Enoseos; mains €6-14, fish
per kg from €50; ☺ 11.30am-1am May-Sep, reduced
rest of year) In the quieter eastern harbour,
these well-respected spots for fresh fish and
Cretan dishes are in two separate buildings.
Apostolis II is the more popular as the owner reigns there, but the other has the same
menu at marginally cheaper prices. A seafood platter for two, including salad, is €30.
Service is friendly and efficient, and there's a
good wine list.

Soul Kitchen
INTERNATIONAL €€

(☑ 28210 44372; Kallergon, cnr Sarpidonos; mains
€7-12; ☺ 6pm-midnight Tue-Fri, noon-midnight Sat,
noon-7pm Sun) Modern, with amber wood-
en stools and tables and clean lines, this
casual contemporary restaurant serves up
everything from Cretan specialities to heaping burgers and salads. There's also a good
beer selection.

Akrogiali
SEAFOOD €€

(☑ 28210 71110; Akti Papanikoli 20; mains €7-12;
☺ lunch & dinner May-Oct; ☎) This airy white-
and-blue space on Nea Hora beach, to the
west of town, does fabulously fresh fish and
seafood, including some inspired stuffed-
squid varieties.

Ela
CRETAN €€

(☑ 28210 74128; www.ela-chania.gr; Kondylaki 47;
mains €7-16; ☺ noon-1am; ☎) Built as a soap factory in 1650, Ela has also seen incarnations
as a school, distillery and cheese-processing
plant and is now a charismatic roofless lair
serving upscale Cretan specialities. The multilingual menus arrayed in the street signal
tourist trap, but they do solid meals.

★ Thalassino Ageri
SEAFOOD €€€

(☑ 28210 51136; www.thalasino-ageri.gr; Vivilaki 35;
fish per kg €55; ☺ from 7.30pm Apr–mid-Oct) This
solitary fish taverna in a tiny port 2km east
of the centre among the ruins of Hania's old
tanneries is one of Crete's top eateries. Take

in the sunset from the superb setting and
peruse the changing menu, dictated by the
day's catch. Most dishes, like the fisherman's
salad, hum with creativity, or transcendent
simplicity like melt-in-your-mouth calamari.

Take a taxi or follow El Venizelou, turning
left at Noel St as soon as you veer away from
the coast. The owners also operate excellent
To Maridaki (p65), in the Splantzia quarter
of Hania.

🍷 Drinking & Entertainment

The cafe-bars around the Venetian harbour
are nice places to sit, but charge top euro.
For a more local vibe, head to Plateia 1821
in the Splantzia quarter, the interior streets
near Potie, or to alt-flavoured Sarpidona on
the eastern end of the harbour.

Kleidi
BAR

(☑ 28210 52974; Plateia 1821; ☺ 8am-late) By day
locals fill the shady plaza tables and sip iced
coffee, and by night the place buzzes with
party life. There's no written sign, just the
image of a keyhole (*kleidi* means key).

Sinagogi
BAR

(☑ 28210 95242; Parodos Kondylaki 15; ☺ 1pm-
late Jun-Sep; ☎) Housed in a roofless Venetian building on a small lane accessible only
from Kondylaki street in the old town, this
popular summer-only lounge bar is a laid-
back place to relax and take it all in.

Kibar
BAR

(☑ 28210 50172; Chatzimichali Daliani 22; ☺ 2pm-
late; ☎) Beautifully set in the courtyard of
a 16th-century monastery turned art centre (Monastiri Tou Karolou), this cafe has a
vibrant ambience and lots of international
bottled beer.

Ta Duo Lux
CAFE, BAR

(☑ 28210 52519; Sarpidona 8; ☺ 10am-late; ☎)
Just off the eastern edge of the harbour, in
a strip of local bars, arty cafe-bar Ta Duo
Lux remains a perennial favourite hang-out
among wrinkle-free alternative types and is
popular day and night.

Garage
BAR

(Skalidi 8; ☺ 8pm-late) This cocktail bar turns
into a dance club on nights when DJs are
in town.

Koukouvagia
BAR

(www.koukouvaya.gr; Venizelos Graves; ☺ 10am-
late) If you have wheels, 5km east and uphill from Hania town you'll find the spot

where great statesman Eleftherios Venizelos is buried. The site and its neighbouring owl-themed cafe and bar enjoy panoramic views of Hania. It's a popular hang-out for students from the nearby technical university, and pastries and snacks are delish. Taxi from/to Hania costs about €7.

★ **Fagotto Jazz Bar** BAR, LIVE MUSIC
(🖉 28210 71877; Angelou 16; ⊙7pm-2am) This Hania institution in a Venetian building offers smooth jazz, soft rock and blues (sometimes live) in a setting brimming with jazz paraphernalia, including a saxophone beer tap. The action picks up after 10pm.

🔒 Shopping

Hania offers top shopping, especially in the back streets. Theotokopoulou is lined with souvenir and handicraft shops. Skrydlof offers a vast array of imported sandals, belts and bags. Find some of the most authentic crafts in the Splantzia quarter, along Chatzimichali Daliani and Daskalogianni.

Most stores in the old town tend to stay open until 11pm, while the new town shopping district keeps regular shop hours.

The outdoor *laïki* (street market) on Saturday morning fills Minoos with stalls of local produce and dry goods. On Thursday another market lines the waterfront west of the Firkas Fortress.

Miden Agan FOOD & DRINK
(🖉 28210 27068; www.midenaganshop.gr; Daskalogianni 70; ⊙10am-3pm Mon-Sat & 6-10pm Tue, Thu-Sat) Food-and-wine lovers are spoiled for choice at this excellent shop, which stocks more than 800 Greek wines, as well as its own wine and liquors. There's a variety of beautifully packaged local traditional gourmet deli foods, including olive oil and honey, and its own line of spoon sweets (try the white pumpkin).

Exantas Art Space CRAFTS, BOOKS
(🖉 28210 95920; Zambeliou & Moschon; ⊙10am-2pm & 6-11pm) This high-concept store has great postcards with old photos and engravings, handmade gifts and games, Cretan music as well as a good range of travel, coffee-table and art books.

Georgina Skalidi ACCESSORIES
(🖉28215 01705; www.georginaskalidi.com; Chatzimichali Daliani 58; ⊙11am-2pm Mon-Sat & 6-9pm Tue, Thu & Fri) This internationally distributed local designer creates wonderful contemporary leather bags, jewellery and accessories.

CRETAN FOODSTUFFS

Crete is famous for its local produce like olive oil and thyme honey. You will typically find the best quality (and prices) at humble local shops in the villages rather than at souvenir shops in the cities. Look beyond snazzy packaging with submerged twigs for big unmarked bottles, fresh from the farm.

Sifis Stavroulakis JEWELLERY
(🖉28210 50335; www.sifisjewellery.gr; Chatzimichali Daliani 54; ⊙10am-2pm Mon-Sat & 5.30-8.30pm Tue, Thu & Fri) Beautiful naturalistic jewellery made with semi-precious stones and metals create floral and human forms in this small shopfront and jeweller's workshop.

Agora MARKET
(Central Market; www.chaniamarket.com; Chatzimichali Giannari; ⊙8am-3pm Mon-Sat) Hania's cross-shaped market hall bustles mostly with souvenir-hunting tourists, though a few authentic produce, meat and cheese stands – along with cafes – are still part of the mix.

Terra Verde FOOD & DRINK
(🖉28210 52201; www.terraverde-chania.gr; Chatzimichali Daliani 5; ⊙9.30am-2.30pm & 7-10pm Mon-Fri, to 2.30pm Sat) Shop for organic local products, from *raki* and wine to olive oil and honey.

Karistianis CLOTHING, OUTDOOR EQUIPMENT
(🖉28210 93573; Skalidi 9-11; ⊙9am-9pm Mon-Fri, to 4pm Sat) This is the place to go for serious outdoor clothing and hiking shoes; its more hard-core army supply store across the road sells camping and climbing gear.

Chroma ARTS
(🖉28210 46334; Daskalogianni 42; ⊙11am-2pm Mon-Sat & 6-9pm Tue, Thu & Fri) Elegant serigraph and lithograph prints and old-school maps, in the Splantzia quarter.

Handmade Hats ACCESSORIES
(🖉28210 57037; Skoufon 14; ⊙noon-9pm Mon-Sat) This small shop is both an atelier and boutique crammed with unique handmade hats, beribboned, in felt or in canvas, and printed textiles.

Roka Carpets HANDICRAFTS
(🖉28210 74736; Zambeliou 61; ⊙11am-9pm Mon-Sat) This is one of the few places in Crete where you can buy genuine, hand-woven

goods (note, though, they are not antiques). Amiable Mihalis Manousakis and his wife weave wondrous rugs on a 400-year-old loom, using methods that have remained essentially unchanged since Minoan times.

Omen Art Gallery ART, CRAFTS
(☑ 28210 08685; www.omenart.gr; Daskalogianni 4; ⊙ 11am-2pm Mon-Sat & 6-9pm Tue, Thu & Fri) Pottery, graphic art and other Crete-made art features at this gallery in the Splantzia quarter.

Pelekanakis BOOKS, MAPS
(Halidon 89; ⊙ 8.30am-9pm Mon-Sat, plus Sun Jun-Sep, shorter hours Oct-Mar) This classic Hania bookshop sells driving and hiking maps, guidebooks and otherwise hard-to-find books about Crete in 11 languages.

Mediterraneo Bookstore BOOKS
(☑ 28210 86904; Akti Koundourioti 57; ⊙ 8am-late) On the waterfront, this bookshop sells an extensive range of English-language novels and books on Crete, as well as international press.

❶ Information

EMERGENCY
Tourist Police (☑ 28210 25931, emergency 171; Irakleiou 24; ⊙ 8am-2.30pm) From the central market (agora) square, the police station is 1.2km southeast on Apokoronou, which turns into Irakleiou street.

INTERNET ACCESS
Free wi-fi is widely available in public spaces, including the harbour, around the central market, and at Plateia 1866, as well as at most hotels, restaurants, cafes and bars.

POST
Post Office (☑ 28210 28444; Peridou 10; ⊙ 7.30am-8pm Mon-Fri, to 2pm Sat)

MEDICAL SERVICES
Chania General Hospital St George (☑ 28210 22000; www.chaniahospital.gr; Mournies) Located 4.5km south of town – take a local bus, or a taxi (€8 to €10).

MONEY
Banks cluster around Plateia Markopoulou in the new city, but there are ATMs in the old town on Halidon. **National Bank of Greece** (cnr Tzanakaki & Giannari) has a 24-hour exchange machine.

TOURIST INFORMATION
Hania City Tourist Office (☑ 28213 41665; www.chania.gr; Milonogianni 53; ⊙ 8.30am-2.30pm Mon-Fri) Modest selection of brochures, maps and transport timetables at the town hall. Open some Saturdays.

TRAVEL AGENCIES
Diktynna Travel (☑ 28210 41458; www.diktynna-travel.gr; Archontaki 6; ⊙ 9am-6pm Mon-Fri) Organises a range of cultural and ecotourism activities and tours.
Tellus Travel (☑ 28210 91500; www.tellus-travel.gr; Halidon 108; ⊙ 8.30am-10pm) This major agency hires cars, changes money and arranges air and boat tickets, accommodation and excursions.

BUSES FROM HANIA

DESTINATION	FARE (€)	DURATION	FREQUENCY
Elafonisi	10	2½hr	1 daily
Falasarna	7.60	1½hr	3 daily
Hora Sfakion	7.60	1hr 40min	3 daily
Iraklio	13.80	2¾hr	half-hourly
Kissamos (Kastelli)	4.70	1hr	13 daily
Kolymbari	3.30	45min	half-hourly
Lakki	2.60	1¾hr	2 daily
Moni Agias Triadas	2.30	30min	2 daily
Omalos (for Samaria Gorge)	6.90	1hr	3 daily
Paleohora	7.60	1hr 50min	4 daily
Rethymno	6.20	1hr	half-hourly
Sougia	7.10	1hr 50min	2 daily
Stavros	2.10	30min	3 daily

USEFUL WEBSITES

Chania Old Town Walks (www.chania-old town-walks.com) Excellent historic walking tours.

Chania Tourism (www.chaniatourism.com) The city's tourism portal.

Western Crete Information (www.west-crete. com) Tourism info for Hania province.

ℹ Getting There & Away

AIR

Hania's airport (p262) is 14km east of town on the Akrotiri Peninsula, and is served year-round from Athens and Thessaloniki and seasonally from throughout Europe. Carriers include Aegean Airlines and Ryanair.

BOAT

Hania's port is at Souda, 7km southeast of town (and the site of a NATO base). The port is linked to town by bus (€1.50) and taxi (€9). Hania buses meet each boat, as do buses to Rethymno. The **Port Police** (☑ 28210 89240) provide ferry information.

Anek (☑ 28210 27500; www.anek.gr; Plateia Venizelou) Nightly overnight ferry between Piraeus and Hania (per person/car from €42/83, nine hours). Buy tickets online or at the port; reserve ahead for cars.

BUS

Hania's **KTEL bus station** (☑ info 28210 93052, tickets 28210 93306; www.bus-service-crete-ktel.com; Kydonias 73-77; @ �) has a cafeteria, minimarket and left-luggage service (per day per piece €2). Check the excellent website for the current schedule; it changes month by month. Beaches are usually not served October to April.

Air-conditioned buses connect Hania regularly with towns and major beaches throughout the region, plus larger towns elsewhere in Crete. For several people, hiring a car is often more economical and convenient.

ℹ Getting Around

Hania town is best navigated on foot, since most of it is pedestrianised.

TO/FROM THE AIRPORT

KTEL (www.bus-service-crete-ktel.com) buses link the airport with central Hania up to 27 times daily (€2.30, 30 minutes). Taxis to/from the airport cost €20 (plus €2 per bag).

BUS

A handily central **Giannari stop** (☑ 28210 27044; www.chaniabus.gr; tickets €1.10 or €1.50, if bought on bus €1.50 and €2), near the Agora market hall, has local city buses to/from Souda port, Halepa, Nea Hora and other local destinations.

CAR & MOTORCYCLE

Major car hire outlets are at the airport or on Halidon. Companies at Agia Marina are competitive and deliver to Hania.

Most of the old town is pedestrianised. There's free parking just west of Firkas Fortress and along the waterfront towards Nea Hora beach, or by the eastern edge of the harbour off Kyprou; but avoid areas marked residents-only.

Europrent (☑ 28210 27810; www.europrent.gr; Halidon 87; car hire per day from €32)

TAXI

Taxi (☑ 28210 98700)

EAST OF HANIA

The northeastern corner of Hania prefecture includes the rocky Akrotiri Peninsula with a couple of interesting monasteries, and the Apokoronas Peninsula (which is more like a promontory). The island's only natural freshwater lake, Lake Kournas, is a highlight of the area. Beach resorts such as Kalyves, Almyrida and Georgioupoli are slightly less over-built than the resorts spread along the coast west of Hania, but they can't hold a candle to the beaches in the south and west. You'll find the most Cretan character at the restored village of Vamos, the ancient site of Aptera, and in traditional villages such as Gavalohori.

Akrotiri Peninsula

Χερσόνησος Ακρωτήρι

The Akrotiri (ak-roh-*tee*-ree) Peninsula, to the northeast of Hania, is a barren, hilly stretch of rock covered with scrub. It has a few coastal resorts, Hania's airport, a massive NATO naval base on Souda Bay and two interesting monasteries. There are few buses and the poorly signposted roads make it difficult to explore, but if you have a car you can make a day trip combining a swim and lunch with a visit to the monasteries. If you want to stay at the beach near Hania, Akrotiri's Kalathas and Stavros are much quieter than the overblown package-tour strip west of Hania, but overall, southwest Crete has much better beaches than Akrotiri.

The beach settlement of **Kalathas**, 10km north of Hania, has two sandy beaches lined by pine trees. It is the preferred weekend haunt of Haniots, many of whom own summer and weekend houses nearby.

Three kilometres north of Kalathas is the small beach settlement of **Tersanas**, signposted off the main Kalathas–Stavros road.

Stavros, 6km north of Kalathas, is little more than a dilapidated scattering of houses and an array of restaurants and hotels, plus a famous cove.

◉ Sights

Moni Agias Triadas MONASTERY
(Agia Triada Tsagarolon; www.agiatriada-chania. gr; adult/child €2/free; ⊘8am-sunset Jun-Aug, 8am-2pm & 4pm-sunset Sep-May) Akrotiri Peninsula's major cultural site, the impressive 17th-century Moni Agias Triadas, is a visitor-friendly monastery. It was founded by Venetian monks, Jeremiah and Laurentio Giancarolo, who were converts to the Orthodox faith. There was a religious school here in the 19th century and it is still an active monastery with a rich library. It's worth visiting for its altarpiece, Venetian-influenced domed facade, small museum, and its store selling the monastery's fine wine, oil and *raki*.

Moni Gouvernetou MONASTERY
(Our Lady of the Angels; ⊘9am-noon & 5-7pm Mon, Tue & Thu, 9-11am & 5-8pm Sat & Sun) The 16th-century Moni Gouvernetou, 4km north of Moni Agias Triadas, may date as far back as the 11th century, from a time when an inland sanctuary was an attractive refuge from coastal pirates. The building itself is rather plain, but the church inside has an ornate sculptured Venetian facade. Visitors must park in the car park before the monastery and be dressed respectfully (they do not provide long pants or skirts). Swimming in the cove below is not permitted.

The monastery was attacked and burnt down during the War of Independence but the monks were warned and managed to save the treasures (though not themselves) and shipped them off to Mt Athos in northern Greece. The monastery is now run by a handful of monks from the Holy Mountain who keep a strict regime and have banned tour buses.

Moni Ioannou Erimiti MONASTERY
(Moni Katholikou) From Moni Gouvernetou it's a 2km or so walk (uphill on the way back) down to the coast to the ruins of Moni Ioannou Erimiti. In disuse for many centuries, the monastery is dedicated to St John the Hermit, who lived in the cave behind the ruins, at the bottom of a rock staircase.

When St John died in the cave, his 98 disciples are said to have died with him.

Near the entrance to the cave there's a small pond believed to be holy.

Beaches

Marathi Beach BEACH
On the eastern side of Akrotiri Peninsula the pleasant beach of Marathi is a lovely spot beyond the NATO base with two sandy coves and turquoise waters on either side of a small pier. The ruins of Ancient Minoa are next to the car park. Marathi gets crowded with local families at weekends and has a couple of tavernas.

Further south along this coastline you'll find another nice swimming and snorkelling spot at the small white-stone cove of **Loutraki**.

Stavros Cove BEACH
Near Akrotiri Peninsula's northern tip, Stavros' sandy beach is covered with umbrellas and lines a cove dominated by a mammoth rock. It famously served as the dramatic backdrop for the final dancing scene in the classic movie *Zorba the Greek*. The beach and its neighbouring clump of cafes and tavernas can get crowded. Other thin, windswept beaches line Stavros' western shores.

🛏 Sleeping

Artemis Apartments APARTMENT €
(☑28210 39005; www.artemis-village.gr; Stavros; apt €45-100) This well-kept peach-coloured apartment complex 1km back from the cove at Stavros is a welcoming spot to while away your holiday. Well-furnished apartments come with a kitchen, terrace or balcony. The large pool beckons when you can't make it down to the beach.

Blue Beach APARTMENT €
(☑28210 39404; www.bluebeach.eu; Stavros; d €50-70, apt €100-130; ❋ ❋) On a pretty promontory on the western edge of Stavros, Blue Beach is a low-key hotel complex with comfortable, self-contained rooms equipped with fridge, kitchenette and TV. There's also a bar.

Georgi's Blue Apartments APARTMENT €€
(☑28210 64080; www.blueapts.gr; Kalathas; apt incl breakfast €100-180; P❋@❋❋❋) Georgi's is an immaculate complex of well-furnished studios and apartments with phone, satellite TV, fridge and kitchenette. Unwind at the pleasant lounge area near the

pool, or swim off the rocks at a private little cove. The owner advises on local outdoor activities and car hire.

Lena Beach Hotel HOTEL €€
(☑ 28210 64750; www.lenabeach.gr; Kalathas; s/d/tr from €70/90/110; ❄ ⬥ 🖥 🏊) Simple seafront rooms make this tidy hotel tops for a carefree holiday. Rooms have small TVs and refrigerators, plus there's a big pool. Discounts online.

✗ Eating

Sunset Beach CAFE €
(Iliovasilema; ☑ 28210 39780; Stavros; dishes €4.50-7.50; ⊙ 10am-10.30pm Jul & Aug, noon-8.30pm Apr-Jun & Sep, Sat & Sun only Nov-Mar) On the beach on the southwestern edge of Stavros, have a drink or light meal at the Sunset Beach cafe, tucked under a huge tree with a shady timber deck and thatched umbrellas evoking the tropics. The French and Greek proprietors serve a range of local and international-style snacks.

Patrelantonis SEAFOOD €€
(☑ 28210 63337; Marathi; mains from €15; ⊙ noon-1am Easter-Oct) On Marathi beach, this dependable seafood taverna is well regarded by locals and visitors. Lunch under the shady beachside tamarisk trees on dishes like cuttlefish with fennel and olives or grouper fricassee. There's a good wine list too.

ℹ Getting There & Away

From Hania there are three buses daily to Stavros beach (€2.10) that stop at Kalathas and two buses daily to Moni Agias Triadas (€2.30, 30 minutes, 6.30am and 2.15pm). If coming by car from Hania follow signs to the airport and branch off at the turn-offs from there.

Aptera Απτέρα

★ **Aptera** RUIN
(adult/child €3/free; ⊙ 8am-3pm Tue-Sun) The ruins of the ancient city of Aptera, about 13.5km east of Hania, spread over two hills that lord grandly over Souda Bay. Founded in the 7th century BC, Aptera was one of the most important city-states of western Crete and was continuously inhabited until an earthquake destroyed it in the 7th century AD. Aptera revived with the Byzantine reconquest of Crete in the 10th century, and became a bishopric. In the 12th century, the

monastery of St John the Theologian was established; the reconstructed monastery is the centre of the site. There's no public transport to Aptera.

The site is still being excavated. Diggers have exposed the remains of a fortified tower, a city gate and a massive wall that surrounded the city. You can also see Roman cisterns and a 2nd century BC Greek temple. At the western end of the site, a Turkish fortress, built in 1872, enjoys a panoramic view of Souda Bay. The fortress was built as part of a large Turkish fortress-building program during a period when the Cretans were in an almost constant state of insurrection.

Notice the 'Wall of the Inscriptions' – this was probably part of an important public building and was excavated in 1862 by French archaeologists. The Greek Ministry of Culture is continuing to restore the site, installing signs and paths.

Armenoi & Around Αρμένοι

South of the ruins at Aptera, interlocking valleys are quilted with vineyards and groves, and punctuated by traditional Cretan villages. A wonderful drive, it could take you to the village of Armenoi where **Tzitzikas** (☑ 28250 41144; www.tzitzikas.com; mains €4-9; ⊙ 10am-late May-Sep, Sat & Sun only Oct-Apr; 🅿 ♿) ☕ serves fresh Cretan meals and coffee on the edge of a river, under lush, shading trees, with horses and goats grazing nearby. The focus is on all things organic, from sausage to salad.

Almyrida Αλμυρίδα

POP 56
The former fishing village of Almyrida, 21km east of Hania, is considerably less developed than its neighbour, Kalyves, although it's pretty built up, with ever more new hotels going in. It has a long, exposed beach and is popular for windsurfing. History buffs can find the remains of an early Christian basilica at the western end of the village.

🏃 Activities

Flisvos Tours BICYCLE RENTAL
(☑ 28250 31337; www.flisvos.com; mountain bike per 3 days €15; ⊙ 8am-1.30pm & 5-9.30pm) Flisvos Tours, just off the main road, hires mountain bikes, as well as cars and scooters.

UCPA Sports
WINDSURFING, KAYAKING

(☑28250 31443; www.ucpa.com) French-run UCPA Sports offers windsurfing to experienced surfers only outside of high season and also hires kayaks. It has its own resort too.

Dream Adventure Trips
SNORKELLING

(☑6944357383) Dream Adventure Trips offers snorkelling trips to nearby caves, islets and Marathi beach (€15).

🛏 Sleeping & Eating

Almyrida Studios
APARTMENT €€

(☑28250 32075; www.almyridaresort.com; studio incl breakfast €80-100) Studios perched on the water's edge are just the way to soak up the summer sun. Some are large enough for four, and all have kitchens, telephones and satellite TV. Some have sea-facing balconies. There are two other hotel properties as well.

Lagos
GREEK €

(☑28250 31654; mains €6-9; ⊙noon-late) Located at the entrance to Almyrida, this popular taverna serves good-value traditional cooking on a lovely shaded terrace.

Dimitri's
TAVERNA €

(☑28250 31303; mains €4-9; ⊙11am-late) This family tavern is recommended for its friendly service and produce from its farm, as well as fresh seafood.

ℹ Getting There & Away

There are four to five KTEL buses from Almyrida to Hania (€2.90, 45 minutes) via Kalyves in high season.

Vamos
Βάμος

POP 706

The 12th-century village of Vamos, 26km southeast of Hania, was the capital of the Sfakia province from 1867 to 1913 and was the scene of a revolt against Turkish rule in 1896. It is now the capital of the Apokoronas province, and in 1995 a group of villagers banded together to preserve the traditional way of life of Vamos. They got EU funding to showcase the crafts and products of the region, and restored the old stone buildings using traditional materials and crafts and turned them into guesthouses.

Fifty metres from the Vamos Traditional Village reception house, you can buy local *raki*, herbs, organic oil and other Cretan products.

🛏 Sleeping & Eating

★ Vamos Traditional Village
VILLAS €€

(☑28250 22190; www.vamosvillage.gr; villas €75-250; ⊙10am-7pm Mon-Fri, to 6pm Sat, 11am-2pm Sun; ❋ 🛜 👜) The Vamos village organisation rents out the village's many restored homes. The lovely stone cottages have kitchens, fireplaces and TVs and are decorated in traditional style. Most accommodate up to four people, but there are larger cottages that also have a pool. Also rents cars, books excursions and runs Cretan cooking lessons in a restored olive press.

★ I Sterna tou Bloumosifi
TAVERNA €€

(☑28250 83220; mains €6-14; ⊙12.30-11pm; 🛜) The old stone taverna I Sterna tou Bloumosifi has a welcoming tree-shaded courtyard garden and is known far and wide for its excellent Cretan cuisine. For starters try the *gavros* (anchovy) wrapped in vine leaves, or the garlic and herb mushrooms, and then move on to the *hilopites* (tagliatelle) with rooster or lamb tart.

ℹ Getting There & Away

There are three to five KTEL buses to Vamos from Hania (€3.30, 45 minutes), Monday through Saturday in high season.

Gavalohori
Γαβαλοχώρι

The charming village of Gavalohori, 25km southeast of Hania, makes an interesting stop. The main attraction is the **Folklore Museum** (☑28250 23222; http://odysseus.culture.gr; adult/child €2/free; ⊙9am-3pm Mon-Sat, 11am-3pm Sun), which is located in a renovated building that was constructed during Venetian rule and then extended by the Turks. The exhibits are well labelled in English and include examples of pottery, weaving, woodcarving, stone-cutting and other Cretan crafts, including the fine *kapaneli* (intricately worked silk lace). A historical section documents Cretan struggles for independence.

The **Women's Cooperative** (⊙10am-10pm Apr-Oct), on the main square, sells a few rare pieces of *kapaneli* made by local women. You can normally see women hard at work on this painstakingly long process. Prices for quality lacework range from €15 to €1500, depending on the size.

Signs direct you to the Byzantine wells, Venetian arches and Roman tombs about 1.5km above the village.

Georgioupoli Γεωργιούπολη

POP 455

No longer the quiet getaway that it once was, Georgioupoli has been swamped by coastal hotel development and is popular with holidaying foreign families.

Nature lovers look beyond the sprawl to appreciate its setting at the junction of the Almyros River and the sea. It's a nesting area for the endangered loggerhead sea turtle. The marshes surrounding the riverbed are known for bird life, especially egrets and kingfishers which migrate into the area in April. They also produce hordes of mosquitoes in summer.

Picturesque **Agios Nikolaos chapel** perches on a narrow rocky jetty in the sea. The long narrow stretch of hard-packed sand east of town, spliced by another river leading into the sea, becomes a long sandy beach that continues for about 10km towards Rethymno.

Activities

Talos Express Tourist Train   TOUR
(☑ 6973907018; www.facebook.com/talosexpress; return adult/child €8/free) If you don't have wheels, a small tourist train connects Georgioupoli to nearby Kournas Lake and Argiroupoli.

Adventure Bikes   CYCLING
(☑ 28250 61830; www.adventurebikes.org; bicycles per day €12) Hires bikes and runs bike tours around the region (€35 to €65).

Sleeping

Large hotels and resorts on the beach are aimed at package tourists.

Zorba's   HOTEL €
(☑ 28250 61381; studio/apt from €50/60; ❄ 🅿 🏊) Zorba's is set back from the beach near the town's main square. Studios and apartments are contemporary and come with kitchenettes, flat-screen TVs and balconies.

Egeon   PENSION €
(☑ 28250 61161; www.the-egeon-crete.com; studio €40; ❄) Near the bridge at the entrance to Georgioupoli, but a fair walk to the beach, these pleasant rooms and studios are run by friendly Greek-American Polly and her fisherman husband. Some rooms have kitchenettes and TV.

Porto Kalyvaki   APARTMENT €
(☑ 28250 61316; www.kalivaki.com; studio €40-50; ❄ Apr-Oct; 🅿 ❄ 🏊) Located behind a taverna on the more isolated northern beach, Kalyvaki has a mix of plain studios spread across two buildings in well-established gardens.

Eating

Arolithos   TAVERNA €
(☑ 28250 61406; www.arolithos-georgioupolis. gr; mains €5-9; ⊘ noon-11pm May-Sep, shorter hours Oct-Apr) Near Georgioupoli's central church, Arolithos has an extensive selection of appetisers and traditional Greek dishes such as *spetsofaï* (sausage and pepper stew).

Poseidon Taverna   SEAFOOD €€
(☑ 28250 61026; www.poseidon.georgioupoli.eu; fish per kg €30-50; ⊘ 11.30am-11pm May-Oct, shorter hours Nov-Apr) Signposted down a narrow alley to the left as you come into Georgioupoli, this well-regarded fish taverna is run by a fishing family. You can choose from the day's fish and seafood laid out on the counter and enjoy an excellent meal under the mulberry trees in the lovely courtyard.

ℹ Information

The main street from the highway leads to the town centre, dotted with travel agencies and ATMs. Find basic info at www.georgioupoli.net.
    Ballos Travel (☑ 28250 83088; www.ballos. gr; ⊘ 9am-1.30pm & 4-8pm) organises boat tickets, excursions and accommodation, and hires out cars.

ℹ Getting There & Away

KTEL buses between Hania and Rethymno stop on the highway outside Georgioupoli (€4.50, 45 minutes, hourly).

Lake Kournas
Λίμνη Κουρνάς

Lake Kournas, 4km inland from Georgioupoli, is a lovely, restful place to have lunch or to pass an afternoon. The island's only natural lake, it is about 1.5km in diameter, 45m deep and is fed by underground springs. There's a narrow sandy strip circling the lake and you can walk two-thirds of the way around. The crystal-clear water is now off limits for swimming (to protect the environment) and changes colour according to the season and time of day. You can hire **pedal boats** (€7 per hour) and **canoes** (€4 per hour) and view the turtles, crabs, fish and snakes that make the lake their home.

Tourist buses crowd the lake in the peak of summer, and the basic tavernas around the lake fill up. To stay over, try **Korrisia Taverna & Rooms** (☑ 28250 61753; www.kournas-lake-apartments.gr; d/tr/q €40/50/60), on the northern edge of the lake, which has simple but immaculate rooms and a good taverna.

To get away from the summertime lakeside fray, head up the hill to **Ambrosia** (☑ 28250 83008; www.ambrosialakekournas.com; mains €8-12; ☺ 9am-11pm May-Oct) where you can sup on traditional Cretan dishes, like *gamopilafo* (lamb and stock-cooked rice) or faves like homemade pizza in a stone-built restaurant with a balcony high above Lake Kournas. Or just grab an iced coffee and take in the excellent vista.

The lake sits below **Kournas village**, a steep 5km southeast up the hill. Kournas is a simple village with a couple of *kafeneia* (coffee houses). The reason to go is for a delicious meal at the **Kali Kardia Taverna** (☑ 28250 96278; grills €5-7; ☺ 12.30-10pm) on the main street. Owner Kostas Agapinakis is known for his award-winning sausages, excellent *apaki* (smoked pork) and meats cooked on the grill outside the taverna. If you are lucky you might get to try his delicious *galaktoboureko* (custard pastry) while it is still warm.

A tourist mini-train (p73) runs from Georgioupoli to Lake Kournas in summer, but there's no public transport.

Vryses   Βρύσες

Most travellers just pass through ho-hum Vryses (population 740), 30km southeast of Hania, on their way to or from the south coast. Buses from Hora Sfakion to Hania stop here, and it's the transfer point for service to Rethymno or Iraklion. If you are stuck waiting, head to the spot where the rivers Voutakas and Vrysanos run through the centre of the village, watering the giant plane trees along the banks, and cool off in one of the shady tavernas. It's also a centre for the region's agricultural products, so you will find good produce and excellent yoghurt and honey, a speciality of the town.

SOUTHWEST COAST & SFAKIA ΣΦΑΚΙΑ

The mountainous province of Sfakia extends from the Omalos Plateau down to the southern coast, and has some of the island's most spectacular landmarks, including Samaria (sa-ma-*ria*) Gorge, the Lefka Ori (White Mountains) and Mt Gingilos (2080m) in the rugged interior. The memorable drive from Hania to Hora Sfakion – descending through the mountains on numerous loop-back turns overlooking the sea – is one of the most stunning sights in Crete.

The stark, muscular Lefka Ori meet the Libyan Sea along Crete's corrugated southwestern coast indented with a handful of laid-back beach communities, such as Frangokastello and Loutro. Hora Sfakion is Sfakia's main village, and a small outpost, perfect for relaxing and boat-hopping further down the coast. Sougia and the larger Paleohora, west of Sfakia proper, are also some of the best places in Crete to unwind.

This rocky southern coast is arguably the least changing place in Crete – thanks to the massive cliffs running to the sea. Some of the villages and beaches are accessible only by boat and therefore completely untouched by mass tourism. You can walk or boat-hop to perfectly isolated little coves or soak up the majestic scenery and fragrant air on a scramble through wildly romantic gorges. The gorges, including famous and busy Samaria Gorge, slice through the mountains to the coast. Samaria Gorge, for example, ends at the beach village of Agia Roumeli.

Summer winds blast through the gorges and across the Libyan Sea, which means there is often good windsurfing to be had, especially at Paleohora.

The interior of Sfakia is known for being the only part of Crete never subdued by the Arabs, Venetians or Turks. It was the centre of resistance during the island's long centuries of domination by foreign powers, and its steep ravines and hills made effective hideaways for Cretan revolutionaries. The Sfakiot people are renowned for their proud fighting spirit and strong culture, and they have a colourfully tragic history of clan vendettas. Their local cuisine includes the delicious *Sfakianies pites* (thin, flat cheese pie drizzled with honey).

Askyfou   Ασκύφου

POP 450

The road to Hora Sfakion takes you across the formerly war-torn plain of Askyfou, which was the scene of one of the most furious battles of the Cretan revolt of 1821. The Sfakiot forces triumphed over the Turks in a bloody battle here, which is still recounted in local songs. More than a century later the plain was the scene of more strife as Allied troops retreated towards their evacuation point in Hora Sfakion.

The central town on the plateau is also called Askyfou, and stretches out on either side of a hill. The post office is at the top of the hill with a minimarket and several tavernas with inexpensive rooms to rent.

◉ Sights

Askyfou War Museum   MUSEUM

(☐ 6979149719; www.warmuseumaskifou.com; ☺ 8am-7pm Mon-Sat) FREE Signs direct you to the small museum displaying the extensive gun and military odds-and-ends collection of the Hatzidakis family, who are happy to show you around.

🛏 Sleeping & Eating

For a glimpse of traditional Sfakiot village life, seek out the small square flanked by *kafeneia* and statues of local resistance heroes. Just above the small square you'll probably see black-clad gents under the mulberry tree. You can normally get a simple meal of local sausage and *Sfakiani pita,* or at weekends traditional wild goat or lamb *tsigariasto* (sautéed) or *vrasto* (boiled), charged by the kilo – and lots of *raki.*

Lefkoritis Resort   RESORT €€

(☐ 28250 95455; www.lefkoritis.com; apt €65-95; P @ ≋ 🐕) This massive stone retreat with a taverna and large swimming pool operates year-round. Its tastefully furnished apartments sleep up to six and enjoy sweeping views of the surrounding mountains. It offers child-friendly activities such as horse and pony riding, along with mountain biking.

ℹ Getting There & Away

Askyfou (€6.20) is on the Hania to Hora Sfakion KTEL (www.bus-service-crete-ktel.com) bus route.

ℹ SFAKIA TIPS

➡ Hora Sfakion has the only ATM along the southern coast until you reach Paleohora.

➡ Check www.sfakia-crete.com for useful information on Sfakia.

➡ Peter Trudgill's *In Sfakia: Passing Time in the Wilds of Crete* (Lycabbetus Press, 2008), sold in local shops, is a memoir documenting the life, legends and values of the Sfakiots.

Imbros Gorge   Φαράγγι Ιμπρου

Half the length of its illustrious sister at Samaria, the 8km-long **Imbros Gorge** (admission €2; ☺ year-round), 57km south of Hania, is no less beautiful and a lot less busy, especially in the afternoon. The hike takes you past 300m-high walls buttressed by cypresses, holm oaks, fig and almond trees and redolent sage. Landmarks include the narrowest point of the ravine (near the 4.5km mark), which is just 2m wide, and a giant arch 2km from the southern end.

Most people begin the walk in the mountain village of **Imbros** and then hike down to the southern coastal village of **Komitades**. But it's possible to park at either and taxi (€22) or bus between. Both villages serve gorge hikers and have minimarkets and tavernas. In Imbros, you'll find the well-marked entrance to the gorge next to Porofarango taverna on the road to Hora Sfakion. Hania's EOS (p62) has more information on gorge hikes.

🛏 Sleeping & Eating

Imbros village has no hotels.

Villa Archodiko   VILLA €€

(☐ 28310 55289; www.marybeach.gr; per night from €180; ❄ 🛜) Villa Archodiko is a full house for rent which can sleep up to eight.

Porofarango   TAVERNA €

(mains €7-10; ☺ noon-10pm) At the start of the gorge in Imbros village, the friendly family taverna Porofarango has a big balcony with great panoramic views of the gorge and serves good-value Cretan cuisine and generous *raki.* The meat is usually the taverna's own and it often has wild goat. Try the special pork *tsigariasto* (stew).

🛈 Getting There & Away

There are three daily buses from Hania to Hora Sfakion (€7.60, one hour 40 minutes), which stop at Imbros. The southern end of the gorge path ends at Komitades, served by two buses to Hora Sfakion; or, walk 5km or take a taxi to Hora Sfakion (€22).

Frangokastello
Φραγγοκαστέλλο
POP 148

Marked by a striking 14th-century fortress, Frangokastello is a low-key resort 15km east of Hora Sfakion, with a fabulous wide and sandy beach that slopes gradually into shallow warm water, making it ideal for kids. There's no actual village, just a few tavernas, small markets, a gas station, and low-rise holiday apartments and rooms scattered along the main street. Development has been kept to a minimum with most accommodation set back from the shore, leaving the natural beauty largely untouched. In summer, occasional concerts and folk dance performances are held.

◉ Sights

Frangokastello   RUIN
(Frankish Castle; adult/child €1.50/free; ◷10am-7pm Apr-Oct or Nov) Frangokastello is a ruined 14th-century fortress, constructed soon after the Fourth Crusade (1204) by the Venetians, who sought a stronghold against pirates and Sfakiot warriors. The legendary Ioannis Daskalogiannis, who led a disastrous rebellion against Ottoman oppression in 1770, was persuaded to surrender at the fortress but was later flayed alive by the Turks. On 17 May 1828, 385 Cretan rebels made a last stand in one of the bloodiest battles of the war for independence. About 800 Turks were killed along with the rebels.

Legend has it that at dawn each anniversary their ghosts, the *drosoulites,* can be seen marching along the beach. The name comes from the Greek word *drosia* meaning 'moisture', which may refer to the dawn moisture during the hours when the ghosts are said to appear.

Orthi Ammos Beach   BEACH
Adjoining the Frangokastello fortress is the stunning Orthi Ammos beach, a long stretch of fine sand with shallow, warm waters. It is blissful and child-friendly, unless (as is frequently the case) the wind whips up the sand and forces you to retreat into the nearby cafe.

🛏 Sleeping

Accommodation is mostly designed for longer stays and is reasonably good value, especially a bit further from the beach across the east–west road.

Milos   APARTMENT €
(✆28250 92162; www.milos-sfakia.com; r €45-55, apt €70; P❄🛜🐾) A renovated, century-old stone windmill (*mylos* in Greek), turned into an apartment on a pretty spot on the beach, is the most captivating of several atmospheric rooms and studios. Four stone cottages sit under the tamarisk trees, and modern well-equipped studios are nearby. To stay in the mill in high season book ahead. There's also a good taverna.

Stavris Studios   APARTMENT €
(✆28250 92250; www.studios-stavris-frangokastello-crete.com; studio/2-bedroom apt from €35/60; ◷Apr-Oct; P❄🛜🐾) This collection of 24 studios and apartments is great value, especially considering its position smack on the beach. Studios have kitchenettes, balconies and sea views. There is a leafy garden and big open area for kids to run around in, and the owners are happy to advise about local activities.

Fata Morgana   APARTMENT €
(✆28250 92077; www.fatamorgana-kreta.com; studio €40-60; P❄🛜🐾) Set among an olive grove above Orthi Ammos beach, this simple complex has a range of fully equipped, but a bit old-fashioned, studios and larger apartments for families, as well as two cosy mock castles. There's a playground and a chook/bird pen to amuse the kids.

🍴 Eating

Oasis Taverna   CRETAN €
(✆28250 92136; www.oasisrooms.com; mains €6-8; ◷lunch & dinner; @🛜) Part of an excellent family-run studio and apartment complex at the western end of the beach, this is the best place to eat. The taverna's well-executed Cretan specials include a delicious *kreatopita* (meat and cheese pie). The spacious apartments (€50 to €60) have full-sized kitchens, are set in a lovely garden, and you can walk to a quiet stretch of beach.

Taverna Babis & Popi   TAVERNA €
(✆28250 92092; www.babis-popi.de; mains €5-7; ◷lunch & dinner) This taverna serves decent,

good-value meals under a shady vine canopy tucked behind the family's rooms and minimarket.

ⓘ Getting There & Away

KTEL buses stop at several spots along the main road. To/from Hania there's one daily bus (€8.40, 2½ hours). For Rethymno, change at Vryses. In summer, two daily buses from Hora Sfakion to Plakias stop at Frangokastello (€2, 25 minutes).

Hora Sfakion
Χώρα Σφακίων
POP 212

The more bullet holes you see in the passing road signs, the closer you are to Hora Sfakion (*ho*-ra sfa-*kee*-on), long renowned in Cretan history for its rebellious streak against foreign occupiers. But don't worry, the pint-sized fishing village is an amiable, if eccentric, place that caters well to today's foreign visitors – many of whom are Samaria Gorge hikers stumbling off the Agia Roumeli boat on their way back to Hania.

Most pause here only long enough to catch the next bus out, but the village, the main town in the region, and the only one with an ATM, can be a relaxing stay for a few days and is the access point to several beaches, including the isolated **Sweetwater** and **Ilingas Beaches** to the west. Ilingas is a small scrim of grey-sand beach backed by craggy mountains. Hora Sfakion is also convenient for ferrying westward to other hamlets and Paleohora, or for catching a ferry to Gavdos Island.

Hora Sfakion gift shops stock books about local traditions, linguistics and local cookery.

History

Under Venetian and Turkish rule Hora Sfakion was an important maritime centre and (with the upland regional capital of Anopoli) the nucleus of the Cretan struggle for independence. The Turks inflicted severe reprisals on the town's inhabitants for their rebelliousness in the 19th century, after which the town fell into an economic slump that lasted until the arrival of tourism several decades ago. Hora Sfakion played a prominent role during WWII when thousands of Allied troops were evacuated by sea from the town after the Battle of Crete. Today, a memorial to the last British, Australian and New Zealand soldiers evacuated after the battle stands on the eastern bluff over the town.

◉ Sights & Activities

Bungee jump (p79) off the Aradena bridge over the Aradena Gorge, northwest of town.

Vrissi Beach   BEACH
Abutting the western edge of town, tiny grey-sand Vrissi Beach makes for an easy dive or sunset viewing.

Sweetwater Beach   BEACH
(Glyka Nera) West of Hora Sfakion, lovely Sweetwater Beach is accessible by a small daily ferry (May to October, per person €4), by taxi boat (one-way/return €20/30) or on foot via a stony and partly vertiginous one-hour coastal path starting at the first hairpin turn of the Anopoli road. A small cafe rents umbrellas and sun chairs.

Notos Mare Diving Centre   DIVING
(☑ 6947270106; www.notosmare.com; 1 dive from €49) Offers dives and certifications for beginners and experienced divers, as well as snorkelling and boat excursions along the south coast.

Yoga on Crete   YOGA
(☑ 6937363890, 28250 91109; www.yogaoncrete. gr; ☻ Jun-Sep) Warm and welcoming Eugenia Sivitou runs excellent all-inclusive weeklong yoga retreats and seminars (from €590) in different disciplines with teachers from all over the world. Offers a work-exchange option (€490).

⨼ Sleeping

Xenia Hotel   HOTEL €
(☑ 28250 91490; www.sfakia-xenia-hotel.gr; d incl breakfast €55; ❋ 🛜) The best-value, and best-located, rooms in town are to be found at this refurbished hotel well positioned at the western edge overlooking the water. The 21 rooms have mod cons such as air-con, satellite TV and a fridge.

Hotel Stavris   HOTEL €
(☑ 28250 91220; www.hotel-stavris-sfakia-crete. com; s/d/tr from €30/35/40; ❋ 🛜) Up the steps at the western end of the port, this long-running place owned by the Perrakis clan has clean, basic rooms – some with kitchenettes and fridges and harbour-facing balconies. Rooms vary; aim for the renovated main building.

Lefka Ori HOTEL €
(☑28250 91209; www.chora-sfakion.com; s/d €25/35; ❄☎) This long-established little hotel on the western end of the port has 10 rooms and two studios with kitchenettes, all clean and well kept, though fairly basic. Avoid the sub-par taverna below.

✗ Eating

Be sure to try the local *Sfakiani pita* – this thin, circular pancake filled with sweet *myzithra* (sheep's-milk cheese) and flecked with honey makes a great breakfast when served with a bit of Greek yoghurt on the side.

★**Nikos** TAVERNA €
(☑28250 91111; mains €5-12; ☺8am-midnight) Hora Sfakion's best harbour-front taverna stands out for its friendly, family-run service, special care with all of its dishes and top *Sfakiani pita,* and it's always fun to have the grilled garlic bread, which is usually thrown in for free. Mains run from seafood to traditional Greek taverna fare and Cretan specialities like smoked pork or sautéed snails.

Three Brothers TAVERNA €
(www.three-brothers-chora-sfakion-crete.com; Vrissi Beach; mains €5-12; ☺8am-midnight; ☎) The menu features all the staples, but it's the location overlooking Vrissi Beach that sets this taverna apart from the others in the harbour. It's especially crowded when Giannis fires up the barbecue. Great at sunset. Rooms for rent too (doubles from €35).

Delfini SEAFOOD €€
(☑20250 91002; www.chorasfakion.com; mains €6-15, fish per kg €40-55) Among the row of seafront tavernas, Delfini is recommended for fresh fish dishes.

❶ Information

Hora Sfakion has two petrol stations and one ATM. The post office is on the square, opposite the police station.

The small **Hora Sfakion Tourist Kiosk** (www. chora-sfakion.com; ☺9am-2pm & 5-7pm Easter-Sep) near the entrance to the harbour has maps and transport info in high season.

❶ Getting There & Away

BOAT
The ferry quay is around the point on the eastern edge of the village harbour. Hora Sfakion is the western terminus for the south-coast **Anendyk** (☑28210 95511; www.anendyk.gr) ferry route to/from Paleohora via Loutro, Agia Roumeli and Sougia, and also has boats to Gavdos Island.

Buy tickets at the **ticket booth** (☑28250 91221) on the eastern edge of the harbour. Schedules vary seasonally, so always check ahead. Often boats only run as far as Agia Roumeli, where you must change for a boat to Sougia (€14) and Paleohora (€17, three hours). In low season, it is usually impossible to ferry a car all the way to Paleohora, as some of the boats are passenger-only.

From June through August there are three daily boats from Hora Sfakion to Agia Roumeli (€11, one hour) via Loutro (€5, 15 minutes). There are four additional boats to Loutro only. There are two to three boats per week to/from Gavdos Island (€17, 1½ hours).

Boat taxis (☑6978645212) serve the coast around Hora Sfakion. Private hire to Sweetwater beach is €20, and from May to September set group taxi departures cost €4 per person.

BUS
KTEL Buses (www.e-ktel.com) leave from the square up the hill above the municipal car park. Schedules change seasonally; check online. In summer there are three daily services to Hania (€7.60, two hours); to reach Rethymno change in Vryses (€7.30, one hour). The last bus tends to wait for the boat from Agia Roumeli. There are also two to three daily buses to Frangokastello (€2, 25 minutes) and one daily to Anopoli/Aradena (€2, 30 minutes) in summer.

CAR
The municipal car park (€3 per day Easter to October) is at the entrance to town; there's also parking near the ferry quay.

Sfakia Tours (☑28250 91272; www.sfakia-tours.com; ☺9am-1.30pm & 4-9pm) Sfakia Tours, next to the post office, has hire cars and can help with accommodation.

Around Hora Sfakion

The forbidding, rocky moonscape of Inner Sfakia rises up from the sea behind Hora Sfakion. Although now almost unpopulated due to past clan vendettas and emigration, it was in fact once a powerful provincial area teeming with life.

Anopoli Ανώπολη

A scenic, hair-raisingly steep 12km winding road west from Hora Sfakion takes you to Anopoli, a quiet village in a fertile plateau at the base of the Lefka Ori, with a memorial to resistance fighters in the main square. It was one of the few areas that did not fall to the Venetians or Turks. In earlier centuries, Anopoli was the Sfakiot capital, presiding over the regional port of Loutro (still accessible, albeit on an extremely steep path, by hikers).

Hearty lunches are served at **Platanos** (☑ 28250 91169; www.anopoli-sfakia.com; mains €4-9), a restaurant on the main roundabout in Anopoli, known for its roast lamb and other local delicacies. The friendly English-speaking owner, Eva Kopasis, can also advise about hikes to Loutro and local beaches, and has rooms (doubles €33).

Don't miss the delicious baked goods at **Cretan Divine Family Bakery** (☑ 28250 91524; ⊘ 8am-8pm daily), where friendly Angeliki serves up cookies, *kalitsounia* (Cretan cheese pies) and hot Greek coffee at wonderful outdoor tables with views around the plateau.

Aradena Gorge
Φαράγγι Αράδαινας

The virtually abandoned stone hamlet of Aradena, about 2km west of Anopoli, is famous for the **Vardinogiannis bridge**, named for the wealthy local businessman who endowed it, which crosses over the Aradena Gorge. Look down into the depths in fascinated horror as the structure rattles under your wheels. At weekends you may see people jumping into the gorge from this bridge – at 138m, the highest bungee jumping bridge in Greece. Contact **Liquid Bungy** (☑ 6937615191; www.bungy.gr; per jump €100; ⊘ noon-6pm Sat & Sun Jul & Aug, by appointment Jun & Sep) to join in.

At the *kantina* (small kiosk) next to the bridge you can get directions for the remote **Church of Agios Ioannis**, a whitewashed early-Byzantine structure. It's only about a 15-minute walk (roughly 800m), but the church is rarely open. From it, however, begins a forking path down to the sea: the western fork leads to Agia Roumeli via the Byzantine **Church of Agios Pavlos**, the eastern to **Marmara Beach** with its brilliant teal waters.

The more-often-used **Aradena Gorge hiking route** to Marmara Beach goes through the gorge and is a 1½-hour (3.5km) trek of moderate difficulty. The trailhead is signposted before the bridge (when coming from Anopoli). From the beach, you can walk to the glittering nearby port of Loutro, with its creature comforts, and catch a ferry to get out.

Loutro   Λουτρό
POP 56

A peaceful crescent of flower-festooned white-and-blue buildings hugging a narrow pebbly beach, the pint-sized fishing village of Loutro lies between Agia Roumeli and Hora Sfakion and is only accessible by boat and on foot. It's the departure point for several coastal walks to isolated beaches, such as **Finix** (also spelled Phoenix; 1km west), Marmara Beach (5km west) and Sweetwater (3.3km east; p77). Ask locally for directions, hire a **mini-canoe** (per hr/day €5/15) from the Hotel Porto Loutro, or take a summer-only small **boat**. You can also explore the **castle ruins** on the point.

Loutro is the only natural harbour on the south coast of Crete, an advantage that made it strategically vital in ancient times when it was the port for Finix and Anopoli. St Paul is said to have been heading to Finix from here when he encountered a storm that blew him off course past Gavdos Island; the journey ended with him being shipwrecked in Malta.

Today it is a marvellous escape and a great base for exploring the south coast.

🛏 Sleeping

Loutro has good budget accommodation, with most overlooking the cove, and each place has a taverna. Confirm whether they'll accept credit cards as not all do.

Apartments Niki   APARTMENT €
(☑ 28250 91213; www.loutro-accommodation. com; studio/apt from €50/110; ❊ 🤶) These beautifully furnished studios with beamed ceilings and stone floors accommodate two to four people. The three-bedroom villa-apartment is unique in Loutro: it houses up to six. Each has its own kitchenette, and since Niki is located just above the village, you get great views over the water from the balconies.

Blue House   PENSION €
(☑ 28250 91035; www.bluehouse.loutro.gr; d €45-50; ❊ 🤶) Midway along the white buildings lining the port, the Blue House has spacious, well-appointed rooms with big verandahs overlooking the water. The nicest rooms are in the refurbished top-floor section. The taverna downstairs serves excellent *mayi-refta* (mains €5 to €7), including delicious *boureki* (Turkish-influenced filo pie) baked with zucchini, potato and goat's cheese.

Rooms Sofia PENSION €

(☑ 28250 91354; www.sofiarooms-loutro.gr; d/tr
€35/45; ☺ Apr-Oct; ❋ 🛜) Above the Sofia minimarket, one street back from the beach, these
plain and clean rooms can be a bit cramped,
but have a fridge and kettle. They share a verandah with sea and mountain views.

Hotel Porto Loutro HOTEL €€

(☑ 28250 91433; www.hotelportoloutro.com; s/d/
tr incl breakfast €55/65/75; ☺ Apr-Oct; ❋ @ 🛜)
The Porto Loutro is the classiest hotel in
town. Spread across three buildings, it offers rooms and studios that are simply decorated in understated island style. Two of
the buildings are smack on the beachfront,
the other has balconies overlooking the harbour. Does not accept children under age
seven. No credit cards.

✖ Eating

Given the captive market, the tavernas that
line the waterfront in Loutro are surprisingly good. Most display a wide range of *mayirefta* and you can't miss the dazzling range
of cakes and sweets.

Notos CRETAN €

(☑ 28250 91501; http://notos.loutro.gr; dishes
€2.50-7; ☺ noon-late) Excellent mezedhes, set
back from the beach. Order a range of small
plates, like stuffed onions, and dig in.

Pavlos TAVERNA €

(☑ 28250 91336; www.pavlos.loutro.gr; mains €6-
10; ☺ 11am-midnight) Sit harbourside while
feasting on all manner of freshly grilled
meat and fish.

Ilios SEAFOOD €€

(☑ 28250 91160; www.iliosloutro.gr; mains €5-15;
☺ 8am-midnight; 🛜) Ilios is the best spot in
town for fish and seafood, though it also
offers a full range of Cretan classics and
breakfast, too. Ilios also has rooms.

❶ Information

There's no bank, ATM or post office, and many
places do not accept credit cards (and there is
no cash back option). Bring plenty of cash (the
nearest ATM is in Hora Sfakion). There is internet
access (per hour €4) at the Daskalogiannis Hotel.

❶ Getting There & Away

Loutro is on the **Anendyk** (www.anendyk.gr)
Paleohora–Hora Sfakion boat routes. Boats
dock in front of the Sifis Hotel. The ticket booth
opens an hour before departures. Boats serve
Hora Sfakion (€5, 15 minutes), Agia Roumeli (€6,
45 minutes) and occasionally Paleohora (€16,

2½ hours) and Sougia (€13, 1¾ hours), or you
can change in Agia Roumeli to reach those ports.
September to June, boats from Hora Sfakion to
Gavdos Island also stop in Loutro.

High season taxi boats go to Sweetwater
Beach (ferry/private €5/25, 15 minutes) and
Hora Sfakion.

Agia Roumeli Αγία Ρουμελή

POP 57

The coastal hamlet of Agia Roumeli is a collection of tavernas and pensions serving Samaria Gorge hikers, since it is the southern
terminus of the famous gorge hike. While
not spectacular in itself, it is undoubtedly a
divine sight for tired trekkers stumbling out
of the canyon. Stop for a swim and lunch at
this tiny beach settlement, or stay overnight,
before catching a boat, which is the only way
out. The black pebble beach is pretty, but ab-
sorbs an exceptional amount of heat so becomes impossible to sit on for long unless you
hire a beach umbrella and sun lounge (€6).

There are no tourist facilities or banks and
ATMs, and not much to see, other than to walk
up to the well-preserved ruins of the **Venetian
castle** above the village (about 1km, or 30
minutes, one-way), or check out the **Panagia
church** in the village, which has some surviving remnants of a Roman mosaic floor.

Agia Roumeli is also a good access point
to the southern bits of Samaria Gorge, for
families with small children or those eager
to peer into the gorge a bit, rather than do
the whole hike.

🛌 Sleeping & Eating

Paralia Taverna & Rooms PENSION, TAVERNA €

(☑ 28250 91408; www.taverna-paralia.com; d €35-
40; ❋ 🛜) Right on the waterfront, Paralia
Taverna & Rooms offers excellent views, the
best Cretan cuisine in town, cold beer and
simple, clean rooms.

Calypso Hotel & Taverna HOTEL €

(☑ 28250 91314; www.calypso.agiaroumeli.gr; s/d/
tr from €25/35/45; ❋ 🛜) Beachfront and well-
established, Calypso offers tidy rooms with
refrigerators, and a spacious taverna-bar
(mains €5 to €11).

Artemis Studios APARTMENT €

(☑ 28250 91225; www.agiaroumeli.com; s/d/tr
€45/55/70; ☺ Apr-Oct; ❋ 🛜 👪) Fifty metres
from Agia Roumeli's pebble beach, the
family-run Artemis has 12 self-catering studios accommodating up to five people. It is a

REMOTE GORGE HIKES

Samaria Gorge isn't western Crete's only canyon worth conquering. For the gorges below, which are more remote, it's always wise to go with a guide or with thorough pre-planning if you are an experienced trekker. Check in first with **Hania's EOS** (p62) for advice on local conditions, water sources and lodgings, and pick up the Anavasi hiking maps, marked with GPS coordinates, trails and other key details, available in Hania bookshops. Find additional info at www.west-crete.com.

➡ **Agia Irini Gorge** (p81) More lush than most, ends 5km north of Sougia.

➡ **Imbros Gorge** (p75) Half as long as Samaria and open year-round, ends at Komitades near Hora Sfakion.

➡ **Aradena Gorge** (p79) Moderate-to-steep hike ends at Marmara Bay, 5km west of Loutro.

➡ **Trypiti Gorge** (p82) Tough and little visited, ends 12km east of Sougia. Guide essential.

➡ **Klados Gorge** This gorge, marked by its sheer and unforgiving rock face, runs between and parallel to Samaria and Trypiti Gorges. This is the place to go for serious rock climbers; it offers great abseiling (rappelling) too. It lets out on the barren south coast. Mountaineers only.

good bet if you want to be near the water and away from the crowds. The owners provide info on local hill walks too.

Gigilos Taverna & Rooms PENSION €
(☑ 28250 91383; www.gigilos.gr; s/d/tr €25/35/40; ﷽) Right on the beach at the western end of the village, the best rooms are at the front, on the beach road. They are clean and nicely furnished, with decent new bathrooms and a communal fridge in the hall. The taverna, which serves good home-cooked Cretan fare, has a pleasant, huge, shady deck on the beach.

🛈 Getting There & Away

The Anendyk boat **ticket office** (☑ 28250 91251; www.anendyk.gr) is 50m inland from the ferry quay. Served by the southern ferries on a seasonally changing schedule, you can head east to Loutro (€6, 45 minutes) and Hora Sfakion (€11, one hour) and connect with the last bus back to Hania. Or go west to Sougia (€9, 45 minutes) and Paleohora (€15, 1½ hours). Many Gavdos Island boats (€17.50) also call in here.

In high season, it is usually possible to time a round-trip from Hora Sfakion in order to visit Agia Roumeli as a day trip.

Sougia   Σούγια
POP 136

Sougia (*soo*-yah), 67km south of Hania, and on the Hora Sfakion–Paleohora ferry route, is one of the most laid-back and refreshingly undeveloped beach resorts along the south-

ern coast. It lies at the foot of a narrow, twisting road that deters most tour buses. Cafes, bars and tavernas line a tamarisk-shaded waterfront promenade while most lodging options enjoy a quieter inland setting. Sougia was once a popular hippie hang-out and many nostalgic ex-hippies return each year. It retains its chilled-out atmosphere and there is little to do other than relax or take nearby gorge hikes, or the walk to ancient Lissos.

Sougia's tranquillity has been preserved largely because archaeological remains on the eastern edge of the beach prohibit development. The ancient town of Sougia was on the western side of the existing modern village. It flourished under the Romans and Byzantines when it was the port for Elyros, an important inland city (now gone). A 6th-century basilica contained a fine mosaic floor that is now in Hania's Archaeological Museum.

🅞 Sights & Activities

Sougia has a lovely 1km-long grey sand-and-pebble **beach**, but its drop-off is quick, so it's not the best swimming spot for families with small children (seek shallower waters at Frangokastello, Paleohora and Elafonisi).

Like most southern coast villages, it's also great hiking territory. A taxi to the Samaria Gorge trailhead is €60, but with a day or two advance notice, staff at the taxi kiosk can put together a pool of hikers to share the cost.

⭐ **Agia Irini Gorge** HIKING
(admission €1.50; ☺ year-round) Pretty Agia Irini Gorge starts some 13km north of Sougia.

The 7km well-maintained trail (with a 500m elevation drop) brings you through redolent and varied verdure, plus a few caves hidden in the gorge walls. You'll emerge at excellent **Taverna Oasis** (☑ 28230 51121; mains €6-10; ☺ lunch & dinner Apr-Oct), from where it's another 7km walk via a quiet, paved road (or a €15 taxi ride) to Sougia.

Of course, it's also possible to do the hike in reverse. To trek without a tour, take the Omalos bus from Paleohora or the Hania bus from Sougia, and get off at Agia Irini.

Trypiti Gorge   HIKING

Little-visited Trypiti Gorge near Mt Gingilos is one of Crete's most strenuous and longest, starting from Omalos and ending on the southern coast 12km east of Sougia at Cape Trypiti. You will have blissfully little company on the 10-hour jaunt, making Trypiti great for those seeking unspoilt nature and solitude. But the trail is difficult and you should be with a guide, and equipped with maps, water and food.

🛏 Sleeping

A small settlement of campers and nudists sometimes crop up at the eastern end of the beach.

Aretousa Studios & Rooms   APARTMENT €

(☑ 28230 51178; s/d/studio €35/40/45; ☺ Apr-Oct; [P][✳][🛜][🐾]) This lovely pension on the road to Hania, 200m from the sea, has bright and comfortable refurbished rooms and studios, most with kitchenettes. There's a relaxing garden and playground for kids out back.

Rooms Ririka   PENSION €

(☑ 28230 51167; www.sougia.info/hotels/ririka; d €45; [✳][🛜]) This cosy place consists of eight double rooms with a leafy garden, just up from the eastern side of the beach.

Santa Irene
Apartments & Studios   APARTMENT €€

(☑ 28230 51342; www.santa-irene.gr; apt €60-80; ☺ late Mar-early Nov; [P][✳][🛜][🐾]) This smart hotel on the beach has airy rooms with marble floors, TV and kitchenettes, while there are also two family apartments (€80 to €90) with baby cots available. Prices drop dramatically in low season.

Syia Hotel   HOTEL €€

(☑ 28230 51174; www.syiahotel.com; studio/apt incl breakfast from €70/90; [P][✳][🛜]) This professionally run family hotel is as fancy as things get in laid-back Sougia. Set in a quiet garden environment, units have plenty of elbow room along with a balcony, contemporary furnishings and full kitchens with upmarket appliances.

🍴 Eating

Taverna Rembetiko   CRETAN €

(☑ 28230 51510; dishes €5-9; ☺ noon-late; [🌿]) On the road to Hania, this popular taverna serving mezedhes is a great place for a quick snack or a varied meal at good prices. Friendly owners offer an extensive menu of Cretan dishes like *bourekia* (filo pies shaped into thin long rolls, batons and pinwheels) and stuffed zucchini flowers. Good vegetarian options too.

Polyfimos   TAVERNA €

(☑ 28230 51343; mains €5-8; ☺ lunch & dinner; [🛜][🌿]) Tucked away off the Hania road behind the police station, ex-hippie Yianni makes his own oil, wine and *raki* and even makes dolmadhes (vine leaves stuffed with rice) from the grapevines covering the shady courtyard.

★ Omikron   INTERNATIONAL €€

(☑ 28230 51492; mains €5-14; ☺ 8am-late; [🛜][🌿]) At this elegantly rustic lair, Jean-Luc Delfosse has forged his own culinary path in a refreshing change from taverna staples. Mushroom crêpes to *Flammekuch*e (Alsatian-style pizza), seafood pasta to pepper steak – it's all fresh, creative and delicious.

Kyma   SEAFOOD €€

(☑ 28230 51688; mains €6-17; ☺ noon-late) Near the waterfront T-junction with the Hania road, you'll know Kyma by the fish tank in front. It's known for its seafood, supplied by the owner's brother, and the restaurant raises its own meat. Try the goat *tsigariasto* (sautéed) in wine sauce or the rabbit *stifadho*. Fried *kalamari* or the langoustine spaghetti (€70 per kilogram) are top seafood picks.

☆ Entertainment

Sougia has two summer-only open-air clubs that can get surprisingly lively (after midnight) for such a small town. **Alabama** (☺ 11pm-late Jun-Sep), on the eastern side of the beach, is the age-old favourite, while **Fortuna** (☑ 6977423023; ☺ 11pm-7am Jun-Sep), on the left before the entrance to the town, is a great place for a late-night drink. Both kick off after midnight.

❶ Information

There is no ATM, bank or petrol station; Paleohora has those. Visit www.sougia.info for area information.

❶ Getting There & Away

BOAT

Sougia is on the **Anendyk** (☑ 28230 51230; www.anendyk.gr) Paleohora–Hora Sfakion boat route. In high season, daily boats serve Agia Roumeli (€9, 45 minutes), Loutro (€13, 1½ hours) and Hora Sfakion (€14, 1¾ hours) to the east and Paleohora (€9, 50 minutes) to the west. Twice-weekly boats from Paleohora to Gavdos Island (€18 from Sougia) pass through as well.

Captain George's Water Taxi (☑ 6947605802) serves the coast near Sougia.

BUS & CAR

There's no petrol station in Sougia. There is one road into Sougia and the bus drops you on the coastal road near the T-junction. Buy tickets at Roxane's minimarket, nearby.

In high season, two to three daily buses (www.e-ktel.com) connect Hania and Sougia (€7.10, one hour 50 minutes), and can stop at Agia Irini to let off gorge hikers. There are also thrice-weekly buses to Paleohora and daily buses to Omalos in high season only.

Various **taxi drivers** (☑ 6972370480, 6977745160, 28230 51362; www.taxi-selino.com) serve Sougia, and have a central kiosk on the waterfront.

Lissos   Λισσός

The ruins of ancient Lissos are a 3.5km walk from Sougia on the coastal path to Paleohora, which starts at the far end of Sougia's small port. The only other option is to take a water taxi to the nearby cove and hike up.

Lissos arose under the Dorians, flourished under the Byzantines and was destroyed by the Saracens in the 9th century. A port for inland Elyros (now gone), it was part of a league of city-states, led by ancient Gortyna, which minted its own gold coins inscribed with the word 'Lission'.

At one time there was a reservoir, a theatre and hot springs, but these have not yet been excavated. Most of what you see dates from the 1st through 3rd centuries BC, when Lissos was known for its curative springs. The 3rd-century-BC Temple of Asklepion was built next to one of the springs and named after the Greek god of healing, Asclepius.

Excavations here uncovered a headless **statue of Asclepius**, along with 20 other statue fragments now in Hania's Archaeological Museum. You can still see the marble altar base that supported the statue next to the pit in which sacrifices were placed.

The other notable feature is the **mosaic floor** of multicoloured stones intricately arranged in beautiful geometric shapes and images of birds. On the way down to the sea there are traces of Roman ruins, and on the western slopes of the valley are unusual barrel-vaulted tombs.

Nearby are the ruins of two early Christian basilicas – **Agios Kyriakos** and the **Panagia** – dating from the 13th century.

Lissos has a lovely beach to cool off at after the walk, and if you come on 15 July you will stumble on the annual festival, held in honour of Agios Kyriakos.

Paleohora   Παλαιόχωρα

POP 1675

Appealing, laid-back and full of character, Paleohora (pal-ee-*oh*-hor-a) lies on a narrow peninsula flanked by long, curving tamarisk-shaded and sandy **Pahia Ammos beach** (Sandy Beach) on one side, and pebbly **Halikia beach** (Pebble Beach) on the other. Shallow waters and general quietude also make the town a good choice for families with small children.

The most picturesque part of Paleohora is the maze of narrow streets around the castle. Tavernas spill out onto the pavement and occasional cultural happenings, as well as Cretan and international music, inject a lively ambience. In spring and autumn, Paleohora attracts many walkers. It's also the only beach town in Crete that does not go into total hibernation in winter.

⊙ Sights

Venetian Castle   CASTLE

FREE It's worth clambering up the ruins of the 13th-century Venetian castle for the splendid view of the sea and mountains. The fortress was built so the Venetians could monitor the southwestern coast from this commanding position on the hilltop. There's not much left of the castle, as it was destroyed by the Venetians, the Turks, the pirate Barbarossa in the 16th century, and the Germans during WWII.

Museum of the Acritans of Europe
MUSEUM

(☎ 28230 42265; ⏰ 10am-1pm Mon-Fri) FREE
This little museum next to the town's ornate church is dedicated to the border fighters and heroes of Europe's medieval and Byzantine times. It has a well-displayed historical exhibition along with musical instruments, weapons and other items from the period.

🏃 Activities

There are several great **walking trails** nearby. From Paleohora, a six-hour walk along a scenic coastal path (p86) leads to Sougia, passing ancient Lissos. An easier inland loop goes to Anydri then through small, lush Anydri Gorge (p87) to the sea.

When a stiff summer breeze is blowing, **windsurfing** off sandy Pahia Ammos is excellent. Private dolphin-spotting trips are also run from Paleohora.

Tours

You can hike Samaria and Agia Irini Gorges from Paleohora, either with local organised tours or by using taxis or the KTEL bus service to reach the trailheads, then returning by ferry from the trails' coastal end-points (at Agia Roumeli, for Samaria Gorge, and Sougia for Agia Irini). Mid-May to October you can take a day trip to Elafonisi by boat. Tickets are sold at Selino Travel (p86), which also offers other excursions.

🛏 Sleeping

★ **Joanna's Place**
APARTMENT €

(☎ 28230 41801; www.joanna-place.com; studio €45-55; ⏰ Apr-Nov; P ❄ 🛜) This charmer sits in a quiet spot across from a small stone beach at the southeastern tip of the peninsula. Spacious and spotless studios are outfitted with locally made furniture, and there's a kitchenette for preparing breakfast to enjoy on your balcony.

Paleohora

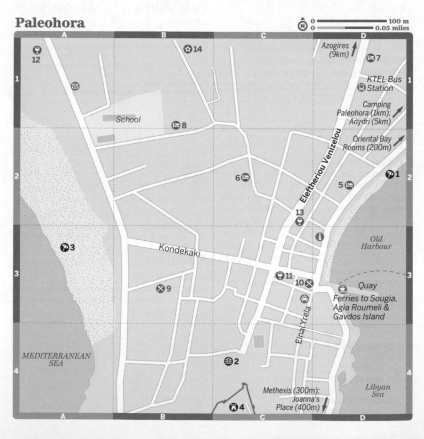

Homestay Anonymous PENSION €
(☑ 28230 42098; www.anonymoushomestay.com; s/d/tr/2-bedroom apt €25/30/35/55; ❄ 🛜 🍴) This simple but good-value pension with private bathrooms and shared cooking facilities in the courtyard garden is a good bet. Friendly, well-travelled owner Manolis cultivates a welcoming atmosphere and is a mine of information on local activities. The rooms are clean and tastefully furnished, in a quaint stone building, though a bit cramped. Rooms can connect to accommodate families.

Oriental Bay Rooms PENSION €
(☑ 28230 41076; www.orientalbay.gr; s/d/tr €30/ 35/50; ❄ 🛜) These immaculate rooms in a large modern building at the northern end of Halikia beach have balconies with sea or mountain views and come with kettle and fridge.

Villa Anna PENSION €
(☑ 28103 46428; www.villaanna-paleochora.com; apt €50-80; ❄ 🛜 🍴) Set in a lovely shady garden bordered by tall poplars, these well-appointed, family-friendly apartments can sleep up to five people. There are cots, and swings and a sandpit in the garden, and the grounds are fenced.

Camping Paleohora CAMPGROUND €
(☑ 28230 41120; www.campingpaleohora.gr; camp sites per adult/child/tent €6/3.50/5; 🛜) This

large campground is 1.5km northeast of the town, about 500m east of the stony Halikia beach. There is a taverna and it is near the sea, but there's no minimarket, and facilities in general are a bit run-down. You can hire tents (small/large €6/10).

★**Corali** APARTMENT €€
(☑ 6974361868; www.corali-studios.com; d studio from €65; ❄ @ 🛜) A friendly Greek-Italian family runs these immaculate studios which are a distinct cut above standard studios for rent. A series of luxe studios with kitchenettes and waterfront balconies are kitted out with top-end modern furniture and large pristine bathrooms. Some come with computers in the room. The central location and water views are excellent.

Libyan Princess HOTEL €€
(☑ 28230 42030; www.libyanprincess.gr; d incl breakfast from €100; ❄ @ 🛜 ≋) This full-service hotel is Paleohora's highest-end option. Thirty-three rooms and one executive suite curl around a sparkling pool and boast all the mod cons from flat-screen TV and phone to safe and tea- and coffee-making facilities. There's a gym and massage service as well. Downside: it's on the busy main street.

🍴 Eating

Paleohora has good Cretan restaurants and the olive oil produced in this region is among the best in Greece. In summer, little tavernas spill onto the pedestrian-only central street and make for great ambience. In the Paleohora region, the excellent *myzithra* cheese is generally unsweetened, unlike the sweetened *myzithra* usually served elsewhere in Crete.

Third Eye VEGETARIAN €
(☑ 28230 41234; www.thethirdeye-paleochora.com; mains €6-7; ⏱ 8.30am-3pm & 5.30-11pm; 🛜 🍴) A local institution, the Third Eye, Crete's only vegetarian restaurant, has an eclectic menu of curries, salads, pastas, and Greek and Asian dishes. There's live music weekly in summer. The restaurant is just inland from sandy Pahia Ammos.

Christos Taverna CRETAN €
(☑ 28230 41359; www.christospaleochora.com; mains €6-10; ⏱ noon-late May-Oct) Straightforward Cretan and Greek dishes are the order of the day in this long-standing summer-only taverna near the stony Halikia beach. Pick from what's fresh, arrayed in casseroles behind the glass.

PALEOHORA–SOUGIA COASTAL WALK

From the town centre of Paleohora, follow signs to the camp sites to the northeast. Turn right at the intersection with the road to Anydri and soon you'll be following the coastal path marked as the E4 European Footpath. After a couple of kilometres, the path climbs steeply for a beautiful view back to Paleohora. You'll pass **Anydri Beach** and several inviting **coves** where people may be getting an all-over tan. Take a dip because the path soon turns inland to pass over **Cape Flomes**. You'll walk along a plateau carpeted with brush that leads towards the coast and some breathtaking views over the Libyan Sea. Soon you'll reach the Dorian site of Lissos (p85). After Lissos the path takes you through a pine forest. The road ends at Sougia Harbour. The 14.5km walk (allow about six hours) is nearly shadeless, so take several litres of water and sunscreen. From June through August, it's best to start at sunrise in order to get to Sougia before the heat of the day. You can boat back.

Vakakis Family Bakery
BAKERY €

(📞 28230 41850; baked goods from €1; ⏱ 7am-late) Load up on fresh bread and sweet treats paired with hot or iced coffees.

★ Methexis
CRETAN €€

(📞 28230 41431; www.methexistaverna.com; mains €6-15; ⏱ 12.30-11.30pm Tue-Sun, later Jul & Aug; 📶🅿) It's well worth the short saunter to the peninsula's southeastern tip to sample the authentic comfort food and warm hospitality at this locally adored taverna across from a small beach. All the classics are here along with such surprises as the meat-free and superb chestnut *stifado* (stew), salt cod with garlic sauce, and other Cretan delicacies.

🍸 Drinking & Entertainment

Agios
BAR

(📞 28230 41258; www.agiosbar.gr; ⏱ noon-late year-round) Casual lounge, bar and music venue, Agios is one of Paleohora's best hang-outs.

Nostos Club
CLUB

(⏱ 6pm-2am Apr-Oct) Nostos Club has an outdoor terrace bar and a small indoor club playing Greek and Western music.

La Jetee
BAR

(⏱ 9am-2am May-Sep; 📶) A beachside tourist haunt known for its cocktails, La Jetee has a lovely garden and sunset views, plus snacks (€2.50 to €5) are served all day.

Open-Air Cinema
CINEMA

(⏱ Jun-Sep) Three nights a week in summer, films (usually in English and subtitled in Greek) are screened at Paleohora's outdoor cinema.

ℹ Information

Paleohora has an attractive seafront promenade and it, along with the main road (Venizelou), are cut off to traffic May to September. There are petrol stations and ATMs on Venizelou. Stock up before heading to places like Sougia, which have neither.

Post Office (⏱ 7am-2pm Mon-Fri) Just across from Pahia Ammos (sandy beach).

Selino Travel (📞 28230 42272; selino2@otenet.gr; Kondekaki; 3hr trip €18; ⏱ 8am-1.30pm & 6-9.30pm Apr-Oct, shorter hours rest of year) General information, boat and airline tickets and excursions, including to the gorges of Samaria and Agia Irini. Mid-May to October they offer a daily boat to Elafonisi beach on the western coast.

Tourist Kiosk (📞 28230 41507; ⏱ 10am-1pm & 6-9pm Wed-Mon May-Oct) On the beach road near the ferry quay with basic brochures.

Tsiskakis Travel (📞 28230 42110; www.notoscar.com; Eleftheriou Venizelou 53; ⏱ 9am-1pm & 5-9pm) Organises rental cars and local tours and excursions, including Samaria, Agia Irini and Ardena Gorges.

ℹ Getting There & Away

BOAT

Boats leave from the quay at the far southern end of Halikia pebble beach. Buy tickets for all boats at Selino Travel.

From mid-May to late October an excursion boat serves the west-coast beach of Elafonisi (adult/child one-way €9/4.50, one hour) once daily, weather permitting.

Paleohora is the westernmost stop on the **Anendyk** (www.anendyk.gr) south coast boat routes. Schedules change seasonally; always check ahead online or at local travel agencies. Ferries go east to Sougia (€9, 50 minutes) and Agia Roumeli (€15, 1½ hours), where you can change for a boat to Loutro (€16, 2½ hours) and Hora Sfakion (€17, three hours). Usually you cannot take a car the whole way as some of the boats carry passengers only. Three times per week in summer a ferry goes to Gavdos Island (€19, 2½ hours).

BUS
Buses from the **KTEL bus station** (☑ 28230 41914; www.e-ktel.com) go on ever-changing schedules to Hania (€7.60, 1¾ hours, three to four daily). In summer one daily service, departing 6.15am, goes to Omalos (€6.40, two hours), for Samaria Gorge, and also stops at the entrance to Agia Irini Gorge (€4.50). Also in summer, thrice-weekly buses serve Sougia and Elafonisi.

CAR
Do not attempt to drive the route to Elafonisi that was once signposted from Grameno (5km west of Paleohora). The road becomes impassable after Maniatiana village except for the most rugged 4WD. **Notos Rentals** (☑ 28230 42110; www.notoscar.com; Eleftheriou Venizelou 53; ⏰ 8am-10pm) has cars, motorcycles and bicycles for hire.

ⓘ Getting Around
Paleochora Taxi (☑ 6979594667, 28230 41128; www.paleochora-taxi.com) Get a ride to gorge trailheads or remote beaches.

Around Paleohora

The hills around Paleohora offer excellent walking, some along the coastal E4 and some through verdant small gorges. Loop from Paleohora to Anydri and back, or go (by taxi) to Azogires and hike down to Anydri and back. Maps are available in Paleohora shops.

Anydri   Ανύδροι
The village of Anydri, 5km northeast of Paleohora, is a popular destination for walkers and is reached via a picturesque drive or walk through the lush Anydri Gorge carved by a small stream. The founding fathers of the village were two brothers from Hora Sfakion fleeing a murderous vendetta, which is why most villagers have the same surname. A path from the village leads to the **Church of Agios Georgios**, which has 14th-century frescoes.

🏃 Activities
Anydri Gorge   HIKING
A popular, beautiful circuit route leads from Paleohora to Anydri then down Anydri Gorge to return along the coast.

From Paleohora, take the road that goes past the campground and follow the paved road that forks off to the left, which is bordered by steep rocks. As you enter Anydri village you'll see a sign directing you to Anydri Gorge. After a few hundred metres on a footpath you'll encounter an overgrown path on the left. Red markers direct you to the gorge.

After walking along the dried-out riverbed, signs direct you to wide **Gialiskari Beach** at the end of the gorge. The nicest stretch is the area with coarse sand at the eastern end, left of the *kantina*. You can take a different path back to Paleohora following the E4 markers, which will take you along the coastal cliffs. The beach is also accessible by a drivable dirt road, from where it is signposted to the right, well before the gorge.

🛏 Sleeping & Eating

Christos Place   COTTAGES €€
(☑ 28230 41330; www.christosplace.gr; cottage €80-130; P❄☎) Just opened in 2015, these lovely small cottages in an olive grove above Anydri house three to five people and have a kitchenette, private terrace and satellite TV. Note: showers are outdoors. Views sweep to the Libyan Sea.

★ To Skolio   MEZEDHES €
(☑ 28230 83001; dishes €3-7; ⏰ from 9am for coffee, noon-11pm for food daily Easter-Sep, Wed-Sun Oct-Easter) Whether gorge walker or hire-car driver, do not miss the chance to dine at wonderful To Skolio. 'The School' is in a converted schoolhouse, and cheerily painted tables fill a shady cliff-side courtyard with grand valley views. Menus of mezedhes rotate with the season, incorporating the best local produce. Though prices are low, portions are huge.

Dishes might be aubergine rolls with feta, fennel pie or heaping salads, and the homemade sweets such as cheesecake (€2.50) are divine.

Azogires   Αζογυρές
An eccentric hill village 9km north of Paleohora, Azogires and its sylvan valley are the place of legends involving river Nereids in its waterfalls and medieval ascetics who inhabited cave dwellings. Both the waterfalls and the caves can be visited today, and a handy local map lists these and other attractions.

Maps, more info and good food and drink can be found at **Alpha Restaurant** (mains €4-7; ☺ lunch & dinner). There, American-born local guide Lakkis 'Lucky' Koukoutsakis leads tours of the village and **Azogires Gorge**. Or you can walk on your own down the gorge to join up with the Anydri Gorge (p87) trail.

Elafonisi   Ελαφονήσι

Tucked into Crete's southwest corner, this symphony of fine pink-white sand, turquoise water and gentle rose dunes looks like a magical dreamscape. As the azure water swirls across the sands, prismatic rainbows shimmer across the surface. Off the long, wide strand of Elafonisi beach lies Elafonisi Islet, occasionally connected by a thin sandy isthmus, which creates a lovely double-beach, but otherwise easily reached by wading through 50m of knee-deep water. The islet is marked by low dunes and a string of semi-secluded coves that attract a sprinkling of naturists. A walk to its high point offers mind-blowing views of the beaches, sea and raw mountainscape. The entire area is part of Natura 2000, the environmental protection program of the EU.

Alas, this natural gem is hardly a secret and less than idyllic in high summer when hundreds of umbrellas and lounge chairs (€7) clog the beach (dash out to the island where you can find peace). The invasion puts enormous pressure on this delicate ecosystem and on the minimal infrastructure, especially the toilets. Come early or late in the day or, better yet, stay overnight to truly sample Elafonisi's magic. And outside of high season, when there is no public transport to the beach and very few tours, you may have it all to yourself.

◉ Sights

Kedrodasos Beach   BEACH
If you'd like to get even more off the beaten track than gorgeous pink-sand Elafonisi, head 1km east to similarly gorgeous Kedrodasos, a soft arc of pink-white sand favoured by nudists and backed by junipers. You can reach it via 2.5km of dirt lanes through the greenhouses behind the beaches, or by the E4 coastal trail.

🛏 Sleeping & Eating

In addition to the lodging right near the beach, there are several more pensions around Hrysoskalitissas. Elafonisi Resort has the best restaurant, and other decent tavernas line the road in Hrysoskalitissas. There are a few snack bars on the beach.

★**Elafonisi Resort**   HOTEL, TAVERNA €
(✆ 28250 61274; www.elafonisi-resort.com; s/d €35/45; ❄ ☎) More a small, well-run hotel than a resort, these 21 spacious rooms have fridges, and there are nicely furnished cottage rooms in back among peaceful olive groves, as well as apartments with kitchens. The shared patio has sea views and there's an excellent attached restaurant (open to all) serving the catch of the day and classic Greek fare. Book well ahead.

Elafonisi Village   HOTEL €
(✆ 6942254382, 28220 61548; www.elafonisi-village.gr; d/q from €55/75; ☺ Apr-Oct) Just 250m from Elafonisi Beach, these 10 rooms string across an arid courtyard and offer refrigerator, TV and a small outdoor terrace area.

Rooms Panorama & Taverna   PENSION €
(✆ 28220 61548; s/d studios €40/50) One of the closest options to Elafonisi beach, these basic rooms have a kitchenette with fridge. The taverna overlooks the sea but that's the best that can be said of it; food and service are erratic.

❶ Getting There & Away

There is one boat (p86) daily from Paleohora to Elafonisi (€8, one hour) from mid-May through September. Those same months there is one **KTEL bus** (www.e-ktel.com) daily from Hania (€15, 2½ hours) and Kissamos (Kastelli; €8.10, 1¼ hours), which return in the afternoon. There is no public transport from October to mid-May.

Hrysoskalitissas
Χρυσοσκαλίτισσας

Five kilometres north of Elafonisi is the small hamlet of Hrysoskalitissas (hris-os-ka-*lee*-tiss-as) with its beautiful seaside monastery. It makes an alternative base to Elafonisi.

◉ Sights

Moni Hrysoskalitissas Monastery   MONASTERY
(admission €2; ☺ 7am-7pm) Five kilometres north of Elafonisi is this beautiful monastery perched on a rock high above the sea. The church is recent but the monastery is allegedly a thousand years old and may have

been built on the site of a Minoan temple. The monastery has created two small rudimentary **museums** on-site, a folk museum with a selection of weavings and objects from rural life and an ecclesiastical museum with mostly icons and manuscripts. Buses to Elafonisi drop passengers here.

Hrysoskalitissas means 'golden staircase'. Some accounts suggest the top step of the 98 steps leading to the monastery was made of gold, but could only be seen by the faithful. Another version says one of the steps was hollow and used to hide the church's treasury. In any case, during the Turkish occupation the gold, along with much of the monastery's estate, was used to pay hefty taxes imposed by the Ottoman rulers.

🛏 Sleeping & Eating

There are a handful of good tavernas and accommodation options strung along the road through Hrysoskalitissas hamlet.

Glykeria   HOTEL €€

(🖉 28220 61292; www.glykeria.com; d/tr incl breakfast €60/80; ❋ ❋) A small and friendly family-run hotel with neat and simple rooms with fridges and balconies overlooking the sea, as well as an inviting pool and a beloved taverna across the road. It's on the main road before the monastery.

Gavdos Island   Γαύδος
POP 45

Gavdos (*gav*-dos) is as much a state of mind as it is an island. If you want to get away from it all, there is no better place for peace and isolation. Located in the Libyan Sea, 65km from Paleohora and 45km from Hora Sfakion, Gavdos is the most southerly place in Europe, and with only a smattering of rooms and tavernas, it's a blissfully remote spot. The island attracts a loyal following of campers, nudists and free spirits happy to trade the trappings of civilisation for unspoilt beaches, long walks and rustic holidays. This is the place for chilling out, letting your beard grow, rolling cigarettes and spending the nights gazing at starry skies.

Geographically, Gavdos is more akin to Africa than Europe, and it enjoys a very mild climate. You can swim as early as February. For a sandy island it is surprisingly green, with almost 65% of the island covered in low-lying pine and cedar trees and vegeta-

tion. There are several stunning beaches, some of which are accessible only by foot or boat. Most of the beaches are on the northeastern coast, as the southern coastline is all cliffs.

Until the late 1960s Gavdos had little water and no electricity or phones, and most residents emigrated to Paleohora or other parts of Crete, or to Athens. While water is now plentiful, there can still be electricity shortages and blackouts (particularly in summer) as only part of the island has grid power – the rest uses generators, which are often turned off at night and in the middle of the day. Take a torch. Strong winds can prevent boats from coming, and leave visitors stranded for days, but you won't find too many people complaining. At its tourist peak, the island's permanent population of about 45 residents may swell to 1000.

History

Archaeological excavations indicate that the island was inhabited as far back as the neolithic period. In the Graeco-Roman era Gavdos, then known as Clauda, belonged to the city of Gortyna. There was a Roman settlement on the northwestern corner. Under the Byzantines, Gavdos was the seat of a bishopric, but when the Arabs conquered Crete in the 9th century the island became a pirates' nest. It is thought to be the legendary island home of Calypso, in Homer's 'Odyssey', where the nymph held Odysseus captive for many years.

◉ Sights & Activities

There are no villages per se on the island. Just tiny hamlets and loose encampments.

Boats land at **Karave** on the eastern side of the island, which has a couple of tavernas and a minimarket. The teeny capital **Kastri** is in the centre of the island and also has a couple of tavernas.

The biggest beach community is at **Sarakiniko**, just north of Karave, and has a wide swath of sand, several tavernas, a minimarket and showers.

The stunning **Agios Ioannis** beach, on the northern tip of the island, has a ragtag summer settlement of nudists and campers and is a 15-minute walk to the nearest taverna (which only has intermittent electricity) or road. Some camp out here for months.

Lavrakas beach is a half-hour walk from Agios Ioannis, and offers one of the most remote beach encampments. There is a natural freshwater well, and tanned, naked campers with dreadlocks blend in with the surroundings.

Potamos and **Pyrgos** are even more remote, but gorgeous, beaches on the northern coast (no facilities). You can reach them on foot from Kastri along the path leading north to **Ambelos** and beyond. The restored 1880 **lighthouse** on the road to the village of Ambelos has a museum and cafe. Before it was bombed by the Germans in 1941 it was the world's second-brightest lighthouse after Tierra del Fuego in Argentina.

South of Karave, **Korfos** has a pebbly beach and a couple of tavernas with rooms. From here a 3.5km trail leads down via near-unpopulated **Vatsiana** to **Tripiti** – the southernmost tip of Europe. Three giant arches carved into the rocky headland at Tripiti are the island's best-known natural feature. You can also come by small boat.

In Vatsiana, the island's priest has created a small **museum** (☑28230 42167; ⊙10am-6pm Jul & Aug) in an old stone house with items collected from the island, including agricultural and domestic tools, a loom and weavings. Outside of July and August, knock next door for admission.

Despite the meagre population, there are 16 small **churches** dotted around the island. Most local boat owners offer full- and half-day **cruises**, including trips to the remote, uninhabited island of Gavdopoula, although there are no good beaches there. Ask at the tavernas.

🛏 Sleeping

In addition to the rooms, people free camp around the island. The folks running the website www.gavdos-online.com can help with reservations. Gavdos has a short season, running June to August, and most tavernas and rooms start closing in early September.

Consolas Gavdos Studios
STUDIO €
(☑210 324 0968, 28230 42182; www.gavdostudios.gr; Sarakiniko Beach; d/tr studio incl breakfast €50/70; ❄🛜) These comfortable studios perch right above Sarakiniko beach. Villas sleeping up to five are also available (€80 to €100). Taverna customers may use the satellite internet connection. Bicycles rent for €5. Phone ahead for harbour pick-up.

Akrogiali Taverna & Rooms
PENSION €
(☑28230 42384; www.gavdoshotel.com; Korfos Beach; d/tr €35/50; ❄) Right on Korfos beach,

Akrogiali offers simple rooms with fridge and air-conditioning (and electricity), and the pension overlooks the beach. The adjacent taverna is famed for its local cooking.

Sarakiniko Gavdos
APARTMENT €
(☑28230 41103; http://gavdos-crete.info; Sarakiniko Beach; r/studio €40/50) This solar-powered place at Sarakiniko beach has a taverna run by a fisherman and his wife. The rental rooms and apartments are bare-bones.

Sofia Rooms
PENSION €
(☑6947003533; www.sofiaroomsgavdos.com; near Agios Ioannis Beach; r €45-50; ⊙May-Oct; ❄) Sofia Rooms is a solid 10- to 15-minute walk from Agios Ioannis beach in the clutch of tavernas nearest that remote beach encampment. Ecofriendly tidy rooms and a welcoming taverna beckon. Air-conditioning runs 9am to midnight, but solar power is 24 hours.

Gavdos Princess
APARTMENTS €€
(☑28230 41181; www.gavdos-princess.com; Kastri; apt €55-105; ❄🛜🐾) Open year-round in the small hamlet of Kastri, Gavdos Princess offers pretty stone cottages with one or two bedrooms sleeping four to six people, and air-conditioning and small kitchenettes and terraces. There's wi-fi in the public areas and a restaurant.

🍴 Eating

Fresh fish, of course, is the singular highlight of dining in Gavdos. Most pensions have attached tavernas.

Theophilos Taverna
TAVERNA €
(mains €5-10; ⊙lunch & dinner May-Oct) Above Agios Ioannis beach and about a 10-minute walk, this place has excellent trays of *mayirefta* catering to the campers coming up from the beach.

Taverna Sarakiniko
SEAFOOD €€
(☑28230 41103; Sarakiniko Beach; mains €5-15; ⊙lunch & dinner) Run by Manolis the fisherman and his wife Gerti, this taverna serves Manolis' fresh catch daily. Try the tangy grilled octopus or red snapper braised with lemon and olive oil.

ℹ Information

The island's port is Karave, on the eastern side of the island, where there's a small **police station** (☑28230 41109). There are no banks, ATMs or petrol stations, but you can send mail in Sarakiniko. There's a minimarket in Karave, and one in Sarakiniko for basic supplies, and usually a doctor on the island in summer. Mobile coverage is patchy but cardphones are available. Most tavernas have wi-fi but the signal can be interrupted due to weather and wind.

If camping, be sure to find out about local water sources before setting out. The website www.gavdos-online.com has lots of good tips about the island and what to bring.

ℹ Getting There & Around

Anendyk (☑ 28230 41222; www.anendyk.gr) ferry services to Gavdos vary throughout the year and can take between 2½ to five hours depending on the boat and where it stops. There are two routes: one serves Hora Sfakion (€17) via Agia Roumeli (€17) and Loutro (€17) two to three times per week, and one serves Paleohora (€19) via Agia Roumeli and Sougia (€18) two times per week. Check online for ever-changing schedules; the Anendyk site also lists which buses you can connect with.

The most direct route to Gavdos is from Hora Sfakion, which is sometimes direct (2½ hours) in summer. Only some ferries take cars, so check ahead.

Bike, scooter and car hire are available in Karave and Sarakiniko. Enquire about boat taxis to take you to remote beaches. From Karave, it takes about 30 minutes to walk to Sarakiniko, one hour to Korfos and 1½ hours to Agios Ioannis.

LEFKA ORI & SAMARIA GORGE
ΣΦΑΚΙΑ & ΛΕΥΚΑ ΟΡΙ

Deep in central Hania province, the Omalos Plateau breaches the towering Lefka Ori (White Mountains) and marks the northern entry to the Samaria (sa-ma-*ria*) Gorge. Many will approach the region from Hania and start the gorge hike in little Omalos. But you can also reach Omalos easily from Paleohora and Sougia on the southern coast. The Samaria Gorge trail descends to Agia Roumeli, also on the southern coast.

Hania to Omalos

The road from Hania to the beginning of Samaria Gorge in Omalos is varied and, in places, spectacular. After heading through orange groves you'll get to the village of **Fournes**.

If you detour up a left fork in the road after Fournes, you'll twist and turn along a gorge offering beautiful views to **Meskla**. Although the bottom part of the town is not particularly attractive, the road becomes more scenic as it winds uphill to the modern, multicoloured **Church of the Panagia**. Next to it is a 14th-century chapel built on the foundations of a 6th-century basilica

---

WORTH A TRIP

THERISO

For a day trip or an alternative route to Omalos, take the scenic road from Hania via the village of Perivolia to Theriso (Θέρισο), 14km south. This spectacular drive follows a coursing stream through a green oasis and the 6km Theriso Gorge. At the foot of the Lefka Ori (White Mountains), at 500m above sea level, Theriso was the site of historical battles against the Turks and is famous for its connection with Eleftherios Venizelos and the late-19th-century revolutionary period in Crete. These days it's popular for its fine tavernas that host marathon Sunday lunches.

Two tavernas vie for top billing. **Leventogiannis Taverna** (☑ 28210 74095; https://sites.google.com/site/leventogiannistherisso; Theriso; mains €6-11) has a lovely courtyard under a giant canopy of plane trees and makes a delicious and sizeable *kreatotourta* (local meat pie). **Antartis** (☑ 28210 78833; Theriso; mains €6-11; ☺ lunch & dinner) has excellent mezedhes and Cretan food like *staka*, a goat's-milk sauce over juicy cubes of goat meat.

Just past the village on your right, the small **Museum of National Resistance** (☑ 28210 78780; admission €1.50; ☺ hours vary) chronicles Crete's resistance movement from 1941 to 1945. It has a monument outside paying tribute to a female resistance fighter. The millstone on display was used by Turkish occupiers in 1821 to crush Chrysi Tripiti to death in the local olive press.

A steep and winding road takes you through rugged mountain terrain and around an ever-changing landscape of plane, olive, orange, eucalyptus and pine trees through the villages of Zourva to Meskla and Lakki, where you can continue to Omalos or head back to Hania.

that might have been built on an even earlier Temple of Aphrodite. At the entrance to the town a sign directs you to the **Chapel of the Metamorfosis Sotiros** (Chapel of the Transfiguration of the Saviour) that contains 14th-century frescoes. The fresco of the Transfiguration on the southern wall is particularly impressive.

On the main Hania–Omalos road south of Fournes, the excellent **Botanical Park** (☑ 6976860573; www.botanical-park.com; Km 17 on Hania–Omalos road; ☼ 9am-7.30pm Jul & Aug, to 5pm Apr-Jun & Sep–mid-Nov) is well signposted about halfway between Fournes and Lakki. It was created by four brothers who transformed the family's 80 hectares of agricultural land into a hilly park of medicinal, tropical, ornamental and fruit trees, all well signed and beautifully arrayed from mountaintop to valley floor. Their restaurant (mains €5 to €11) is a must for heaping regional dishes using locally sourced ingredients, some grown right in the park. Tables fill a hilltop terrace with sweeping views. The kitchen closes at 6pm.

The main road continues to the unspoilt village of **Lakki** (*la*-kee), 24km from Hania, which affords stunning views in all directions, and has a striking **church**. The village was a centre of resistance during both the uprising against the Turks and against the Germans in WWII.

Rooms for Rent Nikolas (☑ 28210 67232; Lakki; d €35) has comfortable, simple rooms above a taverna, with magnificent views over the valley.

Omalos   Ομαλός

POP 30

Most tourists only hurry through Omalos, 36km south of Hania, on their way to Samaria Gorge 4km further on, but for those inclined towards solitude or the outdoors, this plateau settlement warrants a longer stay. During summer, the air is bracingly cool here compared with the steamy coast and there are great mountain walks offering magnificent views, birding, caving and climbing.

Omalos itself is little more than a few hotels on either side of the main road cutting across the plateau. After the morning Samaria rush, there's hardly anyone on the plateau except goats and shepherds. It is practically deserted in winter.

🛏 Sleeping & Eating

Some Omalos hotels are open only when the Samaria Gorge is open. Most have restaurants that do a bustling trade serving breakfast to hikers and are open at mealtimes the rest of the day. Many proprietors will drive you to the start of the gorge. As at other mountain locations, air-conditioning is not necessary.

Hotel Neos Omalos   HOTEL €
(☑ 28210 67269; www.neos-omalos.gr; s/d/tr incl breakfast €35/45/55; P🛜) A rustic mountain feel pervades this comfortable and contemporary hotel where views from your balcony will get you in the mood for hiking. The owners are a fount of information on local hikes and other outdoor activities and can also shuttle you to the Samaria Gorge. The restaurant dishes up good, fresh food.

Hotel Exari   HOTEL €
(☑ 28210 67180; www.exari.gr; s/d/tr €30/40/45; ☼ Apr-Oct; P) This traditional-style stone-built hotel has 24 simply furnished rooms with TV and balconies. The attached restaurant has a fireplace. The owner shuttles people to Samaria Gorge.

Kallergi Hut   MOUNTAIN REFUGE €
(☑ 28210 44647; www.kallergi.net; dm with shared bathroom members/nonmembers €15/20) The bare-bones Kallergi Hut is located in the hills between Omalos and the Samaria Gorge. It has four rooms of bunk beds and is maintained by Hania's EOS. It makes a good base for exploring Mt Gingilos and surrounding peaks. It is a 2km hike to reach the hut, or arrange in advance for a ride.

Agriorodo   VILLAS €€
(☑ 28210 67237; www.omalos.com; 2-/3-bedroom villa €80/120; ☼ year-round; P🛜🗕) These new and lovely individual stone cottages are the closest accommodation to the Samaria Gorge. Each sleeps four to five people and is fully kitted out with satellite TV, wi-fi, kitchens, and living rooms with fireplaces. The owners also operate the good restaurant Xyloskalo (p95), with spectacular views at the very entrance to the gorge.

Omalos Village   VILLAS €€
(☑ 28210 67169; www.omalosvillage.gr; 2-bedroom villas €80; ☼ year-round; P🛜🗕) Omalos Village is a cluster of three well-equipped, spacious, two-bedroom stone villas with large

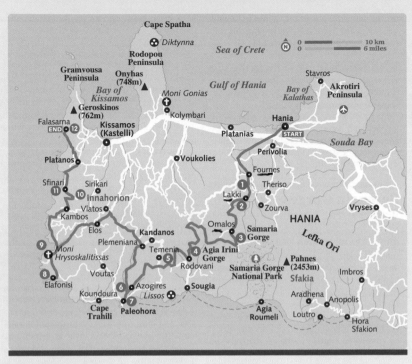

Driving Tour
Southwestern Hania Province

START HANIA
FINISH FALASARNA
LENGTH 45KM; ONE DAY

This southwestern driving tour is a swerving mountain adventure into the wildest stretches of Crete – a DIY dream through bucolic villages, past stunning ravines where olive trees cling precipitously to cliffs, and to the island's most serene beaches. It's a full-day trip, so start early.

From Hania, head south towards Fournes, making your first stop at the **1 Botanical Park** (p92), where you can have a quick jaunt among the plants and a coffee with views, before heading on to the unspoilt mountain hamlet of **2 Lakki** (p91). Continue on to mountain-shrouded Omalos and peek into awe-inspiring **3 Samaria Gorge** (p94) at Xyloskalo. Next, turn back a few kilometres and go west across the Omalos Plateau to return to the jagged north–south road. Going south you'll reach the top of **4 Agia Irini Gorge** (p81), equally stupendous as Samaria. The zigzagging road south requires

concentration and passes through several traditional villages.

Turning west at Rodovani, you will soon reach a junction near **5 Temenia**; if in need of cool refreshment, stop in at this tiny hamlet, known for its juices. Keep heading west and then south to **6 Azogires** (p87), a curious village of unusual local legends. Drop to the coast at colourful, laid-back **7 Paleohora** (p83) for a fish-taverna lunch, and a quick dip. Next up are the magnificent pink sands of **8 Elafonisi** (p88), Crete's most sublime beach. This requires you to loop north again via Plemeniana and Elos; don't take the more direct-looking dirt road shown on some maps, suitable only for serious 4WDs. After luxuriating here, drive 4km north to visit ethereal **9 Moni Hrysoskalitissas** (p88). Continue along the coast through the **10 Innahorion villages** (p96), with traditional architecture and delicious honey, cheese and olive oil. Stop at **11 Sfinari** (p96) for a seaside fresh fish meal, then plan to spend the night at relaxing **12 Falasarna** (p97), a lovely rose-sand beach with good accommodation.

dining and kitchen areas, including a dishwasher. They have a fireplace and outdoor seating area with great views, too.

ℹ Getting There & Away

Three daily buses (www.e-ktel.com) serve Hania (€6.90, 1½ hours). One bus daily in summer comes from Paleohora via Sougia.

To hike the gorge and return to your room (and luggage) in Omalos, you can take the afternoon boat (www.anendyk.gr) from the hike terminus at Agia Roumeli to Sougia, then taxi back to Omalos (about €50).

Samaria Gorge
Φαράγγι της Σαμαριάς

Hiking through **Samaria Gorge** (☑ 28210 67179, 28210 45570; adult/child €5/free; ☉ 7am-sunset May-late Oct) is considered one of the 'must-do' experiences of Crete, which is why you'll almost never be without company. In peak season, up to 3000 people per day tackle the stony 16km-long trail, and even in spring and autumn, there are rarely fewer than 1000 hikers. The vast majority arrive on organised coach excursions from the big northern resorts. You'll encounter a mix of serious trekkers as well as less experienced types attempting the trail in flip-flops.

Samaria Gorge

Nevertheless, there's an undeniable raw beauty to Samaria, whose vertical walls soar up to 500m high and are just 3m apart at the narrowest point, 150m at the broadest, all carved by the river that flows between the peaks of Mts Avlimaniko (1858m) and Volakias (2115m). The hike begins at an elevation of 1230m just below the Omalos Plateau and ends in the coastal village of Agia Roumeli. It's especially scenic in April and May when wildflowers brighten the trail.

Samaria is also home to the *kri-kri*, a rarely seen endangered wild goat. The gorge was made a national park in 1962 to save the *kri-kri* from extinction. You are unlikely to see these shy animals, which show a marked aversion to hikers, but you might spot golden eagles overhead.

Hiking the Gorge

The trail begins at **Xyloskalo**, a steep and serpentine stone path that descends some 600m into the canyon to arrive at the simple cypress-framed **Agios Nikolaos chapel**. Beyond here the gorge is wide and open for the next 6km until you reach the abandoned settlement of **Samaria**, whose inhabitants were relocated when the gorge became a national park.

Just south of the village is a 14th-century **chapel dedicated to St Maria of Egypt**, after whom the gorge is named. Every 1 May, numerous locals attend the *panigyri* (saint's day) of St Mary. This is the only night during which anyone can stay inside in the old village of Samaria – a few old houses are opened for the purpose, and camping is allowed. (For further details, check with Hania's EOS.)

Further on, the gorge narrows and becomes more dramatic until, at the 11km mark, the walls are only 3.5m apart. These are the famous **Sideroportes** (Iron Gates), where a rickety wooden pathway leads hikers the 20m or so across the water.

The gorge ends at the 12.5km mark just north of the almost abandoned village of Palea (Old) Agia Roumeli. From here it's a further basic 2km hike to the seaside hamlet of Agia Roumeli (p80), whose fine pebble beach and sparkling water are a most welcome sight.

Few people miss taking a refreshing dip or at least bathing sore and aching feet. The entire trek takes from about four hours for the sprinters to six hours for the strollers.

LOCAL KNOWLEDGE

TOP TIPS FOR HIKING SAMARIA GORGE

➡ An early start (before 8am) helps to put you ahead of the crowd. Sleep over in Omalos to be first. During July and August even the early bus from Hania can be packed. Or start after noon, and plan to sleep over in Agia Roumeli.

➡ Hikers starting after about 2pm are only allowed to walk a distance of 2km from either end. There's no spending the night in the gorge – expect to be out by sunset.

➡ There's a 1200m elevation drop going north to south. Wear sturdy shoes and take sunscreen, sunglasses, some food, a hat and a water bottle, which you can refill from taps with potable water along the way. Drink plenty!

➡ There are several rest stops with toilets, water, trash bins and benches along the trail.

➡ Falling rocks occasionally lead to injuries but generally it's the heat that's a far bigger problem. Check ahead as park officials may close the gorge on rainy or exceptionally hot days (generally, over 40°C), and the gorge season can end early if the rains have started.

➡ Early in the season it's sometimes necessary to wade through the stream. Later, as the flow drops, the stream-bed rocks become stepping stones.

➡ If the idea of a 16km hike does not appeal, get a taste of Samaria by doing it 'the easy way', ie starting in Agia Roumeli and heading north for as long as you feel like before doubling back. The Sideroporta, for instance, can be reached in about an hour. Or consider some of the other gorges (p81) in the area, like Agia Irini or Imbros.

🛏 Sleeping & Eating

It is forbidden to camp in the gorge. Stay at Omalos on the northern end, or Agia Roumeli in the south. The trailhead, Xyloskalo, near Omalos, has one restaurant and a clutch of refreshment stands selling souvenirs, snacks, bottled water and the like, when the gorge is open.

Xyloskalo   CRETAN €
(☑ 28210 67237; www.omalos.com; dishes €5-10; ⊙10am-7pm or 8pm daily Apr-Oct, Sat & Sun Nov-Mar; ☏) Perched just over the spectacular drop of Samaria Gorge, with eagles occasionally circling outside its wrap-around windows, this cosy restaurant dishes up classic Cretan and Greek meals. And offers that last chance to use indoor plumbing and wi-fi.

❶ Getting There & Away

Most people hike the gorge one way going north–south on an organised day trip from every sizeable town and resort in Crete. Note that prices listed usually don't include the €5 admission to the gorge or the boat ride from Agia Roumeli to Sougia or Hora Sfakion.

With some planning, it's possible to do the trek on your own. There are daily early morning public buses to Omalos from Hania (€6.90, 45 minutes) and Rethymno (€15, 1¾ hours) as well as services from Sougia (€4.20, one hour) and Paleohora (€6.40, one hour), once or twice daily in high season. Check www.e-ktel.com for the seasonally changing schedule. Taxis are another option.

At the end of the trail, in Agia Roumeli, ferries (p81) go to Sougia or Hora Sfakion, some of which are met by public buses to Hania; or you can continue on to Paleohora, Gavdos Island or other destinations, if you carried your pack with you the whole way (or started from Sougia or Paleohora).

NORTHWEST COAST

Far northwestern Crete is less affected by tourism than the city of Hania and its satellite resorts. Once you move past the overbuilt Platanias region west of Hania, the northern coast is defined by the virtually uninhabited Gramvousa and Rodopou Peninsulas. Kolymbari, at the foot of the Rodopou Peninsula, is the most developed tourist town (but more famous for its nationally distributed olive oil).

The Kissamos province is a rugged region of scattered villages and towns sustained by agriculture. Its capital, Kissamos (Kastelli), is the port for boats from the Peloponnese. On the western coast you'll find two of Crete's finest beaches, which are surprisingly underdeveloped: Falasarna and the even more remote Balos (Gramvousa). The Selino province includes the Innahorion region of small mountain villages.

Innahorion Villages
Ινναχωριών

Some of western Crete's most scenic and unvisited mountain villages, the Innahorion (derived from *Enneia Horia*, or nine villages), are spread across the far western coastal region, along the route connecting Moni Hrysoskalitissas and Elafonisi beach in the south with Falasarna and Kissamos (Kastelli) in the north. This quiet area, renowned for its chestnuts and olives, is one of the lushest and most fertile parts of the island. The coastal road from Kefali to Sfinari is one of Crete's most beautiful: it winds around cliffs with magnificent coastal views unfolding after every bend.

For the area's best eating, as well as blissfully serene traditional lodgings, plan to visit the area's remote ecotourism settlement in Milia (p97).

◉ Sights

Elos
VILLAGE

Elos, near the south of the Innahorion Villages region, is the area's largest town and centre of the chestnut trade – hence the annual **chestnut festival**, on the third Sunday of October. The plane, eucalyptus and chestnut trees around the main square make Elos a cool and relaxing place to stop. Behind the taverna on the main square stand remains of a once-working **aqueduct** that used to power the old mill.

Perivolia & Kefali
VILLAGES

Two and half kilometres west of Elos, atmospheric Perivolia leads to Kefali, with its 14th-century frescoed **church**. Kefali has a handful of tavernas taking advantage of the lovely setting and view. From here, you can travel south to Elafonisi beach or loop north along the coast.

Pappadiana & Amygdalokefali
VILLAGES

The western Innahorion villages that line the coastal road enjoy a stunning location between mountains and ravines. First is the hamlet of Pappadiana, about 2km west of Kefali, from where the road rises into the mountains before manifesting superlative sea views from a bluff at Amygdalokefali.

Kambos
VILLAGE

Good hiking, beach access and decent accommodation can be found at Kambos, a tiny village on the edge of a gorge along the winding Innahorian region's coastal road.

Sfinari
BEACH, VILLAGE

The Innahorian coastal road winds along by Sfinari, 9km north of Kambos and 9km south of Platanos. It's a languid, laid-back agricultural village with a long grey-stone beach. The northern end is backed by greenhouses and the cove holds a basic camp site and several excellent beachside fish tavernas.

Voulgaro
VILLAGE

Idyllic Voulgaro is located 9km southeast of Kissamos (Kastelli) on the inland road towards Elafonisi. Its name (by allusion, 'Bulgarian village') is said to descend from the identity of settlers brought to the place when Byzantine Emperor Nikiforos Fokas recaptured Crete from the Arabs in the 961 expedition to Crete.

Latsiana & Mouri
VILLAGES

Testaments to the Byzantine period remain with the ruined 15th-century **Basilica of Agia Varvara**, 2km from Voulgaro down a southeastern side road in tiny Latsiana, and the church of **Agios Nikolaos**, 2km beyond that in the hamlet of Mouri. The former was built on an ancient Greek temple site, while the latter has distinctive surviving frescoes. There are fantastic views from both sites.

Topolia Gorge
CANYON

Three kilometres south of Voulgaro, the main road towards Elafonisi reaches Topolia, a lovely village clustered with whitewashed houses overhung with plants and vines. Beyond it, the road skirts the edge of the 1.5km-long Topolia Gorge, bending and twisting and affording dramatic views. The gorge ends at tiny **Koutsomatados**, from where hikers can access the gorge.

Agia Sofia Cave
CAVE

Just south of the village Koutsomatados, and after a narrow tunnel, the Agia Sofia cave contains evidence of settlement from as far back as the neolithic era. The cave is often used for baptisms and celebrates the patron saint's day on 13 April. A third of the way up the 250 rock-cut steps to the cave, the taverna has great views over the ravine.

🛏 Sleeping

There's rough camping and rooms for rent in Sfinari, and many villages have some very basic rooms to let. Milia has the premier accommodation in the area.

WORTH A TRIP

MILIA ECOVILLAGE

One of Crete's ecotourism trailblazers is the isolated mountain resort village of **Milia** (28210 46774; www.milia.gr; cottages incl breakfast €70-135; year-round;). Inspired by a back-to-nature philosophy, 16 abandoned stone farmhouses were transformed into ecocottages sleeping one to four, with only solar energy for basic needs. Milia is one of the most peaceful places to stay in Crete, but it's also worth a visit just to dine at the superb organic restaurant (mains €5 to €11).

Milia makes a great base for those wishing to unwind and see the Innahorion region. The cottages have antique beds, rustic furnishings, and fireplaces or wood-burning stoves. With the solar power, it's best to shelve the laptop and hairdryer.

The restaurant's frequently changing seasonal menu sources organic produce cultivated on the farm, including its own oil, wine, milk, cheese and free-range chickens, goats and sheep. Try the *bourekia* (filo pies shaped into thin long rolls, batons and pinwheels), stuffed rabbit with *myzithra* (sheep's-milk cheese) or yoghurt, or pork with lemon leaves baked slowly overnight. We loved the winter favourite – potatoes, chestnuts and baby onions in red-wine sauce. There is nothing processed.

To reach Milia, follow the signposted turn-off north of the village of Vlatos. The narrow access road becomes a drivable 3km dirt road.

Sunset Rooms PENSION €

(28220 41128; Kambos; s/d €25/30;) In Kambos, Sunset has great views over the valley. Rooms are basic but pleasant enough. The attached taverna serves up good-value grills and salads.

Hartzoulakis Rent Rooms PENSION €

(28220 41445; manolis_hartzoulakis@yahoo.gr; Kambos; r €30-50;) Small and basic but very clean, with large verandahs, the rooms here make a good base for walkers. The taverna on the terrace serves up good Cretan fare and excellent *raki*.

✕ Eating

Iliovasilema SEAFOOD €

(Sunset; 28220 41627; Sfinari; mains €7-12; lunch & dinner May-Oct) Seafront in Sfinari, this simple taverna grills up the fresh catch of the day and locally grown (and some organic) produce with tables lining the gravel beach, and back under the shade trees. And it does, indeed, have views of the sunset.

Thalami SEAFOOD €

(28220 41632; www.thalami-kissamos.gr; Sfinari; mains €6-12; 11am-10pm May-Sep) One of Sfinari's excellent fish tavernas, Thalami offers the local catch on the seafront, perfect for taking a midday dip before your grilled fish and mountain greens.

Panorama Taverna & Rooms TAVERNA €

(Kefali; mains €4-10; lunch & dinner May-Oct) Dramatic views down the valley let this little taverna and rooms-for-rent in Kefali village live up to its name, and then some.

Falasarna   Φαλάσαρνα

POP 25

Some 16km west of Kissamos, Falasarna is little more than a long sandy beach – but what a beach! This broad sweep is considered among Crete's finest, even though views are somewhat marred by greenhouses set among the olive groves. Like Elafonisi, Falasarna has magical-looking pink-cream sands and teal waters. It is known for its stunning sunsets.

Along with superb water clarity, Falasarna has wonderfully big waves – long rollers coming from the open Mediterranean. It gets busy from mid-July to mid-August, primarily with day trippers from Hania and Kissamos (Kastelli).

Spread your towel on the **Big Beach** (Megali Paralia) at the south end or pick a spot in one of the coves separated by rocky spits further north.

Falasarna has no centre as such, although there are hotels and several tavernas, bars and small supermarkets.

History

The mysterious word 'Falasarna' is of unclear provenance – it may even pre-date the Greek language itself. The area has been occupied at least since the 6th century BC, but reached the height of its power as a city-state in the 4th century BC. Although originally built next to the sea, the town's ruins are now about 400m inland because the western coast of Crete has risen over the centuries.

Falasarna owed its wealth to the agricultural produce from the fertile valley to the south. It was the west-coast harbour for Polyrrinia but later became Polyrrinia's chief rival for dominance over western Crete. By the time of the Roman invasion of Crete in 67 BC, Falasarna had become a haven for pirates. Stone blocks excavated around the entrance to the old harbour indicate that the Romans may have tried to block the harbour to bar entrance to the pirates.

⊙ Sights

Ancient Falasarna   RUIN

Wander among Falasarna's ancient ruins reached via a 2km dirt road which starts where the paved road ends. The entrance is just past the 'stone throne'. Further on there are the remains of the wall that once fortified the town and a small harbour. Notice the holes carved into the wall, which were used to tie up boats. At the top of the hill there are the remains of the acropolis wall and a temple, as well as four clay baths.

⊨ Sleeping

Magnolia Apartments   APARTMENT €

(☑28220 41407; www.magnolia-apartments.gr; studio/apt from €45/55; ⊙year-round; ❋🕾) The modern cluster of creamy stone apartments sits just a short walk back from Falasarna's Big Beach (Megali Paralia) and offers well-equipped studios and apartments with balconies. They are immaculate and comfortable.

Rooms Anastasia-Stathis   PENSION €€

(☑28220 41480; www.anastasiastathis.com; d/apt from €45/60; ❋🕾) Set back from the sea and the day crowds, the airy, attractively furnished rooms with fridges and large balconies are perfect for stress relief, as the friendly owner Anastasia puts it. Her enormous breakfasts are open to all comers and guests can pick vegies from the rose-rimmed garden.

Sunset Taverna
& Apartments   APARTMENT €€

(☑28220 41204; www.sunset.com.gr; d/tr/apt/villa €40/45/65/160; 🅿🕾) Sunset Taverna

(mains €7 to €8) has a terrace with fig trees and wonderful views, its own natural spring and beach access, along with simple but comfortable rooms. There are also multi-room apartments and relatively luxurious free-standing villas. The entire outfit is run by a welcoming family.

Falassarna Beach Hotel   HOTEL €€

(☑28220 41436, 28220 41257; www.falassarnabeach.gr; studio/apt from €40/50; ❋🕾) This well-kept modern hotel (situated right where the bus from Kissamos stops) is a good bet for those who want to have the creature comforts of a full-service hotel with quick access to the beach (a two-minute walk downhill). There are good views from most of the sea-facing rooms and from the shady patio taverna. Each room has a kitchenette.

✗ Eating

Galasia Thea   CRETAN €

(☑28220 41421; mains €4.50-8; ⊙10am-11.45pm late Apr-Oct; 🕾) On the cliff overlooking the great expanse of Falasarna beach, this cafe has spectacular views from its huge terrace and full children's play area. They offer a full range of Cretan *mayirefta* such as the *Sfakiano* lemon lamb and are quite friendly, but service can be slow when it's crowded.

⊙ Getting There & Away

From June through August there are three buses daily from Kissamos (€3.50, 20 minutes) and Hania (€7.60, 1¼ hours). Check www.e-ktel.com for seasonal schedules.

Gramvousa Peninsula
Χερσόνησος Γραμβούσα

Northwest of Kissamos (Kastelli) is the beautifully wild and remote Gramvousa Peninsula, whose main attraction is the stunning lagoon-like sandy beach of Balos, on Cape Tigani on the west side of the peninsula's narrow tip. Kalyviani village is a good base for visiting the peninsula.

History

The offshore island of Imeri Gramvousa was an important vantage point for the Venetians, who built a fortress here to protect ships on their way to and from Venice. Considered impregnable, and outfitted with a huge cache of armaments, the fortress was not conquered by the Turks with the rest of Crete in 1645; it remained in Venetian hands. Eventually the Venetians left, and the fort fell into disuse until it was taken over in 1821 by Cretan revolutionaries. It later became a notorious base for piracy before the Turks took it and used it to blockade the coast during the War of Independence. Local legend has it that the pirates amassed a fabulous fortune that they hid in caves around the island.

The **Kalyviani shipwreck**, rusting on the west side of Kalyviani beach, is a Lebanese-registered ship that struck trouble on its way from Libya to Crete in 1981.

◎ Sights & Activities

★ Balos
BEACH, RUIN

The idyllic Balos beach and looping lagoons of shallow, shimmering turquoise waters are overlooked by islets **Agria** (wild) and **Imeri** (tame). It's a heavenly remote stretch of Crete that merits its inclusion on brochures everywhere. The beach is gorgeous, with lapping translucent waters dotted with tiny shellfish and darting fish.

In summer, the crowds do come, usually by day-trip boat (May to October only), filling the beach from 11am to 4pm. To go independently by car or KTEL bus (July and August only) the final descent to the beach requires 4WD or a long, hot hike.

There is no shade and umbrellas with sunbeds cost €7.

The 12km, very rough dirt road (best in a 4WD) to Balos begins at the end of the main street of Kalyviani village and follows the eastern slope of **Mt Geroskinos** (762m). From here, the views over the shoreline and the Rodopou Peninsula are spectacular. It ends at a car park with snack kiosk from where the path to the lagoon is 1.2km down the sandy cliffs. Nondrivers could try hitching a ride or walk, although you'll be eating a lot of dust from passing vehicles.

If you come by boat, it usually stops at the island of Imeri, which is crowned with a ruined **Venetian fortress** from which there are stunning views of the peninsula. It's a steep 20-minute walk to the top and there is a rocky and generally unusable beach below with a (modern and not particularly compelling) shipwreck.

Gramvousa

Balos Cruises
BOAT TOUR

(☑ 28220 24344; www.gramvousa.com; adult/child €25/12; ⊙ May-Oct) The easiest way to get to gorgeous Balos is by day-trip boat. Boats stop at different places along the way. Book online for discounted tickets. Reasonably priced food and drink is available on board. If it's windy the trip can be rough – or cancelled – so check the day before. Summer-only KTEL buses from Hania are timed to boat departures.

🛏 Sleeping

The best base for touring this region is the village of Kalyviani, 7km west of Kissamos (Kastelli). There are also other great studios arrayed along the coast nearby. There is no lodging at Balos.

Olive Tree Apartments
APARTMENT €

(☑ 28220 24336; www.olivetree.gr; Kalyviani; apt/maisonette from €45/75; [P] [※] [≋]) This attractive complex in an olive grove just east of Kalyviani village has spacious, comfortable and well-presented apartments and maisonettes suitable for families and longer stays, as well as an inviting pool and great sea views.

Kaliviani
INN €€

(☑ 28220 23204; www.kaliviani.com; Kalyviani; d/q from €60/75; [P] [※]) This welcoming stone-built guesthouse has comfortable, tastefully furnished rooms with fridge and balcony. There is also an excellent and modestly priced restaurant and a kids' play area.

Patriko
VILLA €€€

(☑ 6977575080; www.villapatriko.com; Kalyviani; villa per week from €1600; [※][🛜][≋]) This fully kitted out luxury villa in the heart of Kalyviani village sleeps nine and has everything from iPod docking stations to a dishwasher, laundry, swimming pool and organic bath products.

🍴 Eating

★ Gramvousa
CRETAN €

(☑ 28220 22707; www.gramboussa-restaurant.gr; Kalyviani; mains €6-15; ⊙ noon-midnight) In the centre of Kalyviani village, Gramvousa serves fine traditional Cretan cuisine in an elegantly decorated stone building set in a superb garden. It's a cut above other

LOCAL KNOWLEDGE

SAMPLING CRETAN CUISINE

Leventis (☑ 28210 68155; www.leventis -tavern.com; Ano Stalos; mains €6.50- 14.50; ☺ 5pm-late Mon-Fri, noon-late Sat & Sun & daily mid-Jul–Aug, closed Mon Jan & Feb), an award-winning taverna about 10km west of Hania, attracts locals and visitors for its authentic and refined Cretan cuisine. Tables fill an elegant stone-and-wood-beam dining room and an alfresco terrace and have views of the lush hills all around. It's a super place to get the best sampling of Crete's top cuisine.

restaurants, and offers the chance to sample the freshest regional cuisine Crete has to offer, as well as wood-oven specials like suckling pig or lamb with honey.

❶ Getting There & Away

Take a day-trip cruise from Kissamos to get to Balos May through October, or bring a 4WD. Westbound buses from Kissamos will let you off at the turn-off for Kalyviani.

Kissamos (Kastelli)
Κίσσαμος (Καστέλλι)

POP 4236

About 40km west of Hania, the north coast port town of Kissamos (Kastelli) exudes an unpolished, almost gritty, air compared to other north-coast towns. This is not a place given entirely over to tourism, and although the setting on a broad azure bay ringed by peninsulas and mountains is spectacular, the town itself is a bit rough and tumble. Tourist hotels, cafes and tavernas line the seafront promenade, and bustling streets press inland. There are two beaches separated by a murky canal: sandy **Mavros Molos** in the west and the pebbly **Telonio beach** to the east.

The largest town and capital of Kissamos province, it is referred to interchangeably as either Kissamos or Kastelli (though the official name is the former). The port serves ferries to/from the Peloponnese or Kythira, and day boats to Balos beach.

History

Kissamos was the harbour of important Dorian city-state Polyrrinia, 7km inland, and reached its heyday during Roman times,

artefacts of which are now displayed in the local museum and archaeological museums in Hania and Iraklio. Most of the ancient city, however, lies beneath modern-day Kissamos and cannot be excavated.

Kissamos gained independence in the 3rd century AD and then became a bishopric under the Byzantines. It was occupied by the Saracens in the 9th century and flourished under the Venetians who built a castle here, at which point it became known as Kastelli. That name persisted until 1966 when authorities decided that too many people were confusing it with Crete's other Kastelli, near Iraklio. The official name reverted to Kissamos, though it is still often called Kastelli or Kissamos-Kastelli. Ruins of the castle wall survive to the west of Plateia Tzanakaki.

⊙ Sights

Archaeological
Museum of Kissamos   MUSEUM
(☑ 28220 83308; http://odysseus.culture.gr; Plateia Tzanakaki; adult/child €2/free; ☺ 9am-3pm Tue-Sun) Located in an imposing two-level Venetian-Turkish building on the main square, this museum presents locally excavated treasure, including statues, jewellery, coins and a large mosaic floor from a Kissamos villa. Most items are from the Hellenistic and Roman eras, though there are also some Minoan objects. There are also exhibits from Falasarna, Polyrrinia and Nopigia.

⎧⎭ Sleeping

Thalassa   STUDIO €
(☑ 28220 31231; www.thalassa-apts.gr; Paralia Drapanias; studio from €40; P ✱ @ 🎧 🐾) The isolated Thalassa complex is ideal for a quiet beach retreat about 5km east of Kissamos at Drapanias beach. The immaculate studios are airy and well fitted. There's a barbecue on the lawn, and a small playground. It's helpful to have a car.

Camping Mithymna   CAMPGROUND €
(☑ 28220 31444; www.campingmithimna.com; Paralia Drapanias; camp sites per adult/child/ tent €7/3.50/5; P 🎧 🐾) About 5km east of Kissamos, Camping Mithymna is an excellent shady site near a great stretch of beach. There's a restaurant, bar and shop. Take a bus to the village of Drapanias, from where it's a pleasant 15-minute (800m) walk through olive groves to the campground.

Nautilus Bay APARTMENT €€
(☑28220 22250; www.nautilusbay.gr; apt €75-145; P❀🅿🛜♨) Spacious modern apartments fill this newly built complex right on the sandy beach and in the centre of town. Balconies have sweeping views and there's a restaurant and bar and a large pool area.

Christina Beach Hotel APARTMENT €€
(☑28220 83333; www.christina-beach.gr; studios €50-80; P❀@🛜♨) This smart studio complex on the west side of Kissamos represents the upper end of accommodation in town. Right across from the water, the modern studios are large and airy, and the sandy beach is right nearby.

✖ Eating & Drinking

Taverna Sunset TAVERNA €
(☑28220 41627; Paraliaki; mains €7-10; ⊘11am-late Apr-Oct; 🛜) Locals mix with in-the-know visitors at this quintessential family taverna presided over by Giannis, who's usually ensconced behind the grill coaxing meat and fish into succulent perfection. It's right on the waterfront.

Papadakis SEAFOOD €
(☑28220 22340; Paraliaki; mains €4-10; ⊘noon-late May-Oct; 🛜) This classic taverna on the central waterfront is known for fresh fish (caught by the iconic owner), but also has plenty of *mayirefta* and grills. Try the roast aubergines or *keftedhakia* (meatballs).

Taverna Petra FAST FOOD €
(souvlaki €2.30; ⊘lunch & dinner) This unassuming place cornering the main square serves the best souvlaki in town (along with a range of grilled meats), accompanied by pungent local olive oil.

★Babel Cafe Bar CAFE, BAR
(☑28220 22045; ⊘9am-2am; 🛜) Not only a good choice for a quick breakfast or snack, this waterfront cafe-bar is a great place for coffee and gets lively at night with young locals. It has one of the most extensive beer and cocktail lists in town, and is worth swinging in for a pit stop simply for the amazing bay views from its bustling patio.

❶ Information

The main commercial drag, Iroön Polytechniou, has supermarkets, banks with ATMs, the post office and the bus stop. Kissamos' basic information site is www.kissamos.net.

Horeftakis Tours (☑28220 23250; www.horeftakistours.com; Skalidi; ⊘9am-1.30pm & 5-8pm) is a good source of information, sells boat tickets and organises car hire.

❶ Getting There & Away

BOAT
From the port 3km west of town, **Lane** (☑27360 37055; www.lane-kithira.com) operates twice-weekly ferries to Piraeus (12 hours), and goes four times per week to Antikythira (€10, two hours), Kythira (€17, four hours) and Gythio (€25.10, five hours). It's far quicker to go to Piraeus from Hania. In summer, a bus meets ferries; otherwise taxis into town cost around €5. For tickets, try **Chalkiadaki Travel** (☑28220 22009; Skalidi 49). Schedules change seasonally. Check www.openseas.gr.

BUS
Buses leave from the **KTEL office** (☑28220 22035; www.e-ktel.com; Iroön Polytechniou 77) opposite the EKO gas station. Check the website for seasonally changing schedules. There are as many as 14 buses to Hania (€4.70, one hour) every day; change in Hania for Paleohora, Rethymno and Iraklio. There are also two to three daily buses to Falasarna (€3.50, 15 minutes) in summer only and one daily to Elafonisi (€8.10, 1¼ hours) from May to October.

CAR
Kissamos Rent a Car (☑28220 23740; www.kissamosrentacar.com; Iroön Polytechniou; car hire per day from €25) One of several car hire agencies along Kissamos' main street. Can deliver or pick up from Hania airport.

Polyrrinia Πολυρρηνία

★Polyrrinia RUIN
The wonderful mountain-top ruins of the ancient city of Polyrrinia (pol-ee-ren-*ee*-a) lie about 7km south of Kissamos, above the village of Ano Paleokastro (also called Polyrrinia). Sea, mountain and valley views from this defensible spire are stunning and the region is blanketed with wildflowers in spring.

The most impressive feature of the site is the acropolis built by the Byzantines and Venetians. There's also a church built on the foundations of a Hellenistic temple from the 4th century BC.

The city was founded by the Dorians in the 6th century BC and was constantly at war with the Kydonians from Hania. Coins from the period depict the warrior-goddess Athena, who was evidently revered by the warlike Polyrrinians.

Unlike their rivals the Kydonians, the Polyrrinians did not resist the Roman invasion, and thus the city was spared destruction. It was the best-fortified town in Crete and the administrative centre of western Crete from the Roman through to the Byzantine period. The Venetians used it as a fortress. Many of the structures, including an **aqueduct** built by Hadrian, date from the Roman period. Near the aqueduct is a **cave** dedicated to the nymphs; it still contains the niches for nymph statuettes.

There is no public transport to the site.

Rodopou Peninsula
Χερσόνησος Ροδοπού

The barren, rocky Rodopou Peninsula has a few small villages clustered at its base, but the rest is uninhabited. A paved road goes as far as **Afrata**, which has a couple of great tavernas like **Tis Litsas Ta Kamomata** (🖉6976228778; Afrata; mains €6-10; ⏲10am-10pm daily Apr-Oct, Sat & Sun Nov-Mar), but then becomes a dirt track that meanders through the peninsula.

If you are travelling by foot, 4WD, motorcycle or boat you can reach the Diktynna sanctuary at the end of the peninsula, but make sure you have planned your journey and are well supplied; there is not a drop of petrol or water, nor a morsel of food, beyond Afrata. From Afrata a road winds down to the small, gravelly **Afrata Beach**, with a small summer-only snack bar.

Kolymbari   Κολυμπάρι
POP 1088

Kolymbari, 23km west of Hania, is at the eastern base of the Rodopou Peninsula, and appeals to those seeking a low-key holiday. This former fishing hamlet has developed into a small tourist resort, taking advantage of the village's long pebbly beach. It's a good base for hiking Moni Gonias, and is known for its seafood tavernas.

🅞 Sights & Activities

Moni Gonias   MONASTERY
(admission free, museum €2; ⏲8am-12.30pm & 4-8pm Mon-Fri, 4-8pm Sat, 7am-noon & 4-8pm Sun) Founded in 1618, Moni Gonias was damaged by the Turks in 1645, but rebuilt in 1662 and extended in the 19th century. The monastery houses a unique collection of icons dating from the 17th and 18th cen-

turies. Some are in the church while others are in the monastery's two-room museum. The most valuable icon is that of Agios Nikolaos, painted in 1637 by Palaiokapas (in the museum). It perfectly exemplifies the Cretan school of icon painting that flourished in the 17th century.

The monastery, which also incorporates Crete's Theological College, is easy to reach from Kolymbari. Take the beach road north from the town centre for about 500m.

Oceanis Dive   DIVING
(🖉28244 00113; www.oceanisdive.com; ⏲year-round) Full roster of dives and courses for beginners (intro course €80) and advanced divers (per dive €50), plus snorkelling (adult/child €35/25).

🛏 Sleeping

Aeolos Apartments   APARTMENT €
(🖉28240 22203; studio/apt from €40/50; 🅟❄🛜) Signposted up the hill from town, this dated but well-maintained complex has big balconies with sea views. Breezy studios and two-room apartments are spacious, with carved timber beds, TV and kitchenettes.

Grand Bay Beach Resort   RESORT €€
(🖉28240 83380; www.grandbay.gr; d €125-155, ste €150-250; 🅟❄@🛜🏊) This luxe resort complex on the eastern beachfront section of Kolymbari is an 'adults-only' haven of holidaymakers. Guests must be 16 or over and the place caters to your every whim.

🍴 Eating & Drinking

Argentina   SEAFOOD €€
(🖉28240 22243; Kolymbari Harbour; fish per kg €40-55; ⏲noon-late) Considered one of the best fish tavernas in the area, the classic Argentina has tables on the main road and across the street overlooking the harbour. It serves seafood dishes such as octopus with olives and top-quality fish.

Diktina   SEAFOOD €€
(🖉28240 22611; Kolymbari Harbour; fish per kg €40-60) This modern fish taverna has harbour views and a range of reliable seafood dishes.

Milos tou Tzerani   CAFE
(🖉28240 22210; Kolymbari Harbour; ⏲9am-late) In a beautiful restored stone mill on the sea, this cafe-bar is a great place for a coffee or an evening drink and also serves light snacks and mezedhes.

❶ Information

There is an ATM on the main street and a post office in the centre of the village.

❶ Getting There & Away

Buses from Hania to Kissamos stop at Kolymbari (€3.30, 45 minutes, half-hourly) on the main road, from where it is a 500m walk down to the settlement.

Diktynna   Δίκτυνα

On the eastern tip of the Rodopou Peninsula are the remains of a temple to Cretan goddess Diktynna. Diktynna was the goddess of hunting and she was worshipped fervently in western Crete. The most important religious sanctuary in the region under the Romans, the temple was desecrated after the collapse of the Roman Empire. Now you'll find foundations and a sacrificial altar as well as Roman cisterns. There's also a lovely sandy beach.

Diktynna is accessible only by dirt road from Kolymbari; travel agencies in Hania offer boat excursions.

Legend has it that Diktynna's name derives from the word *diktyon,* meaning 'net'. It was a fisherman's net that saved her when she leapt into the sea to avoid the amorous desires of King Minos. The temple dates from the 2nd century AD, but it was probably built on the site of an earlier temple.

Rethymno

Best Places to Eat

➡ Castelvecchio (p114)
➡ Avli (p114)
➡ Tasomanolis (p128)
➡ Vrisi (p129)
➡ To Steki tou Sifaka (p134)

Best Places to Stay

➡ Enagron (p122)
➡ Casa Vitae (p112)
➡ Idili (p134)
➡ Kapsaliana Village (p121)
➡ Sohora (p111)

Why Go?

Rethymno (Ρέθυμνο) is a wild beauty. Endless ribbons of mountain roads wind through the timeless interior, passing fields of wildflowers and tiny, traditional hamlets cradled by olive groves. It's a region peppered with historic sites and natural wonders. Descend into the spooky darkness of grotto-like caves; explore steep, lush gorges; and rest in the shade of lofty Mt Psiloritis, Crete's highest peak. Visit enduring monasteries, Minoan tombs and Venetian strongholds. Rethymno is also a magnet for artists, many practising age-old trades with modern twists.

The eponymous capital on the northern coast is a bustle of atmosphere-soaked, cobbled lanes, laden with shops, restaurants and bars and flanked by a wide, sandy beach. The southern coast is graced with bewitching beaches in seductive isolation. Weave your way through this spellbinding land from shore to shore.

Road Distances (km)

	Agia Galini	Anogia	Plakias	Rethymno
Anogia	99			
Plakias	47	94		
Rethymno	53	56	39	
Argyroupoli	58	79	24	23

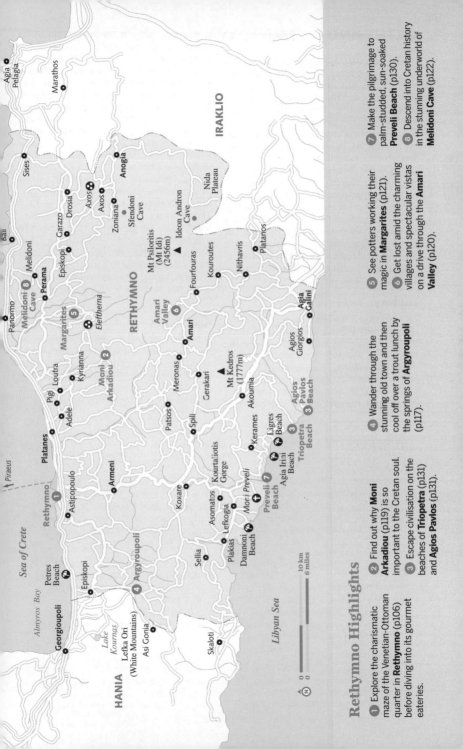

Rethymno Highlights

1 Explore the charismatic maze of the Venetian-Ottoman quarter in **Rethymno** (p106) before diving into its gourmet eateries.

2 Find out why **Moni Arkadiou** (p119) is so important to the Cretan soul.

3 Escape civilisation on the beaches of **Triopetra** (p131) and **Agios Pavlos** (p131).

4 Wander through the stunning old town and then cool off over a trout lunch by the springs of **Argyroupoli** (p117).

5 See potters working their magic in **Margarites** (p121).

6 Get lost amid the charming villages and spectacular vistas on a drive through the **Amari Valley** (p120).

7 Make the pilgrimage to palm-studded, sun-soaked **Preveli Beach** (p130).

8 Descend into Cretan history in the stunning underworld of **Melidoni Cave** (p122).

RETHYMNO ΡΕΘΥΜΝΟ

POP 32,468

Basking between the commanding bastions of its 15th-century fortress and the glittering azure waters of the Mediterranean, Rethymno (*reth*-im-no) is one of Crete's most enchanting towns. Its Venetian-Ottoman quarter is a lyrical maze of lanes draped in floral canopies and punctuated with graceful balconied houses, ornate monuments and minarets that add an exotic flourish. But Rethymno is more than its history; thanks largely to a sizeable student population, it has a lively nightlife, excellent restaurants and a hopping, stylish shopping district. There's also a worthwhile, sandy beach right in town. The busier beaches, with their requisite resorts, are all outside of town, along a nearly uninterrupted stretch all the way to Panormo, some 22km away.

History

Archaeological findings suggest that the site of modern Rethymno has been occupied since Late Minoan times. Around the 4th century BC, 'Rithymna' emerged as an autonomous state of sufficient stature to issue its own coinage. It waned in importance during Roman and Byzantine times but flourished again under Venetian rule (1210–1645), when it became an important commercial centre as well as a cultural and artistic hub.

The Venetians built a harbour and began fortifying the town in the 16th century against the growing threat from the Turks. Nevertheless, the massive hilltop fortress was unable to withstand the Turkish assault of 1646. Rethymno was an important seat of government under the Turks, but it was also a centre of resistance to Turkish rule, resulting in severe reprisals.

The Ottomans ruled until 1897, when Russia became overseer of Rethymno during the European Great Powers' occupation. The town's reputation as an artistic and intellectual centre grew from 1923, when the mandated population exchange between Greece and Turkey brought many refugees from Constantinople.

These days, the students of the University of Crete keep the town lively outside the tourist season.

◉ Sights

Rethymno is fairly compact, with most sights, accommodation and tavernas wedged within the largely pedestrianised old quarter off the Venetian Harbour. The beach is east of the harbour, and Arkadiou, one block inland, is the main shopping street.

THREE PERFECT DAYS

Day One

Head south from Rethymno to the fascinating **Cemetery of Armeni** (p125), for a peaceful visit filled with morning birdcall. From there, head west to quaint **Argyroupoli** (p117) to explore the ruins. Cool off by the springs and enjoy a fresh seafood lunch. Return to Rethymno to explore its **Venetian fortress** (p107) and labyrinth-like historic quarter. Dine at **Avli** (p114) and then wander along the picturesque harbour to catch the sunset.

Day Two

Get an early start in Plakias and beat the crowds to **Preveli Beach** (p130). Later, head back uphill for a dose of Cretan history at **Moni Preveli** (p130). Say goodbye to civilisation and get lost in the maze of winding coastal roads leading to the fabulously secluded beaches of **Triopetra** (p131) and **Agios Pavlos** (p131). When you're done splashing, head back to Plakias and drive north, taking in the stunning **Kotsifou Gorge** (p128). On your way back down, stop in Myrthios for a modern Cretan country dinner at **Vrisi** (p129).

Day Three

From Panormo or Bali, take the short drive to moody **Melidoni Cave** (p122), site of a horrendous massacre under Turkish rule. Carry on to **Margarites** (p121) to browse for handmade pottery and lunch on a scenic taverna terrace. Next, visit the atmospheric, history-soaked **Moni Arkadiou** (p119). For an authentic Cretan feast, make dinner reservations at **Agreco Farm** (p107), near Adele.

A MODEL FARM

Embedded in the rolling hills near the village of Adele, about 13km southeast of Rethymno, **Agreco Farm** (☑ 28310 72129; www.agreco.gr; Adelianos Kampos; tour & lunch or dinner €58; ☉ 11am-10pm Tue-Sat May-Oct, farm tours & dinner 6pm Tue-Sat & noon Sun) is a replica of a 17th-century estate and a showcase of centuries-old, organic and ecofriendly traditional farming methods. It uses mostly traditional machinery, including an old donkey-driven olive press, a flour watermill and winepress. You'll also find small shops selling local produce and artwork. Call ahead first to make sure it's open.

The farm is usually open May to October, but private events, such as weddings or baptisms, often keep it closed to the public. Normally, farm tours culminate in a 30-course Cretan feast in the taverna. Most of the dishes are prepared with produce, dairy and meat grown on the farm.

If you're more the hands-on type, swing by on Sunday at 11am when visitors are invited to participate in traditional agricultural activities. Depending on the time of year, you could find yourself shearing a sheep, milking a goat, making cheese or smashing grapes; see the website for the schedule. This is followed by a buffet-style Harvest Festival Lunch. Reservations are essential for the farm tour and the Sunday experience.

If you're just stopping by during the day, you can do an independent tour (€5) and enjoy a drink in the *kafeneio* (coffee house).

★ **Fortezza** FORTRESS
(adult/family €4/10; ☉ 8.30am-7.30pm Jun-Oct, 10am-5pm Nov-May; Ⓟ) Looming over Rethymno, this Venetian fortress cuts an impressive figure with its massive walls and imposing bastions. Built in the 1570s as a reaction to pirate raids and the threat of invasion, it was still unable to stave off the Turks in 1646. Views are fabulous from up here and it's fun to poke around the ramparts, palm trees and remaining buildings, most notably the meticulously restored **Sultan Bin Imbrahim Mosque**.

The mosque was converted from a Venetian cathedral by the Turks and is now used occasionally for art exhibitions. Its architecture is stunning, especially the dome, held up by eight arches and the ornate mihrab (a niche that points in the direction of Mecca). The pint-sized church near the east gate is of more recent vintage (1899) and commemorates the eviction of the Turks. Also within the compound is the **Erofili Theatre**, a modern amphitheatre surrounded by pine trees, which gets busiest during the **Renaissance Festival** (www.rfr.gr).

Archaeological Museum MUSEUM
(☑ 28310 54668; Argiropoulon; admission €3; ☉ 8am-3pm Tue-Sun; Ⓟ) In a Turkish-era building that served as a prison until the 1960s, this small museum showcases treasures from neolithic to Roman times, including bronze tools, Mycenaean figurines, Roman oil lamps and a 1st century AD sculpture of Aphrodite. You'll also find

Minoan pottery and artefacts gathered from the tombs at the Cemetery of Armeni (p125). Other star exhibits include fine examples of blown glass and a precious coin collection.

Venetian Harbour HISTORIC SITE
Rethymno's compact historic harbour is chock-a-block with tourist-geared fish tavernas and cafes. For a more atmospheric perspective, walk along the harbour walls, past the fishing boats to the landmark **lighthouse**, built in the 16th century by the Turks.

Agios Spyridon Church CHAPEL
(Kefalogiannidon) Built right into the cliff beneath the Venetian fortress, tiny Agios Spyridon has enough atmosphere to fill a cathedral. This Byzantine chapel is filled with richly painted icons, swinging bird candleholders and the sound of the nearby pounding surf. You'll see pairs of slippers, baby shoes and sandals in crevices in the rock wall, left as prayer offerings for the sick. Find the chapel at the top of a staircase on the western side of the fortress. Opening hours are erratic.

Neratzes Mosque MOSQUE
(Vernardou) This beautiful, triple-domed mosque was converted from a Franciscan church in 1657 and is now used as a music conservatory and concert hall. Even if there's no show on, it's definitely worth peeking in for a look. The building's minaret, the former bell tower, was built in 1890 and is undergoing lengthy restoration.

Rethymno

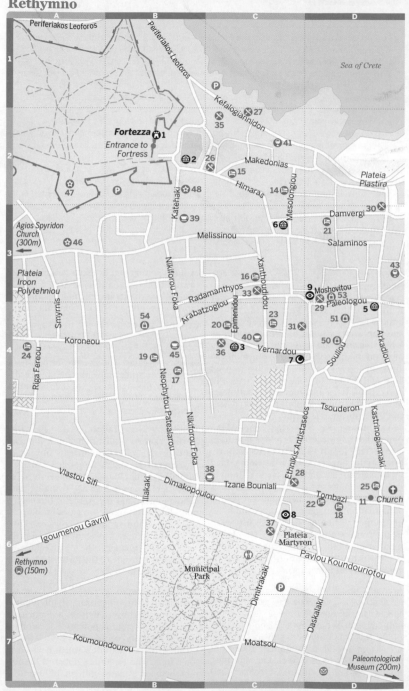

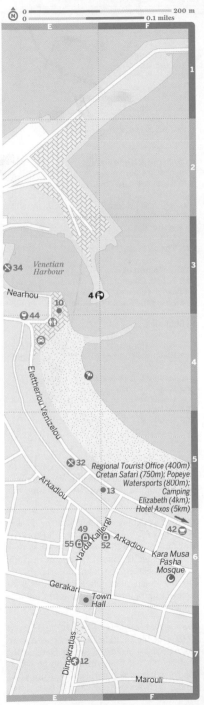

Rimondi Fountain
FOUNTAIN

(cnr Paleologou & Petihaki Sq) Pride of place among the many vestiges of Venetian rule goes to this fountain with its spouting lion heads and Corinthian capitals, built in 1626 by city rector Alvise Rimondi. Water spouts from three lions' heads into three basins flanked by Corinthian columns. Above the central basin you can make out the Rimondi family crest.

Loggia
HISTORIC BUILDING

(cnr Paleologou & Souliou; ⊘ 7.30am-2.45pm Mon-Fri) This well-preserved 16th-century landmark originally served as a meeting house for Venetian nobility to discuss politics and money. Converted into a mosque complete with minaret during the Turkish era, it now houses the Archaeological Museum's gift shop.

Museum of Contemporary Art
ART GALLERY

(☑ 28310 52530; www.cca.gr; Himaras 5; admission €3; ⊘ 9am-2pm & 7-9pm Tue-Fri, 10am-3pm Sat & Sun) Near the fortress, this gallery exhibits well-known and upcoming local and international artists. The permanent collection showcases the oils, drawings and watercolours of local lad Lefteris Kanakakis, as well as modern Greek artists since 1950. Entrance is off Mesologiou.

Porta Guora
HISTORIC SITE

(Great Gate; cnr Ethnikis Antistaseos & Dimakopoulou) On the southern edge of the old quarter, this arched stone gate is the only remnant of the 16th-century defensive wall. It was originally topped with the symbol of Venice – the Lion of St Mark – which can now be found in the Archaeological Museum.

Historical & Folk Art Museum
MUSEUM

(☑ 28310 23398; Vernardou 26-28; admission €4; ⊘ 9.30am-2.30pm Mon-Sat) In a lovely 17th-century mansion, this five-room exhibit documents traditional rural life with a collection spanning from clothing to baskets, weavings to farm tools. Labelling is also in English.

Paleontological Museum
MUSEUM

(☑ 28310 23083; www.gnhm.gr; Temple of Mastaba; adult/child €3/free; ⊘ 9am-3pm Tue, Thu & Sat) Dwarf Cretan elephants and hippopotami aren't likely to start a ticket stampede, but it's well worth swinging by this museum for its setting in the restored 17th-century Temple of Mastaba (aka Veli Pasha Mosque). Nine domes shape its silhouette, overlooked by the city's oldest minaret, while the once-communal gardens are steeply scented with thyme and oregano. The permanent

Rethymno

exhibit displays tusks and fossils from hippos hunted to extinction 10,700 years ago. It's located southeast of the Municipal Park.

The complex, a branch of Athens' Goulandris Natural History Museum, often has touring exhibits from the capital and abroad.

Municipal Park PARK
(Igoumenou Gavriil) Located between Iliakaki and Dimitrakaki, the trails and tree-shaded benches found here offer a respite from the heat and crowds. Old men doze and chat while children romp around the playground.

🏃 Activities

Paradise Dive Centre DIVING
(☑ 28310 26317; www.diving-center.gr; dives from €42, open-water certification €400) Runs diving trips for all grades of divers from its base at Petres, 14km west of Rethymno. Offers cave dives, night dives and various PADI courses. Book through travel agencies or phone.

Happy Walker HIKING
(☑ 28310 52920; www.happywalker.com; Tombazi 56; day walk €32; ☺ 5-8.30pm Mon-Fri) Runs day walks for four to 18 people through gorges, along ancient shepherd trails and to traditional villages in the lush hinterland. Add €10 for lunch and coffee en route. Book the evening before. Multiday tours are also available.

Popeye Watersports ADVENTURE SPORTS
(☑ 6973434275, 28310 52803; www.popeyewatersports.gr; Sofokli Venizelou; ☺ 10am-6pm) At the western end of Rethymno's sandy beach, Popeye will take you parasailing (from €60), jet skiing (from €40) or banana boat riding (from €25).

☞ Tours

Dolphin Cruises BOAT TOUR
(☑ 28310 57666; www.dolphin-cruises.com; Venetian Harbour; cruises €12-38; ⊙ 9.30am-5pm)
Runs one- to four-hour boat trips, visiting pirate caves, cruising to Bali or fishing.

World of Crete TOUR
(☑ 28310 50055, 6949791242; www.ecoevents.gr; 30 Eleftheriou Venizelou; tours €18-70; ⊙ 10am-2pm & 5-9pm) These guys organise a huge array of tours, from hikes through the Samaria Gorge to boat trips and photo safaris. Its ecotours take you to traditional villages where you might see *raki* distillation or take a cooking lesson. Also sells boat and plane tickets.

Cretan Safari ADVENTURE TOUR
(☑ 28310 20815; www.cretansafari.gr; 4 Sofokli Venizelou; tour €75; ⊙ 10am-2pm & 5-9pm) Join an all-day, off-road 4WD adventure to beaches, gorges and traditional villages.

✸ Festivals & Events

Carnival CARNIVAL
(www.carnival-in-rethymnon-crete-greece.com) The annual pre-Lent celebrations bring four weeks of dancing and masquerading, games and treasure hunts, and a grand street parade. Festivities usually fall around February or March.

⌂ Sleeping

The old town has an ample supply of lovely restored mansions, boutique hotels and friendly pensions to cater for all budgets. Many hotels are open year-round. Along the beach east of town is an uninterrupted stretch of mostly uninspired hotels and resorts.

Atelier PENSION €
(☑ 28310 24440; www.frosso-bora.com; Himaras 25; s €35, d €45-55; ❄🛜) Nearly next door to the fortress, the four spotless, comfortable rooms here are attached to the pottery studio (p116) of local ceramic artist Frosso Bora. With exposed stone walls, small flat-screen TVs, new bathrooms and kitchenettes, they are the best deal in town. The upstairs rooms have small balconies while the ground floor has Venetian architectural features and a beamed ceiling.

Rethymno Youth Hostel HOSTEL €
(☑ 28310 22848; www.yhrethymno.com; Tombazi 41; dm €10; ⊙ reception 8am-1pm & 5-11pm; 🛜) This cheerful, well-run hostel sleeps six to eight people in clean, functional dorms.

Centrally located, it has a private, sociable patio, bar and a flowering garden to relax in. Laundry facilities, hot showers, snacks and breakfast (€2) are available, as are female-only dorm rooms.

Camping Elizabeth CAMPGROUND €
(☑ 28310 28694; www.camping-elizabeth.net; 84 Ionias, Missiria; camp sites per adult/child €7.50/4, tent/car/caravan €6.50/4/6.50; ⊙ year-round; @🛜) The closest campground to Rethymno is 4km east, adjacent to beautiful Missiria beach. Bamboo, palm and olive trees provide plenty of shade, and there's a taverna, snack bar and minimarket, plus a communal fridge, laundry facilities and free beach umbrellas and sun lounges. It also rents out simple bungalows and caravans from €38 and tents from €9. An Iraklio-bound bus can drop you here.

Anna's Apartments PENSION €
(☑ 6987830516; www.facebook.com/Annas.apartments.rethymno; Mesologiou 38; d/tr €35/60; ❄🛜) These five basic but tidy rooms are seriously easy on the budget. Some are much brighter and more comfortable than others; try to get one at the front. They come with kitchenettes and are just steps away from the heart of things.

★ Sohora BOUTIQUE HOTEL €€
(☑ 2831 300913; www.sohora.gr; Plateia Iroön Politehniou; studio/d/apt €60/80/100; ❄🛜) Extremely comfortable and slightly quirky, the four rooms in this 200-year-old home incorporate original architectural features alongside vintage, upcycled furnishings. A solar-water heater, luxury organic bath products and a hearty, homemade breakfast make staying here a guilt-free treat. Service is both friendly and professional.

Beneath the shadow of the fortress, it's set on a square popular with locals and is just a short walk from the heart of the old town.

ⓘ RETHYMNO RESOURCES

Rethymno (ww.rethymnon.gr) Official site with local history, maps, festivals, accommodation and sights.

Crete Travel (www.cretetravel.com/guide/rethymno) Tourist company site with links to hotels, ferry tickets and activities.

Rethymnon.biz (www.rethymnon.biz) For event listings, local business guide and local news.

THE BIRTH OF THE ONE-EYED MONSTER

The Rethymno region seems to have had more than its share of fossil-filled caves. In fact, it's the richest area in the Mediterranean for endemic fossils, including those of the dwarf elephant. Some scientists believe that when ancient Greeks entered the shore caves and discovered the skulls of dwarf elephants, they were taken aback by what they saw. About twice the size of a human skull, the large, central nasal cavity for the trunk may well have been interpreted as an enormous, single eye-socket. The possible result? The birth of the Cyclops. Visit Rethymno's Paleontological Museum (p109) to see the skeletons for yourself.

★ **Casa Vitae**   BOUTIQUE HOTEL €€
(✆ 28310 35058, 6973237897; www.casa-vitae.gr; Neophytou Patealarou 3; r €95-150; ❀ 🛜) This charismatic Venetian-era hotel has eight quietly elegant rooms mixing exposed stone and wood and wrapped around a peaceful courtyard where breakfast is served beneath the vine-covered pergola. Romance rules in the larger suites with iron four-poster beds, jacuzzi and private terrace.

Casa dei Delfini   BOUTIQUE HOTEL €€
(✆ 28310 55120, 6937254857; www.casadeidelfini.com; Nikiforou Foka 66-68; studio/maisonette €70/110; ❀ 🛜) The four individual rooms in this elegant guesthouse orbit a small courtyard and burst with historic character. In one you'll find a *hammam* (Turkish bath), and in another, a covered, lit, Venetian well. All have modern kitchenettes and quality linens. For extra room, book the two-storey maisonette with a large private terrace.

Hotel Veneto   BOUTIQUE HOTEL €€
(✆ 28310 56634; www.veneto.gr; Epimenidou 4; s/d/ste €70/110/120; ❀ 🛜) Soak up that Venetian vibe in these 10 rooms boasting traditional features like polished wood floors and ceilings, alongside a satisfying range of mod cons. Each room tells a story; stay in No 101, once a monk's cell, or No 106, a long-ago *hammam*. It's in the heart of the old town. Optional breakfast is €6.

Palazzino di Corina   BOUTIQUE HOTEL €€
(✆ 28310 21205; www.corina.gr; Damvergi 9; d €80-120; ❀ 🛜 ❄) This regal Venetian mansion is a classy place to unpack. Antique furniture, exposed stone walls and timber vaulted ceilings create an ambience of period plushness. You'll also find a good dose of mod cons, including jacuzzi tubs. In the courtyard, a small, deep pool begs you to dive in, while the lounge is overflowing with antiques – from gramophones to sewing machines.

Vetera Suites   BOUTIQUE HOTEL €€
(✆ 28310 23844, 6972051691; www.vetera.gr; Kastrinogiannaki 39; r €110-190; ❀ 🛜) Quaint and extremely comfortable, this four-suite gem is brimming with character and attention to detail. Four-poster beds, antique wooden furnishings, quality bath products and neatly concealed kitchenettes make each room individual. The hotel is graced with Venetian architecture, including stone work and wooden beams. DVD players and wi-fi lend a modern touch. Optional breakfast is €10.

Casa Moazzo   BOUTIQUE HOTEL €€
(✆ 28310 36235; www.casamoazzo.gr; 57 Tobazi; r incl breakfast €85-155; ❀ 🛜) Once the home of Venetian nobles, these nine rooms are elegant and bright. Just a stone's throw from the harbour, they exude privacy. Rooms are each unique, combining wallpaper, exposed stone and wooden beams for a classy Italian feel. Some have balconies, claw-foot tubs and kitchenettes, while they all have king-sized beds and an option for goose-down pillows. Service is impeccable.

Check out the Venetian stone door fame from the street to the courtyard. It was built in 1276 and is the only one of its kind left in Rethymno.

Axos Hotel   HOTEL €€
(✆ 28310 54472; www.axos-hotel.gr; Maxis Kritis 167, Platanes; studio/apt €65/80; ❀ 🛜 ❄) Never mind the busy thoroughfare: this mid-sized hotel in Platanes, some 5km east of Rethymno, is a sweet retreat and a great deal. Modern and well-proportioned units wrap around a sparkling pool. There's a supermarket across the street and a lovely beach 200m away. Optional breakfast is €4.

Avli Lounge Apartments   BOUTIQUE HOTEL €€€
(✆ 28310 58250; www.avli.gr; Xanthoudidou 22; r incl breakfast €140-270; ❀ 🛜) Luxury is taken very seriously at this hushed retreat, where you'll be ensconced in warmly furnished studios sporting stone walls, beamed ceil-

ings and jacuzzi tubs. Retire to plush beds after a first-rate dinner downstairs in Avli's romantic, courtyard restaurant.

Rimondi Estate BOUTIQUE HOTEL €€€
(☎28310 51001; www.rimondiestate.com; Xanthoudidou 21; ste incl breakfast €190-390; ❋❂☒) Tucked in the heart of the old town, this luxurious Venetian mansion has historical ambience and cushy furnishings. The 13 studios in the Estate building feature original domes and stone arches, while rooms in the Palazzo are equally plush but offer a little less atmosphere. There's a glittering pool in the relaxing courtyard and the breakfast buffet is a feast.

✖ Eating

After visiting Rethymno, you will likely need to loosen your belt a notch or two. The dining here is fantastic, with the best eats found in the tiny side streets of the old quarter. Despite the magical setting, the majority of the tourist-geared tavernas in the Venetian Harbour are mediocre at best. Better waterfront dining options are along Kefalogiannidon below the fortress. Set menus (two or three courses, plus wine, water, *raki* and coffee) are popular.

★ Raki Baraki GREEK €
(☎28310 26213; Arabatzoglou 17; mains €6-9; ⊙lunch & dinner; ☎) Rustic, colourful and lively, this is a fantastic place to while away the evening over mezedhes (small dishes) such as sardines stuffed with herbs, sausage with grilled vegetables, or mussels steamed with sage. The fried feta with caramelised figs and mint is divine. Dine to live music Thursday to Sunday.

Taverna Knossos GREEK €
(www.knosos-rethymno.com; Venetian Harbour; mains €6-12, set menu for 2 €30; ⊙lunch & dinner; ☎⊞) Nestled next to the Venetian Harbour, Taverna Knossos stands out from its neighbours for superb food and swift, gracious service. It's been run by the Stavroulaki family for half a century; pop your head in the kitchen and you'll likely see grandma whipping up dinner. The menu is simple but authentic, with excellent fish. Tables are topped with fresh flowers and set close together – it's like dining with family. You'll find a kids menu too.

Mojo Burgers AMERICAN €
(☎6987328252, 28310 50550; www.facebook.com/mojoburgers; Damvergi 38; meals €3-7; ⊙1pm-midnight) With a funky, graffitied interior and a size-large menu, Mojo's delivers some of the best burgers and hot dogs this side of the Atlantic. Try the Alabama Mama with crispy pork, coleslaw and pickles or the Boston dog with blue cheese. Slap on some extras like jalapeños or caramelised onions and order a side of hand-cut cheese fries. They deliver.

Peperoncino PIZZA €
(Eleftheriou Venizelou 45; mains €6-12; ⊙lunch & dinner; ☎) Come here for pizzas piled with fresh ingredients and baked in a stone oven even the Italians would approve of. Or fill up with fresh pasta, complemented by a decent wine list. Sit outside with a view of the beach or in the small, classy interior.

yum...me BAKERY €
(Plateia Martyron; pastries €1.50-4; ⊙breakfast & lunch) Perfect for a quick breakfast or snack, this is the place to fill up on spinach pie, focaccia with barbecued chicken, giant pretzels and pastries. There's also self-serve, frozen yoghurt with all the toppings, as well as lots of strong coffee. Park yourself at a sidewalk table among the city's sociable youth or get it to go.

Meli ICE CREAM €
(☎28310 50847; ice cream €2-5; ⊙10am-9pm) Locals swear by Meli where the countless flavours of ice cream and sorbet will leave you spoiled for choice. You'll find a branch next to Rimondi Fountain.

Gaias Gefseis BAKERY €
(☎28310 22440; Ethnikis Antistaseos 15; pastries €1-4; ⊙7am-late) For *loukoumadhes* (doughnut-like concoctions drizzled with honey and cinnamon), follow your nose to Gaias Gefseis. This bakery creates some of the city's best traditional cakes and biscuits,

DON'T MISS

BAKLAVA & KATAÏFI

One of the last traditional filo masters in all of Greece, **Yiorgos Hatziparaskos** (Vernardou 30; pastries €2-4; ⊙10am-2pm & 5.30-7pm) still makes superfine pastry by hand in his workshop. The highlight is when he whirls the dough into a giant bubble before stretching it over a huge table. His wife, Katerina, encourages passers-by to watch the spectacle and try some of the best baklava and *kataïfi* ('angel hair' pastry) they will ever eat.

MAROULAS

If you're into herbs, aromatherapy, organic teas or natural beauty products, make the 10km drive southeast of Rethymno to Maroulas, a pretty, higgledy-piggledy village with panoramic sea views. The protected town has a mix of nicely restored late Venetian and Turkish architecture, including 10 olive presses and a 44m tower jutting above the village. After stocking up on healthy herbs, have lunch at a cheerful outdoor restaurant.

Marianna's Workshop (☑ 28310 72432; www.mariannas-workshop.gr; Maroulas; ⊙ 10am-3pm & 5-7pm summer, call for winter hours) Right on the main road of Maroulas, you'll find tiny Marianna's Workshop. Marianna Founti-Vassi collects aromatic medicinal herbs from the mountains to make her unique range of teas and oils from natural extracts using traditional methods. There are potions for all manner of ailments, including a tea made from 40 herbs once used by midwives.

Marianna's interest in alternative therapies became a full-time obsession when she moved to Maroulas in the mid-1990s and consulted locals about identifying Crete's many herbs. Marianna says animals were another guide to herbs and flowers, as they don't touch toxic plants. Indeed, *kri-kri* (Cretan goats) have been observed using Crete's endemic *diktamo* to heal their wounds.

Katerina (Maroulas; ⊙ May-Oct) Report for a traditional lunch at Katerina, an outdoor restaurant with sensational sea views. It's located down a small lane beyond the Venetian tower.

as well as homemade sheep's-milk gelato. If your sweet tooth needs a break, there's a mammoth supply of savoury breads; try one stuffed with feta and olives.

★ **Castelvecchio**　　　　GREEK €€
(☑ 28310 55163; Himaras 29; mains €15-21; ⊙ dinner Jul & Aug, lunch & dinner Sep-Jun) Classy yet chilled, family-run Castelvecchio is perfect for date night – especially if your date is a plate of the smoked pork in wine or the boneless lamb in creamy tomato and feta sauce. Be sure to save room for homemade dessert. If it's the walnut cake, you'll be pining for seconds. The terrace is hopping and the service is impeccable.

En Plo　　　　GREEK €€
(☑ 28310 30950; Kefalogiannidon 28; mezedhes €10-15; ⊙ lunch & dinner; 🗟🍴) Right at the water's edge, snug beneath the fortress, En Plo kicks Greek and Cretan comfort food into high gear. Mountain greens get a tangy twist with tamarind dressing, plump bacalao is paired with a feisty garlic sauce, and the creamy fish soup is hearty and satisfying. Sit in the arty interior or snag a table next to the waves. For the younger buccaneers of your party, there's a Little Pirates' Menu.

Veneto　　　　CRETAN €€
(☑ 28310 56634; www.veneto.gr; Epimenidou 4; mains €15-20; ⊙ dinner May-Oct; 🗟) In a 14th-century manor house that doubles as a boutique hotel (p112), Veneto oozes histor-

ic charm from every nook and cranny. The kitchen adds a contemporary streak to traditional Cretan recipes, with results like fish with fennel and lime or meatballs with basil sauce. The owner is a wine buff and will happily help you pick a bottle to complement your meal. The impressive cellar is housed in what was once the monks' quarters.

Thalassografia　　　　MEDITERRANEAN €€
(☑ 28310 52569; Kefalogiannidon 33; mains €5-20; ⊙ lunch & dinner May-Oct; 🗟) With cascading terraces from fortress to sea, this is where locals head for dinner. The eclectic Mediterranean menu offers up skilfully created dishes like stuffed mushrooms, Cretan cheese in filo with tomato and spearmint, and fish with a horseradish crust. It's all best washed down with local Brink's beer. If it's windy, dress warmly.

Othonas　　　　CRETAN €€
(☑ 28310 55500; Plateia Petihaki 27; mains €7-15; ⊙ breakfast, lunch & dinner) With its streetside 'host' and multilingual menus, Othonas may scream 'tourist trap' but it's actually well respected for its regional fare. Menu stars include the lamb with artichokes and the lip-smacking 'Zeus Chicken' (with *raki*, feta, mustard and onions).

★ **Avli**　　　　CRETAN €€€
(☑ 28310 58250; www.avli.com; Xanthoudidou 22; mains €13-30; ⊙ lunch & dinner; 🗟) This Venetian garden villa has a well-deserved rep-

utation for serving some of the city's most creative Cretan food in a lovely patio setting. Farm-fresh fare has bold flavour pairings: kid goat meets honey and thyme, sea bass comes with lemon saffron sauce, and octopus with caramelised onions. It's all flawlessly prepared and beautifully presented. Check the website for cooking classes.

 Drinking & Nightlife

The main bar and cafe strip, popular with students and tourists, is along Eleftheriou Venizelou. Another cluster is around Rimondi Fountain and on Plateia Petihaki. Wander the side streets to find quieter places. Most open around 9am or 10am, operating as cafes until the evening, when they morph into bars.

Nightclubs are concentrated around the Venetian Harbour. Doors open around 11pm, but most of the shiny, happy people don't arrive before midnight or 1am. Some in-town clubs move to a seaside location in summer.

Livingroom　　　　　　　　　　CAFE, BAR
(www.livingroom.gr; Eleftheriou Venizelou 5; ⊙ 9am-3am; 🛜) Kick back on stylish, waterfront sofas during the day or head inside in the evening to join Rethymno's young and restless amid big mirrors, velvet chairs and stylish lamps. The Livingroom has been a permanent fixture on the scene for over a decade.

Chalikouti　　　　　　　　　　CAFE, BAR
(🖉 28310 42632; Katehaki 3; ⊙ 9am-1am; 🛜) In the artsy quarter below the Fortezza, this cafe collective draws talkative locals who appreciate the coffee from Mexican Zapatistas, sugar from landless workers in Brazil, and *raki* from a Cretan women's cooperative. The tiny interior is overflowing with books and chessboards, while tables spill onto the cobbled street.

Inomena Voistasia　　　　　　　　　　BAR
(🖉 28310 54758; Kefalogiannidon 20; ⊙ 9.30am-1am) With an interior of tiles, wood and newsprint, this place has a cool, rustic vibe. The bar is well stocked, including a good selection of Greek beers and a decent cocktail menu. Come back the next day for healing Cretan mountain teas or a shot of Arabic or Guatemalan coffee.

Ali Vafi's Garden　　　　　　　　　　CAFE, BAR
(Tzane Bouniali 65a; ⊙ 10am-2am; 🛜) In summer there are few locations more enchanting than the laid-back garden behind the

pottery workshop of Natasha and Giorgos. Some of the artist-owners' choice pieces are showcased in niches in the stone-vaulted front room and between the branches of the orange and lemon trees in the garden. Frequent live music performances draw big crowds who sip wine and cocktails.

Figaro　　　　　　　　　　CAFE, BAR
(www.facebook.com/FigaroSocial; Vernardou 21; ⊙ 8pm-1am) Housed in a handsomely restored old building, Figaro attracts a slightly older, mostly local crowd and is great for socialising in an unpretentious setting. Regular live music performances make it even better.

Tholos　　　　　　　　　　CAFE, BAR
(Nikiforou Foka 86; ⊙ 10pm-2am) At this charismatic hang-out in a quiet street of the old quarter, you can unwind beneath the stone arches and dome of a former Venetian-Ottoman bathhouse. Serves beer, coffee and simple cocktails.

Metropolis　　　　　　　　　　CLUB
(Nearhou 12; ⊙ 11pm-dawn) Hobnob with hipsters at this hot-and-heavy party palace. In summer, DJs spin mostly international chart music for the tourist crowd, while Greek pop dominates in low season.

Mini Bar　　　　　　　　BAR, DANCE CLUB
(🖉 28310 20771; Petihaki 6; ⊙ 9pm-dawn) A classic Rethymno hang-out, this place has been renamed and revamped but continues to house two bars and a dance floor that gets filled nightly by tourists and local students.

☆ **Entertainment**

Asteria Cinema　　　　　　　　　　CINEMA
(🖉 28310 22830; Melissinou 21; tickets €7; ⊙ 9pm summer) This small open-air cinema near the fortress shows mostly new-release movies.

Kaloumba Puppet Theatre　　　　　　THEATRE
(Katehaki; ⊙ shows 11am Sun, cafe 9am-midnight) While performances are often in Greek, kids (and kids at heart) will be mesmerised by the puppets that take the stage in this tiny, relaxed theatre. Shows are usually Sunday at 11am, but stop by to confirm. The neighbouring cafe here has information on the theatre.

You can also join workshops to build your own puppet or to design and build your own wooden board game (€10, three hours). The cafe has dozens of games from around the world to get your imagination fired.

🛍 Shopping

Rethymno's old quarter is fodder for any would-be shopper. The narrow, cobbled pedestrian streets are tightly packed with mainly tourist-geared stores. There are also some gems worth searching for. Try Mellissinou, Souliou and Arabatzoglou. The mainstream shopping strip is along Arkadiou.

For English-language books, travel guidebooks, international periodicals and maps, try **Ilias Spondidakis** (📞 28310 54307; Souliou 43), **Mediterraneo** (Paleologou) and **Xenos Typos** (📞 28310 29405; Ethnikis Antistaseos 21).

Agora   FOOD & DRINK
(www.avli.gr; Avli, Xanthoudidou 22; ⊘9am-2pm & 5-9pm) Foodies will love Avli's Raw Materials store that's packed with a huge range of gourmet delights from around Greece, including great wines, olive oils and soaps.

Liranthos   MUSIC
(📞 28310 29043; Arkadiou 66; ⊘9am-2pm & 5-8pm) This tiny store filled with musical instruments is the place to get that bouzouki or Cretan *lyra* (three-stringed instrument similar to a violin). You can also pick up CDs of local Cretan music.

Frosso Bora   CERAMICS
(www.frosso-bora.com; Himaras 27; ⊘9am-2pm & 5-7pm) This local artist makes beautiful pots, vases, candlesticks, bowls and other vessels from local clay using the wheel or slabs. Prices are very reasonable.

Handmade Stories   CERAMICS
(📞 28310 42410; Varda Kallergi 46; ⊘9am-2pm & 5-9pm) The brightly glazed pottery here makes great, useable souvenirs. Choose a Minoan-designed salt shaker, olive bowls or *raki* shot cups. Much of it is produced in the nearby town of Margarites. The owner will pack your purchases to make them nearly indestructible for travel.

Leather Studio Kanakakis   ACCESSORIES
(www.leatherstudio.gr; 23 Souliou; ⊘9am-2pm & 5-8pm) At this small store-cum-workshop you can watch the owner crank out handmade leather belts in all sorts of colours and designs. There's also a good assortment of leather handbags, wallets and shoes.

DON'T MISS

TRADITIONAL ARTISAN SHOPS

Many of the crafts you see touted as being local aren't local at all, but mass produced elsewhere and imported. Nevertheless, you can still find a few artisans who practise traditional techniques, often intertwined with modern styles. These shops are worth visiting, and not just for the masterly crafted goods. The artists you'll meet have a passion for what they're doing that's keeping tradition alive.

Spantis (www.leather-workshop.com; Koroneou 9; ⊘9am-2pm & 5-9pm) John Spantidakis works with raw leather – not pre-dyed or pre-cut – to create bags, belts and wallets that will make you crave leatherware like never before. Paint strokes and unusual cuts lift this traditional art to a new playing field (wallets/belts/bags start at €18/80/130). Earthy greens, deep reds, Aegean blues and smoky blacks appear in varying levels of vibrancy. John will also craft special orders, right here in his workshop.

Wood Art (www.siragas.gr; Varda Kallergi 38; ⊘9am-2pm & 5-8pm) Many of the wooden ware you find in Greece has been imported from Tunisia. But Niko Siragas creates his own here using woodturning techniques dating back to the Minoans. An internationally acclaimed artist and teacher, his handcrafted bowls, vases and objects are each unique and silky smooth. His designs are intricate and often have a whimsical, organic feel. Niko also offers classes in woodturning. Check his website for details.

Spanoioakis (Nikiforou Foka 93; ⊘9am-2pm & 5-8pm) Found across Greece, the fading tradition of *koulouri* (embroidered bread) has its roots in Crete. In a tradition passed down by his grandfather, baker Spanoioakis continues to create intricately decorated bread, including the wedding roll, the original Greek wedding cake. Each beautiful design is symbolic: pomegranates bring luck; trees, longevity; and rings, an eternal bond. This bread isn't edible; it's lacquered and will last for years. With traditional designs, such as bread shaped like dinosaurs and flamingos, this may be the most unique souvenir you'll find.

BUSES FROM RETHYMNO

DESTINATION	FARE (€)	DURATION	FREQUENCY
Agia Galini	6.50	1½hr	up to 5 daily
Anogia	5.50	1¼hr	2 Mon-Fri
Argyroupoli	3.30	40min	up to 3 daily
Hania	6.20	1hr	hourly
Hora Sfakion	7.30	2hr	1 daily
Iraklio	7.60	1½hr	hourly
Margarites	3.50	30min	2 Mon-Fri
Moni Arkadiou	2.80	40min	up to 3 daily
Omalos (Samaria Gorge)	15	1¾hr	3 daily
Plakias	4.50	1hr	up to 5 daily
Preveli	4.50	1¼hr	2 daily

❶ Information

There are free public wi-fi hot spots at the town hall, Plateia Iroön, the Venetian Harbour and the Municipal Garden, all within the old town. The vast majority of restaurants and hotels offer free wi-fi.

Cool Holidays (☑28310 35567; Melissinou 2; ◷9am-2pm & 5-9pm) Helpful office that handles boat and plane tickets, hires out cars and motorcycles, and books excursions.

Cybernet (Varda Kallergi 44-46; per hr €2.50; ◷10am-4am) Internet access.

General Hospital of Rethymno (☑28210 27491; Triandalydou 17; ◷24hr) Has 24-hour accident and emergency. A few blocks inland from the port, in the newer part of the city.

National Bank (cnr Dimokratias & Gerakari; ◷8am-2pm) Usually has better exchange rates and lower fees than most other banks. Across the road from the town hall.

Post Office (Moatsou 21; ◷7am-7pm Mon-Fri) Accepts letters and parcels.

Regional Tourist Office (☑28310 29148; www.rethymno.gr; Sofokli Venizelou; ◷8am-2pm Mon-Fri) Has local maps and offers regional information. Next to the water in the Commercial Harbour.

Tourist Police (☑28310 28156, 28310 54340, emergency 171; Sofokli Venizelou; ◷on call 24hr) In the same building as the Regional Tourist Office.

❶ Getting There & Away

The **bus station** (cnr Igoumenou Gavriil & Kefalogiannidon) is on the western edge of the centre. Services are reduced at weekends and outside high season. Check **KTEL** (www.bus-service-crete-ktel.com) for the current schedule.

❶ Getting Around

Rethymno is compact and the downtown is easy to manoeuvre on foot, which is a good thing as many of the streets in the old quarter are too narrow for cars. City buses and taxis can take you to anywhere on the outskirts or rent a bike for an easy, flat ride to the far reaches of the beach.

Auto Moto Sports (☑28310 24858; www.automotosport.com.gr; Sofoklis Venizelou 48; bicycle/car per day from €10/32; ◷10am-7pm) Hires out bicycles, cars and motorbikes.

Rent-a-Bike (Paleologou 14; per day from €7; ◷9am-2pm & 5-9pm) Rents new, durable mountain bikes, including kids' models.

WEST OF RETHYMNO

The villages southwest of Rethymno, in the foothills of the Lefka Ori (White Mountains), make for a lovely afternoon drive. The main destination is the mountain village of Argyroupoli, built on an ancient settlement and famous for its springs and waterfalls. The road also passes through Episkopi, a pretty market town with winding lanes and traditional houses.

Argyroupoli   Αργυρούπολη

POP 400

When the summer heat becomes too intense, you'll find a natural cooling system at Argyroupoli, 25km southwest of Rethymno. At the bottom of this village is a watery oasis formed by springs from the Lefka Ori that keep the temperature markedly cooler here than on the coast. Running through aqueducts, washing down walls, seeping from

> ## ❶ GETTING AROUND THE RETHYMNO REGION
>
> The roads in Rethymno are generally good. The E75 highway connects Rethymno with Iraklio and Hania, while coastal communities are accessed via the parallel Old National Rd. Southern-coast driving, meanwhile, means negotiating a maddening warren of tiny roads off the Rethymno–Agia Galini road. The going is scenic but slow, here and in other rural areas, such as the Amari Valley and the foothills of Mt Psiloritis. It's worth investing in a decent map, rather than relying on the basic ones handed out with car rentals. From about April to October, buses link Rethymno with major towns and tourist attractions on a regular basis.

stones and pouring from spigots, the gushing springs supply water for the entire city of Rethymno.

Argyroupoli is built on the ruins of the ancient city of Lappa, one of the most important Roman cities in western Crete – of which very few remnants survive. Being in the foothills of the Lefka Ori also makes the town a gateway to some fine walking and hiking trails.

◉ Sights

Argyroupoli is divided into an upper town and a lower town. Most historical sights are near the main square at the top, while the springs and tavernas are at the bottom. Approaching from Rethymno, the turn-off to the lower village is on your right before the road climbs to the upper village.

Necropolis   ANCIENT SITE
Ancient Lappa's cemetery lies north of the town and is reached via a signed 1.5km footpath from the main square. Hundreds of tombs have been cut into the rock cliffs here, especially around the Chapel of the Five Virgins. The path leads on to a plane tree that is supposed to be 2000 years old.

◉ Upper Town

Begin your exploration in the main square, dominated by the stately 17th-century Venetian church of **Agios Ionnis**. This is also where you'll find the remains of **Ancient Lappa**.

Carry on up the cobbled road, passing the crumbling remains of buildings constructed of ruins, set next to brightly painted homes. Exploring the riddle of alleyways, you'll find ancient Venetian columns and olive presses.

On your left, watch for a **Roman portal**, with the inscription Omnia Mundi Fumus et Umbra (All things in this world are smoke and shadow). At the T-junction, head right to the **Church of St Paraskevi**, where the lid of a baby's sarcophagus now serves as the entrance step to the courtyard. Then head left, looping around to an impressive 7000-piece Roman **mosaic floor** from the 1st century BC. The road then returns you to the square.

◉ Lower Town

Heading downhill from the main square, then taking your first main left will get you to the tavernas clustered around the springs in the lower village. Towering chestnut and plane trees and luxuriant vegetation create a shady, restful spot for lunch among the waterfalls and fountains that have been incorporated into all the tavernas. It's especially lovely on a summer night. Aside from the tavernas, you'll find a 17th-century water-driven **fulling machine**, once used to thicken cloth by moistening and beating it, as well as the overgrown remains of a **Roman bath** and **St Mary's Church**, built atop a temple dedicated to Poseidon.

🛏 Sleeping

Villa Eleva   PENSION €
(☑ 28310 81269; s/d incl breakfast €20/30) The Zografakis family rents basic, clean rooms above their taverna. Views from the balconies are stupendous and breakfast is a big, traditional spread. It's next to the square in the upper town.

Arcus Villas   BOUTIQUE HOTEL €€
(☑ 28312 00201; www.arcus.com.gr; Argyroupoli; ste €110-120, apt from €180; ❄ @ 🛜 ☒) In the heart of the upper town, this traditional Venetian home has been given a plush, new lease on life. Each of the five suites have kitchenettes and stone fireplaces and apartments sleep up to six people. BBQ in the garden next to the pool and feel miles away from anywhere.

🍴 Eating

The tavernas around the springs cater to tourists, but the quality is actually quite good and the shaded glen setting is spectacular. There's little difference in terms of quality, so just pick the one that looks most inviting to you. All have outdoor seating amid imaginative (and often noisy) water features. Most close around 7pm except on balmy summer nights.

Local specialities are farm-raised trout and sturgeon, which can sometimes be seen swimming around in tanks. Lamb and pork, spit-roasted over olive wood, are good non-piscine choices.

O Kipos Tis Arkoudenas   CRETAN €€
(☑28310 61607; mains €5-12; ⊙lunch & dinner) One of the best tavernas around here, the 'Garden of Arkoudenas' turns superb organic produce into gorgeous dishes, many of them prepared in the wood oven.

🛍 Shopping

Lappa Avocado Shop   BEAUTY
(☑28310 81070; www.lappa-avocado.gr; ⊙10am-7pm Mar-Nov, 11am-3pm Dec-Feb) Across the street from the remains of Ancient Lappa and under the stone archway, you'll find the Lappa Avocado Shop. Not only does it sell excellent avocado-based beauty products, but it doubles as an unofficial tourist office. Ask here for a free town map, which outlines a quick loop around the old quarter, starting behind the store.

❶ Getting There & Away

From Monday to Friday three buses ply the route from Rethymno to Argyroupoli. Before you head out, be sure to check that there is in fact a return bus to Rethymno (€3.30, 40 minutes).

THE HINTERLAND & MT PSILORITIS

Rethymno's mountainous hinterland offers lots of options for interesting routes and detours. In a single day, you could easily combine a visit to the historic Moni Arkadiou with a poke around the pottery village of Margarites while also taking in the ruins of Ancient Eleftherna.

Further east, the foothills of Mt Psiloritis beckon with a couple of charismatic caves and traditional villages like Axos and Anogia; the latter is also the launch pad for the precipitous drive up to the Nida Plateau.

Moni Arkadiou
Μονή Αρκαδίου

★**Moni Arkadiou**   HISTORIC SITE
(Arkadi Monastery; ☑28310 83136; www.arkadimonastery.gr; admission €2.50; ⊙9am-8pm Jun-Aug, shorter hours Sep-May) The Arkadi Monastery, in the hills some 23km southeast of Rethymno, has deep significance for Cretans. As the site where hundreds of cornered locals massacred both themselves and invading Turks, it's a stark and potent symbol of human resistance and considered a spark plug in the struggle towards freedom from Turkish occupation. When visiting, be sure to cover your shoulders out of respect. There are three buses (two on weekends) from Rethymno to the monastery (€2.80, 40 minutes).

In November 1866, massive Ottoman forces arrived to crush island-wide revolts. Hundreds of Cretan men, women and children fled their villages to find shelter at Arkadiou. However, far from being a safe haven, the monastery was soon besieged by 2000 Turkish soldiers. Rather than surrender, the Cretans set fire to their kegs of gunpowder, killing everyone, Turks included, except for one small girl who lived to a ripe old age in a village nearby. A bust of this woman and one of the abbot who lit the gunpowder stand outside the monastery. Also here (next to the cafeteria, skip the food), in the monastery's old windmill, is the macabre **ossuary** with skulls and bones of some of the 1866 victims neatly arranged in a glass cabinet.

Arkadiou's most impressive structure, its Venetian **church** (1587), has a striking Renaissance facade marked by eight slender Corinthian columns and topped by an ornate triple-belled tower. Inside, its interior is hushed, ornate and filled with ancient relics.

DON'T MISS

RETHYMNO'S BEST HISTORIC SITES

➡ **Moni Arkadiou** (p119) Ultimate symbol of Cretan resistance.

➡ **Rethymno fortress** (p107) Massive Venetian fortifications.

➡ **Moni Preveli** (p130) Famous for its key role in WWII.

➡ **Melidoni Cave** (p122) Site of a terrible massacre.

➡ **Cemetery of Armeni** (p125) Site of over 200 Minoan tombs.

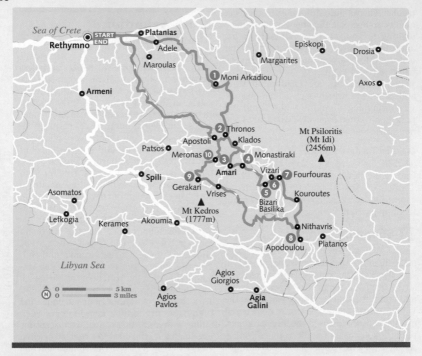

Driving Tour
Amari Valley

START RETHYMNO
FINISH RETHYMNO
LENGTH 150KM; ONE DAY

The Amari Valley is a quilt of unspoilt villages punctuated by Byzantine churches and framed by olive groves and orchards. Mt Psiloritis looms grandly above the landscape. You will need a good map.

Begin with a visit to the ever-impressive **① Moni Arkadiou** (p119). To reach it, head east from Rethymno, take the turning for Adele and follow the signs. Continue south to **② Thronos**, whose Agia Panagia has extraordinary, if faded, 14th-century frescoes (key at next-door cafe). From here, head downhill and turn left for Fourfouras.

Follow the signs to **③ Amari**, an enchanting medley of Venetian buildings and a square filled with cafes and overflowing flowerpots. Climb the 19th-century bell tower to share beautiful views with the pigeons. Continue on to **④ Monastiraki**, home to a (badly signposted) Minoan site. Carry on through

Lamiotes, turning east after Petrochori. Pass through olives groves, stopping at the remains of the 7th-century **⑤ Bizari Basilica**, destroyed in 824 by the Arabs.

In **⑥ Vizari**, visit olive woodworking shops, then head east to pretty **⑦ Fourfouras**, where trails climb up Mt Psiloritis and you can refuel at the gas station and bakery. Head south to **⑧ Apodoulou**, with the manor of Kalitsa Psaraki, named for a girl abducted by Turks and rescued (and married) by an English traveller. Follow a dirt track west of town to Agios Georgios, with its still-colourful 17th-century frescoes.

Return north, taking the turning for Agios Ioannis, through the western valley. Turn north for Anomeros and on to modern, colourful **⑨ Gerakari**, a market town famous for its cherries, wild tulips and its nicely frescoed 13th-century Church of Agios Ioannis.

Complete the loop in **⑩ Meronas**, where the 14th-century Church of Maria and its frescoes are a highlight of the trip. Carry on to Agia Fontini, from where you can continue north to Rethymno.

Left of here is a cypress trunk that was scorched by the explosion and still has a bullet embedded in its bark. Beyond is the former refectory (dining room), now a small museum of religious objects, icons and weapons used in 1866, as well a gift shop for your iconic needs. At the end of the left wing is the old wine cellar where the gunpowder was stored.

🛏 Sleeping

★ **Kapsaliana Village**   HOTEL €€€
(☎ 28310 83400; www.kapsalianavillage.gr; s €120, d €170-210, all incl breakfast; P✻🛜🏊) Once a hamlet whose olives supplied nearby Moni Arkadiou, these small homes have taken on new life as an unrelentingly charming and stylish hotel. The 12 original and five new villas offer top-notch amenities, including ultracomfy beds, fireplaces and view-filled verandahs. The ambience is peaceful, even around the pool and in the restaurant, which serves expertly prepared organic meals.

Eleftherna   Ελεύθερνα

Ancient Eleftherna   ARCHAEOLOGICAL SITE
Continuing 7km east from Moni Arkadiou takes you to the archaeological site of Ancient Eleftherna. This Dorian-built settlement was among the most important in the 8th and 7th centuries BC and also experienced heydays in Hellenistic and Roman times. Excavations have been ongoing since 1985 and archaeologists continue to make new finds all the time. The 2010 discovery of the gold-adorned remains of a woman in a 2700-year-old double tomb made international news. The excavation of the tomb of a high priestess and three acolytes a year earlier even prompted the Archaeological Institute of America to include Eleftherna in its Top 10 Discoveries of 2009.

Alas, most of the site is fenced off for now and none too visitor-friendly. The most easily accessible section is the Acropolis and the remains of a tower atop a long narrow ridge behind the Akropolis taverna. From here, an uneven, overgrown path leads down to vast Roman cisterns carved into the hills and, further along, to a Hellenistic bridge.

Down in the valleys flanking the ridge, active digs include the huge 2800-year-old necropolis of Orthi Petra to the west, where findings have produced evidence of human sacrifice. For a closer look, follow the dirt road down a steep hill from the village of Eleftherna.

On the eastern slope, the remains of residential and public buildings from the Roman and Byzantine periods are being dug up. You can peek through the fence by following the main road east towards Margarites, turning off at the sign to the Church of the Sotiros and taking the dirt road just past this lovely Byzantine chapel.

Margarites   Μαργαρίτες

POP 270

Tiny Margarites' well-regarded pottery brings droves of tour buses in the morning. By the afternoon, all is calm and you can wander through the studios and enjoy wonderful valley views from the eucalyptus-lined taverna terraces on the main square.

Margarites has only one road, and no bank or post office, but boasts more than 20 ceramics stores and studios. Much of the pottery is bright and usable.

◎ Sights

Keramion   GALLERY
(www.keramion.gr; ⊙9am-7pm) Much of George and Marinki's pottery is created using Minoan techniques and designs and is fired in wood, resulting in a brown finish. (The red finish is achieved by using electricity.) The clay is of such fine quality that it needs only one firing and no glazing – the outside having been smoothed with a pebble. The gallery is a cool oasis where the potters will happily explain their work to you.

Ilys   GALLERY
(www.ilysceramics.gr; ⊙9am-7pm) This gallery is an explosion of colour. Brightly glazed bowls, plates, magnets, *raki* cups and other small (and not so small) keepsakes line the shelves. Watch Ilys at work at his wheel from where he's happy to share his local knowledge.

Ceramic Art   GALLERY
(⊙9am-7pm) Down a side road at the top of the village, Konstantinos Gallios makes some beautiful pieces, displayed in his inviting gallery.

🛏 Sleeping & Eating

Kouriton House   BOUTIQUE HOTEL €€
(☎28340 55828; www.kouritonhouse.gr; Tzanakiana; r incl breakfast €60-110) Bunches of dried herbs and flowers dangling from the wood-beamed ceiling welcome you to this gem on the northern outskirts of Margarites in Tzanakiana. The beautifully restored stone-built manor was built in 1750

and now offers seven rooms, each with a kitchenette. Owner Anastasia Friganaki is a wealth of local knowledge and demonstrates traditional methods of making honey, picking herbs and greens, and cooking Cretan and Minoan cuisine.

Mandolos GREEK €
(mains €5-7; ☺ lunch & dinner) On the shady main square, Mandolos is a well-regarded taverna. Dig into big portions of local standards like rabbit meatballs while relaxing under the plane trees, drinking wine and taking in the countryside views.

❶ Getting There & Away

Two buses make the trip from Rethymno to Margarites (€3.50, 30 minutes) from Monday to Friday.

Perama to Anogia
Πέραμα Προς Ανώγεια

The roads linking the small commercial hub of Perama and Anogia pass through some of the most dramatic scenery in northern Crete. Stop to explore fabulous caves or enjoy lunch in a timeless village along the foothills of Mt Psiloritis.

Melidoni Μελιδόνι

Melidoni Cave CAVE
(Gerontospilios; ☑ 28340 22650; admission €3.50; ☺ 9am-7pm Apr, May & Oct, 9am-8pm Jun-Sep) Melidoni Cave, about 2km outside the village of Melidoni, has an eerie beauty and carries heavy, historical significance. A place of worship since neolithic times, it became the site of a nasty massacre in 1824 under the Turkish occupation when 370 villagers and 30 soldiers sought refuge here from the Ottoman army. After a three-month siege, the Turks lit a fire and asphyxiated them inside, including 340 women and children. Pay your respects in the Hall of Heroes before exploring this evocative underworld of stalactites and stalagmites. Wear decent walking shoes as the cave is poorly lit and the ground uneven and slippery in places. You'll need to descend 70 steps into the cave. Also bring a sweater; at 24m below ground, it never gets above 18°C.

Episkopi Επισκοπή

This charming village 9km from Melidoni served as a bishopric under Venetian rule and is a maze of lanes lined with well-preserved stone mansions. Stop to admire the faded frescoes gracing the crumbling ruins of the 15th-century **Church of Episkopi**. Also watch for the Venetian **water fountain** next to the bridge at the end of the town.

Zoniana Ζωνιανά

Sfendoni Cave CAVE
(☑ 28340 61734; www.zoniana.gr; adult/child incl tour €4/2; ☺ 10am-5pm Apr-Oct, to 3pm weekends Nov-Mar) Guided tours take you 270m below ground and through seven chambers with such fanciful names as Sanctuary of the Fairy and Zeus' Palace. All teem with illuminated stalagmites and stalactites shaped into drapery, organ pipes, domes, curtains, waves and other strange formations. The cave is home to over 400 bats, who may greet you if you visit in the morning.

Tours run roughly every 45 minutes and take about 40 minutes. A new 270m-long walkway makes it accessible to everyone.

Zoniana itself is modern and not particularly attractive. From Monday to Friday, two buses make the trip out from Rethymno (€5.50, one hour).

Axos Αξός

The village of Axos has the kind of lazy Cretan ambience that has made it a popular stop for tour buses. During the day, the village is quiet, but at night the tavernas with open-air terraces are hopping.

◉ Sights

Museum of Wooden Sculptures MUSEUM
(☑ 6937691387; www.woodenmuseum.gr; admission €5; ☺ 9am-8pm) Fronted by a massive sculpture of Hercules killing the lion, this private museum is essentially a showcase of the work of self-taught artist Georgios Koutantos. An enthusiastic and voluble man, he'll happily show visitors around his workshop and explain the stories and cultural references behind each of his sculptures. He has completed over 100, each carved from local trees. None of the pieces are for sale.

The large-scale works, including an eagle with a 6m wing span, are the most impressive. Others depict family members, often in a highly personal fashion.

🛏 Sleeping

★Enagron RESORT €€
(☑ 28340 61611; www.enagron.gr; studio & apt €90-150; ❄ @ ❄ ❄) Set in the valley below

Axos, Enagron flawlessly blends ecotourism and comfort, meaning a guilt-free, cushy stay. The traditional, stone-built studios are large and comfortable, with kitchenettes and fireplaces. There's a pool overlooking the mountains and a taverna serving the estate's organic produce. Guests can participate in activities like Cretan cooking classes, botanical walks, bread- and cheese-making and *raki* distilling.

Guided walks are also available. You can visit the farm and eat at the restaurant by booking ahead.

Anogia
Ανώγεια
POP 2380

Anogia presides over the so-called 'Devil's Triangle' of macho mountain villages that occasionally get involved in armed stand-offs with the police (usually, over illicit cannabis cultivation, but also because of perceived affronts to local honour), much to the excitement of the Athenian media. The village is the centre of a prosperous sheep husbandry industry, and is a popular stopover for day trippers and those headed for the Nida Plateau. It has also spawned several of Crete's best-known musicians.

During WWII, Anogia was a centre of resistance and suffered heavily for it. The Nazis burned down the town and massacred all the men in retaliation for their role in sheltering Allied troops and aiding in the kidnapping of German commander General Heinrich Kreipe.

Hence, most of the buildings you see today are actually of relatively recent vintage, yet Anogia has a reputation for clinging to time-honoured traditions. Black-shirted men lounge in the *kafeneia* (coffee houses), their traditional baggy pants tucked into black boots and vying for the largest moustache, a sign of strength. Gunshot holes pepper the street signs while elderly women hunch over their canes, aggressively flogging woven blankets and the traditional embroidered textiles displayed in their shops.

◉ Sights

Anogia clings to a hillside, with the tourist shops in the lower half and most accommodation and businesses above.

Museum of Grylios MUSEUM
(☑ 28340 31593; donation welcome) A short walk uphill from the lower village square, this humble museum presents the paintings and sculptures of Anogia-born folk artist Alkiviadis Skoulas (1900–97), aka Grylios. Many depict local war scenes; there are few English explanations but the paintings largely speak for themselves. It's now run by Grylios' son Yiorgos, who is known to hold impromptu *lyra* concerts. Opening hours are unpredictable; if the museum's not open, knock next door or ask at the square for Yiorgos.

ANOGIA: MUSICAL TALENT FACTORY

Anogia is known for its stirring music and has spawned a disproportionate number of Crete's best-known musicians. The main instrument is the *lyra,* a three-sided, pear-shaped string instrument played sitting down and often accompanied by lutes and guitars. Local boy Nikos Xylouris (1936–80) took the world by storm with this instrument and his handle-bar moustache and is still considered Crete's best singer and *lyra* player more than 30 years after his death.

Nikos' somewhat eccentric brother Psarantonis has since taken up the reins. He is wildly popular nationwide for his timbre voice and often plays internationally. Brother Giannis Xylouris (Psaroyiannis) is Greece's most accomplished lute player. His heir apparent is Psarantonis' charismatic son, Giorgos Xylouris (Psarayiorgis), known for playing the lute as a solo instrument rather than in its traditional accompaniment role. Giorgos' sister, Niki, is one of the few female Cretan singers.

Other notable musicians from Anogia include the *lyra* players Manolis Manouras, Nikiforos Aerakis, Vasilis Skoulas (son of the folk painter Alkiviadis Skoulas) and Giorgos Kalomiris. The talented but capricious Georgos Tramoundanis, alias Loudovikos ton Anogion (Ludwig from Anogia), sells his brand of folksy, ballad-style Cretan compositions to audiences all over Greece. He's also the mastermind behind the annual **Yakinthia Festival** (www.yakinthia.com), with open-air concerts held on the slopes of Mt Psiloritis the first week of July.

Nikos Xylouris' Home   MUSEUM

(⊙9am-2pm & 5-8pm) FREE Musician Nikos Xylouris was born in this little house on the lower village square that is now a *kafeneio* run by his sister. The tiny room is completely plastered in posters, letters and other memorabilia related to the singer and *lyra* player, attesting to the extent of the adulation he still receives some 30 years after his death.

🛏 Sleeping

Hotel Aristea   HOTEL €

(✆28340 31459; www.hotelaristea.gr; s/d incl breakfast €35/40, apt €70-110; P🅿🛜) In the upper village, the friendly Aristea enjoys spectacular valley views and cool breezes in straightforward, clean rooms with TV, private bathrooms and big balconies. For more space and comfort, spend a little extra for one of the slightly newer apartments next door, some sleeping up to six people.

Delina Mountain Resort   HOTEL €€

(✆28340 31701; www.delina.gr; d incl breakfast €100-150; ❄🛜🏊) If you're planning on hiking Mt Psiloritis, this is a great place to unwind. About 1km outside of Anogia, en route to the Nida Plateau, this stylish resort exudes calm with spacious, modern rooms. Relax your weary muscles in the sauna, pool or spa, or in your private in-room jacuzzi. All rooms have verandahs with views to the mountain. The resort is owned by renowned local *lyra* player Vasilis Skoulas, who also gives the occasional concert.

🍴 Eating

Melissa   CAFE €

(sweets & ice cream €1-3; ⊙9am-9pm) Come here for homemade sheep's-milk ice cream and sweets, *raki* and coffee strong enough to stand a spoon in. Sit in the cool grotto-like interior or at a sidewalk table to watch life in the upper village slowly wander by.

Ta Skalomata   CRETAN €

(✆28340 31316; mains €4-9; ⊙lunch & dinner; 🛜) In the upper village, Skalomata has fed locals and travellers for about 40 years, making it the oldest restaurant in town. When you peel your eyes away from the huge windows with panoramic views, check out the open kitchen and traditional decor. It does great grills, handmade sausages, homemade wine and bread, and tasty meat-free options.

Arodamos   CRETAN €

(✆28340 31100; www.arodamos.gr; mains €6-10; ⊙lunch & dinner; @) This big restaurant in a new stone house in the upper village is held in high regard by villagers and visitors for its fresh Cretan fare and gracious hospitality. Anything with lamb is tops, but so is the *saganaki* (fried cheese) made with *katsohiri* (a local goat's cheese). Free sweet pie with ice cream caps off every meal.

Aetos   CRETAN €

(✆28340 31262; grills €5-8.50; ⊙lunch & dinner) This traditional taverna in the upper village has a giant charcoal grill out front and fantastic mountain views out back. A regional speciality is *ofto* (a flame-cooked lamb or goat). Aetos also serves another local staple: spaghetti cooked in stock with cheese.

ℹ Information

An ATM and the post office are in the upper village. Yakinthos, across from the Hotel Aristea, offers internet access.

ℹ Getting There & Away

There are up to three buses daily from Iraklio (€3.80, one hour) and two buses Monday to Friday from Rethymno (€5.50, 1¼ hours).

Mt Psiloritis
Ορος Ψηλορείτης

Imposing Mt Psiloritis, also known as Mt Ida, soars skyward for 2456m, making it Crete's highest mountain. At its eastern base is the **Nida Plateau** (1400m), a wide, fertile expanse reached via a paved 21km-long road from Anogia. The winding road affords beautiful mountain views and passes several *mitata* (round, stone shepherd's huts). It culminates at a huge parking lot where a simple taverna offers refreshment and spartan rooms (€25). It gets chilly up here, even in summer, so bring a sweater or light jacket.

About 1km before the road's end, an asphalt spur veers off to the left, ending after about 3km at the **Skinakas Observatory** (www.skinakas.org.gr; ⊙full moons 5-11pm), Greece's most significant stargazing vantage point. The observatory opens to the public once a month during the full moon from May to September, between 5pm and 11pm (English-speaking guides in July and August only). The website has details.

The mountain's most important feature is **Ideon Cave** (also known simply as Ideon) – the place where, according to legend, the god Zeus was reared (although Dikteon Cave in Lasithi claims the same). Ideon was a place of worship from the late 4th millennium BC onwards and many artefacts, including gold jewellery and a bronze shield, have been unearthed here. The cave itself is really just one huge and fairly featureless cavern about 1km from the parking lot.

Back on the plateau itself, you can make out a sprawling landscape sculpture called **Andartis – Partisan of Peace** against the hills. Created by German artist Karina Raeck in 1991, it commemorates the Cretan resistance in WWII. The monument itself is a pile of local rocks arranged in such a way that it looks like an angel when seen from above. Ask the taverna staff to point it out if you can't spot it on your own. It's a flat and easy 1.25km walk out there.

To reach Mt Psiloritis, you really need your own wheels. Buses run from Rethymno to Anogia (€4, two hours, twice daily weekdays).

COAST TO COAST

From Rethymno, the fastest and most direct route to the southern coast is via Armeni and Spili. For a more leisurely pace, travel via the almost ridiculously pastoral Amari Valley, a part of Crete that seems frozen in time.

Armeni   Αρμένοι

Heading away from Rethymno, it would be easy to fly right through Armeni, 10km south. With modern architecture and not much going on, it's not a natural draw. But you should stop, since it's here that you'll find one of the region's top Minoan sites.

◉ Sights

★ **Cemetery of Armeni**   CEMETERY
(admission €2; ◕8am-3pm Tue-Sun) Wandering through this beautiful oak forest is both eerie and fascinating. Some 231 tombs were carved into the rock between 1300 and 1150 BC and their long, sunken corridors and damp chambers are open for you to explore. Head up the hill for some of the most impressive. Excavation began in 1961 and finds included pottery, bronze ornaments, weapons, jewellery and a boar's tusk helmet, all on display at Rethymno's Archaeological

Museum, 7km to the south. Coming from the sea, watch for the turn-off to the right.

Upon entry to the cemetery, there are details in English on the site's history, including the interesting fact that there wasn't a sizeable town nearby to account for this number of tombs.

✕ Eating

Alekos Kafeneio   TAVERNA €
(mains €4-9; ◕lunch & dinner) A good choice for lunch, this little taverna has a small but superb daily selection of traditional dishes. There's no menu, but staff will take you downstairs to their kitchen and let you choose from simmering pots. It's popular with locals and has a few tables outside.

Spili   Σπήλι
POP 700
About halfway between Rethymno and Agia Galini, Spili (*spee*-lee) is a pretty mountain village with cobbled streets, flowered balconies, vine-covered rustic houses, and plane trees. Tourist buses stop here during the day, but in the evening Spili belongs to the locals. It's a good spot for lunch, and a haven for hikers. The rugged Kourtaliotiko Gorge, which culminates at the famous palm grove of Preveli Beach, starts not far south of town.

◉ Sights

Venetian Fountain   FOUNTAIN
The main local attraction is this restored charming fountain that spurts water from 19 stone lion heads into a long trough. Fill

up your own bottle with some of the island's best water. A walkway leads from the fountain uphill to the village's quiet and picturesque backstreets.

Folk Museum of Spili   MUSEUM
(by donation; ⊘ 10am-6pm) Up a footpath at the northern end of town, this place is a treasure trove of local vintage artefacts. The giant traditional loom or the coffee bean roaster might catch your eye, or the shoemaker's room and the traditional kitchen from 220 years ago. Well maintained and run by the knowledgeable Manolis, this museum is worth hunting down.

Monastery   MONASTERY
Spili is a bishop's see (seat of a bishop) based at the massive modern monastery at the west end of town. You're free to walk around and admire the arched entryways, marble-floor courtyard, stunning valley views and opulently decorated church. Hours are unpredictable.

🛏 Sleeping

Heracles   PENSION €
(☑ 28320 22111, 6973667495; www.heracles-hotel. eu; s/d €30/40; ❋ 🛜) These five balconied rooms are quiet, spotless and simply furnished, but it's the friendly Heracles himself who makes the place memorable. A geologist by profession, he's intimately familiar with the area and can put you on the right hiking trail, birdwatching site or hidden beach. Optional homemade breakfasts start at €4. Heracles also operates the worthwhile Creta Natura shop nearby.

Green Hotel   HOTEL €
(☑ 28320 22225; www.maravelspili.gr; s/d/tr €25/30/35; ⊘ Mar-Oct; 🛜) The 12 rooms here don't exactly fuel the imagination, but each has a balcony and the in-house sauna (€5) is a good spot to unwind. The owner also operates the Maravel Shop, which sells organic beauty products made with ingredients grown in his huge garden nearby. Optional breakfast is €5.

🍴 Eating

Stratidakis   CRETAN €
(specials €5-7; ⊘ lunch & dinner) A mother-and-son team presides over the oldest taverna in town. There's meat grilling on the spits outside and robust Cretan daily specials stewing in pots that you're free to inspect. Local honey and yoghurt is served for break-

fast. The leafy garden verandah has jaw-dropping mountain views.

Maria Kostas Taverna   TAVERNA €
(mains €5-10; ⊘ lunch & dinner) Come here for the home cooking and dine on the patio hung with gourds and overflowing with flowers. You'll likely find Maria in the kitchen stuffing tomatoes and dishing up fantastic grills and casseroles. It's on the main road, at the northern end of town.

Yianni's   GREEK €
(☑ 28320 22707; Main Rd; mains €5-8; ⊘ lunch & dinner) Past the Venetian fountain, this friendly place has a big roadside terrace, reliably good traditional cooking and a decent house red. Try the delicious rabbit in wine or the local mountain snails.

Panorama   CRETAN €€
(☑ 28320 22555; mains €6-13; ⊘ dinner daily, lunch Sun; 🛜) Pantelis Vasilakis and his wife Calliope are the masterminds behind this fine traditional taverna on the outskirts of Spili. Enjoy memorable views from the terrace while munching on homemade bread, toothsome mezedhes or such tempting mains as succulent kid goat with *horta* (wild greens). It's an accredited Concred taverna.

ℹ Information

There are two ATMs and a post office on the main street. Some of the cafes near the fountain have wi-fi.

ℹ Getting There & Away

Spili is on the Rethymno–Agia Galini bus route (€3.50, 40 minutes), which has up to five services daily.

SOUTHERN COAST

Rethymno's southern coast is bookended by the resort towns of Plakias and Agia Galini, which are linked by a string of marvellously isolated beaches, including the famous palm beach at Preveli. Massive summertime winds have spared the area from the tourism excesses that typify the northern coast.

Approaching from the north, the scenery becomes increasingly dramatic and takes in marvellous views of the Libyan Sea. From the Rethymno–Agia Galini road, it's a fabulous drive through the rugged Kotsifou Gorge to Plakias. The road to Preveli travels via the equally spectacular Kourtaliotiko Gorge.

CRETAN BREW

When Dortmund-born mathematician Dr Bernd Brink moved to Crete after marrying a local girl, he did what any self-respecting German would do – he opened a brewery. In business since 2001, **Brink's Brewery** (☑ 28310 41243; www.brinks-beer.gr) is a sophisticated operation producing full-bodied organic blonde and dark lagers that are sold all over Greece. You'll pass the brewery some 12km south of Rethymno, just past Armeni. It's no longer open for tours but you'll have no problem finding locations across Crete to try it.

The unfiltered and unpasteurised beer is brewed in accordance with a 16th-century German law that permits only the use of water, hops, yeast and malt in beer making.

Plakias   Πλακιάς

POP 145

Set beside a long southern-coast beach, between two immense wind tunnel gorges, Plakias was once a humble fishing village. In 1961, the official census recorded a population of just six. Today its population explodes each summer with Central European package tourists and the international legions quartered at the popular youth hostel. It's hopping.

Plakias has some decent restaurants and plenty of accommodation options. While the town itself isn't particularly peaceful, from here you can walk through olive groves, along seaside cliffs and to some sparkling hidden beaches. It's also a good base for regional excursions.

🏃 Activities

Diving

Several diving operators run shore and boat dives to nearby rocky bays, caves and canyons, as well as all manner of courses.

Dive 2gether   DIVING
(☑ 28320 32313, 6974031441; www.dive2gether.com; dive packages incl gear from €110; ⊗8.30am-12.30pm & 2-7pm Apr-Oct) A topnotch, Dutch-run operation in town with state-of-the-art equipment and super-high safety standards. Also runs a one-on-one Discover Scuba Diving (€86) and Bubblemaker sessions for kids as young as eight.

Kalypso Rock's Palace Dive Center   DIVING
(☑ 06983666422; www.kalypsodivecenter.com; Kalypso Cretan Village Resort & Spa; dive packages incl gear from €95; ⊗9am-2pm & 5-8pm Apr-Oct) Based at the Kalypso Holidays Village, just outside Plakias, it runs PADI courses, night snorkelling trips and shore dives alongside lots of options for dive locations.

Hiking

There are well-worn walking paths to the scenic village of Selia, Moni Finika, Lefkogia, and a lovely walk along the Kourtaliotiko Gorge to Moni Preveli. An easy 30-minute uphill path to Myrthios begins just before the youth hostel.

Anso Travel   HIKING
(☑ 6944755712, 28320 31444; www.ansotravel.com) For guided walks, including the one to Preveli Beach that gets you back by boat, contact Anso Travel.

Horse Riding

Horseback Riding Plakias   HORSE RIDING
(☑ 28320 32033; www.cretehorseriding.com; adult €25-100, child €15-25; ⊗8am-5pm) Set within olive groves outside Plakias, these family-run stables offer horse-riding tours along beaches and up into the surrounding mountains. With over 30 horses and 11 routes, there's plenty to choose from. Tours are one to four hours and there's a whole string of ponies for children to ride.

☞ Tours

Baradakis Lefteris   BOATING
(☑ 28320 31940, 6936806635; smernabar@gmail.com) In summer, Baradakis Lefteris, owner of the Smerna Bar, runs boats to nearby beaches like Preveli (€15) and Frangokastello (€39).

Elena Tours   TOUR
(☑ 6936371451, 28320 20465; tours €40-60; ⊗9.30am-1.30pm & 6-9pm) Hop in Elena's minibus for an excursion into the less touristy side of the area. Hike through gorges, take boats to unheard of beaches, visit ancient churches and meet locals in quaint villages. Each tour includes a maximum of eight people. The office is located in the centre of Plakias, just over the bridge.

DON'T MISS

KOTSIFOU GORGE

Narrow and lush, a drive through this gorge is jaw-droppingly beautiful. Blanketed in wildflowers, the road north from Plakias winds and twists its way from the coast like a piece of yarn. Heading north, stop at pretty **Agios Nikolas**, a small chapel built directly into the side of the mountain.

At the top of the gorge, the mountainside **Taverna Iliomanolis** (📞 28320 51053; Kanevos; mains €4-7; ⊙ lunch & dinner Tue-Sun, closed Nov) makes the trip worth it in itself. The hearty homestyle Cretan food is superb, and while there's no menu, you'll be invited into the kitchen to peruse the tempting array of stews, casseroles, soups and local specialities prepared daily. Meat, wine, olive oil, cheese and *raki* all come from the family farm. You can also buy bags of local herbs and mountain teas.

If you have a compass and plenty of time, head north of here. The roads are narrow and winding and badly signposted, but the scenery – mountaintop farms and forested ravines – is worth getting lost in. You can eventually wind your way all the way to Rethymno.

🛏 Sleeping

Livikon Beach Hotel
HOTEL €

(📞 28320 31420; www.hotel-livikon-plakias.com; d/tr €45/50; P❄🛜) A family-run affair across the street from the beach, this hotel has 10 spotless, spacious, comfortable rooms that have had a recent lick of paint. Each has a balcony and kitchenette. Service is ace.

Plakias Youth Hostel
HOSTEL €

(📞 28320 32118; www.yhplakias.com; dm €10; ⊙ Easter-Oct; P@🛜) Set around a hammock-filled lawn amid olive groves, about 500m from the waterfront, this purposely lazy hostel fosters an atmosphere of inclusiveness and good cheer that appeals to people of all ages and nationalities. The hostel has eight-bed dorms with fans and well-kept facilities. Inexpensive breakfast and drinks are available. Book ahead.

Gio-Ma
APARTMENT €

(📞 28320 32003; www.gioma.gr; d/apt €35/40; ⊙ check-in 8am-midnight; ❄🛜) Located at the quiet end of town and fronted by a flower-filled balcony, the rooms here are basic but clean. The fabulous sea views, however, give it an edge. Snag one of the upper units for postcard-perfect photos. The owners also run the waterfront taverna across the street.

Camping Apollonia
CAMPGROUND €

(📞 28320 31318; camp sites per adult/tent/car/caravan €9/6/5/8; ⊙ May-Oct; 🛜🖼) You won't find much privacy here but you can settle in under some olive and eucalyptus trees. Sites have cafeteria-style picnic tables, there's a big pool and pool bar, and the beach is your neighbour. The facilities could use a little TLC. It's on the main road into town.

Plakias Suites
APARTMENT €€

(📞 28320 31680, 6975811559; www.plakiassuites. com; ste €100-150; ⊙ Apr-Oct; P❄🛜) This stylish outpost has modern yet warm aesthetics and plush touches such as large flat-screen TVs and mini hi-fis, rainforest showers and a chic kitchen. Staying here puts you within a whisker of the best stretch of local beach.

Alianthos Garden Hotel
HOTEL €€

(📞 28320 31280; www.alianthos.gr; s/d incl breakfast from €75/95; P❄@🛜🖼🦽) Rooms at this modern hotel complex sparkle in breezy turquoise and come with high-end mattresses and flower-filled balconies, many with sea views. Common areas include a stylish bar, pool, library and snooker table. A children's pool, games and a playground give it an edge with families.

🍴 Eating

To Xehoristo
GREEK €

(mains €3-8; ⊙ lunch & dinner) Never mind the picture menu: locals swear by the tasty souvlaki and grills. It's at the eastern end of the main road, across from the sea.

Lisseos
INTERNATIONAL €

(📞 28320 31479; dishes €6.50-13.50; ⊙ breakfast, lunch & dinner) This unfussy eatery by the bridge has excellent homestyle cooking; try the pork in lemon sauce with almonds. They also do their bit for the international crowd – goulash, shrimp cocktail and a fabulous chocolate cake.

★ Tasomanolis
SEAFOOD €€

(📞 28320 31129; mains €4-16; ⊙ lunch & dinner; 🛜) Head to this friendly, nautical-themed taverna, at the quiet end of town, for the local catch, hauled in by Manolis and cooked by his wife, Eleni. Park yourself on the colourful patio for seafood lasagne, anchovy bruschetta or the grilled daily catch paired with wild greens and wine.

Taverna Christos   CRETAN €€
(☑ 28320 31472; mains €5-15; ☺ lunch & dinner; ☎) This established taverna has a romantic tamarisk-shaded terrace right next to the crashing waves, and lots of interesting dishes that you won't find everywhere, including home-smoked sea bass, black spaghetti with calamari, and lamb *avgolemono* (meat or vegetables cooked in an egg-lemon stock) with fresh pasta. Finish off with the orange pie.

🍷 Drinking & Nightlife

A whole string of cafes and bars line the western end of the waterfront.

Ostraco Bar   CAFE, LOUNGE BAR
(☺ 9am-late; ☎) With a stylish downstairs cafe, waterside tables and an upstairs bar, you could spend all day at this old favourite. In the evening, the gregarious gather for drinking and dancing. In the daytime, it's great for chilling.

Joe's Bar   BAR
(Nufaro; ☺ 9am-late; ☎) Sooner or later everyone seems to end up at Joe's, a dark, warehouse-like joint that's officially called Nufaro and is right on the central waterfront. It plays a good selection of rock and pop and service is friendly.

❶ Information

There are two ATMs on the central waterfront. The post office is on the first side street coming from the east. Most waterfront cafes offer free wi-fi with purchase.

Plakias' well-stocked, multilanguage **lending library** (☺ 9.30am-12.30pm Sun, Mon & Wed, 5-7.30pm Tue, Thu & Sat) is 250m beyond the youth hostel.

❶ Getting There & Away

There are up to five buses daily to Rethymno (€4.50, one hour) and one to Preveli (€2.30, 30 minutes).

❶ Getting Around

Anso Bike Hire (☑ 28320 31444; www.anso travel.com; per day €10-25; ☺ 9am-2pm & 5-9pm) Anso Travel rents out mountain bikes, speed bikes and even electric bikes for taking to the mountains around town. Multiday rates available.

MYRTHIOS

The postcard-pretty village of Myrthios (Μύρθιος), draped across the hillside above Plakias, makes for a quieter and more villagelike alternative to staying beachside. You might also be lured by great food and good deals on accommodation. Myrthios is a short drive (about 4km) or 30-minute walk (about 2km) from Plakias.

Anna Apartments (☑ 6973324775; www.annaview.com; d/tr from €50/60; ❄) Run by a welcoming family, these attractive, roomy units have cranked up the comfort and hominess. Balconies are a quiet kick-back zone, especially at sunset. Recently renovated, they are clean and modern with full kitchens.

Stefanos Village Hotel (☑ 28320 32252; www.stefanosvillage.gr; d & apt €80-95; ☺ May-Nov; ❄ ☀) On the outskirts of the village, rooms here are spotless and well cared for with fireplaces, kitchenettes and view-filled balconies. The infinity pool has the most amazing view of Plakias and the beach.

Vrisi (www.tavernavrisi.gr; mains €8-12; ☺ 9am-midnight May-Sep) Set below the main road, this stylish restaurant creates delicious Cretan cuisine with panache. Dishes like chicken with honey and mustard, fig and chicken salad, and smoked pork with bulgur lettuce are all served on a secluded patio. Service is first-rate. If you're very lucky, Fidel, the in-house parrot, might speak (or bark) at you. The restaurant is named after a neighbouring traditional fountain, once a major water source for the village.

Plateia (mains €6-13; ☺ lunch & dinner) With a view over Plakias, the fairly fashionable Plateia gives Greek standards a creative spin. Try chicken with ocra, rabbit *stifado* or one of the tempting stews.

Cars Alianthos (☑ 28320 32033; www.alian thos-group.com; per day from €36; ⊘ 24hr) Reliable car-hire outlet.

Around Plakias

Between Plakias and Preveli Beach, there are several secluded coves popular with freelance campers and nudists. **Damnoni Beach** is pleasant out of high season, despite being dominated by the giant Hapimag tourist complex.

To the west is **Souda**, a quiet beach with a couple of tavernas with rooms. Continuing west are the low-key beach resorts of **Polyrizos-Koraka** (also known as Rodakino), with a handful of tavernas and a few small hotels scattered along a pleasant stretch of beach. It's ideal if you want a quiet retreat at which to chill for a few days.

Set on the edge of Rodakino village, **Panorama** (☑ 28320 32179; Rodakino; d €45; P ✷ 🛜) has basic, good-value rooms with a view built on a rise above the beach, behind the thatched-roof taverna. For more elbow room, get a self-catering studio.

Preveli   Πρέβελη

A smooth, curving ribbon of a road winds from the bottom of Kourtaliotiko Gorge towards the southern coast, soaring up to Moni Preveli and plunging down to Preveli Beach. With two of the region's biggest draws, Preveli sees a lot of visitors but retains a feeling of remoteness.

Before the road begins its ascent, 3km before Moni Preveli, you'll pass the blackened **Lower Monastery**. Steeped with atmosphere but now unused, this is where the 'working' monks once lived. It was these monks who, in the 1800s, hand built the

RETHYMNO'S BEST BEACHES

➜ **Preveli Beach** (p130) Famous palm grove at the mouth of a gorge.

➜ **Triopetra** (p131) Long, sandy and remote.

➜ **Agios Pavlos** (p131) Isolated, cliff-fringed cove.

➜ **Karavostasi** (p135) Kid-friendly, sandy crescent in Bali.

nearby stone bridge that spans the river Megalopotamos.

Strictly a farming region, there is no town here so come prepared. In summer, there are two daily buses to Moni Preveli from Rethymno (€4.50, 1¼ hours) and one from Plakias (€2.30, 30 minutes). Hop off at the turn-off for Preveli Beach, 1km before the monastery.

Driving, the turn-off for Preveli is 27km from Rethymno. During high season, you can also get to Preveli Beach by boat from Plakias and Agia Galini.

⊙ Sights

Moni Preveli   MONASTERY
(Μονή Πρεβέλης; ☑ 28320 31246; www.preveli. org; admission €2.50; ⊘ 9am-6.30pm mid-Mar–May, 9am-1.30pm & 3.30-6.30pm Jun-Oct) The historic Moni Preveli stands in splendid isolation high above the Libyan Sea. Like most Cretan monasteries, it was a centre of anti-Ottoman resistance and was burned by the Turks during the 1866 onslaught. Inside stand the stunning, ornate chapel and small museum packed with icons and portions of a 13th-century fresco. The monastery is active, with out-of-bounds monks' quarters; women who aren't covered up will be given skirts and shawls to wear.

Look out for the Benedictine Cross, believed to be miracle-inducing (particularly for eye ailments), which has been carried at the front of battles since its creation in the 18th century. After the Battle of Crete in WWII, many Allied soldiers were sheltered here before their evacuation to Egypt, commemorated by a monument overlooking the cliffs just before the monastery.

Preveli Beach   BEACH
(Παραλία Πρεβέλης) Also known as Palm Beach, dazzling Preveli Beach is one of Crete's most celebrated strands. At the mouth of the Kourtaliotiko Gorge, where the river Megalopotamos empties into the Libyan Sea, the palm-lined river banks have freshwater pools good for a dip. The beach is backed by rugged cliffs and punctuated by a heart-shaped boulder at the water's edge.

A steep path leads down to the beach (10 minutes) from a car park (€2), 1km before Moni Preveli.

There's some natural shade, and umbrellas and lounges can be hired from a couple of seasonal snack bars. Once on the beach, you'll have to cross the ankle-deep river to reach the sandiest stretch.

Eating

Taverna Gefyra   TAVERNA €
(mains €4-9; ⊙lunch & dinner) Cool off at tree-shaded tables, with a view to the river and a stone bridge built by local monks. The food here is fresh and traditional and the service is friendly.

Beaches Between Plakias & Agia Galini

No amount of hyperbole can communicate the dramatically rugged beauty of Rethymno's pristine southern sandy beaches. East of the more popular Preveli Beach, remote and peaceful Ligres, Triopetra and Agios Pavlos are perfect for stress-free escapes surrounded by photogenic splendour and popular with yoga and meditation groups. There's no megaresort to distort the idyllic ambience, only a few lone tavernas with modest rooms. Strong summer winds are common on these beaches. There is no public transport to any of them.

Ligres   Λίγκρες

Serene Ligres is a long sweep of greyish sand with some good swimming. Access to Ligres is via a tiny winding road. Get off the main highway at Akoumia and follow the signs.

If you want to be in the thick of things, best not stay at **Villa Maria** (☑28320 22675, 6973232793; www.ligres.eu; d from €45, studio from €70; ⊙Apr-Oct; ❀🛜). With only the waves and a rushing creek for entertainment, this friendly, family-run property on a stunning, isolated beach is great for quiet relaxation. Rooms are comfortable without being fanciful and come with balcony and kitchenette. The excellent taverna specialises in grilled meats and just-caught fish (mains €5 to €10).

Triopetra   Τριόπετρα

Triopetra is named after the three giant rocks jutting out of the sea. A headland divides the beach into Little Triopetra on the eastern side and Big Triopetra on the other. Because of submerged sand shelves, Little Triopetra is not ideal for swimming; head to the much longer western beach for that.

Triopetra can be reached via a 12km winding asphalt road from the village of Akoumia, on the Rethymno–Agia Galini road. A new road to Ligres starts at the western end of Big Triopetra beach (the first 200m or so are dirt track), sometimes closed due to storms.

🛏 Sleeping

Pension Girogiali   PENSION €
(☑6974559119; s/d/tr €30/35/40; ⊙Apr-Oct; ❀) Right on Triopetra's long beach, this place is run by two brothers, with their mother whipping up a storm in the kitchen. The rooms are clean and basic with marble floors and balconies. The mattresses are on the thin side.

Pension Pavlos   PENSION €
(☑28310 25189; www.triopetra.com.gr; s/d/tr €33/43/48; ⊙Apr-Oct; ❀) Set on Little Triopetra, simple rooms are down to earth (no TV), with kitchenettes and balconies that catch the sea breeze, but it's looking thirsty for a lick of paint. The attached taverna serves mostly home-grown fare (mains €5 to €12). Aside from lounging on the beach or hiring boats in the small harbour, there is nothing to do but chill. Rooms are often booked by participants in monthly yoga workshops.

Agios Pavlos   Αγιος Παύλος

Agios Pavlos is little more than a couple of small hotels and tavernas set around a picture-perfect sandy crescent cradled by rugged cliffs. In the distance you can make out the distinctive silhouette of Paximadia Island. The village claims to be the location from where Icarus and Daedalus took their historic flight in ancient mythology (though nearby Agia Galini makes the same claim).

Despite its isolation, the main cove gets busy in July and August, but you can escape the bustle by heading for the beaches behind the headland to the west, which can only be reached by hiking down a steep sand dune. The furthest cove is the least busy and is popular with nudists. Agios Pavlos' beauty and tranquillity have made it a popular destination for yoga retreats organised by UK-based **Yoga Plus** (www.yogaplus.co.uk).

At **Agios Pavlos Hotel** (☑28320 71104; www.agiospavloshotel.gr; d €32-40, apt €45-60; ⊙Apr-Oct; ❀) recently renovated rooms are fresh and modern, with gorgeous views over the little bay. Uphill from the hotel, apartments sleep four and are sparklingly new with full amenities. The taverna has worthwhile Cretan food while the adjacent palm-thatched cafe does breakfast and drinks, which you can take while lazing in a hammock. There's also a small children's playground.

To get to Agios Pavlos, look for the turnoff to Kato Saktouria on the Rethymno–Agia Galini road and follow the winding road down to the sea.

Agia Galini Αγια Γαλήνη

POP 860

An erstwhile picturesque fishing village, Agia Galini (a-ya ga-*lee*-nee) has had much of its original charm trampled out of it by package tourism and overdevelopment. With scores of ageing hotels and apartment buildings clinging to a steep hillside and hemmed in by cliffs and a busy harbour, it has a bit of a retro-resort look but can feel claustrophobic, especially in high season.

While it doesn't see the crowds of northern resorts, Agia Galini attracts mostly a middle-aged crowd, families, bus loads of package holidaymakers and long-term expat residents. In the shoulder seasons, it is a convenient base for visits to Phaestos, Agia Triada and the remote beaches of Agios Pavlos and Triopetra. The town all but shuts down in winter.

The centre is built along a main road that plunges down to the little harbour where it terminates in a huge car park overlooked by statues of Daedalus and Icarus. From here, two pedestrianised lanes climb back uphill. Souvenir stores and travel agencies line the first one on the left, which is therefore nicknamed Shopping St. Paralleling it is Food St which, you guessed it, is chock-a-block with tavernas. The beach is about 1km east of the town, along the main road.

Activities

Elizabeth Boat   FISHING
(6936848445; tour incl lunch €30) Cruise the Libyan Sea on this little boat. Tour local caves and coves, try your luck at prime fishing sites, and then stop at a remote beach for a barbecue lunch. Trips depart the harbour at 10.30am and return around 3.30pm.

Acrogiali   WATER SPORTS
(6946905781) The owner of the Acrogiali taverna on the main beach also organises water sports like paragliding, wake boarding and windsurfing. There's a banana boat, too.

Tours

Argonaftis   BOAT TOUR
(28320 91346) From late May to September, the owner of the Faros taverna runs daily cruises to Preveli Beach (€25) and the deserted offshore island of Paximadia (€30, including small lunch). Departures depend on weather conditions. For enquiries, stop by the taverna the night before or go to the port at around 10am.

Sactoris Cruises   BOAT TOUR
(6976693729; boat trip €20; 9.30-10.30am & 6-10pm) This modern, well-equipped motorboat will take you to Preveli Beach for a four-hour play on the beach. To book, visit the stand at the harbour during opening hours.

Sleeping

There's no shortage of places to stay in Agia Galini, but a large percentage of the accommodation is bland and prebooked by tour operators in peak season.

Camping No Problem   CAMPGROUND €
(28320 91386; camp site per person/tent/car/caravan €6/4/2/4; year-round; P🛜🏊) With a bright, blue pool and shady spots to pitch a tent, this well-maintained campground is about 100m from the beach and a 10-minute walk from the town centre. There's also a pleasant garden, an excellent taverna and a small supermarket.

Palazzo Greco   BOUTIQUE HOTEL €€
(28320 91187; www.palazzogreco.com; d €85-110; P❄🛜🏊) A passion for design is reflected in the stylish details at this gem overlooking the sea. Match your mood to the wall colours – greens, blues and purples – in peaceful, modern rooms with view-filled decks, flat-screen TVs, fridges and fabulous showers. Breakfast on the beautiful patio above the pool. At the top of town, it's halfway between the beach and the harbour.

Irini Mare   RESORT €€
(28320 91488; www.irinimare.com; d/f incl breakfast with sea view €110/150; May-Oct; ❄@🛜🏊♿) Great for families, this beautifully landscaped low-key resort sits a short walk from the main beach and has 98 bright, modern rooms, most with sea views and terraces, in different configurations. Diversions include a gym, sauna and tennis court, while kids can romp in their own pool or clamber around the playground. Wi-fi is available in common areas only.

Glaros Hotel   HOTEL €€
(28320 91151; www.glaros-agiagalini.com; s €60-75, d €80-100; ❄🛜🏊) These well-maintained rooms have a modern edge in a town full of

ho-hum hotels. Some have balconies overlooking the pool and there's a stylish common area and breakfast room. Excellent, friendly service seals the deal. It's at the back of town, straight up from the harbour.

✕ Eating

Platia
CAFE €

(⊙ 8am-2pm & 6pm-1am; 🛜) Set in a square just up from the harbour, this cafe-cum-bistro-cum-bar is popular with locals. Excellent breakfasts (€6 to €10) offer everything from yoghurt and museli to ham and eggs, while dinner sees spaghetti with leeks and goat's cheese or king prawn salad. When the sun goes down, the long list of cocktails come out.

Taverna at Camping No Problem
GREEK €€

(pizza & pasta €4-8, mains €7-13; ⊙ 9am-midnight Apr-Oct; 🛜) Giorgos and Yiannis' tree-shaded and flower-filled patio is a peaceful setting for both classic and creative local fare, including spit-roasted lamb and pork fillet with honey and walnuts. In summer, there's live Cretan music on Friday. It's about 750m from town to the eponymous campground. Bring a swimsuit to cool off in the big pool.

Faros
SEAFOOD €€

(☑ 28320 91346; Shopping St; mains €7-13, fish per kg €30-55; ⊙ lunch & dinner) This no-frills family-run fish taverna is usually packed to the gills, and for good reason: the owner himself drops his nets into the Med, so you know what's on the plate that night was still swimming in the sea in the morning. Squid cooked in their own ink, lobster spaghetti and fish soup are specialities.

Onar
GREEK €€

(Food St; mains €7-16; ⊙ lunch & dinner; 🛜🍴) Even after many years in business, Onar still hasn't lost its grip on the crowd. There are plenty of other tavernas with romantic views over the port, but Onar's tasty mezedhes and finger-lickin' grills make it a standout option. There's a kids menu too.

🍷 Drinking & Nightlife

The harbour is none too shy of a party, with countless bars booming out the beat. Most are indistinguishable. Follow the crowd.

Blue Bar
BAR

(Shopping St) This been-there-forever pub has a reputation for playing the best music in town. Owner Heinz himself is a singer-songwriter with eclectic sound tastes, which is why turntables get a workout with everything from R&B to rock and soul to pop.

❶ Information

Buses stop near the port, right in the commercial heart of Agia Galini. The post office is just past the bus stop and ATMs are nearby. Most cafes and restaurants offer free wi-fi. For information try www.gogalini.com and www.agia-galini.com.

❶ Getting There & Away

In high season there are up to six buses daily to Iraklio (€8, two hours), up to five to Rethymno (€6.20, 1½ hours) and to Phaestos (€2.10, 30 minutes), and two to Matala (€3.30, 45 minutes), in Iraklio.

Galini Express (www.galiniexpress.com) has direct buses to the airport in Iraklio (€20) and Hania (€25).

❶ Getting Around

Galini Express runs regular buses to Matala Beach (€6). A number of car-rental agencies are located just behind the harbour. For a taxi, call ☑ 6936906217 or 6942989520.

Auto Galini (☑ 28320 91241; www.autogalini.com; ⊙ 9am-2pm & 5-8pm) For car and 4WD rentals.

Ostria (☑ 28320 91555; www.ostria-agiagalini.com; ⊙ 9am-2pm & 5-8pm) Rents small cars for booting around, as well as convertible 4WDs.

NORTHEASTERN COAST

Once you clear the resort strip, the coastline east of Rethymno is indented and pockmarked with watery caves and isolated coves that are accessible only by boat. The chief resorts along the northern coast are Bali and Panormo, both good bases for exploring the villages in the Mt Psiloritis foothills, such as Axos and Anogia.

Panormo
Πάνορμο
POP 880

Panormo, about 22km east of Rethymno, is one of the few relatively unspoilt beach towns on the northern coast. Despite a couple of big hotel complexes, it retains an unhurried, authentic village feel and makes for a quieter alternative to the overcrowded scene immediately east of Rethymno and at nearby Bali. In summer, concerts and other events are held in a carob mill turned cultural centre.

In Panormo, cats are king. You'll see a number of wooden snack huts around town, built just for them by local expats.

Sights & Activities

Church of Agios Yiorgos CHURCH
Ecclesiastic art fans should stop in town at Panormo's parish church, which has some stunning modern frescoes.

Basilica of Aghia Sophia ANCIENT SITE
Coins unearthed in Panormo indicate that a village flourished here between the 1st and 9th centuries AD, but the only in situ evidence from this period are the crumbling bits and pieces of this 6th-century church. It's built on the slopes above the village but gated off. Look for signs directing you to the site.

Rodialos COOKING COURSE
(☎28340 51310; www.rodialos.gr) Regularly hosts one- to seven-day cooking classes in a stunning villa. Learn first-hand the principles of Cretan cooking and take the recipes away with you. Workshops cost €50 per day and include sharing a meal of what you've created. Stays at the villa cost €30. Rodialos also hosts an annual yoga retreat and Greek language course. Check the website for details.

Atlantis Diving Center DIVING
(☎28310 71640; www.atlantis-creta.com; 2 dives incl gear €100, snorkelling gear per day €15; ⏲9am-2pm & 5-8pm) Based at the Grecotel Club Marine Palace, this five-star PADI outfit offers both shore and boat dives as well as the gamut of courses from beginner to instructor level. Snorkellers can accompany the dive boat if there's room (€22).

Tours

Tourist Train TRAIN
(⏲2.30-11pm in town, 9.30am-2.15pm to Margarites & Melidoni, May-Sep) In summer, a cute little train chugs around Panormo (adult/child €4/2) and out to the pottery village of Margarites and the Melidoni Cave (adult/child €15/7.50). You'll find it on the eastern side of town, across from the Carob Factory.

Aitidis Travel TOUR
(☎28340 52040; www.aitidistravel.com; ⏲9am-2pm & 5-8pm) Offers a whole gamut of tours including excursions to Samaria Gorge, out to the island of Gramvousa and to Preveli Beach.

Sleeping

Captain's House APARTMENT €
(☎28103 80833; www.captainshouse.gr; apt €40-60; ⏲Apr-Oct; ❄📶) Above the port, these big apartments have a touch of character. They're all different, both in size and appearance, but comfortable and with sea breezes.

Christina APARTMENT €
(☎28340 51277; www.apartments-christina.gr; studio €50, apt from €60; ⏲Apr-Oct; ❄📶) Meticulously kept and efficiently run, rooms here are a little dated but spotless. All have a seafront balcony or terrace but the studios are snug. Unexpected bonus: the enclosed hydromassage showers.

★**Idili** APARTMENT €€
(☎28340 20240, 6972405863; www.idili.gr; apt €60-75; P❄📶) If cookie-cutter rooms don't do it for you, you'll love the three traditionally furnished apartments in this protected stone house, which has seen incarnations as a courthouse, a carpenter's workshop and a residence. Arches, wooden ceilings and sleeping lofts endow each unit with charm and uniqueness, while the fireplace and verandah are welcome unwinding stations. The flowering garden offers a shady retreat.

Dalabelos Estate RESORT €€
(☎28340 22155; www.dalabelos.gr; d/apt from €70/90; ❄📶) Hemmed in by grapes, olives and herbs, these 10 traditional-style houses have a view over the rolling hills to the sea. Modern rooms have stone fireplaces, private terraces and beautiful bathrooms. Seasonal activities include olive harvesting and *raki* distilling, as well as hands-on Cretan cooking classes. It's about 15 minutes west and inland from Panormo. You'll definitely need your own transport.

In the high season, there's a minimum three-night stay, but who would want to leave?

Kastro APARTMENT €€
(☎28340 51362, 6937097757; www.kastro.com; studio/apt €75/85; ❄📶) Back from the seafront on the road out of town, these rooms are older but have some nice touches like four-poster beds. Apartments sleep four and have private entrances, while studios have views.

Eating

The touristy harbour tavernas serve standard Greek and international dishes as well as fish. More traditional places can be found a block or two inland.

★**To Steki tou Sifaka** CRETAN €
(mains €5-10; ⏲lunch & dinner) Also known as George & Georgia's, this couple serve up satisfying homestyle Cretan food. Scrumptious

oven-roasted dishes, including a great selection of vegie options, keep this cheerful little place hopping. Find it between the waterfront and the main road, near the post office.

Kharas To Kafeneio
CAFE €

(snacks €3-5; ⊙9am-9pm) Near the post office, friendly Kharas gives you a glimpse into local life. This is where locals come to drink coffee, eat snacks and play cards. Tables spill into the big windowed room across the street.

Porto Parasiris
CRETAN €

(mains €5-10; ⊙breakfast, lunch & dinner) This upbeat, colourful harbourside patio is a great place to relax. Meals have a creative streak – try pork with dried fruit or chicken with lavender. The salmon risotto and homemade pasta are sure hits.

Taverna Kastro
CRETAN €€

(mains €7-12; ⊙dinner May-Oct; 🕾) The flower-festooned terrace is a great place to sit, but it's what's on the plates that will truly wow you. Classic Cretan recipes get a modern makeover here, which translates into such palate teasers as lentils with *apaki* (cured pork), hake with potatoes, or rabbit in oregano. It's on the eastern side of town, back from the seafront.

Angira
SEAFOOD €€

(mains €6-12; ⊙lunch & dinner) Right at the harbour, seafood doesn't get any fresher. Choose from marinated anchovies, shrimp salad or grilled fish, along with the usual suspects.

ℹ Information

The bus stop is on the main road outside of town. The post office and an ATM are right in town. For car rentals, try **Rent-A-Car** (www.bestcars-rental. gr; ⊙9am-2pm & 5-8pm), across from the Carob Factory. Further information can be found at www.panormo.gr.

ℹ Getting There & Away

In high season, hourly buses go from Rethymno to Panormo (€2.20, 25 minutes). Buses stop on the main road just outside of town.

Bali
Μπαλί

POP 330

Bali, 38km east of Rethymno and 51km west of Iraklio, has one of the most stunning settings on the northern coast, with a series of little coves strung along the indented shore, marked by hills, promontories and narrow, sandy beaches. But helter-skelter development has significantly marred the natural beauty, and the former fishing hamlet has all but disappeared under the weight of package tourism. Beaches can get crammed with sun-worshippers in summer. In low season, though, it's a fun place to come and enjoy the dramatic scenery and take advantage of lodging bargains.

The name Bali has nothing to do with its Indonesian namesake; it means 'honey' in Turkish, as excellent honey was once collected and processed here. In antiquity Bali was known as Astali, but no traces of ancient Astali now remain.

◯ Sights & Activities

Bali is rather spread out and it's a long and undulating walk from one end to the other – 25 minutes or more. The town has four grey-sand beaches, all of them rather kid-friendly.

Livadi
BEACH

Livadi is the biggest and widest beach, with a party vibe. It's packed with chairs and umbrellas and backed along its entire length by bars, tavernas and cafes.

Varkotopo
BEACH

Next after Livadi beach is Varkotopo, a tiny, narrow strip of sand flanked by young palm trees. There are a couple of quite classy bars here that are nice for sunset cocktails.

Limani
BEACH

Further north of Varkotopo beach is the old port of Limani, a rather narrow crescent but with easy access to water sports and dining options.

Karavostasi
BEACH

Karavostasi, the last of the Bali beaches, is also the smallest and quietest, with just a couple of tavernas curled up beneath the rocky cliffs. A coastal footpath leads here from the port and the Bali Express tourist train goes out here as well.

Lefteris
WATER SPORTS

(📞6937200333; cat_cruises@yahoo.gr; Limani; ⊙9am-6pm) At the port, Lefteris hires canoes (per hour €8), motorboats (per hour €35), jet skis (€50 for 20 minutes) and pedal boats (€12). Hop on a three-hour catamaran trip (€30) for swimming, snorkelling and fishing, or take a 1½-hour cruise to check out some local caves (€15).

Hippocampos Dive Centre
DIVING

(📞28340 94193; www.hippocampos.com; Limani; 1 dive incl gear €50, snorkelling gear per day €15; ⊙9am-1pm & 5-9pm, closed Mon Apr-Jun,

Sep & Oct, closed Sun Jul & Aug) This well-run outfit does shore and boat dives as well as the gamut of courses, including one-week open-water certifications (€410). In high season, it's best to reserve two or three days ahead. It's at the port.

☞ Tours

Bali Travel TOUR
(www.balitravel.gr; Livadi; ☺9am-2pm & 5-9pm) Whether you're yearning to visit Preveli (€30), Hania (€40), Knossos (€30) or the Samaria Gorge (€45), Bali Travel has a tour for you. It also runs overnight trips to Santorini.

Mellisi Travel TOUR
(☑28340 94500; www.mellisitravel.com; Varkotopo; ☺9am-2pm & 5-9pm) These guys organise day excursions to well-known beaches and sites across the region, throwing some more off-the-beaten-track stops in to offer a genuine glimpse into local life.

🛏 Sleeping

★Petrino Horio RESORT €
(☑28340 94125; Vlihada; d incl breakfast €45-65; ☺year-round; ❄@☎≋) In the quiet hills above Bali, the traditional rooms at 'Stone Village' feel like your own small Cretan house. The village features 37 carefully crafted apartments with terraces or balconies, kitchens and fireplaces set amid flowering trees and potted plants. It's 600m from the beach and close to the Bali Express tourist train stop. Three pools, a petting zoo, a sauna and seasonal hands-on activities, such as grape crushing and cheesemaking, provide distractions. There's a good restaurant and friendly service.

Lisa Mari HOTEL €
(☑28340 94072; lizamary.hotel@hotmail.gr; Livadi; s/d/tr incl breakfast €50/60/70; P❄☎≋🍴) This hotel offers excellent value for money. There's a whole gamut of rooms and, while many are filled with package travellers, they are all clean, comfortable, have modern furnishings and you can request one with a sea view. The real bonus is the lovely, private pool with a bar and garden. The staff is ultra-friendly and the restaurant is bright and satisfying.

Sunrise Apartments APARTMENT €€
(☑28340 94267; Karavostasi; d/apt €60/80; ❄) Right on Karavostasi beach, these spacious, well-kept studios with kitchenettes are great value-for-money and perfect for escaping the frenzy of Bali while still staying right on the beach. The patios overlooking the sandy cove are perfect for sunset drinks. This place is very popular so book ahead.

Bali Blue Bay HOTEL €€
(☑28340 20111; www.baliblue bay.gr; Limani; d incl breakfast €75; ❄☎≋) Modern and comfortable, but not fancy, rooms here are spacious and have great sea views. Common areas are welcoming and open to the sea and the service is top-notch.

🍴 Eating

★Taverna Karavostasi GREEK €
(Karavostasi; specials €5-10; ☺lunch & dinner May-Sep) With vegies straight from their garden and local wine from the barrel, this taverna on pint-sized Karavostasi beach offers local dishes that are bursting with flavour. The speciality is stuffed aubergines (eggplants) or try the lentil soup and baked chicken with lemon. There's an awesome view, a kids menu and friendly service.

Taverna Nest CRETAN €
(mains €4-14; ☺lunch & dinner May-Oct) For honest-to-goodness, farm-to-table fare, report to this vine-covered terrace where home-cooked meals are served in ample portions and with big smiles. Regulars crave the barbecue and the grilled fish, nicely paired with the homemade dolmadhes and hand-cut fried potatoes. It's a few steps inland from the port. Satisfying breakfasts, too.

Bonsai CAFE €
(Limani Beach; meals €3-5; ☺9am-late) Next to Limani beach, this is a great spot for breakfast or lunch with crêpes, sandwiches, burgers and wraps. At night it morphs into a bar with a long cocktail list.

❶ Information

There's an ATM and **internet cafe** (per hr €2; ☺9am-11pm) in town, behind Limani beach.

❶ Getting There & Around

Buses on their Rethymno–Iraklio run (€7.60) drop you at the main road, from where it is a 2km walk to the port of Bali (€6.30).

A good way to get around is by the **Bali Express** (one-way/return €3/5; ☺9am-11pm May-Sep), a tourist train that makes 11 stops in town and at the beaches.

Auto Bali (☑28340 94504; www.autobali. com; Varkotopo; ☺9am-2pm & 5-9pm) rents cars that they will bring to you at the airport. You can also hire cars through the tour agencies.

STEVE OUTRAM / GETTY IMAGES ©

Best of Crete

The brilliant azure seas, rugged mountains marching inland, crumbling ancient ruins, and traditional hilltop villages of Crete invite a visitor into the fold. Explore life on this gorgeous, independent-minded island in the middle of the Mediterranean, through the millennia and today, from beach to trail.

Contents

➡ **Witnesses to History**
➡ **Life's a Beach**
➡ **Hitting the Trail**

Above: Loutro (p79)

138

MARKUS LANGE / GETTY IMAGES ©

1. Minoan container, Palace of Malia (p185) 2. Odeion (p171), Gortyna
3. Koules Venetian Fortress (p150), Iraklio 4. Moni Toplou (p209)

Witnesses to History

At the crossroads of three continents, Crete's turbulent history has been shaped by many players. Hear the whispers of the past as you visit grand Minoan palaces, remnants of a Roman city, showcases of Venetian architecture, and monasteries with military pedigrees. If only stones could talk...

Magic Malia

Smaller than Knossos, and without the reconstructions and embellishments, the Palace of Malia (p185) is Crete's most accessible and easily understood Minoan site. Its sophisticated layout and infrastructure attest to this ancient society's advanced level of civilisation. Excavations are still ongoing.

Glorious Gortyna

Get lost amid the moody ruins of Roman Crete's capital, stop to admire what's left of a beautiful early Christian church and marvel at 2600-year-old stone tablets engraved with a surprisingly modern legal code.

Fortified Monastery

Despite its fortifications, 15th-century Moni Toplou (p209) was sacked by pirates, looted by the Knights of Malta and finally captured by Turks in 1821. Its church shelters a precious icon by Ioannis Kornaros.

Mighty Fortresses

The most impressive vestiges of Venetian rule are the many stalwart fortresses built to keep pirates and Turks at bay. Visit those in Hania, Rethymno, Iraklio and Frangokastello.

Monastery Seige

The hauntingly beautiful Moni Arkadiou (p119) is a window into the Cretan soul. During the revolt of 1866, local Cretans trapped within opted to blow up their gunpowder supplies rather than surrender to the Turks, killing nearly everyone, Turks included.

BANET12 / GETTY IMAGES ©

. Triopetra (p131) **2.** Matala (p174) **3.** Falasarna (p97)

Life's a Beach

Crete has been blessed with many off-the-chart splendours, including bewitching beaches lapped by clear waters shimmering in myriad shades of turquoise. From bar-backed busy strips to romantic palm-fringed strands and footprint-free crescents where solitude reigns, there's a beach with your name on it.

Secluded Splendour

Escaping the crowds means pointing the compass to Agios Pavlos and Triopetra, two hauntingly beautiful and tranquil beaches tucked into the jagged southern coastline of Rethymno. At nearby Preveli you can seek shade beneath a grove of swaying palm trees.

Caribbean Crete

If you like nothing better than wriggling your toes in white shimmering sand and splashing in turquoise waters, make a beeline to beautiful Balos beach (p99) on the untamed Gramvousa Peninsula.

Wave Action

Find your favourite among the tiara of coves separated by rocky spits on Falasarna beach (p97). Work on your tan while relaxing in the pinkish sand, then cool off by jumping headlong into the high, long waves rolling in from the open sea.

Triple Treats

Each of Iraklio's southern beaches has its own personality. Matala is a lovely but busy crescent, while Kommos beckons with its long, undeveloped strand and Agiofarango is so remote that it can only be reached by boat or on foot.

Tropical Paradise

A sweeping crescent of powdery pink-white sand, Elafonisi (p88) is one of Crete's most stunning beaches. Only a shallow lagoon with dazzlingly clear azure waters separates it from a little islet where dunes rise above secluded coves.

Zakros Gorge (p213)

Hitting the Trail

Like a fine wine, Crete's landscape wants to be sipped, not downed in one big gulp. So get out of the car and onto the trail for a slow-mo close-up at gorges chiselled by time and the elements, a mountain where Zeus was born and a valley haunted by the ghosts of the Minoans.

Samaria's Little Sister

Samaria may hog the spotlight, but the Imbros Gorge (p75) is no slouch in the beauty department either. Easier, shorter and quieter, it's tailor-made for families with kids. Cypress, oak, fig and almond trees accompany you on your journey.

Lovely Loutro

The secluded natural harbour of Loutro (p79) is the southern terminus of a tangle of trails accessing the spectacular and blissfully tranquil Aradena Gorge, as well as little-visited beaches otherwise only reachable by boat.

Epic Meander

Hats off to those who've walked the entire 10,000-plus kilometres of the E4 European long-distance path. But even tackling just a short stretch in Crete (p34), where it culminates on the pebbly shore of Kato Zakros, has its rewards.

Ghost Canyon

A hike through the dramatic Valley of the Dead (p213), also known as Zakros Gorge, takes you past towering walls pockmarked with caves used by Minoans as burial sites and spills out at the cute beach town of Kato Zakros.

Crete's Rooftop

Grand Mt Psiloritis (p124) serenades a green quilt of valleys and villages from high above, and often wears a monk's tonsure of snow well into spring. Climbing Crete's tallest mountain is no walk in the park, but it doesn't require technical skills either.

Iraklio

Best Places to Eat

➡ Elia & Diosmos (p166)

➡ Kritamon (p164)

➡ Pizza Ariadni (p179)

➡ Peskesi (p153)

➡ Vegera (p168)

Best Places to Stay

➡ Eleonas Cottages (p168)

➡ Villa Kerasia (p166)

➡ Villa Ippocampi (p184)

➡ Thalori Guest House (p181)

➡ Pension Kofinas (p181)

Why Go?

Iraklio (Ηράκλειο) is Crete's most dynamic region, home to almost half the island's population and its top-rated tourist site, the Minoan Palace of Knossos. Priceless treasures unearthed here, and at the many other Minoan sites around Crete, have catapulted the archaeological museum in the capital city of Iraklio onto the world stage.

Admittedly, the coastal stretch east of Iraklio is one continuous band of hotels and resorts. But a few kilometres inland, villages sweetly lost in time provide a pleasing contrast. Taste the increasingly sophisticated tipple produced in the Iraklio Wine Country, walk in the footsteps of painter El Greco and writer Nikos Kazantzakis, and revel in the rustic grandeur of remote mountain villages such as Zaros.

On the quieter southern coast, the ex-hippie hang-out of Matala is the only developed resort, while in the charming villages the laid-back life unfolds much the way it has since time immemorial.

Road Distances (km)

	Iraklio	Malia	Matala	Peza
Malia	37			
Matala	69	106		
Peza	17	48	70	
Phaestos	57	90	10	61

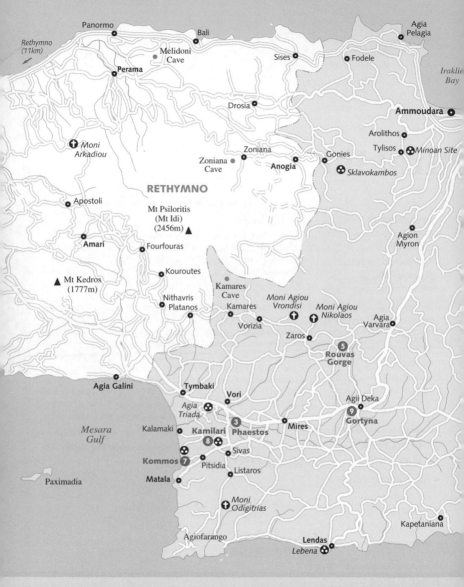

Iraklio Highlights

1 Stand in awe of Minoan artistry at the **Heraklion Archaeological Museum** (p146).

2 Sample the tasty local tipple in the **Iraklio Wine Country** (p165).

3 Get high on knockout views from **Phaestos** (p172).

4 Make a date with King Minos at the **Palace of Knossos** (p157).

5 Marvel at nature's creativity while hiking the **Rouvas Gorge** (p168).

Dia

Sea of Crete

Iraklio ①

Gournes (Cretaquarium)
Kato Gouves

Hersonisos

Skotino Cave ◎ Gouves

Koutouloufari

Stalida

Palace of Malia

Sisi

Milatos

Knossos ④

Skalani

Anopoli

Malia

Agios Nikolaos (14km); Ierapetra (49km)

Anemospilia

Fournis

⑥ Myrtia

Avdou

Arhanes ② Peza

Iraklio Wine Country

Vathypetro

Agies Paraskies

Kastelli

Tzermiado

LASITHI

Profitis Ilias

Livada Lake

Houdetsi

Thrapsano

Psyhro

Dikteon Cave

Agios Georgios

IRAKLIO

Arkalohori

Mt Dikti (2143m)

Vorias

Ano Viannos

Pyrgos

Kastri

Keratokambos

Mt Kofinas (1231m)

Libyan Sea

⑥ Get an insight into the genius of Cretan-born author Nikos Kazantzakis in **Myrtia** (p166).

⑦ Cool off in the clear waters of **Kommos** (p176) in the shadows of Minoan ruins.

⑧ Walk among the olive groves to a Tholos tomb in **Kamilari** (p178).

⑨ Get up to speed on Roman Crete at **Gortyna** (p162).

IRAKLIO ΗΡΑΚΛΕΙΟ

POP 140,730

The birthplace of El Greco and Nikos Kazantzakis, Iraklio (also called Heraklion) is perhaps Crete's most underrated destination. Sure, if you arrive with a tranquil Greek holiday in mind, Greece's bustling fifth-largest city can initially be an assault on the senses. But although it's not pretty in a conventional way, Iraklio can grow on you if you take the time to wander its backstreets and explore its nuances.

In recent times, the city has undergone a period of intense urban renewal and is riding high on energy if not money. The waterfront invites strolling and the attractive pedestrianised historic centre is punctuated with bustling squares framed by buildings from the time when Columbus set sail.

Iraklio has a certain urban sophistication, with a thriving cafe and restaurant scene, the island's best shopping and lively nightlife, in part thanks to its many students. Plus there are blockbuster sights such as the amazing archaeological museum and the Palace of Knossos.

History

Settled since neolithic times, Iraklio was conquered by the Saracens in AD 824 and reputedly evolved into the slave-trade capital of the eastern Mediterranean and the launching pad for the region's notorious pirates. Byzantine troops ousted the Arabs after a long siege in 961 and the city became known as Handakas. This was changed to Candia in 1204 when Crete was sold to the Venetians.

Under the Venetians, the city became a centre for the arts and home to painters such as Damaskinos and El Greco. The magnificent fortress and many of the great public buildings and lofty churches date to this period. The Candians fought tooth and nail to keep the Ottomans at bay, even extending the fortress walls. But the Turks overran Crete in 1645, and began besieging Candia in 1648.

Under the Turks the city became known as Megalo Kastro (Big Castle). Artistic life withered and many Cretans fled or were killed. In August 1898, a Turkish mob massacred hundreds of Cretans, 17 British soldiers and the British Consul. Within weeks, a squadron of British ships steamed into Iraklio's harbour and ended Turkish rule.

Iraklio got its current name in 1922. At the time Hania was the capital of independent Crete, but Iraklio's central location soon saw it emerge as the island's commercial centre. The city suffered badly in WWII, when bombs levelled much of the old Venetian and Turkish town. It resumed its position as Crete's capital in 1971.

◎ Sights

Iraklio's main sights are wedged within the historic town, hemmed in by the waterfront and the old city walls. Many of the finest buildings line up along the main thoroughfare, 25 Avgoustou, which skirts the lovely central square, Plateia Venizelou (also called Lion Square after its landmark Morosini Fountain). East of here, Koraï is the hub of Iraklio's cafe scene, which leads towards the sprawling Plateia Eleftherias and the archaeological museum nearby.

★ Heraklion Archaeological Museum MUSEUM

(http://odysseus.culture.gr; Xanthoudidou 2; adult/child €6/free, incl Knossos €10; ⊙ 8am-8pm Apr-Oct, 11am-5pm Mon, 8am-3pm Tue-Sun Nov-Mar) Reopened in 2014 after a long renovation, the Archaeological Museum of Heraklion is Crete's outstanding jewel. The two floors of the restored 1930s Bauhaus building make a gleaming showcase for the exhibits that span 5500 years, from neolithic to Roman times, and an extensive Minoan collection. The rooms are colour coded, and artefacts are displayed both chronologically and thematically and are beautifully presented with descriptions in English. A visit here enhances any understanding of Crete's rich history. Don't skip it.

The museum's treasure trove includes pottery, jewellery, sarcophagi, plus famous frescoes from the sites of Knossos, Tylissos, Amnissos and Agia Triada. The pieces are grouped into comprehensive themes such as settlements, trade, death, religion and administration. Along with clear descriptions, these bring to life both the day-to-day functioning and long-term progression of the societies.

➡ Ground Floor

Rooms I–III focus on the neolithic period to the middle Bronze Age (7000 BC to 1700 BC), showing life in the first settlements in Crete and around Knossos. Don't miss the golden pendant with bees from Malia, a sophisticated jeweller's masterpiece, and

THREE PERFECT DAYS

Day One

Kick off early and make a beeline for **Knossos** (p157) to get a head start on the tour-bus crowd. Explore the site's main features in relative peace, then move on to the less popular corners when it gets busy. Enjoy a gourmet Cretan lunch at **Elia & Diosmos** (p166), in Skalani on the edge of the Iraklio Wine Country, followed by paying your respects to Crete's most revered 20th-century writer, Nikos Kazantzakis, in **Myrtia** (p166). Swing by **Arhanes** (p163), visiting the town's Minoan sites if you have time, before returning to Iraklio for a gourmet dinner at **Peskesi** (p153).

Day Two

Allow an entire morning at the **Heraklion Archaeological Museum** (p146) to get your mind and body around the Minoan civilisation (and view the extraordinary findings from Knossos). Grab lunch on the run and head to the **wine country** (p165) around Dafnes and Siva for an afternoon of tastings. If you prefer kid-focused fun, an alternative to wine tasting is to head to the **Cretaquarium** (p182) or the neighbouring **Dinosauria** (p182) in Gournes, or fossick in **Skotino Cave** (p183), a spooky underground world.

Day Three

Today you're off to a site inspection of the **Palace of Phaestos** (p172) and nearby **Agia Triada** (p173). Head south to grab lunch on the way at **Kafeneio Ksa Sou** (p180). After lunch, head straight to **Agiofarango Gorge** (p180) for the short hike to a lovely, secluded beach with crystal-clear water. For dinner find your favourite among the tavernas in **Kamilari** (p178).

IRAKLIO IRAKLIO

the extensive jewellery collection. The elaborately embellished set of **Kamares tableware** is possibly a royal dinner service.

Rooms IV, V and **VI** illustrate life in the Late Bronze period (1700 BC to 1450 BC). This is when Minoan culture reached its zenith, as reflected in the foundation of new palaces, elaborate architecture and prolific trading practices. Not surprisingly, these are among the most visited rooms and the collection is vast. Highlights include the **small clay house from Arhanes** and a stunning **ivory-and-crystal inlaid draughts board**. Most hone in on the **Phaistos disc**, a stunning clay piece embossed with 45 signs which has never been deciphered. Nearby, the massive **copper ingots** from Agia Triada and Zakros Palace, demonstrate important units of economic exchange. Other gems include the **bull-leaping fresco** and incredible **bull-leaper sculpture** (Room VI) that show daring sporting practices of the time.

Rooms VII and **VIII** reveal the importance of Minoan religion and ideology with cult objects and figurines. Room VII houses the **Chieftain's cup** from Agia Triada that portrays two men, one holding a staff, the other a sword. Don't miss the so-called **ring of King Minos**, a signet ring

rediscovered and handed to authorities in 2001. The **snake goddesses** and **stone bull's head** (inlaid with seashell and crystal) are two stunning ceremonial items from Knossos.

Room IX and **X** are dedicated to the palace of Knossos and its emergence as a centralised state (after the administrative collapse of other palaces) along with evidence of the Mycenaens. **Linear B clay tablets** reveal the first 'Greek' script and indicate Knossos' complex administrative system and bureaucratic processes. In Room X, look for the extraordinary **boar's helmet** and **gold-handled swords**, displaying the importance of the aristocratic warrior status.

Rooms XI and **XII** highlight settlements, sanctuaries and graves of the Late Bronze Age, including fascinating visual representations of death. The extraordinary sarcophagus from **Agia Triada** (Room XXII) is presumed to be that of a ruler, given its detailed, honorific scenes.

➡ **1st Floor**

Room XIII showcases Minoan frescoes (1800 BC to 1350 BC) including Evans' famous (or infamous) recreations. The paintings reflects the interest in art and nature at

Iraklio

the time. All are highlights, but for your at-a-glance reference, it's home to **The Prince of the Lilies**, the **Ladies in Blue**, and the **bull head**.

Rooms XV–XIX focus on the Geometric and Archaic periods (10th to 6th century BC), the transition to the Iron Age and formation of the first Greek cities. The **Apollonian Triad**, bronze statues from Deros, are the earliest known Greek hammered bronze statues and the **bronze shields of the Idaean Cave** are extravagant votive offerings.

Rooms XX–XXII We move to the Classical, Hellenistic and Roman periods (5th to 4th century BC) where utensils and figurines and stunning mosaic floors and amphorae set the scene for the foundation of the autonomous Greek city-states, followed by civil wars and, finally, the Roman period. The huge **Phalagari hoard of silver coins** (Room XXI) is thought to be a military state fund. The cemetery finds of these periods are especially fascinating: look out for the skull with the gold wreath (Room XXII).

Room XXIII exhibits two private collections donated to the museum.

Rooms XXVI and **XXVII** (7th to 4th century BC) exhibit the role of Crete in the development of monumental sculpture, plus Roman sculptures and the obsession with rendering (and copying) statues of heroes and Gods of the preceding Classical era.

Note: at the time of research a multimedia and conference room (those missing numbers) were still being organised, as was a cloakroom and multimedia exhibition hall.

Historical Museum of Crete MUSEUM
(www.historical-museum.gr; Sofokli Venizelou 27; admission €5; ⊙9am-5pm Mon-Sat Apr-Oct, to 3.30pm Mon-Sat Nov-Mar) If you're wondering what Crete's been up to for the past, say, 1700 years, a spin around this highly engaging museum is in order. Exhibits hopscotch from the Byzantine to the Venetian and Turkish periods, culminating with WWII. There's excellent English labelling, multimedia and listening stations throughout. A small cafe offers post-browse drinks.

The undisputed highlights on the 1st floor are the only two El Greco paintings in Crete – *View of Mt Sinai and the Monastery of St Catherine* (1570) and the tiny *Baptism of Christ* (1569). Other rooms contain 13th- and 14th-century frescoes, exquisite Venetian

IRAKLIO IRAKLIO

Iraklio

gold jewellery and embroidered vestments. A historical exhibit charts Crete's road to independence from the Turks in the early 20th century.

The most interesting rooms are on the 2nd floor. Fans of Nikos Kazantzakis can admire the famed Cretan writer's recreated study from his home in Antibes, France, and watch snippets from *Zorba the Greek* and other films based on his books. Historically, the focus is on WWII, in particular the Battle of Crete. A state-of-the-art exhibit dramatically details the Cretan resistance, the role of Allied Secret Services, the destruction of Iraklio, the abduction of German General Kreipe and other wartime moments. A highlight is the original office of Cretan-born Emmanouil Tsouderos, who served as Greek prime minister from 1941 to 1944. It was donated by his family.

The top (3rd) floor features an outstanding folklore collection.

Koules Venetian Fortress   FORTRESS
(Venetian Harbour) Iraklio's main landmark is this squat and square 16th-century fortress, which was called Rocca al Mare under the Venetians. It helped keep the Turks out for

21 years and later became a Turkish prison for Cretan rebels. Three walls sport marble reliefs of Venice's symbol: the winged Lion of St Mark. It was closed for renovation at the time of research.

Natural History Museum   MUSEUM
(www.nhmc.uoc.gr; Sofokli Venizelou; adult/concession €8/5; ⊙9am-8pm Jun-Sep, 9am-2pm Mon-Fri & 10am-5pm Sat & Sun Oct-May) In an imaginatively recycled power station, and a 10-minute walk west from 25 Avgoustou along the waterfront, this museum uses huge dioramas and a terrarium wing to introduce you to the flora and fauna of Crete and the Mediterranean. Stars of the show include the life-size (5m by 7m) representation of the elephant-like *Deinotherium gigantum,* the world's third-largest land mamma, and the 3D Earthquake Simulator.

Morosini Fountain   FOUNTAIN
(Lion Fountain; Plateia Venizelou) On Plateia Venizelou, this is the most beloved among the Venetian vestiges around town. These days, unfortunately, water no longer spurts from the four lions into eight marble

troughs. The centrepiece marble statue of Poseidon was destroyed under the Turks.

Municipal Art Gallery — ART GALLERY
(Agios Markos Basilica, 25 Avgoustou; ⊘ 10am-1pm & 6pm-8.30pm Mon-Fri, to 1pm Sat) **FREE** The three-aisled 13th-century Agios Markos Basilica was reconstructed many times and turned into a mosque by the Turks. Today it holds temporary exhibitions of Greek and foreign artists. It's worth swinging by to check what's on.

Church of Agios Titos — CHURCH
(Plateia Agiou Titou; ⊘ 7.30am-1pm & 4.30-7.30pm) This majestic church dominates the eponymous square. It has Byzantine origins in AD 961, was converted to a Catholic church by the Venetians and turned into a mosque by the Ottomans, who also rebuilt it after the devastating 1856 earthquake. It has been an Orthodox church since 1925. Since 1966, it has once again sheltered the much-prized skull relic of St Titos, returned here after being spirited to Venice for safe-keeping during the Turkish occupation.

City Walls — FORTRESS
Iraklio burst out of its walls long ago, but these massive fortifications, with seven bastions and four gates, are still very conspicuous, dwarfing the concrete 20th-century structures around them. Venetians built the defences between 1462 and 1562. You can follow the walls around the heart of the city, though it's not a particularly scenic trip.

Bembo Fountain — FOUNTAIN
(Plateia Kornarou) The delightful fountain on Plateia Kornarou, at the southern end of Odos 1866, was cobbled together in the 1550s from antique materials, including a statue of a Roman official found near Ierapetra. The town's first fountain, it channelled fresh water to Iraklio via an aqueduct running 13km south to Mt Yiouhtas. The adjacent hexagonal building, now a quaint *kafeneio*, was originally a pump-house added by the Turks. The fountain was hidden for repairs at the time of research.

Loggia — HISTORIC BUILDING
(25 Avgoustou) Iraklio's town hall is housed in the attractively reconstructed 17th-century Loggia, a Venetian version of a gentleman's club, where the male aristocracy once gathered for drinks and gossip.

Grave of Nikos Kazantzakis — HISTORIC SITE
(Martinengo Bastion) Crete's most acclaimed 20th-century writer Nikos Kazantzakis (1883–1957) is buried south of the centre in the well-preserved Martinengo Bastion. The epitaph on his grave, 'I hope for nothing, I fear nothing, I am free', is taken from one of his works. To get there, pick up Moussourou at the south end of Odos 1821, follow it to the end and turn right on Plastira. The bastion will loom on your left.

Museum of Christian Art — MUSEUM
(St Catherine of Sinai; St Catherine's Sq; admission €4; ⊘ 9.30am-7pm Apr-Oct, to 1.30pm Nov-Mar) Housed in a 13th-century monastery and later a mosque, this tiny but fascinating museum features historic religious artworks from different monasteries around Crete. Star exhibits include the works by 15th-century icon hagiographer Angelos Akotantos and post-Byzantine painter Michael Damaskinos. Paintings, woodcraft, manuscripts and stone carvings are displayed in a clear manner with English descriptions. It's opposite Agios Minas.

Agios Minas Cathedral — CATHEDRAL
One of Greece's largest cathedrals, Agios Minas was constructed between 1862 and 1895. Agios Minas is the Patron Saint of Iraklio.

Beaches
Ammoudara, about 4km west of Iraklio, and **Amnisos**, 2km to the east, are the closest beaches; the latter is just past the airport and gets quite a bit of noise. The strands in Agia Pelagia, some 20km west of town, are nicer.

🏃 Activities

Cretan Adventures — OUTDOORS
(☏ 28103 32772; www.cretanadventures.gr; 3rd fl, Evans 10) 🖉 This well-regarded local company run by friendly and knowledgeable English-speaking Fondas organises hiking tours, mountain biking and extreme outdoor excursions. It also coordinates fabulous self-guided tours with detailed hiking instructions, plus accommodation with breakfast and luggage transfer (from €740 for one week). Fondas' office is up on the 3rd floor and easy to miss.

🛏 Sleeping

Hotel Mirabello — HOTEL €
(☏ 28102 85052; www.mirabello-hotel.gr; Theotokopoulou 20; d with/without bathroom from €60/45; ✵🐾) This friendly and relaxed hotel

is hardly of recent vintage but it's excellent value for money. Rooms are immaculate if a bit cramped and have TVs and phones. Some have a balcony, fridge and (joy of joys) coffee- and tea-making facilities. The street is mainly quiet, but the student social club next door is not, usually on Friday and Saturday evenings.

Rea Hotel   HOTEL €
(☎ 28102 23638; www.hotelrea.gr; Kalimeraki 1, cnr Hortatson; d with/without bathroom €45/35, tr €55; ❄ ☎) Renovated in 2014, the family-run Rea has an easy, friendly atmosphere. The 16 simple, neat-as-a-pin rooms are set over two floors. All have small TVs and balconies, but some bathrooms are shared. Family rooms are available. There's a book exchange and a communal fridge.

Lena Hotel   HOTEL €
(☎ 28102 23280; www.lena-hotel.gr; Lahana 10; s with/without bath €40/35, d with/without bath €50/40, tr €70; ❄ ☎) Everything's a bit long in the tooth but this no-nonsense hotel is still a good budget pick. Amenities in the 16 rooms vary and not all have their own bathrooms, but communal areas are nicely maintained. Staff is particularly friendly. Breakfast costs €8.

Kastro Hotel   HOTEL €€
(☎ 28102 84185; www.kastro-hotel.gr; Theotokopoulou 22; s/d/tr incl breakfast €55/85/110; ❄ @ ☎) The Kastro's nearly-but-not-quite-there *Home Beautiful*–style rooms feature more curves and shapes than a child's put-the-shape-in-the-cube toy. Plus funky wallpaper, marble desks and leather-padded-walls-cum-bedheads. Rooms come with flat-screen TVs, small fridges and balconies. Pleasant breakfast area and the staff is extremely helpful. A good-value choice.

Atrion Hotel   BUSINESS HOTEL €€
(☎ 28102 46000; www.atrion.gr; Chronaki 9; s/d/t/f incl breakfast from €70/95/120/135; ❄ ☎) This modern, streamlined 60-room business-style hotel has all the electronic gizmos and nondescript mainstream design you'd expect of a place that attracts business folk. Close to El Greco Park and the port, it's also conveniently located for the traveller. A reliable, if pricier, bet.

Capsis Astoria   HOTEL €€
(☎ 28103 43080; www.capsishotel.gr; Plateia Eleftherias 11; s €85-100, d €100-120, tr €115-140, all incl breakfast; P ❄ @ ☎ ☀) The hulking

exterior doesn't impress, but past the front door the Capsis is a class act, all the way to the rooftop pool from where you enjoy a delicious panorama of Iraklio. Rooms sport soothing neutral tones and dashing historic black-and-white photographs. Thirty of the 131 rooms are 'skylight' rooms meaning windows but no vistas. Fabulous breakfast buffet.

Lato Boutique Hotel   BOUTIQUE HOTEL €€
(☎ 28102 28103; www.lato.gr; Epimenidou 15; d incl breakfast €85-120; ❄ @ ☎ ⊞) Iraklio goes Hollywood – with all the sass but sans the attitude – at this mod boutique hotel overlooking the old harbour, recognisable by its jazzy facade. Rooms here are tight in size, but are styled with rich woods and warm reds and have pillow-top mattresses and a playful lighting scheme. A recently opened new section in a separate building is even more modern.

Marin Dream Hotel   HOTEL €€
(☎ 28103 00018; www.marinhotel.gr; Epimenidou 46; s/d incl breakfast from €65/75; ❄ @ ☎) Although the Marin Dream Hotel is primarily a business hotel, it also scores with leisure travellers thanks to its great location overlooking the harbour and the fortress (be sure to get a front room with balcony). The strangely lit corridors are like being in a spaceship, but the rooms are decked out in a more palatable chocolate and cherry, with plain no-nonsense furniture. Check online as prices fluctuate according to demand.

GDM Megaron   HOTEL €€€
(☎ 28103 05300; www.gdmmegaron.gr; Doukos Beaufort 9; s/d incl breakfast from €140/170; ❄ @ ☎ ☀) Don't be put off by the towering hulk of this harbour-front hotel, for inside awaits a top designer abode with comfortable rooms (all with different sizes and configurations), jacuzzis in the VIP suites, and flat-screen TVs. Unwinding in the glass-sided pool and drinking in the sweeping views from the rooftop restaurant and bar are hardly run-of-the-mill features either.

✗ Eating

Iraklio has restaurants to suit all tastes and budgets, from excellent fish tavernas to international cuisine and fine dining. Note that many restaurants close on Sunday. There's a supermarket on the north side of El Greco Park.

Loukoumades BAKERY €
(9 Odos 1821; 6 pieces €2.50; ☺ 5am-10pm Mon-Sat) Come here for delicious fluffy *loukoumadhes* (ball-shaped doughnuts drizzled with honey, sesame seeds and cinnamon).

Bitzarakis Bakery BAKERY €
(7 Odos 1821; snacks from €0.50) Sells excellent freshly baked *kalitsounia* (lightly fried filled pastries) along with other traditional sweets made by a women's cooperative.

Fyllo...Sofies CAFE €
(✎ 2810 284774; www.fillosofies.gr; Plateia Venizelou 33; snacks €3-7; ☺ 6am-late; 🛜) With tables sprawling out towards the Morosini Fountain, this is a great place to sample a breakfast *bougatsa* (creamy semolina pudding wrapped in a pastry envelope and sprinkled with cinnamon and sugar). The less-sweet version is made with *myzithra* (sheep's-milk cheese).

★ Peskesi ✕ CRETAN €€
(✎ 28102 88887; www.peskesicrete.gr; mains €8-16; ☺ noon-late) One of Iraklio's recent additions to the city's upmarket dining scene, and housed in a smartly converted cottage, this lovely eatery comes with a large dollop of snob value. It's best described as 'post-modern ancient Greek' (say what? we hear you ask). Think smoked pork (*apaki*) hanging off a butcher's hook with smoking herbs beneath, and *kandavlos* (an ancient souvlaki). It's located in a tiny lane off the northwest corner of El Greco Park. Worth reserving.

Parasties ✕ GREEK €€
(www.parasties.gr; Historic Museum Square, Sofokli Venizelou 19; mains €7-24; ☺ noon-midnight) Parasties' owner Haris is Iraklio's answer to a city's restaurateur who is genuine about serving great-quality local produce and top Cretan wines, and his passion shows in his small but gourmet menu. Beef liver and grilled mushrooms are our top choices, while a great selection of zingy salads and superb meats will keep you munching more than you planned. Decor is stylish and you can eat alfresco or indoors and watch the chef toss her snails and other delights in the open kitchen.

Brillant/Herbs' Garden GREEK €€
(✎ 28102 28103; www.brillantrestaurant.gr; Lato Boutique Hotel, Epimenidou 15; mains €12-23; ☺ 1pm-midnight) The avant-garde decor at Brillant, the fashionable culinary outpost

> ℹ **IRAKLIO RESOURCES**

Municipality of Heraklion (www.heraklion-city.gr) The municipality website has brief general information on the city.

Heraklion History (http://history.heraklion.gr) Provides an excellent overview of the history of the city and its monuments through the ages.

Historical Museum of Crete (www.historical-museum.gr) The official museum website has an excellent overview of Crete since Byzantine times.

at the Lato Boutique Hotel, might almost distract you from the creatively composed, feistily flavoured Cretan cuisine; the menu changes seasonally. From May to October, the restaurant renames itself Herbs' Garden and moves to the hotel's rather cramped rooftop for alfresco dining with harbour views. While the apostrophe in the name might be redundant, the cuisine and flavours are definitely not – think the likes of tender lamb with tomatoes, Cretan red beans and Greek yoghurt.

Ippokambos SEAFOOD €€
(Sofokli Venizelou 3; mains €6-13; ☺ noon-midnight Mon-Sat; 🛜) Locals give this smart *ouzerie* an enthusiastic thumbs up and we are only too happy to follow suit. Fish is the thing here – it's freshly caught, simply but expertly prepared and sold at fair prices. In summer, park yourself on the covered waterfront terrace. Look for the seahorse (*ippokambos*) sign.

O Vrakas ✕ SEAFOOD €€
(Marinelli 1; mains €8.50-12; ☺ 11am-4am) This spot, along the waterfront on the tourist strip, is neither grand nor out of the pages of a gourmet magazine, but it was started by the owner's grandfather and has morphed from a streetside *ouzerie* grilling fish on the sidewalk (no longer permitted) into a reliable, value-for-money place serving up Greek favourites.

Giakoumis TAVERNA €€
(Theodosaki 5-8; mains €6-13; ☺ 7am-11pm) The oldest among the row of tavernas vying for business in a quiet passageway off Odos 1866, Giakoumis offers myriad *mayirefta* (ready-cooked meals) and grills. Don't go past the lamb chops; the cook has been grilling them for over 40 years and has

perfected the seasoning and method. Giannis the owner says, 'Local servings for everyone!' In other words, generous.

Kouzinerie
GREEK €€

(Marinelli 11; mains €10-18; ⊙lunch & dinner) Those wanting a traditional Greek experience might be disappointed, but a faster paced crowd after an ultra-contemporary experience will be happy with modern music, cutting-edge design and more global dishes, featuring spicy buffalo wings to Cretan pies. One of a range of modern eateries to pop up around town, service here can be abrupt and it's a fill-out-the-menu-yourself kind of deal, but if you have any doubts, then just try the traditional pork knuckle, which is baked in a wood oven. Ironically, done the slow way for up to seven hours.

Thalassinos Kosmos
SEAFOOD €€

(www.thalassinoskosmos.gr; Sofokli Venizelou 11; mains €8-12, fish per kilo from €50; ⊙11am-late) Such are his antics, the owner may have you netted by the time you walk past his eatery, part of which is across the road on the quay side. But locals swear by his fresh fish; he'll show you the daily catch.

🍷 Drinking & Nightlife

Being a student town, nightlife in Iraklio is among the best on the island. The see-and-be-seen scene sprawls in oversized sofas along Koraï, Perdikari and Milatou (known as the Koraï quarter) and around El Greco Park. West of here, Handakos, Agiostefaniton and Psaromiligkon have more alternative-flavoured hang-outs. Most places open mid-morning or at noon and close in the wee hours, changing stripes and clientele as the hands on the clock move on.

Clubs line Epimenidou and Beaufort near the harbour and the western waterfront near the Talos Plaza. Cover charges start at around €5; double that if there's a big international DJ at the deck. The action usually doesn't kick into high gear until 1am.

Bars tend to open and close regularly; check with students as to what's hot and what's not.

Utopia
CAFE

(www.outopia.eu; Handakos 51; ⊙9am-2am) This hushed and formal old-style cafe has the best hot chocolate (€5.50 to €8.50) in town, although the prices are utopian indeed. Other temptations include a decadent chocolate fondue and great ice cream and homemade cookies. Its alter ego – Beer Utopia – across the road offers over 500 beers.

★ Bar Blow-Up
BAR

(http://barblowup.blogspot.de; Psaromiligkon 1; ⊙10pm-late; 🖥) This cool party lair has a funky underground vibe that seems more Berlin than Iraklio and draws an all-ages, unpretentious crowd for good music and cold beers.

Jailhouse Bar
BAR

(Agiostefaniton 19a; ⊙5pm-4am) This place drowns in punk (a fave of the owner, Yiannis) and hard rock tunes from Johnny Cash to Johnny Rotten. The trashy-sophisticated decor in a barrel-vaulted Venetian-era building is a bonus. Happy hour runs from 7pm to 11pm and Monday sees a two-for-one beer offering.

Fix
CAFE, BAR

(cnr Mirabello & Aretousa; ⊙10am-late; 🖥) If the trendy cafes along this pedestrian strip don't do it for you, grab a table in this down-to-earth joint that's sought out by an older crowd of chatty conversationalists.

Miniatoura
BAR

(11 Monis Odigitrias; drinks from €4; ⊙8am-late) Over 80 or so Greek wines are on offer at this cosy spot, along with some good South American beans for those who prefer a java fix to a grape-based journey around Crete and beyond.

ℹ GETTING AROUND IRAKLIO

Iraklio has the best transport infrastructure among the Cretan prefectures. The E75 highway runs along the north coast with individual communities accessed via the parallel Old National Rd. A major road links Iraklio with the Messara Plain and the beach resorts around Matala; another travels through Knossos and the Iraklio Wine Country as far as Arkalohori. Smaller roads, too, are mostly in good condition but be aware driving in villages. The historic streets were not made for cars so they are extremely narrow. This is one time not to follow the 'when in Rome' philosophy; it's best to park at the entrance to any village and walk in. The bus service is extensive, with all major communities served regularly, especially in summer.

Mare CAFE, BAR
(www.mare-cafe.gr; Sofokli Venizelou; ⊙9am-late)
In an enviable location on the beautified
waterfront promenade, opposite the Historical Museum, contempo Mare is great for
post-culture java and sunset drinks.

Veneto CAFE
(www.venetocafe.gr; Epimenidou 9) For a swanky
night out, steer towards this stylish outpost above the Venetian harbour for coffee,
cocktails or a light meal. It's a lofty space
with exposed wooden rafters and clubby
leather chairs hemmed in by a long bar,
panoramic windows and a naive mural of
Venice.

Take Five CAFE, BAR
(Akroleondos) This long-time favourite on El
Greco Park, and one of town's oldest bar-
cafes, mostly draws an older crowd.

Rolling Stone LIVE MUSIC
(Agiostefaniton 19; ⊙closed Jun-Aug) If you're
into rock and roll, this funky place scores
high on the groove-meter.

☆ Entertainment

Odeon CINEMA
(www.talosplaza.gr/gr/cine-odeon) Located in
the Talos Plaza mall on the waterfront west
of the centre, Odeon is good for non-dubbed
Hollywood blockbusters.

**Nikos Kazantzakis
Open-Air Theatre** THEATRE
(Jesus Bastion, nr Evans & Plastira) In summer,
the Nikos Kazantzakis Open-Air Theatre
also screens movies. It's behind the Jesus
Bastion. Follow Evans south for about
700m, turn right on Papandreou and right
on Georgiadou. The theatre will be on your
right.

🛍 Shopping

Iraklio has the most extensive and sophisticated shopping in Crete. Pedestrian Dedal-
ou and Handakos are lined with mostly
mainstream shops. Some specialist choices
include:

Aerakis Music MUSIC
(www.aerakis.net; Koraï Sq 14) An Iraklio landmark since 1974, this little shop stocks the
best range of Cretan music, from old and
rare recordings to the latest releases, many
on its own record label, Aerabus – Cretan
Musical Workshop & Seistron.

IRAKLIO MARKET

An Iraklio institution, if slightly touristy
these days, this busy narrow market
along Odos 1866 (1866 St) is one of the
best in Crete and has everything you
need to put together a delicious picnic.
Stock up on the freshest fruit and vegetables, creamy cheeses, honey, succulent olives, fresh breads and whatever
else grabs your fancy. There are also
plenty of other stalls selling pungent
herbs, leather goods, hats, jewellery and
some souvenirs. Cap off a spree with
a coffee at one of the quaint *kafeneia*
(traditional cafes).

Roadside Travel BOOKS, MAPS
(Handakos 29; ⊙9am-9pm Mar-Oct, 9am-2pm
& 5.30-9pm Nov-Feb, to 2.30pm Sat) One of the
world's better travel specialist bookshops,
with a wonderful selection of guidebooks
and maps plus good publications on Crete
and its ancient sites.

ℹ Information

Iraklio's two hospitals are far from the centre
and work alternate days – call first to find out
where to go. Banks with ATMs are ubiquitous,
especially along 25 Avgoustou.

Main Post Office (Plateia Daskalogianni;
⊙7.30am-8pm Mon-Fri, to 2pm Sat)

Paleologos (☑28103 46185; www.greekislands.
gr; 25 Avgoustou 5; ⊙9am-8pm Mon-Fri, to
4pm Sat) Useful travel agent for ferries, flights
and more. Its handy websites provide up-to-
the-minute schedules.

Tourist Police (☑28103 97111; Halikarnassos;
⊙7am-10pm) In the Halikarnassos suburb near
the airport.

Tunnel Internet Cafe (cnr Agiou Titou &
Milatou; per hr €2; ⊙8am-5am) This centrally
located spot has internet and printing services.

University Hospital (☑28103 92111) At
Voutes, 5km south of Iraklio, this is the city's
best-equipped medical facility.

Venizelio Hospital (☑28103 68000) On the
road to Knossos, 4km south of Iraklio.

ℹ Getting There & Away

AIR

About 5km east of Iraklio city centre, the Nikos
Kazantzakis International Airport (p262) has a
bank, an ATM, a duty-free shop and a cafe-bar.
Aegean Airlines has several flights a day to/
from Athens.

BOAT

The ferry port is 500m to the east of the Koules Fortress and old harbour, and the bus terminal is right outside the port entrance. Iraklio is a major port for access to many of the islands, though services are greatly reduced outside high season. Tickets can be purchased through several of the town's travel agencies, including central Paleologos (p155), which also sells tickets online.

Daily ferries from Iraklio's port include service to Piraeus and faster catamarans to Santorini and other Cycladic Islands. Ferries sail east to Rhodes via Agios Nikolaos, Sitia, Kasos, Kapathos and Halki. See www.openseas.gr for current schedules.

BUS

Iraklio has two major bus stations. For details on services to Rethymnon, see www.bus-service-crete-ktel.com. For bus routes to western Crete, see www.e-ktel.com.

Iraklio Bus Station A (☑ 28102 46530; www.ktelherlas.gr) Near the waterfront east of Koules Fortress, this depot serves eastern and western Crete (including Knossos). Local buses also stop here. Most buses use the main coastal highway, but at least one or two each day use the scenic but slower Old National Rd, so double-check before boarding.

Iraklio Bus Station B (☑ 28102 55965; www.ktelherlas.gr) Just beyond Hania Gate, west of the centre, this station serves Anogia, Phaestos, Agia Galini and Matala. Service is greatly reduced on weekends.

LONG-DISTANCE TAXI

For destinations around Crete, you can order a cab from **Crete Taxi Services** (☑ 6970021970; www.crete-taxi.gr) or **Heraklion Taxi** (www.heraklion-taxi.com). There are also long-distance cabs waiting at the airport, at Plateia Eleftherias (outside the Capsis Astoria hotel) and at Bus Station A. Sample fares for up to four people include Agios Nikolaos (€69), Elounda (€74), Malia (€39), Matala (€78) and Rethymno (€87).

🛈 Getting Around

TO/FROM THE AIRPORT

The airport is just off the E75 motorway. Bus 1 connects it with the city centre every five minutes between 6.15am and midnight (in summer); tickets cost €1.10. Buses stop on the far side of the car park fronting the terminal building. In town, buses terminate at Plateia Eleftherias, near the Capsis Astoria hotel. For city bus routes, see http://astiko-irakleiou.gr. A taxi into town costs around €12 to €15.

CAR & MOTORCYCLE

Iraklio's streets are narrow and chaotic. We strongly recommend against street parking; it's best to head straight to one of the car parks

HIGH SEASON FERRY ROUTES FROM IRAKLIO

ROUTE	COMPANY	FARE (€)	DURATION (HR)	FREQUENCY
Iraklio-Halki	Aegeon Pelagos (Anek)	21	11¾	1 weekly
Iraklio-Ios	Hellenic Seaways	66	4	1 daily
Iraklio-Ios	Sea Jets	63	3½	1 daily
Iraklio-Karpathos	Aegeon Pelagos (Anek)	18	7½	1 weekly
Iraklio-Kasos	Aegeon Pelagos (Anek)	19	5¾	1 weekly
Iraklio-Mykonos	Hellenic Seaways	81	4¾	1 daily
Iraklio-Mykonos	Sea Jets	83	5½	1 daily
Iraklio-Naxos	Sea Jets	70	5	1 daily
Iraklio-Paros	Hellenic Seaways	71	4	1 daily
Iraklio-Piraeus	Minoan	43	6½-7½	1-2 daily
Iraklio-Piraeus	Anek-Superfast	36	6½-9½	1-2 daily
Iraklio-Rhodes	Aegeon Pelagos	27	14	1 weekly
Iraklio-Santorini (Thira)	Sea Jets	60	2	1 daily
Iraklio-Santorini (Thira)	Hellenic Seaways	63	2	1 daily
Iraklio-Sitia	Aegeon Pelagos (Anek)	15	3	1 weekly

IRAKLIO BUS SERVICES

From Bus Station A

DESTINATION	FARE (€)	DURATION	FREQUENCY
Agia Pelagia	3.50	45min	2 daily
Agios Nikolaos	7.10	1½hr	hourly
Arhanes	1.80	30min	hourly
Hania	13.80	3hr	up to 17 daily
Hersonisos	3	40min	at least half-hourly
Ierapetra	11	2½hr	up to 6 daily
Kastelli	3.70	1hr	up to 5 daily
Knossos	1.50	30min	3 hourly
Lasithi Plateau	6.50	2hr	1 daily
Malia	3.80	1hr	at least half-hourly
Rethymno	7.60	1½hr	up to 17 daily
Sitia	14.20	3¼hr	4 daily

From Bus Station B

DESTINATION	FARE (€)	DURATION (HR)	FREQUENCY
Agia Galini	8	2	up to 7 daily
Anogia	3.80	1	up to 3 daily
Mires	5.50	1¼	up to 11 daily
Matala	7.80	2	up to 6 daily
Phaestos	6.50	1½	up to 6 daily

dotted around the city centre. Expect to pay around €6 per day. The cheapest car park is the outdoor Marina car park, on the eastern side of town (€2 per day).

All the international car-hire companies have branches at the airport. Local outlets line the northern end of 25 Avgoustou.

Caravel (☑ 28103 00150; www.caravel.gr; 25 Avgoustou 39; per day car from €42) Competitive car-hire rates and a helpful owner, Elsa.

Motor Club (☑ 28102 22408; www.motorclub. gr; Plateia 18 Anglon; per day car from €40, scooters from €28) Fleet of motorcycles in addition to cars.

Sun Rise (☑ 28102 21609, 6981761340; www. sunrise-cars.com; 25 Avgoustou 46; per day car from €35) In a side lane off 25 Avgoustou.

Hertz (☑ 28103 00744; www.hertz.gr; 25 Avgoustou 4) A useful central location of Hertz with friendly, helpful staff.

TAXI

There are small taxi stands all over town but the main ones are at Bus Station A, on Plateia Eleftherias and at the northern end of 25 Avgoustou. You can also phone for one on ☑ 28102 10102/146/168.

AROUND IRAKLIO

Knossos   Κνωσσός

Crete's must-see historical attraction is the **Palace of Knossos** (☑ 28102 31940; adult/child €6/free, incl Heraklion Archaeological Museum €10; ☉ 8am-8pm May-Oct, to 5pm Nov-April) ✐, a mere 5km south of Iraklio, and the capital of Minoan Crete. To beat the crowds and avoid the heat, get there before 10am. Budget several hours to explore Knossos (k-nos-*os*) thoroughly. There is little signage, so unless you have a travel guide, or join a guided tour, it may be hard to appreciate what you are looking at. Guided tours last about 1½ hours and leave from the little kiosk near the ticket booth. Most tours are in English, though other languages are available, too. Prices vary according to group numbers (around €80 for a private tour, €10 per person in a group).

The on-site cafe and touristy tavernas across the street are mediocre at best, so bring a picnic or save your appetite for a

Palace of Knossos

THE HIGHLIGHTS IN TWO HOURS

The Palace of Knossos is Crete's busiest tourist attraction, and for good reason. A spin around the partially and imaginatively reconstructed complex (shown here as it was thought to be at its peak) delivers an eye-opening peek into the remarkably sophisticated society of the Minoans, who dominated southern Europe some 4000 years ago.

From the ticket booth, follow the marked trail to the **North Entrance** ❶ where the Charging Bull fresco gives you a first taste of Minoan artistry. Continue to the Central Court and join the queue waiting to glimpse the mystical **Throne Room** ❷, which probably hosted religious rituals. Turn right as you exit and follow the stairs up to the so-called Piano Nobile, where replicas of the palace's most famous artworks conveniently cluster in the **Fresco Room** ❸. Walk the length of the Piano Nobile, pausing to look at the clay storage vessels in the West Magazine. Circle back and descend to the **South Portico** ❹, beautifully decorated with the Cup Bearer fresco. Make your way back to the Central Court and head to the palace's eastern wing to admire the architecture of the **Grand Staircase** ❺ that led to what Evans imagined to be the royal family's private quarters. For a closer look at some rooms, walk to the south end of the courtyard, stopping for a peek at the **Prince of the Lilies fresco** ❻, and head down to the lower floor. A highlight here is the **Queen's Megaron** ❼ (Evans imagined this was the Queen's chambers), playfully adorned with a fresco of frolicking dolphins. Stay on the lower level and make your way to the **Giant Pithoi** ❽, huge clay jars used for storage.

South Portico
Fine frescoes, most famously the Cup Bearer, embellish this palace entrance anchored by a massive open staircase leading to the Piano Nobile. The Horns of Consecration recreated nearby once topped the entire south facade.

Fresco Room
Take in sweeping views of the palace grounds from the west wing's upper floor, the Piano Nobile, before studying copies of the palace's most famous artworks in its Fresco Room.

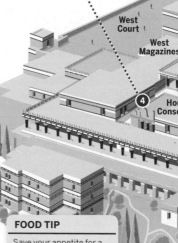

West Court

West Magazines

Horns of Consecration

FOOD TIP

Save your appetite for a meal in the nearby Iraklio Wine Country, amid sunbaked slopes and lush valleys. It's just south of Knossos.

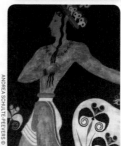

Prince of the Lilies Fresco
One of Knossos' most beloved frescoes was controversially cobbled together from various fragments and shows a young man adorned in lilies and peacock feathers.

PLANNING

To beat the crowds and avoid the heat, arrive before 10am. Budget one or two hours to explore the site thoroughly.

Throne Room

Sir Arthur Evans who began excavating the Palace of Knossos in 1900, imagined the mythical King Minos himself holding court seated on the alabaster throne of this beautifully proportioned room. However, the lustral basin and griffin frescoes suggest a religious purpose, possibly under a priestess.

North Entrance

Bulls held a special status in Minoan society as evidenced by the famous relief fresco of a charging beast gracing the columned west bastion of the north palace, which harboured workshops and storage rooms.

Grand Staircase

The royal apartments in the eastern wing were accessed via this monumental staircase sporting four flights of gypsum steps supported by columns. The lower two flights are original. It's closed to the public.

Piano Nobile

③

①

②

⑤

Central Court

⑥

Royal Apartments

⑧

⑦

Queen's Megaron

The queen's room is among the prettiest in the residential eastern wing thanks to the playful Dolphin Fresco. The adjacent bathroom (with clay tub) and toilet are evidence of a sophisticated drainage system.

Giant Pithoi

These massive clay jars are rare remnants from the Old Palace period and were used to store wine, oil and grain. The jars were transported by slinging ropes through a series of handles.

meal in the nearby Iraklio Wine Country, for instance at the excellent Elia & Diosmos (p166).

History

Knossos' first palace (1900 BC) was destroyed by an earthquake around 1700 BC and rebuilt to a grander and more sophisticated design. It was partially destroyed again between 1500 and 1450 BC, and inhabited for another 50 years before finally burning down.

The second palace was carefully designed to meet the needs of a complex society. There were domestic quarters for the king or queen, residences for officials and priests, homes for common folk, and burial grounds. Public reception rooms, shrines, workshops, treasuries and storerooms flanked a paved central courtyard in a design so intricate that it may have been behind the legend of the labyrinth and the Minotaur.

The ruins of Knossos were unearthed in 1878 by Cretan archaeologist Minos Kalokerinos, then in 1900 by the British archaeologist Sir Arthur Evans (1851–1941). Evans was so enthralled by his discovery that he spent 35 years and £250,000 of his own money excavating and – controversially – reconstructing sections of the palace.

Exploring the Site

As you tour the site, keep in mind that the names and uses ascribed to the buildings do not necessarily reflect Minoan reality. Evans reproductions, too, are controversial, including the reconstructed columns and reproductions of frescoes. For some they provide context, for others interference.

The Minoans' highly sophisticated society is revealed by details like the advanced drainage system and the clever placement of rooms to passages, light wells, porches and verandahs that kept rooms cool in summer and warm in winter.

The first section of the palace you come across is the **West Court**, which may have been a marketplace or the site of public gatherings. On your left is a trio of circular pits, called **kouloures**, that were used for grain storage.

Walk north along the palace's western wall to the **theatral area**, a series of shallow steps whose function remains unknown. It could have been a theatre where spectators watched acrobatic and dance performances, or the place where people gathered to welcome important visitors arriving by the **Royal Road**, which leads off to the west. Europe's first road was flanked by workshops and the houses of ordinary

Palace of Knossos

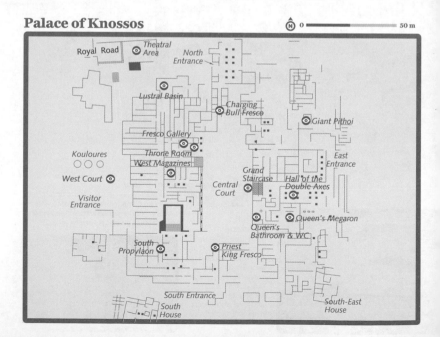

SIR ARTHUR EVANS: THE EXCAVATOR OF KNOSSOS

British archaeologist Sir Arthur Evans was an avid amateur journalist and adventurer, as well as curator of the Ashmolean Museum in Oxford from 1884 to 1908. His special interest in ancient coins and the writing on stone seals from Crete brought him to the island for the first time in 1894. He had a hunch that the mainland Mycenaean civilisation derived originally from Crete. With the help of the newly formed Cretan Archaeological Society, he began negotiating the purchase of the land, originally excavated in 1878 by Cretan archaeologist Minos Kalokerinos, eventually securing it in 1900 after Greek laws changed in his favour. Digging began and the palace quickly revealed itself.

The first treasure to be unearthed in the flat-topped mound called Kefala was a fresco of a Minoan man, followed by the discovery of the Throne Room. The archaeological world was stunned that a civilisation of this maturity and sophistication had existed in Europe at the same time as the great pharaohs of Egypt.

Over the course of 35 years of excavations, Evans unearthed remains of a neolithic civilisation beneath the remains of the Bronze Age Minoan palace. He also discovered some 3000 clay tablets containing Linear A and Linear B scripts and wrote his own definitive description of his work at Knossos in a four-volume opus called *The Palace of Minos*. Evans received many honours for his work and was knighted in 1911.

Evans' reconstruction methods continue to be controversial – with many archaeologists believing that he sacrificed accuracy to his overly vivid imagination.

people. Also here, on your right, is a **lustral basin** where, so Evans speculated, Minoans performed a ritual water cleansing before religious ceremonies.

Near the north entrance to the palace, stop to admire the **Charging Bull Fresco** before continuing to the heart of the palace, the massive **Central Court**, which in Minoan times was hemmed in by high walls. As is typical of a Minoan palace, rooms facing the western side of the courtyard had official and religious purposes, while the residential quarters were on the opposite side.

The central court gives way to the palace's most important rooms, including the **Throne Room**. Peering through security glass, you can make out a simple, beautifully proportioned alabaster throne and walls decorated with frescoes of griffins (mythical beasts regarded as sacred by the Minoans). The room exudes an aura of mysticism and reverence and is thought to have been a shrine. The Minoans did not worship their deities in great temples but in small shrines, and each palace had several.

Walk past the Throne Room and up a staircase to the first floor. Inspired by Italian Renaissance palazzos, Evans called this the **Piano Nobile**, for this is where he believed the reception and staterooms were located. From up here you also have a great perspective on the **west magazines** (storage rooms), where **giant pithoi** (clay jars) once held oil, wine and other staples.

The restored room at the northern end of the Piano Nobile looks down on the aforementioned lustral basin and also houses replicas of the most famous frescoes found at Knossos, including the **Bull-Leaper**, the **Ladies in Blue** and the **Blue Bird**. The originals are now in the Heraklion Archaeological Museum. At the far southern end of the Piano Nobile, a staircase leads down to the **South Propylaion**, where you can admire the Cup Bearer fresco.

Backtrack to the Central Court and cross it to get to the impressive **grand staircase**, which leads down to the royal apartments. Study their layout from above, then walk to the lower level past the **Prince of the Lilies fresco** on the south side of the central court.

Much of the royal apartments is inaccessible but you can still catch glimpses of the king's quarters (megaron) in the **Hall of the Double Axes**, a spacious double room; Evans proposed that the ruler both slept and carried out court duties there. The room had a light well at one end and a balcony at the other to ensure air circulation. It takes its name from the double axe marks (labrys) on its light well, a sacred symbol to the Minoans and the origin of our word 'labyrinth'.

A passage leads from the Hall of the Double Axes to the **queen's megaron**. Above the door is a copy of the **Dolphin Fresco**, one of the most exquisite Minoan artworks. A blue floral design decorates the portal. Next to this room is the queen's bathroom, complete

DON'T MISS

IRAKLIO'S BEST ANCIENT SITES

Knossos (p157) The mother of all Minoan sites.

Malia (p185) Knossos without the reconstructions.

Gortyna (Γόρτυνα; ☑ 28920 31144; adult/child €4/free, combined with Agia Triada €6/free; ⊙ 8am-8pm Jul & Aug, 8am-3pm Sep-Jun) Relic of Roman Crete.

Phaestos (p172) The prettiest location of all Minoan palaces.

with terracotta bathtub and a **water closet**, touted as the first ever to work on the flush principle; water was poured down by hand.

❶ Getting There & Away

Getting here is easy; all roads lead to Knossos, it seems. Bus 2 leaves Bus Station A or from outside Hotel Capsis Astoria in Iraklio every 20 minutes for Knossos (€1.50). If driving, from Iraklio or the coastal road there are signs directing you to Knossos. There is free parking across from the souvenir shops but the spaces fill quickly.

WEST OF IRAKLIO

West of Iraklio, the E75 highway cuts through a particularly scenic stretch with muscular hills plunging down to a couple of small beach resorts.

Agia Pelagia   Αγία Πελαγία

Despite being rather built-up, this beach resort some 20km west of Iraklio hugs a lovely, sandy beach with clear water and excellent swimming. Seafront tavernas are great for people-watching even if they don't offer any culinary flights of fancy. For a glimpse of underwater life, check with **Diver's Club** (☑ 6944565462, 28108 11755; www.diversclub-crete.gr; Agia Pelagia; beginners from per person €75, PADI from €330; ⊙ May-Oct), which offers the gamut of PADI courses and dives to caves, reefs and even a WWII plane wreck.

A 10-minute drive from Agia Pelagia (or a winding 3km), but seemingly a world away, **Mourtzanakis Residence** (☑ 6970709525, 28108 12096; www.ecotourismgreece.com; Achlada;

studio €85-95, apt €95-110; ⊙ Apr-Nov; P ❋ ☎ ✈ 🚗) is a cluster of seven modern loft-style guesthouses offering plenty of elbow room and thoughtfully equipped kitchens. Enjoy a dip in the smallish pool, take in the grand vistas out to sea from your balcony or stroll to the nearby historic village of Achlada. For those who don't want to dirty their hotplates (yeah, great excuse), evening meals are available for €17 and breakfast €9.

Fodele   Φόδελε

POP 460

The tiny village of Fodele, 25km west of Iraklio, snuggles into a fertile valley fed by the little Pantomantris River and dotted with Byzantine chapels. It claims to be the birthplace of El Greco and a small museum is dedicated to him.

❍ Sights

Museum of El Greco   MUSEUM
(www.el-greco-museum-birthplace-fodele.gr; Fodele; adult/child €2.50/free; ⊙ 9am-7pm May-Sep, to 5pm Oct) Despite experts disputing whether this is El Greco's birthplace, it's a quaint little stone building with backlit replicas of his works. Those expecting the real thing on all fronts may be disappointed, but nonetheless, it's in a pretty location, about 1km from the village.

Church of the Panayia   CHURCH
(⊙ Jun-Oct) The beautiful small Byzantine Church of the Panayia, built on the ruins of an 8th-century basilica and opposite El Greco Museum, is in excellent condition. Inside are some evocatively faded frescoes. Unfortunately, at the time of research, there was no official 'keeper of the keys' though it's worth asking at the village tavernas.

✖ Eating

Stousgioustous   CRETAN €
(mains €6.50-11; ⊙ lunch & dinner Tue-Sun) Rustic and homey, Stousgioustous, one of several tavernas on the creek, is one of the best choices for hearty Cretan dishes.

Arolithos   Αρόλιθος

Arolithos   VILLAGE
(☑ 28108 21050; www.arolithos.com; ☎) Built in the mid-1980s as a way to preserve and showcase Cretan life, Arolithos (a-ro-li-thos), 11km southwest of Iraklio, is a reasonably

authentic-looking recreation of a traditional Cretan village. It's a cluster of buildings containing workshops, a *kafeneio* and stores selling local products.

Most visitors arrive on tour buses for a quick wander and peek inside the **Museum of Rural History & Folks Crafts** (☑28108 21050; www.arolithosvillage.gr; adult/child €3/1.50; ☺9am-9pm Mon-Fri, to 5pm Sat & Sun May-Sep, 9am-5pm Mon-Fri, 10am-6pm Sat Oct-Apr), where household and agricultural items illustrate various facets of country life. Some of the buildings have hotel rooms (from €60).

CENTRAL IRAKLIO

South of Iraklio, past Knossos, the urban sprawl segues into an unhurried landscape of undulating hills, olive groves and rows of vineyards clambering up hillsides. It's all lorded over by the proud silhouette of **Mt Yiouhtas** (811m). Several Minoan sites are scattered on and around the mountain. These were once affiliated with ancient Arhanes, the main town in the area and the gateway to the Iraklio Wine Country, where you can sample the local product at several estates. Also of interest is the Nikos Kazantzakis Museum in Myrtia and the pottery town of Thrapsano.

Wine also grows near **Dafnes** and **Venerato** southwest of Iraklio, along the main road to Matala and the south coast. A wonderful detour takes you west to the southern slopes of Mt Psiloritis, where Zaros is a charismatic mountain village known for its spring water and trout.

You'll need your own wheels to explore this region properly.

Arhanes & Around Αρχάνες
POP 4500

Arhanes, 14km south of Iraklio, is an agricultural town with a long history, important archaeological sites, interesting museums and excellent eateries. Considered a model of rural town redevelopment, it comprises a maze of narrow, flower-filled lanes, meticulously restored houses and tree-shaded squares. Wine has been produced in Arhanes since Minoan times.

The modern town sits atop a **Minoan palace**, of which only a tiny section has been excavated. It's believed this may have been the Summer Palace of Knossos. During WWII, Arhanes was the hub of the German military command under General Heinrich Kreipe. Coming from Iraklio, at the turn-off to Kato Arhanes, a modern **monument** by local artist Manolis Tsompanakis commemorates Kreipe's famed 1944 kidnapping.

⊙ Sights

Arhanes is divided into an upper and lower section, with most sights of interest clustered in the latter. Getting around the one-way streets and narrow alleys can be confusing, so it's best to park your car and explore on foot. Fans of Minoan ruins can indulge their passion by visiting several sites within a short drive of Arhanes.

Archaeological Museum of Arhanes   MUSEUM
(Arhanes; ☺8.30am-3pm Wed-Mon) **FREE** This small museum displays many important finds from regional excavations, especially from Minoan times. Among the highlights are clay *larnakes* (coffins) and replicas of musical instruments from Fourni, plus a copy of the dagger presumably used for human sacrifice from the Anemospilia temple. The museum is in a side street just north of the main square.

Anemospilia   ANCIENT SITE
(Wind Caves; Arhanes) Anemospilia packs major importance into its small frame. Excavation of this middle-Minoan three-room temple yielded evidence that human sacrifice played at least some role in Minoan society. The site is closed to the public but you can peek through the fence and enjoy the sweeping views over Arhanes and surrounds. Anemospilia is about 1.5km northwest of Arhanes but not signposted; ask for directions in town.

Fourni   ANCIENT SITE
(Arhanes) On a hill west of town and reached via a steep footpath, Fourni is the most extensive Minoan necropolis on the island. Burials took place here over a period of 1000 years, the oldest going back to 2500 BC. One of the tombs contained the remains of a Minoan noble woman whose jewellery is on display in the Heraklion Archaeological Museum. It was temporarily closed for excavation at time of research.

Mt Yiouhtas Peak Sanctuary   ANCIENT SITE
Driving south from Arhanes, look for a sign and turn-off for Giourtas. The narrow (but driveable) road leads to the top of Mt

Yiouhtas. After a bone-rattling 4km ride, you'll be rewarded with scenic views over to Mt Psiloritis and Iraklio. On the hill near the visible radar station are the fenced-in ruins of a Minoan peak sanctuary dating from around 2100 BC, which is believed to have served the inhabitants of Knossos.

An altar and several rooms are among the unearthed sections.

Vathypetro
ANCIENT SITE

(⊙ 8am-3pm Tue-Sun) FREE About 5km south of Arhanes, and well signposted, Vathypetro was built around 1600 BC, probably as the villa of a prosperous Minoan noble. Archaeologists discovered wine and oil presses, a weaving loom and a kiln in storerooms. The winepress can still be seen; archaeologists believe Vathypetro housed one of the oldest wineries in the world.

🛏 Sleeping

Eliathos
APARTMENT €

(☑ 6951804929, 28107 51818; www.eliathos.gr; Arhanes; studio €110, villas €130-180; ❉ ⛱) Tucked into the hillside about half a kilometre south of Arhanes and with grand views of Mt Yiouhtas, this cluster of six houses is a haven of peace and quiet. The owners can help you get immersed in the local culture through cooking classes, excursions, and olive oil, *raki*- or winemaking workshops.

Arhontiko
APARTMENT €€

(☑ 28107 52985; www.arhontikoarhanes.gr; Arhanes; apt €75-95; ❉ 🛜 🐾) An air of effortless sophistication pervades these four apartments in a villa built in 1893, with incarnations as a military barracks and an elementary school. No hint of either survives in the four bilevel apartments that combine antiques and old embroideries with full kitchens, a fireplace and the gamut of mod cons.

Troullos Traditional Apartments
APARTMENT €€

(☑ 28107 53153; www.troullos.gr; Dimotikis Ananeosis; d/tr/apt €70/90/170; ❉ 🛜 🐾) This laidback place is set around an attractive stone courtyard. Each of the three apartments and one maisonette feature period furniture and paraphernalia. It's not high-end luxury, but charming nonetheless. Delightful owner, Athina, serves up a great breakfast (€12 per person). A garden pagoda is the perfect place for lounging after a day's sight-seeing, walking or taverna hopping.

Kalimera Arhanes
VILLAS €€€

(☑ 28107 52999; www.archanes-village.com; Arhanes; 1-/3-bedroom villas €180/330; ❉) Near the Archaeological Museum, this trio of meticulously restored traditional houses built in the early 19th century sport period furniture, fireplaces, and old-timey decor in a relaxed garden setting. Kitchens are big enough to whip up entire meals and come with attached balcony for alfresco dining.

🍴 Eating

Practically all the tavernas in town have a good reputation, including those on the main square. A couple of attractive *kafeneia* (coffee houses) are in the surrounding laneways.

Bakaliko
GREEK €

(www.bakalikocrete.com; Main Sq; mains €6-8; ⊙ 10am-late daily, Sat & Sun Nov-Mar; 🛜) 🍴 Bakaliko means meeting point; traditionally this meant *kafeneio* and grocery shop in one. This concept has been revitalised in this colourful deli where excellent cuisine (organic produce where possible) and wine complements Cretan products. Although gourmet, prices are reasonable.

It's run by duo Agnes and Susanna (the latter whips up delicious breakfasts, too), while George has all the answers to the local wines.

⭐ Kritamon
CRETAN €€

(www.kritamon.gr; Vathy Petrou 4; mains €9-14; ⊙ dinner daily, lunch Sat & Sun) Send your taste buds on a wild ride at this foodie outpost, in a street off the main square and set attractively around a garden courtyard with walnut trees. Ancient Cretan and creative modern recipes result in soulful salads, rustic mains and to-die-for desserts. Ingredients come either from the family garden or local suppliers.

To Spitiko
GREEK €€

(Main Sq; mains €6-13; ⊙ noon-late) This one-room taverna overlooking the main square gets contemporary flair from whitewashed stone walls, burgundy table cloths and big picture windows. Spaghetti with kid (€7) or the baked lamb (€7.50) are good picks. In fine weather the outdoor tables are the place to be.

ⓘ Information

A couple of ATMs are found around the main square.

❶ Getting There & Away

Drivers coming from Iraklio should take the scenic Knossos road. On weekdays, there's an hourly bus service from Iraklio (€1.80, 30 minutes); weekend service is sparse. Buses stop at the top of the village and close to the main square.

Iraklio Wine Country

Cretan wine is, in a word, superb. While this has long been known among viticulturalists, wine drinkers are beginning to take notice, too. Winemakers cultivate unique indigenous Cretan grape varieties, such as Kotsifali, Mandilari and Malvasia. About 70% of wine produced in Crete comes from the Iraklio Wine Country, which starts just south of Knossos. Almost two dozen wineries are embedded in a harmonious landscape of shapely hills, sunbaked slopes and lush valleys.

There are essentially two clusters of wineries, one around Peza and Arhanes, south of Iraklio via the Knossos road, and another further west around Dafnes, along the main road towards Phaestos and Matala.

Almost all wineries are members of the **Winemakers' Network of Heraklion Prefecture** (www.winesofcrete.gr), an association founded in 2006 and dedicated to promoting Cretan wines by creating an online presence, organising wine fairs and festivals, and producing informative brochures. Look out for the association's excellent *Wine Roads of Heraklion* map, available at the wine estates themselves.

🏃 Activities

There are many wineries in the region where you can sample the local product, sometimes for a small fee. Aside from tasting rooms, some estates also have mini-museums showcasing historic tools and machinery. All sell their wine below retail prices.

Boutari WINERY
(☑28107 31617; www.boutari.gr; Skalani; ⊕9am-5pm Mon-Fri year-round, by appointment on weekends) Near Skalani, about 8km from Iraklio, Boutari is the island's biggest producer (read mass market) and it's a sleek, modern operation. Take the tour (by appointment) to learn about local grapes and winemaking or just stick around to sample the product (most of Crete's grape varieties) in the vast and modern tasting room overlooking the vineyard.

Minos-Miliarikis WINERY
(☑28107 41213; www.minoswines.gr; Peza; ⊕9am-4pm Mon-Fri, 10.30am-3pm Sat) Right on the Peza main street, Minos is a massive winery that, in 1952, was the first to bottle wine in Crete. It makes very respectable vintages, especially under its Miliarakis label, including a full-bodied single-vineyard organic red and a fragrant Blanc de Noirs. Upon appointment, tastings are also held at the winery's **Vineyard House** (⊕11am-6pm Mon-Sat), right next to the grapes in Sambas, about 10km east of Peza towards Kastelli.

Domaine Gavalas WINERY
(☑28940 51060; www.domainegavalas.gr; Vorias; ⊕8am-4pm Mon-Fri) Founded in 2004, this is one of the largest organic wineries in Crete. Try its award-winning Efivos reds and whites. It's in Vorias, about 20km south of Peza.

Douloufakis Winery WINERY
(☑28107 92017; www.cretanwines.gr; Dafnes; ⊕by appointment 10am-3.30pm Mon-Fri) The highly recommended Douloufakis Winery in Dafnes grows Cretan grape varieties, plus uses grapes of surrounding small holdings. It's renowned for its whites (especially Femina) and reds (Aspros Lagos and Enotria). Known also for its colourful and quirky wine labels.

Lyrarakis WINERY
(☑6981050681; www.lyrarakis.gr; Alagni; ⊕10am-5pm Mon-Fri, 11-4pm Sat Apr-Oct) This progressive winery some 6km south of Peza continues to rake in awards, especially for its whites. It's known for reviving two nearly extinct white varietals called Dafni and Plyto. Call to confirm opening times.

Rhous Tamiolakis WINERY
(☑28107 42083; www.rhouswinery.gr; Houdetsi; ⊕by appointment) This organic winery is in a dazzling hilltop location above the village of Houdetsi, 4km south of Peza. It's one of Crete's excellent new-generation wineries, with Bordeaux-trained winemakers, state-of-the-art equipment and visitor-friendly facilities.

Silva Wines WINERY
(☑28107 92021; www.silvawines.gr; Siva) A mother and daughter are among the extraordinary team at this biodynamic winery in Siva. And by biodynamic, we mean it. They cultivate and harvest according to the agricultural (think moon, sun etc) calendar.

The result is ongoing award-winning wines, especially their whites. Reserve tours a day in advance.

🛏 Sleeping

★ Villa Kerasia
PENSION €€

(✆ 28107 91021; www.villa-kerasia.gr; Vlahiana; r incl breakfast €70-95; ☉ Apr-Oct; 🅿 🛜) In a gorgeous location in tiny Vlahiana, on the edge of the western section of the wine region, this converted old farm house has five rooms and two suites that are tranquil, intimate retreats with stone walls, beamed ceilings and wooden floors. Days start with an opulent breakfast entirely composed of local products that will easily tide you over to the afternoon. If dinner is offered during your stay, sign up: owner Babis is a mean cook who makes suppers veritable celebrations of Cretan cuisine.

🍴 Eating

★ Elia & Diosmos
CRETAN €€

(✆ 28107 31283; www.olive-mint.gr; Skalani; mains €10-19; ☉ lunch & dinner Tue-Sun) At this foodie playground on the edge of the Iraklio Wine Country, Argiro Barda turns market-fresh ingredients into progressive Cretan dishes that are a feast of flavours. The menu chases the seasons, but classic choices include succulent lamb chops with honey, fluffy fennel pie, and feisty pork with figs, plums and pistachios. It's only a short drive from Iraklio and about ten minutes south of Knossos.

Roussos Taverna
CRETAN €€

(✆ 28107 42189; Houdetsi; mains €5-10; ☉ lunch & dinner 15 Jun-end Sep, lunch & dinner Sat & Sun Oct-May) Toothsome and original is this simple spot's cooking style. Clued-in gourmets make the trip out to Houdetsi from afar to dine on Roussos' Cretan cooking, including fantastic lamb chops and local *horta* (wild greens) which they gather. It's on the main square across from Ross Daly's Labyrinth, whose musicians sometimes give concerts here.

Taverna Onisimos
GREEK €€

(✆ 28107 41754; Peza; mains €8-10; ☉ 12.30pm-late daily, closed Mon lunch Nov-Mar) On the main road in Peza, near the Minos Miliarakis winery, this handsomely decorated taverna is a good place to re-balance your brain if you've overindulged at a wine tasting. Drop by for tasty fried zucchini balls, grilled meats or *mayirefta* (ready-cooked meals) specials such as lamb in lemon sauce.

Myrtia   Μυρτιά

Myrtia, some 15km southeast of Iraklio, is the ancestral village of Crete's most famous writer and home to the excellent **Nikos Kazantzakis Museum** (✆ 28107 41689; www.kazantzaki.gr; Myrtia; adult/child €3/2; ☉ 9am-5pm Mar-Oct, 10am-3pm Sun Nov-Feb). In a modern building overlooking the *kafeneia*-flanked central plaza, the aesthetically lit presentation zeroes in on the life, philosophy and accomplishments of Kazantzakis. Watch a short

---

DON'T MISS

MUSICAL MUSEUM & WORKSHOP

About 4km south of Peza, Houdetsi is home to a few Byzantine churches but it really got put on the map by **Labyrinth** (✆ 28107 41027; www.labyrinthmusic.gr; Houdetsi; ☉ 9am-2pm & 5-8pm Mon-Sat). This beautiful stone manor is both a Museum of Traditional Musical Instruments and a highly reputable summer-long musical workshop that draws top talent from around the world.

Established in 1982, Labyrinth is the brainchild of renowned musician Ross Daly, an Irishman who's one of the leading exponents of the Cretan *lyra* (lyre). He's also a master of the modal non-harmonic music of Greece, the Balkans, Turkey, the Middle East, North Africa and North India, and has released more than 35 albums. Check him out at www.rossdaly.gr.

Daly is also an avid collector of traditional musical instruments, some 250 of which are displayed in the manor. These are mostly string and percussion instruments from around the world, many of them rare.

On Friday evenings in summer, the lovely grounds make an atmospheric backdrop for concerts in which the teachers and students of Labyrinth participate (free entry). Call or check the website for the schedule.

documentary, then nose around personal effects, movie posters, letters, photographs and other paraphernalia. Rooms upstairs present an overview of his most famous works including, of course, *Zorba the Greek*.

Thrapsano   Θραψανό
POP 1300

All those huge Minoan-style *pithoi* (storage jars) that grace hotel lobbies, restaurants and homes across the island most likely hail from Thrapsano, 32km southeast of Iraklio. Today's designs and even methods have been clearly influenced by those of ancient times. They are fascinating to see if you have appreciated the ancient pots at the archaeological sites and museums. Pottery workshops are scattered around Thrapsano. Note: these aren't your tacky touristy crafty shops, but factories preparing pieces for export around Greece and elsewhere, though they still normally welcome visitors. An annual pottery festival takes place in mid-July.

From Iraklio, Thrapsano is best reached via the Knossos road, turning off at the village of Agios Paraskies, near Peza.

Nikos Doxastakis Workshop   WORKSHOP
(☑28910 41160) Watch the giant clay pots being churned out at the traditional Nikos Doxastakis workshop. From the centre of town, head up to the village's municipal offices and it's beyond that.

Koutrakis Art   CERAMICS
(☑28910 41000; www.cretan-pottery.gr) This wonderful spot has an excellent website, talented potters, and small clay pots for purchase. It's on the Voni–Thrapsano road.

Vasilakis Pottery   CERAMICS
(☑28910 41666) Has small clay pots for sale. It's 300m down the hill from the village school.

Timios Stavros Church   CHURCH
If you're tired of visiting Thrapsano's pottery workshops, stop by the twin-aisled 15th-century Timios Stavros church in the middle of the village to check out its well-preserved frescoes. You might have to ask around for the key.

Livida Lake   LAKE
Just outside Thrapsano on the road north to Apostoli is Livada Lake, a preserved wetland with a rather neglected and undervisited birdwatching lookout and a picnic area. The local bird population includes little egrets, wood sandpipers, red-rumped swallows and whiskered terns. It is said that the lake has doubled in size over time as potters have extracted clay from the lakebed.

Zaros   Ζαρός
POP 2110

At the foot of Mt Psiloritis, the rustic mountain village of Zaros is famous for its natural spring water. Getting here via the scenic road from Agia Varvara (on the main Iraklio–Mires road) is a highly enjoyable ride. Zaros has some fine Byzantine monasteries, excellent walking and delicious trout dishes. Nearby excavations suggest that the fresh water lured Minoans, and later Romans, to settle here. If you look carefully, you can still spot remnants of the water channels that supplied water to the great Roman capital of Gortyna, about 12km south.

⊙ Sights & Activities

Lake Votomos   LAKE
Emerald-green and tree-fringed, this small reservoir just northeast of Zaros was created in 1987 to store the town's natural spring water. It attracts scores of birds and is great for chilling in the shady park or munching away in the excellent taverna-cafe. A path accesses both Moni Agios Nikolaos (1km) and Rouvas Gorge (2.5km).

Moni Agios Nikolaos   MONASTERY
(⊙ sunrise-sunset, closed 1pm-4pm) Just west of Zaros, a sign directs you to this monastery at the mouth of the Rouvas Gorge, about 2km up the valley. The church has some fine 14th-century frescoes. Don't confuse it with the new church under construction in front (with blue domes); the older church is behind this.

Moni Vrondisi   MONASTERY
(⊙ sunrise-sunset) Only 4km northwest of Zaros, this monastery is noted for its 15th-century Venetian fountain with a relief of Adam and Eve, and early 14th-century frescoes from the Cretan School, including one depicting the Last Supper. If you're lucky, an elderly priest will point to the highlights with his walking stick.

Folklore Museum of Zaros   MUSEUM
(Zaros; adult/child €3/2; ⊙ 10am-2pm & 4pm-6pm May-Sep) Opened in 2015, this tiny museum, housed within a traditional stone cottage, is

one of those things you feel you should go to just to support. It houses a quaint selection of donated items from the past, recreating life as it was until the advent of electricity. The 2nd floor houses a quirky geological collection. The most interesting exhibit shows minerals in their pure state next to products they are used in (plastic bottles, batteries and the like).

★Rouvas Gorge HIKING

Part of the E4 European Path, the Rouvas gorge leads to the protected Rouvas Forest, home to some of the oldest oak trees in Crete. It's an especially lovely walk in springtime when orchids, poppies, irises and other wildflowers give the landscape the vibrancy of an Impressionist painting. The trail can be accessed from north of Zaros village; follow the signs to the lake. If starting from the lake, allow around five hours for the return trip.

Domaine Zacharioudakis WINERY

(☎28920 24733; www.zacharioudakis.com; Plouti; ⊙10am-5pm Mon-Sat) Striking architecture and steeply terraced vineyards on the slopes of the Orthi Petra hill characterise this state-of-the-art boutique winery in Plouti, about 7km south of Zaros. The tasting room with views out to sea is a nice spot for sampling its fine wines, including the award-winning white Vidiano and red Orthi Petra Syrah-Kotsifali. Guided tours are also available. If you have time to visit one winery, this one is well worth it.

Sleeping

Studios Keramos PENSION €

(☎28940 31352; www.studiokeramos-zaros.gr; Zaros; s/d/tr incl breakfast €30/45/55; ❄) Close to the village centre, this little old-style pension is run by the friendly Katerina and is decorated with Cretan crafts, weaving and family heirlooms. Many of the rooms and studios pair antique beds and furniture with TV and kitchenettes. Katerina is up early preparing a fantastic and copious traditional breakfast. There is even a small lift.

★Eleonas Cottages COTTAGE €€

(☎28940 31238, 6976670002; www.eleonas.gr; Zaros; studio/cottage incl breakfast from €90/100; P❄@🛜≋👪) In an extraordinary labour of love, owner Manolis has created this paradise for guests. Cradled by olive groves, this beautiful retreat is built into a stunning terraced garden hillside. It's a '*this* is Crete' kind of place, such is the fresh air, relaxing ambience and staff *filoxenia* (hospitality). Its smartly appointed studios and apartments sport tasteful decor.

All offer the gamut of mod cons plus fireplaces. Hang by the pool or head out on a mountain bike, hit the nearby Rouvas Gorge and beyond, or take a cooking class. Plaudits for the sumptuous buffet breakfast of Cretan treats, plus Eleonas' eco-friendly practices. There are discreet spaces for kids galore, including purpose-built playgrounds. Manolis is a spare-no-detail, hands-on kind of host.

Eating

★Vegera CRETAN €

(☎28940 31730; www.vegerazaros.gr; Main St; multicourse meal €12; ⊙8am-late; ✎) The vivacious Vivi has a knack for turning farm-fresh local produce into flavourful and creative dishes based on traditional recipes. Her philosophy is to 'cook the way we cook in our house'. Indeed, with the floral tablecloths, homey setting, and Vivi as your host, you could be in a welcoming Greek home.

A full meal with fresh bread, a garden salad, cheese and olives, several tasty portions, pastries and *raki* is just €12. Cooking classes are also possible (€25 per person, minimum two people).

Limni CRETAN €€

(mains €8-17; ⊙11am-late Mar-Oct) This lakefront taverna is a peaceful oasis serving Cretan specialities and it's just the spot for trout dishes. The starters that come out with the bread add a nice touch.

Eleonos Taverna MEDITERRANEAN €€

(Eleonas Cottages; mains €5-10; ⊙lunch & dinner; 🛜) Scrumptious, fresh Mediterranean fare pulls in punters for fresh salads, delicious fish or meat grills (these change daily) or lighter fare including soups. To top it off, there's an excellent kids' menu and one of the best wine lists on the island. Sitting on the terrace, which is built around an olive tree, amid birdsong, is a delight. It's a couple of kilometres out of town; head north through the village and follow the green and white signs. Lunches start at 1pm; dinner is served from 6pm.

Votomos Taverna GREEK €€

(trout per kg €25, mains €7-10; ⊙noon-late 25 Mar-end Nov) Although you're in the mountains, you can be certain that the fish is

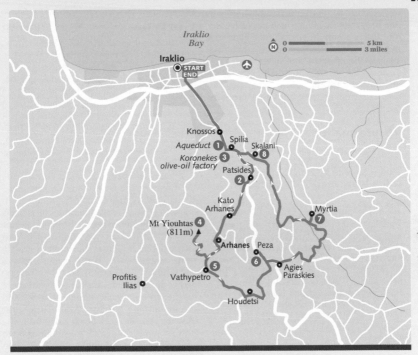

🏃 Driving Tour
Iraklio Wine Country

START IRAKLIO
FINISH IRAKLIO
LENGTH 45KM; ONE DAY

There's something undeniably painterly in the way Iraklio's suburban sprawl rolls itself into luscious wine country with snug villages awash in flowers, sun-dappled vineyards clinging to gentle hillsides and Mt Yiouhtas (811m) looming in the distance. A visit here is especially pretty during the spring bloom and the late-summer harvest.

Coming from Iraklio, follow the Knossos road south. A couple of kilometres beyond the palace ruins, the road skirts an impressive double-arched ❶ **aqueduct** from the early 1800s that once supplied Iraklio with water from Arhanes. Continue through Spilia to Patsides, where a brutalist ❷ **monument** at the turn-off to Kato Arhanes marks the spot where General Heinrich Kreipe was kidnapped in 1944. South of Spilia, pop into ❸ **Koronekes** (http://koronekes.org), a wonderful olive estate, and stock up on oil

and other Cretan products. Arhanes itself is a wine-country hub with Minoan roots. After visiting the village's small museum and soaking of the atmosphere on the leafy plaza, make a detour up ❹ **Mt Yiouhtas** for spellbinding wine-country views and a look at a Minoan peak sanctuary.

Back in Arhanes, head south towards Houdetsi, stopping at ❺ **Vathypetro** (p164) to see what a Minoan winepress looked like. A pretty hamlet wedged into a valley, Houdetsi's main attraction is the wonderful Museum of Traditional Musical Instruments. From here it's a quick drive north to ❻ **Peza**, the centre of wine production in Crete, with several wineries offering tastings and tours. From here, follow signs to ❼ **Myrtia** (p166) to pay your respects to Nikos Kazantzakis, the Cretan-born author of *Zorba the Greek,* at the excellent museum right on the town square. Conclude the day by indulging in a gourmet Cretan dinner paired with excellent local wines at the delightful ❽ **Elia & Diosmos** (p166) in Skalani.

fresh at this family-run taverna, where you can see trout splashing in large tanks before they end up on your dinner plate. It's the second 'Taverna Votomos' as you follow signs to the lake; the first taverna with the same name, located merely 50m away, is just past the Idi hotel. The owner was the first to introduce trout and trout farms to the area.

ⓘ Information

Most businesses are clumped together at the southern end of town. The post office and a supermarket are across the street from the police station. There's an ATM on the main street.

ⓘ Getting There & Away

Travelling on the main road from Iraklio, turn west at Agia Varvara. Coming from the south, there's a smaller road heading north from Kapariana just east of Mires (consult your map carefully and turn at the small road between a bakery and Kafeneio i Zariani Strofi; there's no sign). There is one direct bus daily from Iraklio (€5.50, one hour); the best alternative is to take one of the hourly buses to Mires and catch a taxi from there. A taxi to/from Mires costs around €15.

SOUTHERN IRAKLIO

The south-central region of Crete is blessed with a trifecta of archaeological treasures – Phaestos, Agia Triada and Gortyna – and a cluster of minor sites spanning Cretan history from the Minoans to the Romans. Touring them you'll be weaving your way right through the Messara Plain, one of Crete's most fertile regions, framed by Mt Psiloritis to the north, the Dhiktean mountains to the east and the Asterousia hills to the south.

A major highway links the busy commercial centres of Tymbaki, Mires, Agii Deka and Pyrgos, although they hold little interest for visitors. The nearby coastal towns are another matter. Matala, Kamilari and Kalamaki beckon with long stretches of sandy beach and smaller inland villages such as Sivas make excellent bases for exploring the region's ample charms. There are diversions aplenty: hiking through gorges, visiting ancient monasteries, poking around flower-festooned villages, chilling with locals on the village square or simply getting lost on the winding country roads.

Gortyna   Γόρτυνα

The archaeological site of Gortyna (p162), 46km southwest of Iraklio, is the largest in Crete and one of the most fascinating. Also called Gortyn or Gortys, Gortyna (gor-tih-nah) doesn't have much from the Minoan period because it was little more than a subject town of powerful Phaestos until it began accumulating riches (mostly from piracy) under the Dorians. By the 5th century BC, however, it was as influential as Knossos.

When the island was under threat from the Romans, the Gortynians cleverly made a pact with them and, after the Roman conquest in 67 BC, Gortyna became the island's capital. The city blossomed under the Roman administrators, who endowed it with lavish public buildings, including a Praetorium, amphitheatre, baths, a music school and temples. At its peak, as many as 100,000 people are believed to have lived here. Except for the 7th-century BC Temple of Apollo and the Byzantine Church of Agios Titos, most of what you see in Gortyna dates from the Roman period. Gortyna's splendour came to an end in AD 824 when the Saracens raided the island and destroyed the city.

The city sprawls over a square kilometre of plains, foothills and the summit of plains, hills and fields of which a small percentage has been excavated. An aqueduct used to bring in natural spring water from Zaros, 15km away, to feed fountains and public baths.

There are two main sections to Gortyna, bisected by the main road. Most people only stop long enough to investigate the fenced area on the northern side of the road past the parking lot and entrance gate. However, other important Roman temples, baths and buildings are actually on the other side of the street, albeit scattered around a sprawling open area and thus not as easily explored. Admission to this section is free and there are no closing times.

Buses to Phaestos from Iraklio also stop at Gortyna (€4.70).

Fenced Area

The first major monument visible within the fenced area is the 6th-century Byzantine **Church of Agios Titos**, the finest early-Christian church in Crete. Probably built atop an even older church, its only major surviving feature is the soaring apse flanked by two side chapels, the left of which is still used as a shrine.

A few steps away is the **Odeion**, a Roman theatre from the 1st century BC, which was levelled by an earthquake and rebuilt by Trajan in the 2nd century AD. The covered, arched structure on the far side of the theatre shelters Gortyna's star attraction: the stone tablets engraved with the 6th-century-BC **Laws of Gortyna**. The 600 lines written in a Dorian dialect were the earliest law code in the Greek world and provide fascinating insight into the social structure of pre-Roman Crete. Interestingly, ancient Cretans were preoccupied with the same issues that drive people into court today – marriage, divorce, property transfers, inheritance and adoption, as well as criminal offences. It was an extremely hierarchical society, divided into slaves and several categories of free citizens, each of whom had strictly delineated rights and obligations.

Just past this is an **evergreen plane tree** (or a replacement of), supposedly only one of 50 or so in Crete. According to legend the tree served as a love nest for Zeus and Europa. Europa soon gave birth to triplets, the mythical kings named Minos, Rhadamanthys and Sarpedon. The plane tree, though, which had to witness the lovemaking, felt compromised in its modesty and refused to shed its leaves from thereon. Myths die hard: locals visit the site in the hope of bearing plenty of sons.

South of the Highway

Monuments here are much larger but stretch out over a vast area and are therefore not as easy to locate. It's fun to wander around aimlessly and just stumble upon the ruins, but if you want to explore the site in a more organised fashion, locate the sign pointing to the Temple of Apollo on the main road and follow the stone path. You'll first pass the remains of the **Temple of the Egyptian Gods**, dedicated primarily to Isis, Serapis and Anubis, before arriving at the **Temple of Apollo**, which was the main sanctuary of pre-Roman Gortyna. Built in the 7th century BC, the temple was expanded in the 3rd century BC and converted into a Christian basilica in the 2nd century AD. Its rectangular outline and much of the altar are still in situ. Behind it you can spot the well-preserved **theatre**.

Turn left in front of the Temple of Apollo to reach the huge **Praetorium**. The palace of the Roman governor of Crete, it served both as an administrative building, a church and a private residence. Most of the ruins

IRAKLIO GORTYNA

Gortyna

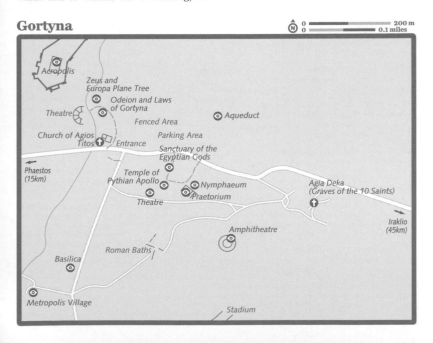

N 0 — 200 m
   0 — 0.1 miles

Acropolis

Zeus and Europa Plane Tree

Odeion and Laws of Gortyna

Theatre

Fenced Area

Aqueduct

Church of Agios Titos

Entrance

Parking Area

Sanctuary of the Egyptian Gods

Phaestos (15km)

Temple of Pythian Apollo

Nymphaeum

Praetorium

Agia Deka (Graves of the 10 Saints)

Theatre

Iraklio (45km)

Amphitheatre

Roman Baths

Basilica

Metropolis Village

Stadium

date from the 2nd century AD and were re-paired in the 4th century. To the north is the 2nd-century **Nymphaeum**, a public bath supplied by an aqueduct bringing water from Zaros. It was originally adorned with statues of nymphs. South of the Nymphae-um is the **amphitheatre**, which dates from the late 2nd century AD.

Buses from Iraklio to Matala or Mires stop here.

Acropolis

It's a 20- to 30-minute hike, but for a bird's-eye view of Gortyna, the hilltop Acropolis is hard to beat. It also features impressive sections of the pre-Roman ramparts. To get there, walk along the stream near the Odeion to a gate that gives way to a scrub-by track to the top. It's also possible to drive reasonably close to the site. Ask for direc-tions at the ticket counter.

Phaestos Φαιστός

The site of **Phaestos** (☑ 28920 42315; adult/child €4/free, combined with Agia Triada cost €6/free; ☺ 8am-8pm May-Oct, to 3pm Nov-Mar), 63km from Iraklio, was the second-most impor-tant Minoan palatial city after Knossos, and also enjoys the most awe-inspiring location,

with panoramic views of the Messara Plain and Mt Psiloritis. The palace layout is simi-lar to that of Knossos, with rooms arranged around a central court. Also like Knossos, most of Phaestos (fes-*tos*) was built over an older palace destroyed in the late Middle Minoan period. But the site also has its own distinctive attractiveness. There's an air of mystery about the desolate, unreconstruct-ed ruins altogether lacking at Knossos. Also in contrast to Knossos, Phaestos has yielded few frescoes; palace walls were apparently covered with white gypsum.

There's a decent on-site cafe but, for bet-ter food, head a few kilometres south to Agios Ioannis where **Taverna Agios Ioan-nis** is known for its succulent roast lamb and grilled rabbit. The tiny 10th-century Church of Agios Pavlos nearby has some moodily faded frescoes.

History

The first palace was built around 2000 BC and destroyed by the same earthquake that devastated other Minoan palaces. The ruins formed the base of a new palace that was begun around 1700 BC and destroyed in an-other catastrophe in 1450 BC. In the inter-vening centuries Phaestos was the political and administrative centre of the Messara Plain. Ancient texts refer to the palace's

Phaestos

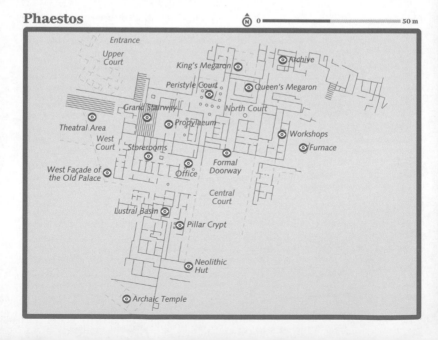

0 ————————————— 50 m

importance and note that it even minted its own coins. Although Phaestos continued to be inhabited, it fell into decline as Gortyna rose in importance. Under the Dorians, Phaestos headed a battling league of cities that included Matala and Polyrrinia in western Crete. Phaestos was defeated by Gortyna in the 2nd century BC.

Exploring the Site

Past the ticket booth, the Upper Court that was used in both the old and new palaces contains the remains of buildings from the Hellenistic era. A stairway leads down to the West Court with the **Theatral Area**, so-called because it may have been the staging ground for performances. The seats are at the northern end, while across to the south you can see the west facade of the Old Palace. The 15m-wide **Grand Stairway** leads to the **Propylaeum**, which was a porch. Below the Propylon are the storerooms that still contain *pithoi* (storage urns).

The square hall next to the storerooms is thought to have been an office, where tablets containing Linear A script were found beneath the floor in 1955. South of the storeroom a corridor led to the west side of the **Central Court**. South of the corridor is a **lustral basin**, rooms with benches and a **pillar crypt**.

The Central Court, which was once framed by columned porticos, is the centrepiece of the palace. It is well preserved and gives a sense of the size and magnificence of the palace. South of the Central Court is a 7th-century **temple** that consists of three parts; it is believed to be of the goddess Leto, mother of Artemis and Apollo. Note the **neolithic hut** in the court's southwestern corner. North of the court are the palace's best-preserved sections, the reception rooms and private apartments. Past a column-flanked **Formal Doorway** a corridor leads to the north court; the **Peristyle Court**, which once had a paved verandah, is to the left. The royal apartments – **Queen's Megaron** and **King's Megaron** – are northeast of the Peristyle Court. The celebrated Phaestos Disc, now in the Heraklion Archaeological Museum, was found in a building to the north of the palace.

ℹ Getting There & Away

Most buses to Matala head to Phaestos from Iraklio (€6.50, 1½ hours), also stopping at Gortyna (but check first with driver and ask for return times, as these can vary). There are also buses from Agia Galini (€2.10, 45 minutes) and Matala (€1.80, 30 minutes, two to three daily).

Agia Triada   Αγία Τριάδα

Pronounced ah-*yee*-ah trih-*ah*-dha, **Agia Triada** (🖉 27230 22448; adult/child €3/free, combined with Phaestos €6/free; ⊙ 9.30am-4.30pm summer; 9am-4pm winter), 3km west of Phaestos, was most likely a smaller palace or a royal summer villa and enjoys an enchanting setting on the tree-covered hillside looking out to the Gulf of Messara. Although it succumbed to fire around 1400 BC, the site was never looted, which accounts for the extraordinary number of masterpieces of Minoan art found here. These include a famous trio of vases (the Harvesters Vase, the Boxer Vase and the Chieftain Cup) now on display in the Heraklion Archaeological Museum.

Exploring the Site

Unfortunately, the site is not very visitor-friendly, as there is no labelling and only a basic pamphlet provided. On the plus side, it drips with historic ambience and rarely sees crowds.

Past the ticket booth, the ruins in front of you are those of the palace, with structures arranged along two sides of a central courtyard. The Byzantine **chapel of Agios Georgios**, on the left, has some beautiful frescoes. To the right of the palace is the **village area**, with the cemetery (closed to visitors) beyond the fence.

To your left, as you go down the stairs, are the ruins of a **Minoan house**, with a shrine dating from the early 14th century BC just behind it. It once featured a frescoed floor painted with octopuses and dolphins, also now at the archaeological museum in Iraklio. Beyond here is the paved central courtyard, with the residential wing on the right beneath a protective canopy. The west wing, at the far end of the courtyard, is a maze of storage rooms and workshops; the 'Chieftain Cup' was found in one of them. One of the most beautiful rooms is in the northwestern corner: called the Fresco Room, and lidded with a modern cement ceiling, it has fitted benches, alabaster walls and gypsum floors.

A ramp running along the northern side of the palace is thought to have led all the way to the sea, which was at a much higher level then; hence the name given to it by archaeologists – **Rampa al Mare**. It leads up

Agia Triada

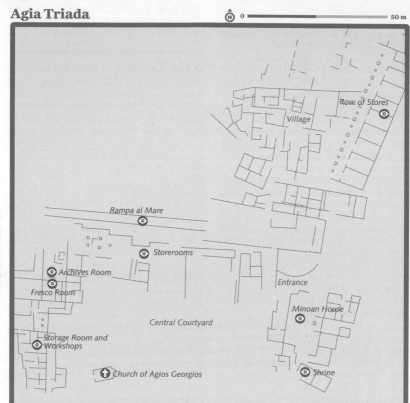

N 0 ▬▬▬▬▬▬▬ 50 m

Row of Stores

Village

Rampa al Mare

Storerooms

Archives Room

Entrance

Fresco Room

Minoan House

Central Courtyard

Storage Room and Workshops

Church of Agios Georgios

Shrine

to the village area with the marketplace and common residential buildings. Of special interest here is the row of stores that were once fronted by a portico.

On the other side of the fence, beyond the stores, is the cemetery that dates from around 2000 BC with two tholos tombs. The famous sarcophagus decorated with funereal scenes was found here; it too is in Iraklio.

ⓘ Getting There & Away

There is no public transport to the site, which is about a 5km walk from any major village. If you're driving, the turn-off to Agia Triada is about 500m from Phaestos on the road to Matala.

Matala   Μάταλα
POP 70

Matala (*ma*-ta-la), on the coast 11km south-west of Phaestos, first made it into the history books as the place where Zeus, in the form of a bull, swam ashore with Europa on his back before dragging her off to Gortyna. The Minoans used Matala as their harbour for Phaestos and under the Romans it became the port for Gortyna. Ruins of these ancient settlements are still visible on the seabed.

Despite such an ancient pedigree, Matala to most means only one thing: hippies. Back in the late 1960s and early 1970s, this little town played host to a colony of flower children, some of them famous (like Joni Mitchell and Cat Stevens) who lived rent-free in the caves. This romantic notion has rather removed the focus of the caves from what they were originally – former Roman tombs – and authorities have made efforts to put them back on the archaeological map.

In summer, or when scores of day trippers flood the village though in low season, it's still possible to discern the Matala magic. The setting along a crescent-shaped bay and beach flanked by headlands is spectacular.

Matala and the area around it is also a popular nesting ground for *Caretta caretta* sea turtles. The Sea Turtle Protection Society has a booth near the car park.

◉ Sights & Activities

Matala Caves CAVE
(Ancient Matala, Roman Tombs; admission €3; ⊙10am-7pm Apr-Sep, 8.30am-3pm Oct-Mar) It's clearly these caves that make Matala unique and not just because of the hippie connection. Hewn into the porous sandstone cliffs in prehistoric times, they were used as tombs by the Romans, under whom Matala was the port town for Gortyna. They were allegedly plundered by the hippies who lived here in the 1960s and 1970s.

Red Beach BEACH
Matala's main beach below the caves is a lovely crescent but often gets uncomfortably crammed. To escape the crowds, follow signs to Red Beach, reached in a 30-minute scramble over the rocks. It's hardly a secret but it does get fewer people, including a smattering of nudists. Bring water and snacks.

Church of Our Lady CHURCH
(Church of Panagia) Easily overlooked, this pint-sized chapel was carved straight out from a cliff, apparently during Venetian times. It contains some lovely icons and carved iconostasis. Follow the signs (enter from opposite Petra and Votsalo Restaurant); note that it's not the small church in the centre of the village.

🛏 Sleeping

Matala Valley Village RESORT €
(☑28920 45776; www.valleyvillage.gr; s/d/bungalow €50/60/90; ⊙May-Oct; P❈🛜🏊🎦) Near the village entrance, this sprawling garden resort is especially popular with families. Various room types are available, the nicest of which are the 23 modernist whitewashed bungalows added in 2008. Each has two bedrooms, a fridge and a spacious bathroom with jacuzzi and separate shower. Frolicking grounds for kids include a lawn, small playground and big pool.

Hotel Nikos HOTEL €
(☑28920 45375; www.matala-nikos.com; Matala; s €25-30, d €40-45, tr €50-55, f €65-70; ❈🛜) The best property on this confined hotel strip, Nikos has 17 recently renovated, pleasant and airy rooms. Rooms are over two floors along a flower-filled courtyard. Breakfast is €7.

Antonio PENSION €
(☑28920 45123, 6932760145; www.antonios -apartments.com.gr; Matala; s €35, d €40-50, tr €50, f €80; ⊙Mar-Oct; ❈) This comfortable pension has a variety of furnished rooms. A recent refurbishment has resulted in a slight mishmash of new and old (some rooms are more modern than others) but all are light and airy and will do the job if you want easy access to the centre.

Coral Hotel HOTEL €€
(☑28920 45785; www.matala-coral.gr; Matala; d/tr incl breakfast €60/75; ⊙Apr-Oct; P❈🛜🏊) This place is a bit like an upmarket trailer park, at least in its design, with 19 clean, simple and compact rooms that are located along a couple of wings; some have their own small front patch-cum-terrace. A lovely pool with sunbeds is a major drawcard. Good buffet breakfast and an efficient owner add to the appeal.

🍴 Eating & Drinking

Eating in Matala is hardly an experience in haute cuisine, and there is little to distinguish any of the tourist joints on the bay. Self-caterers can stock up at the good-sized supermarket next to the big parking lot. Most bars are along the southern side of the beach and stay open until dawn.

Gianni's GREEK €
(mains €5.50-12; ⊙noon-4pm & 6pm-midnight) A refreshing change from the run-of-the-mill waterfront tavernas, this been-there-forever family place just past the central square makes no-nonsense Greek food, including an excellent mixed grill with salad and potatoes.

Scala Fish Tavern SEAFOOD €€
(☑28920 45489; mains €7-15; ⊙11.30am-midnight; 🛜) Past all the bars on the easternmost end of the beach, this modern-looking place is Matala's best restaurant. It's been in the family for over 30 years, so it's doing something right. It gets top marks for its fresh fish, superior service and fabulous desserts (we love the 'tzizkeik' aka cheesecake). The cave views are especially nice at sunset. Reservations recommended.

Lions GREEK €€
(www.lentas-elgreco.com; mains €8-13) Overlooking the beach, down-to-earth Lions has been popular for many years and the food is better than average. It gets buzzy in the evening, making it a good place to wind down the day with a drink.

DON'T MISS

MUSEUM OF CRETAN ETHNOLOGY

The interesting **Museum of Cretan Ethnology** (28920 91110; www.cretan ethnologymuseum.gr; Voroi Pirgiotissis, Vori; admission €3; ⊙11am-5pm Apr-Oct, by appointment in winter) in the village of Vori, 4km east of Tymbaki, provides fascinating insights into traditional Cretan culture. The English-labelled exhibits are organised around themes such as rural life, food production, war, customs, architecture, music and food production. Most of the items are rather ordinary – hoes, olive presses, baskets, clothing, instruments etc – but they're all engagingly and intimately displayed in darkened rooms accented with spotlights. It's well signposted from the main road.

ⓘ Information

The main drag has a couple of ATMs and there's an excellent bookshop with lots of English-language novels and periodicals right on the central square. **Zafiria Internet** (per hr €2; ⊙8am-midnight) is in the centre of Matala.

ⓘ Getting There & Away

There are five buses Monday to Friday, six buses Saturday and three buses Sunday (high season only) to Iraklio (€7.80, two hours), Phaestos (€1.70, 30 minutes) and Mires (€2.80, 45 minutes). There is free parking along the street as you drive into town, and paid parking (per entry €2) on the beach.

Around Matala

If you find Matala too busy, there are several quieter and more authentic bases nearby from which to explore this southwestern pocket of Iraklio. Fine beaches beckon in Kommos and Kalamaki, while inland villages like Pitsidia, Sivas and Kamilari still preserve an unhurried, traditional flair along their impossibly narrow streets. Archaeology fiends can get their fix in Kommos and Kamilari.

Kommos   Κομμός

The Minoan site of Kommos, 3km north of Matala along a fantastic wide and sandy beach, is believed to have been the port for Phaestos. Although fenced off, it's still pos-

sible to discern the ancient town's streets and courtyards as well as the remains of workshops, dwellings and temples. Find the limestone-paved road leading towards Phaestos; look closely and you can make out the ruts from Minoan carts and a sewer running from the northern side. The turn-off for Kommos is signed to the right, several kilometres before Matala (this is more accessible than the old road which is signed from Pitsidia).

✖ Eating

Bunga Bunga   GREEK €
(Kommos Beach; mains €6.50-9; ⊙10am-late) One of two tavernas at Kommos Beach, about 2km north of Matala, the Caribbean-style Bunga Bunga serves tasty, fresh, organic fare. It's named after the WWII bunker in the cliff above.

Mystical View   GREEK €€
(Kommos Beach; mains €7-13; ⊙lunch & dinner; 🐦) Head to this appealing tavern for its million-dollar sunset views over Kommos Beach and fish and meat dishes. It's 1.2km before/after Matala on the Matala–Pitsidia road (at the entry/exit roundabout).

Pitsidia   Πιτσίδια

Quiet and unspoiled, Pitsidia is only 5km northeast of Matala, but could not be more different in look and feel. Its unhurried vibe, nicely restored stone buildings and maze of narrow lanes decorated with potted flowers give it charm and artistic flair. At night, locals mix with visitors for chat and sustenance in one of the low-key tavernas or *kafeneia* around the village square. Buses en route to Matala stop on the main road.

🛌 Sleeping & Eating

Aretoussa   PENSION €
(📞28920 45555; www.pensionaretoussa.com; Main Rd; s/d/tr incl breakfast from €30/40/45; ❄️) This old stone house with lots of trees, flowers and herbs welcomes guests to 17 spiffed-up rooms with mosquito nets over the beds. Some have access to a private garden, making them ideal for families. Light sleepers should avoid the rooms facing the main road (though these are slightly cheaper). Breakfast is served on the cosy verandah. Lovely English-speaking owners.

Patelo   PENSION €
(📞28920 45006; http://patelo.messara.de; Pitsidia; s/d €30/40, studio €45-50; ❄️) Like a miniature

castle, this whitewashed guesthouse crowns the highest point of Pitsidia. Views are predictably fabulous, especially from the large upstairs studio with a kitchen and huge terrace. A communal kitchen is available for use. It's by no means luxurious but a good-value stay. Patelo is run by the humorous and ebullient Maria.

Mike's   CRETAN €
(mains €5-10; ⊘6pm-11.30pm) Near Pitsidia's main square, low-key Mike's is a great place to hang out in the evening and reflect on the events of the day over wine and simple but delicious local fare.

Raftis   INTERNATIONAL €€
(mains €7-14; ⊘from 5pm for coffee, meals 6.30-11.30pm) This small place adds a touch of modern international class to Pitsidia (though their taste in music *à la Hotel California* seems more suited to Matala hippies of old). Serves up not only a lovely garden setting with citrus trees and its own vegie garden but high-quality organic treats, from meats to excellent salads. It is housed in a restored workroom that had been operating since 1914.

🏃 Activities

Melanouri Horse Farm   HORSE RIDING
(☑28920 45040; www.melanouri.com; Pitsidia; rides from €25) Organises horse rides along the beach or into the mountains, including a day trip to the Monastery of Odigitrias near the Agiofarango Gorge for €70.

Sivas   Σίβας

North of Pitsidia, about 2km inland from the main road, the pretty village of Sivas has a homey feel, many heritage-protected stone buildings and a pretty taverna-lined main square.

👁 Sights

**Agia Marina
Donkey Sanctuary**   WILDLIFE RESERVE
(☑28929 42556; www.agia-marina-donkeyrescue. com; nr Sivas; ⊘10am-2pm & 6-8pm Mon-Sat) **FREE** This place is for animal lovers. The passionate folk at Agia Marina Donkey Sanctuary feed and care for abandoned donkeys. At the time of research, 18 were in their care, aged from two to 42 years. Feel free to bring along some carrots or apples and bond with a beast or three. Kids can have short rides. Note: hours are strict. As many of the donkeys are aged, they too need their siesta. Look for the sign on the Matala–Mires road. It's signed 1km on the Matala side of Petrokefali.

🛏 Sleeping & Eating

Horiatiki Spiti   APARTMENT €€
(☑28920 42004; www.horiatiko-spiti.de; Sivas; studio €45, apt €70; 🛜) Run by delightful owners Maria and Mihales, this converted home (where Maria grew up) has maintained touches of history, including both an old well and wood-fired oven in the garden. The house now comprises several homey studios and one larger apartment (with a steep staircase). Upstairs studios with terraces are particularly appealing. It's a low-key place and perfect for lazing.

Sigelakis Studios   APARTMENT €€
(☑6974810905; www.sigelakis-studios.gr; apt €50; 🅿❄🛜) Attractive studios decked out in traditional Cretan style, on the outskirts of town. Owner George also runs the taverna of the same name.

Sigelakis   GREEK €
(mains €6-9; ⊘from 5pm) Sigelakis, slightly north of the main plaza, has a less pretty setting than some of Siva's central tavernas,

---

IRAKLIO FOR KIDS

A plethora of kid-friendly activities are concentrated on the northern coast in Gournes and Hersonisos and surrounds, east of Iraklio. You can get as wet and wild as you like at water theme parks including **Water City** (p182), **Acqua Plus** (p183) or **Star Beach** (p183). Or, in Gournes, get in touch with your inner Brontosaurus Rex, at **Dinosauria** (p182), before flirting with your inner mermaid at **Cretaquarium** (p182). For a hands-on Pythonesque experience, don't miss **Aqua World** (p183) back in Hersonisos. Horsy folk can go on the trot with **Arion Stables** (p183). For something more cultural, but equally as fun, the **Lychnostatis Museum** (p183) will appeal to little minds not so keen on archaeological ruins.

Further south, don't miss feeding the donkeys at the rescue centre **Agia Marina Donkey Sanctuary** (p177) and head off on some sandy rides with **Melanouri Horse Farm** (p177).

but a fabulous range of traditional food, including delicious goat in tomato sauce.

Taverna Sactouris GREEK €
(www.sactouris-sivas.com; mains €6-10; ⊙ lunch & dinner Apr-Oct) The oldest looking spot on the plaza, but with good reason. It makes good salads and vegetable dishes, sometimes featuring wild herbs gathered by owner-chef Jannis himself. With advance notice he also makes a fragrant fish soup.

Kamilari Καμηλάρι

Straddling three hills about 8km from Matala, Kamilari is a beautiful little village in a wonderful location on a hillside, accessible to the beaches around nearby Kalimaki. It's particularly popular among Germans; many have homes here. It's the kind of place where the longer you stay the more you understand its appeal. Excellent tavernas and a quaint *kafeneio* provide excellent nosh. It's home to an incredible Minoan tomb.

◉ Sights

Minoan tomb ARCHAEOLOGICAL SITE
FREE In the middle of fields just outside the village stands an extraordinarily well-preserved circular Minoan tomb. Its stone walls are 2m high. Side rooms were used for ritual purposes. Follow the signs to Tympaki and just after the small white church, look for signs to the right and about 500m on, again to the left. You can drive through the olive groves on a dirt road for about 1.2km. (Alternatively, this is also a pleasant walk). A walking track leads for around 500m to the site.

DON'T MISS

IRAKLIO'S BEST RURAL ESCAPES

Many of the region's rural villages are in wonderful locations and are great places to base yourselves.

Arhanes (p163) The heart of the wine country.

Fodele (p162) Pretty village that claims to be El Greco's birthplace.

Kamilari Charismatic hillside village with a Minoan tomb.

Zaros (p167) Mountain village at the mouth of the Rouvas Gorge.

Sleeping

Ambeliotissa APARTMENT €
(☑ 28920 42690; www.ambeliotissa.com; studio €30-35, apt €50-55; ❈ ☞ ☒ ⋒) A low-key, communal spirit pervades this spot so it doesn't much matter that the studios and apartments are ever so slightly run down. With a playground, toys and a beautiful swimming pool area, children will feel especially well taken care of here. There's also an outdoor barbecue for socialising with fellow travellers.

Asterousia APARTMENT €
(☑ 28920 42832; www.asterousia.com; studio/apt from €35/45; ❈ ☞) Feel your stresses melt away at this enchanting place run by Monica and Jorgos, who seek to impart their love for nature and the simple things in life to their guests. In line with their philosophy, the ageing studios and apartments are no frills, and the wi-fi is average, but this is one place where the hosts make the experience.

Long-term rentals (one week) are required, but they can accommodate shorter terms if these fall between other bookings.

Aloni Villas APARTMENT €
(☑ 6934404574; www.aloni-kamilari.net; d studio €35; ℗ ❈ ☞) Four casual and compact studio apartments with ubiquitous blue and white theme and nothing but a bed, bathroom and kitchen area to prepare a picnic or three. That's it. Oh, plus a great little sun deck with chairs for soaking up the rays. It's propped out on its own and is a five-minute walk from the village of Kamilari, with a view towards the sea (direction Kalamaki). Blissful.

Plaka APARTMENT €
(☑ 28920 42697; www.plakakreta.com; apt €35; ⊙ Apr-Oct; ❈ ☞) These four well-appointed hillside apartments just outside the village have balconies with sea views and are decorated in cool blue and white shades. There is a garden with sun lounges in the back. Ask at Taverna Mylonas.

Eating

Kentriko CAFE €
(www.kafenio-kentriko.gr; drinks from €1; ⊙ 4pm-late; ☞) Kentriko is a beautiful, congenial stone *kafeneio* (established in 1922) on the narrow main drag. Decorated with old photos of village families, it's great for breakfast, a nightcap or anything in between. As friendly owner Irini explains, it runs to a

rhythm: the tourists, then regular elderly men who chat over a coffee, then local youths into the wee hours. Drinks are served with a small plate of mezes.

★ Pizza Ariadni ITALIAN €€
(mains €8-13; ☺ 7.30pm-late May-Oct) It might seem incongruous to consider an Italian pizzeria in a Cretan village, but trust us. For over 20 years Manolis has been kneading pizza dough for hundreds of loyal clients, who head here not only for the lush setting on a candlelit garden terrace, but also for the best (we mean, the *best*) pizzas outside of Italy. Things hot up into party mode later in the evening.

Taverna Acropolis GREEK €€
(mains €5-10.50; ☺ 3pm-late Apr-Nov, Thu-Sat Dec-Mar) This relaxing taverna, housed in an historic building, is delightful for a pre- or post-dinner nip. The walls are lined with eclectic artworks and the interiors reflect effortless good taste. That extends to the cuisine that comes highly recommended – good, wholesome Greek. Head to the kitchen to choose from a selection of daily offerings. The bonus is the terrace overlooking the village.

Taverna Mylonas GREEK €€
(www.milonaskamilari.gr; mains €7.50-12; ☺ 5pm-late Apr-Oct) Kamilari's oldest taverna, this no-nonsense spot headed by the ebullient Giorgos serves tasty traditional Cretan mezedhes and a daily-changing selection of *mayirefta* with some ingredients trucked in from the nearby family farm. Score a terrace table to soak up the stunning views.

Kalamaki Καλαμάκι

With its long sandy beach and attractive setting, 7km from Matala, Kalamaki has all the trappings of an alluring resort town. Despite the presence of several skeletal half-finished buildings, it's a pleasant, low-key spot with good-value lodging and relaxed locals. The taverna- and lounge-lined beach promenade makes for fine strolling and you can walk to Kommos Beach along the strand. Many places close from December to February.

🛏 Sleeping

★ Arsinoi Studios APARTMENT €
(☑ 28920 45475, 6986858923; www.arsinoi-studios.gr; Kalamaki; studios €35-40, apt €50-80; 🅿 ❄ 🛜) Arsinoi would be just another

apartment building near the beach were it not for the friendly Papadospiridaki family who will fall over backwards for you – they epitomise Greek *filoxenia*. You'll instantly feel at home when big-hearted Noi ushers you to your squeaky-clean and roomy digs and proffers fruit and goodies from the family farm. She's also a killer cook and often presents her guests with homemade mezedhes and *raki* on the communal terrace in the evenings. (Fortunately, their local shop, CretaNature, in the village also sells their homemade delights). Sea-view rooms particularly nice. Breakfast costs €6.

Alexandros Beach HOTEL €
(☑ 28920 45195; www.alexandros-kalamaki.com; Kalamaki; d incl breakfast €45-60; ☺ Mar-Nov; ❄ 🛜) Right on the beach at the quiet end of the waterfront promenade, this 28-room peach-coloured hotel provides a fine base for the beach and the local countryside. Sea-facing rooms are the largest, while the cheaper ones out back are cramped; all have balconies. The owners also have larger villas (€70 to €100) on a hill top between Kalamaki and Kalamari. Rates are €8 per person less without breakfast.

✕ Eating

Aristides GREEK €
(mains €5.80-9; ☺ 9am-late) If there's one eatery where diners don't mind sitting cheek by jowl, it's here. This barnlike place, with a ship's steering wheel at the helm, offers a down-to-earth, unlikely-to-offend Greek food experience that pulls in the crowds for its genuine ambience and reasonable prices.

Steer yourself towards a variety ranging from pizza to a selection of fish (some frozen; they will be frank with you) or good home-cooked *mayirefta* such as lamb and beans.

★ Yiannis GREEK €€
(multicourse menu €12; ☺ 11am-late Nov-Mar) A top choice for something with a genuine by-gone local flair, head one block inland from the Kalamaki beach to Yiannis, a bare-bones eatery that has been running for over 30 years. It enjoys cult status with locals and loyal visitors for its scrumptious mezedhes and lovably eccentric proprietor.

It's a go-with-the-flow place, where €12 gets you a selection of spontaneous treats and more. In summer, he'll even arrange picnic boxes (around €8).

DON'T MISS

MONI ODIGITRIAS & AGIOFARANGO GORGE

A detour en route to/from Matala delivers a trifecta of treats: a monastery, gorge walk and lovely swimming cove.

Moni Odigitrias (⊘9am-8pm) **FREE** About 6km south of Sivas, Moni Odigitrias is a historic monastery with a tower from which the monks fought off the Turks, Germans and the odd pirate. A rickety ladder leads to the top for superb views. Afterwards, take a quick spin around the small museum with its wine- and olive presses, and check out the 15th-century frescoes and icons in the church up the hill.

Agiofarango Gorge From the parking lot opposite Moni Odigitrias, it's around 7km to the beach via the Agiofarango Gorge. The gorge is awash with oleander and popular with rock climbers. There are caves, makeshift chapels and hermitages in the cliffs as well as a Byzantine chapel en route. The gorge emerges at a lovely pebble beach with crystal-clear water. Despite its remoteness, it can get busy.

For those who don't want to walk the whole way, drive on the road signed to Kali Limenes for approximately 3.5km, where you turn right at a sharp fork. Continue on this rough dirt road for around 2.5km until the road ends (at a parking area). From here you walk for approximately 1.5km to the sea. A Cretan warning: don't park your car under the shade. Goats sometimes jump on the roofs to reach tree leaves.

Kafeneio Ksa Sou (www.listarossa.gr; mezedhes €4-8; ⊘4-11pm Tue-Sat, 1-11pm Sun, weekends-only in winter) Enjoy a glass of homemade lemonade and other organic treats at this arty spot near the village of Listaros. The owners are active environmentalists. Sylla is also a mean cook: try her special Kessarias pie bulging with *kaseri* (sheep's-milk cheese) and a spicy sausage. And don't miss her 'cretamisu'.

If you want to spend the night, ask if there's a vacancy in Sylla's two traditional guesthouses (€90 to €100).

Delfinia   SEAFOOD €€
(mains €7-10, fish per kg from €55; ⊘9am-late Mar-Nov) Of the many tavernas along the beach (all good), Delfinia is one of the snazziest with its distressed-look, white-washed furniture. It's highly regarded for its fresh fish.

Lendas   Λέντας

POP 80

Lendas appeals to those in search of a remote, laid-back beach retreat. Reached via a long and winding road culminating in a dramatic plunge down to the village, it clings to the cliff overlooking the beach. It attracts mostly longstanding return guests and independent travellers after a budget-focused experience. Aside from the sun, a few beach bars and tavernas, there's not much going on.

⊙ Sights

The beach in town is narrow and pebbly and not particularly attractive, but there are better options not too far away.

Diskos   BEACH
About 1km to the west, over the headland, there's a nice, long stretch of sand called Diskos (or Dytikos), a favourite for 'nudies'.

Loutro   BEACH
The narrow, if pretty, Loutro beach is the launching pad for the scenic 6km-hike to Kronos via the Trakhoula Gorge. It's about 5km east of Lendas.

Lendas Ruins   ARCHAEOLOGICAL SITE
Under the Romans, Lebena (today's Lendas) was a health spa cherished for its therapeutic springs. The ancient settlement stood right above the beach, but only two granite columns of a 4th-century BC temple remain. Next to the temple was a treasury with a mosaic floor that is still visible. Very little else is decipherable and the springs have been closed since the 1960s.

🛏 Sleeping

Villa Tsapakis   STUDIOS €
(☑28920 95378, 6947571900; www.villa-tsapakis. gr; Lendas; d/tr €35/€40, studio €40-45; ❄) Over the headland, on lovely sandy Diskos (Dytikos) beach, which is mostly nudist,

this flower-filled spot has good-value, no-nonsense studios with kitchens and balconies set around an oddly shaped central courtyard.

Casa Doria   HOTEL €€
(☑ 28920 95376; www.casadoria.net; Lendas; d incl breakfast €80; ☻ Apr-end Oct; ❀) There's remote and then there's Casa Doria. The self-proclaimed 'slow-life hotel' has seven rooms, all individually and slightly quirkily decorated with Zen-like simplicity. Its main appeals are the charismatic Italian owners and a restaurant that delivers Mediterranean flavour explosions. Half-board is an extra €15.

Prices decrease significantly outside of high season. With easy access to the Trakhoula Gorge, this is a great base for hikers, climbers and mountain bikers. It's about 3km from Lendas and is signed to the east at the first turn-off out of town (the Loutra–Trakhoulas road).

✖ Eating

El Greco   GREEK €
(www.lentas-elgreco.com; Lendas; mains €6-11) This friendly taverna run by the Delakis family has an good selection of *mayirefta* and traditional Greek dishes in a garden setting overlooking the sea. Its rooms rent for around €40.

Taverna Casa Doria   ITALIAN €€
(☑ 6972648013; www.casadoria.net; Loutra; mains €6-12; ☻ 1-3pm & 7.30-10pm) Given that the owners are Italian, it's little surprise your taste buds will receive a touch of Milanese treatment. Isobella's homemade pasta is to die for, but so too are her main courses such as *vitello tonnato* (using pork loin instead of veal, with tuna and capers). But leave room for the desserts, especially the panna cotta (€4).

The beautiful view, and attractive garden setting, in front of their accommodation (Casa Dora), means you might be in for one long lunch or dinner. If you ring, Alessandro will ferry you to and from the 3km stretch from Lendas.

ℹ Information

It's best to leave your car in the car park on entry to the village; the right fork heads to the main square. The bus stops outside the car park. There are a couple of small markets but no petrol station.

ℹ Getting There & Away

To get here, you must change buses in Mires. In high season, one daily bus plies the route between Mires and Lendas (€4, one hour), none on Sunday. Alternatively, a taxi from Mires costs around €40.

Kapetaniana   Καπετανιανά

In the heart of the Asteroussia mountain range that runs along the entire southern coast of Iraklio, and clinging to the slopes of the highest peak, Kapetaniana is a remote, car-free mountain hamlet that's a mecca for rock climbers and hikers. The last 8km of road corkscrews up into the mountains, making it one of the most exciting drives in Crete.

Kapetaniana is blessed with a couple of excellent sleeping options and one basic taverna. A gorgeous 14th-century Byzantine church graces Kato ('lower') Kapetaniana.

⌂ Sleeping & Eating

★ **Pension Kofinas**   GUESTHOUSE €
(☑ 28930 41440, 6977747797; www.korifi.de; Ano Kapetaniana; s €25, d €35-40, all incl breakfast; ℗ ☎) Located in Ano Kapetaniana, the upper village, is this remote and relaxed ecofriendly haven operated by the ultra-hospitable Austrian Gunnar and Louisa. It has a wonderful old-style ski lodge feel, where you can get as much socialising or privacy as you need around their large wooden table or in the garden. Bookings are essential.

There are just three double rooms (one recently spiffed up and the only one with private bathroom) and a small backpacker-style bunk room. All but one share external bathroom facilities. Owner Gunnar is also a gourmet chef who serves divine dinners (from €14) on the terrace, which has superb views of Mt Kofinas and out to sea. A former hiker and climber, he was also one of the first, along with Czech climber Zbynek Cepela, to map the area's walks and climbs and has a phenomenal knowledge of the region.

★ **Thalori Guest House**   APARTMENT €€
(www.thalori.com; Kapetaniana; studio/apt from €75/85; ❀ ☎ ☎ ⚑) It's almost like a fairytale. Owners Marcos and Poppy have rehabilitated the 'dying' village of Kato Kapetaniana. Twenty-one original stone cottages have been renovated and offer an atmospheric, old-style experience with modern comforts. Strangely, given the focus on sustainability,

it's not the most environmentally friendly of places, with a reliance on electricity for heating and cooling and no solar panels.

If you can turn a blind eye to this, it's a stunning spot. Transfers to the beach (8km) are available, as are use of bikes and boat trips.

Taverno Miro CRETAN €
(Ano Kapetaniana; mains €5-8; ☺10am-late Wed-Mon mid-Apr–mid-Nov) This no-name taverna (referred to as 'Miro's' after its hardworking owner) is relaxed and basic – but anything else would look out of place here. After all, who needs more than freshly grilled meat (from Miro's own farm), seasoned with local herbs, and an incredible vista of the Libyan Sea from the village high ground. On a summer evening you can watch the moon rise over the sea.

🏃 Activities

Korifi Tours HIKING, ROCK CLIMBING
(☐ 28930 41440; www.korifi.de) Based in Kapetaniana, founder Gunnar was responsible for mapping many of the climbs in this remote area, and also sells the informative *Crete Topo Climbing Guide,* detailing eight different climbing areas and 120 routes. Hiking and climbing tours around Kapetaniana are available.

NORTHEASTERN COAST

Ever since the national road along the northern coast opened in 1972, the coast between Iraklio and Malia has seen a frenzy of unbridled development, particularly in the seaside towns of Hersonisos and Malia. Hotels deal almost exclusively with package-tour operators who block-book hotel rooms months in advance. For independent travellers, the chain of villages above Hersonisos (Koutouloufari, Piskopiano and Old Hersonisos) are the most appealing places to stay in this area.

While Hersonisos has some family-friendly attractions, including fun water parks, Malia is primarily a party town. A bit incongruously, it's also home to the area's only significant historical site, the wonderful Minoan palace.

Buses link all the coastal towns along the Old National Rd at least every 30 minutes. If you want to avoid this area altogether, whoosh right past it on the E75 highway.

Gournes & Around Γούρνες

Gournes, about 15km east of Iraklio, was dominated by a huge US air force base until it closed in 1994.

◉ Sights & Activities

Cretaquarium AQUARIUM
(☐ 28103 37788; www.cretaquarium.gr; adult/child €9/6, audio guide €3; ☺9.30am-9pm May-Sep, to 5pm Oct-Apr; ☻) This high-tech indoor sea occupies the site of former military grounds. Inhabited by some 2500 Mediterranean and tropical aquatic critters, this huge aquarium will likely bring smiles to even the most jaded youngster. You can watch jellyfish dance, sharks dart, skates fly and corals sway. There are multimedia features and multilingual displays. Audio guides provide in-depth explanation. It's affiliated with the Hellenic Center for Maritime Research next door.

Dinosauria AMUSEMENT PARK
(☐ 28103 32089; www.dinosauriapark.com; adult/child €9.50/7.50; ☺10am-8pm May-Oct, to 5pm Nov-Apr) Both big and small kids will love tapping into their inner 'aurouses' at this fun and educational theme park. A mind-boggling array of activities is crammed onto the compact premises. You enter a time tunnel (with explanations on the way), and exit into the world of the dinosaurs, complete with moving, roaring life-sized replicas, a sandpit bone yard, a 3D cinema and more besides. It's located to the north of Gournes, towards the coast; follow the signs.

Water City WATER PARK
(☐ 28107 81317; www.watercity.gr; adult/child under 140cm/child under 90cm €25/17/free; ☺10am-6.30pm May-Sep) Not only kids will get their jollies on a hot summer day at Water City, Crete's largest water park, in Anopoli, about 3km inland. Plunge down wicked high-speed slides, brave wave pools or simply chill in the pool. Some of the 34 attractions have height and weight restrictions.

Hersonisos Χερσόνησος

Hersonisos, about 25km east of Iraklio, has grown from a small fishing village into one of Crete's largest and busiest tourist towns that is deluged in summer. The main thoroughfare is lined with sprawling hotels, apartment buildings and a cacophonous

SKOTINO CAVE

Also known as Agia Paraskevi Cave, after the chapel built above it, **Skotino Cave** (Σπήλαιο Σκοτεινού) is one of the largest caves in Crete and deliciously spooky to boot. A gaping arch gives way to a dark chamber as lofty as a Gothic cathedral and teeming with stalactites, stalagmites and massive limestone formations. Let your mind wander and you'll make out all sorts of shapes (a bear, a dragon, a head) in the dim light.

Unless you have some spelunking experience and a flashlight, you probably shouldn't venture beyond here, because the chamber drops another 15m and it gets eerily dark.

Skotino was first explored by Arthur Evans in 1933. Later excavations have unearthed vases, bone needles and figurines dating as far back as Minoan times, suggesting that the cave had religious significance. To this day, pilgrims leave votives and offerings.

There is no admission fee, no guard and few (if any) visitors. In fact, the site has a long-abandoned feel. Wear sturdy shoes and mind your footing at all times.

The cave is near the village of Skotino, some 8km inland from Kato Gouves. About 1km past Skotino, look for the turn-off to the 'Cave of Agia Paraskevi' sign and drive another 2.3km to the cave entrance.

strip of bars, cafes, tourist shops, clubs, fast-food eateries, travel agencies and quad-hire places. Its most decent stretch of sand is the quaint Sarandaris Beach.

To escape the bustle, base yourself uphill in one of three adjoining villages: Koutouloufari, Piskopiano or Old Hersonisos. Although touristy, these are nonetheless charming and have some excellent tavernas and accommodation options.

⊙ Sights & Activities

★ Lychnostatis Museum   MUSEUM
(☑ 28970 23660; www.lychnostatis.gr; adult/child €5/2; ⊙ 9am-2pm Sun-Fri) In a lovely seaside setting on Hersonisos' eastern edge, this family-operated, open-air folklore museum recreates a traditional Cretan village with commendable authenticity. The various buildings include a windmill and a farmer's house. Elsewhere there are weaving workshops, ceramics and plant-dying demonstrations, orchards and herb gardens and a theatre that hosts music and dance performances. Guided tours and audio guides (€1) are available and a *kafeneio* provides refreshments.

Aqua World   AQUARIUM
(www.aquaworld-crete.com; adult/child €6/4; ⊙ 10am-6pm Apr-Oct, last admission 5.15pm) In Hersonisos, behind the big Spar supermarket, this small, private aquarium and reptile centre is run by a friendly Brit. It showcases mostly local fish, including such crowd-pleasers as the venomous scorpion fish and the brightly hued peacock wrasse,

as well as turtles, geckos, a python and other reptiles. Almost all the animals are rescues.

Acqua Plus   WATER PARK
(www.acquaplus.gr; adult/child €26/17; ⊙ 10am-6pm May-Sept, to 7pm Jul & Aug) Wet fun awaits at Greece's oldest water park, in a lovely hillside garden setting 5km inland on the road to Kastelli. Kamikazee and the four extreme water slides are for adrenalin junkies, while nervous nellies might prefer the gentle float down the 270m-long Lazy River.

Star Beach   WATER PARK
(www.starbeach.gr; ⊙ 10am-6pm Apr-May, to 7pm Jun-Sep) **FREE** Part of the hotel complex of the same name, this water park is smaller and more low-key than the competition, making it perhaps less overwhelming for small children. Admission is free but most activities – jet skiing to parasailing – are fee-based.

Crete Golf Club   GOLF
(☑ 28970 26000; www.crete-golf.gr; 9/18 holes €50/80) This is Crete's only 18-hole golf course. It's a desert-style course that makes challenging use of the hillside setting and local nature and is definitely not for hackers. It was having a major overhaul at the time of research.

Arion Stables   HORSE RIDING
(☑ 6973733825; www.arionstables.com; Old Hersonisos; per hr €30) This horsy crowd is praised for its treatment of animals and for its rides. There's even an on-site petting zoo with rescued animals. Minimum two persons.

🛏 Sleeping

If you want to stay away from the resort hubbub, pick a place up the hill in the village of Koutouloufari, Piskopiano or Old Hersonisos.

Camping Creta CAMPGROUND €
(☑ 28970 41400; www.campingcrete.de.ki; camp sites per tent/person/car €7.50/4/3.50) About 7km west of Hersonisos on a sand-and-pebble beach in the hamlet of Gouves. There are some nicely shaded spots catering for both tenters and caravans, as well as a small market and waterfront taverna.

Villa Iokasti APARTMENT €€
(☑ 28970 22607; www.iokasti.gr; Koutouloufari; 1-/2-bedroom apt €65/110; ❋ @ ☒) Iokasti's 20 modern and bright one- and two-bedroom apartments with cheerful aqua-coloured accents and balconies are set off the main drag towards the end of Koutouloufari. What's left of the garden is taken up by the pool, but if sun lounges aren't your thing, there are pleasant seating areas out front. Also operates a Mediterranean restaurant of the same name.

★ Villa Ippocampi APARTMENT €€€
(☑ 28970 22316; www.ippocampi.com; 4G Seferi St, Koutouloufari; apt from €130; ❋ 🤶 ☒) This relaxing place exudes style and mesmerises from the moment you step past its lavender bushes and pool. Once you're ensconced in your apartment (all are decorated in a strong blue and white theme, right down to the checkered bathroom tiles), it's hard to go past two choices – to laze by the pool or chat to the charming owners, Lydia and Nikos.

Breakfasts (€9) are a treat; Nikos prepares a Cretan storm (and even picks mulberries that drip from the garden's tree). Of course, once you've distracted yourself from your book, or from sipping on a cappuccino at the tasteful, bright and airy on-site cafe (so discreet it's an extension of the garden), you might be ready to explore the quaint villages nearby. Note: it's a TV- and radio-free zone. Minimum three nights.

✗ Eating

For a more authentic experience, skip the identikit tourist tavernas and check out what's cooking uphill in Koutouloufari.

David Vegera Kafeneio CRETAN €
(Piskopiano; plates €3-7; ⊙ 5pm-late Mon-Sat) A fabulous spot housed in a former *kafeneio*, expect a buzzy vibe and a bit of table shuf-

fling due to the scores of Greeks and tourists who fill this little spot from the 5pm opening time. It serves old-time mezhedes, efficiently and without fuss. You fill out your own order, but ask about the daily specials too. Cheap. Cheerful. Highly recommended.

Poke your head inside to see the evocative black-and-white photos of Hersonisos of old.

Mythos GREEK €
(Sanoudaki 19, Hersonisos; mains €5-10; ⊙ 11am-midnight Apr-Oct) Honest-to-goodness Greek food is a rare commodity in Hersonisos proper, which is what makes Gianna and Manos' taverna such a find – and a long-standing Lonely Planet entry such is its reliability. It's tucked into a side street off the main strip.

Kostas & Eliotas GREEK €€
(Church Sq, Piskopiano; mains €7-15; ⊙ lunch & dinner Apr-Oct) It's easy to be distracted by the street-facing eateries in Koutouloufari, so you walk right past this gem, on the edge of the church plaza above the main village thoroughfare. Kostas is one of seven brothers, who each has a taverna in Crete, so need we add more? He's perfected the art of the simple grill, plus other traditional Greek dishes. Don't miss the lamb fillet with ouzo. If you're lucky you might catch a wedding at the church on the square, not to mention soccer games, bike-riding lessons and general village life.

Saradari SEAFOOD €€€
(www.saradari.com; Hersonisos; mains €10-25, fish per kilo from €50; ⊙ lunch & dinner) A high-end seafood place set on the upper slopes at the eastern end of Hersonisos, with a lot going for it: top-quality cuisine, snob factor and lovely ocean view. Write off the afternoon.

❶ Getting There & Away

Buses from Iraklio run at least every 30 minutes (€3, 40 minutes).

Malia Μάλια

You won't need to look hard to find the party in Malia, 34km east of Iraklio. The party will find you. The main strip, Dimokratias, is chock-a-block with boisterous bars, pubs and high-energy clubs filled with carousing twenty-somethings from abroad. One pocket of charm saves the town from being outright tacky: tiny Old Town Malia is a classic maze of narrow lanes.

Offering a civilised antidote to the madness, and the reason you must come here, are the ruins and sense of place of the fascinating Palace of Malia, a Minoan palace.

Beaches here are packed, though there's a lovely sandy strip east of town, near the Palace of Malia.

◉ Sights

★ **Palace of Malia** ARCHAEOLOGICAL SITE
(☎ 28970 31597; adult/child €4/free; ⊙ 8am-5pm, closed Mon in winter) The Palace of Malia, 3km east of Malia, was built at about the same time as the great Minoan palaces of Phaestos and Knossos. The First Palace dates back to around 1900 BC and was rebuilt after the earthquake of 1700 BC, only to be levelled again by another temblor around 1450 BC. Most of what you see today are the remains of the Second Palace, where many exquisite Minoan artefacts – including the famous gold bee pendant – were found.

Malia is a relatively easy site to comprehend, especially if you've already visited Knossos, which follows a similar ground plan. A free map and basic labelling throughout also help, as does the exhibition hall just past the entrance, where photographs and scale models of the ruined and reconstructed complex help you visualise the main palace and surrounding sites.

Access to the ruins is from the **West Court**. Instead of entering, though, turn right and walk south along the **West Magazines** to eight circular pits believed to have been **grain silos**. Continue east past the pits to the palace's south entrance and turn left to reach the southern end of the **Central Court**. On your left, in the ground, is the **Kernos Stone**, a disk with 24 holes around its edge. Archaeologists have yet to ascertain its function, but it probably had a religious purpose, possibly for offerings. Immediately adjacent are the four surviving steps of a

IRAKLIO MALIA

Palace of Malia

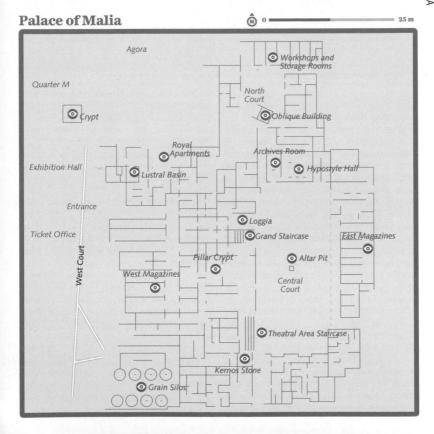

WORTH A TRIP

TOWARDS THE LASITHI PLATEAU

From Malia, the road climbs quickly to the Lasithi Plateau, passing through the charming village of **Krasí** and the monastery of **Kerá** along the way. Krasí's main claim to fame is a 2000-year-old **plane tree** with a mind-boggling 16m girth. It is fed by the adjacent spring spurting from an arcaded stone basin and provides shade for the taverna tables set up beneath its massive canopy.

Aposelemis Dam En route to/from Krasí, you will pass the controversial Aposelemis Dam, the construction of which was completed in 2012. Formerly wedged between the villages of Potamies and Advou, the village of Sfendile was flooded to allow for the damming of the Aposelemis Creek. This will provide drinking water to the greater Iraklio and Agios Nikolaos areas. Depending on the dam levels, you may still see house roofs, including that of Sfendiles village church, plus a tattered Greek flag fluttering.

The dam was still filling at the time of research, helped by the winter snowmelts.

Panagia Kardiotissa (admission €2; ⊘ 7am-7.30pm) Continuing on from the Aposelemis Dam takes you to Kerá, home to one of Crete's most cherished monasteries, the Panagia Kardiotissa. Its teensy chapel is embellished with 14th-century frescoes depicting scenes from the life of Christ and the Virgin, but locals especially venerate an 18th-century icon of the Virgin and Child. Legend has it that the Turks spirited it thrice to Constantinople but it miraculously returned each time, despite being chained to a marble pillar.

You'll find the icon on the left of the iconostasis (the wall that separates the nave from the sanctuary), next to the chains; the marble pillar is outside. There's also a small museum with religious paraphernalia.

Taverna Niki (www.nikitaverna.gr; Kerá; mains €7-13; ⊘ noon-late) After visiting the Panagia Kardiotissa, stop for both a view and a bite at Taverna Niki, on the corner as you leave Kerá. Niki cooks up daily treats in a traditional wood-fired oven; these are the most reliable dishes; you can really taste the smoky flavours. She's renowned, too, for the most simple of dishes: a potato omelette.

large staircase that may have been used as a **Theatral Area**.

Walk to the sunken **altar pit** in the centre of the courtyard and take in its impressive dimensions: 48m long and 22m wide. Beneath a canopy on your right are the **East Magazines**, where liquids were stored in giant *pithoi*. Opposite, the west wing harboured the most important rooms of the palace. These include the **Pillar Crypt** behind a stone-paved vestibule; the 11 remaining steps of the **Grand Staircase**, which might have led to a shrine; and the elevated **Loggia**, which was probably used for ceremonial purposes. Walk to the northern end of the courtyard and look down to see the stumps of the pillars that once held up the portico of the **Hypostyle Hall**. Fitted benches indicate that it may have served as a kind of council chamber. Near here, tablets containing Linear A script were found.

Continue along the paved walkway west of the Hypostyle Hall to the **North Court**, which was once lined with **workshops and storage rooms**. En route you'll pass by an oddly **oblique room** that dates to the more recent Postpalatial period. West of the north court you can spot the **royal apartments** anchored by the cordoned-off **Reception Hall** (labelled Polythyron, meaning 'many doors'), a rectangular structure on a raised platform. Behind it is the **lustral basin** where religious or symbolic cleansings possibly took place.

Malia Palace was surrounded by an entire city, the excavation of which is still ongoing. The canopied structure just west of the compound is described as the **Crypt**, while north of here the **Agora** was essentially one large building wrapped around a central courtyard. The most impressive section is **Quarter M**, a residential area a bit further west. Though fenced off, it's still possible to appreciate its size and complexity. These outer buildings date back to the First Palace period.

Guides are available at the entrance. Highly recommended German-speaking guide is Giorgos Pothos, a charismatic individual who brings the site alive.

Buses from Iraklio stop on the main road, 250m from the site.

Sleeping

Matheo Hotel
HOTEL €€

(📞 28970 32980; www.hotel-matheo.com; Theodoros 1; s €60-80, d €80-160; ❄ 🛜 ⭐) Quiet but close enough to the action, and popular with travel agency bookings, Matheo Hotel's 70 modern rooms occupy sparkling white villas amid olive and lemon trees. The standard ones are a bit teensy (rooms range from standard to suites and many in between). It's about 900m to the beach and 500m into town.

Villa Sonia
PENSION €€

(📞 28970 32221, 6932066776; www.villasonia.gr; d from €45; ❄) On the bustling beach road between Malia and Stalis, Sonia has 18 clean and utilitarian rooms in two buildings surrounded by palm trees. There is no pool, but you can use those at nearby hotels for free. It has a small on-site bar and the beach is only a short walk away, as is the bus stop. Air-conditioning costs €6 per day.

🍴 Eating

Head to Old Town Malia or Potamos beach near the Palace of Malia for better quality food and more authentic flair.

Taverna Kalyva
GREEK €€

(Potamos Beach, Malia; mains €8-14; ⊘ 11am-late Apr-Oct) To the west of the Malia archaeological site and just before you hit Potamos Beach, Taverna Kalyva is a bare-bones, no-nonsense beachside taverna that's been serving locals and visitors since 1964, especially on Sunday when Greeks pour in for *lo-ong* lunches.

The menu changes daily but the owner chefs whip up seafood and *mayirefta* (ready-cooked meals) for both those who haven't had enough sun, and for those who have.

Stablos & Elisabeth
GREEK €€

(Old Town Malia; mains €6-15) The best taverna on Old Town Malia's main square goes for the Crete-meets-English-B&B look with plenty of knick-knacks and lace curtains. The nicely prepared Greek and international foods are best enjoyed on the rooftop garden.

Mylos
GREEK €€

(📞 28970 33150; Giorgio Lapidi 9; mains €9-12; ⊘ 7pm-late Apr-Oct) This is as near to an oasis you can get in Malia – garlic strings hang from the walls, and flowers and leaves drip from the garden's lush trees. But what mainly pulls in the crowds are the *psito* dishes (roasted oven meats) cooked in the garden's wood-fired oven that's lit every afternoon. Best to reserve. It's located at the eastern edge of Old Town Malia.

ℹ Getting There & Away

There are buses to Malia from Iraklio at least every 30 minutes (€3.80, one hour).

IRAKLIO MALIA

Lasithi

Why Go?

Lasithi (Λασίθι) is Crete's wildest area with the richest biodiversity – with its caves, gorges, gas-blue coves and snow-capped mountains, the region seems to have been lavished by the gods. And that's not forgetting its rich ancient history, with Minoan and Mycenaean sites to be explored at every turn.

This is also where you'll find the island's top resorts. Agios Nikolaos' smouldering cosmopolitan cool, while nearby Elounda, the preserve of Tinseltown's finest, glitters with uber-swanky hotels. For adventure and gastro Grecophiles, Lasithi ticks all the boxes. Cyclists head up to misty Lasithi Plateau, trekkers tackle gorges like the dramatic Valley of the Dead, while foodies enjoy some of Crete's finest tavernas and restaurants. Then there are attractions like the historic monastery of Toplou and Vaï's beguiling palm-lined beach, while scores of towns and villages maintain a rich undertow of Cretan history and spirit.

Best Places to Eat

➜ Pelagos (p195)

➜ Arodamos (p200)

➜ Ta Kochilia (p206)

➜ Zorba's Tavern (p207)

➜ Napoleon (p217)

Best Places to Stay

➜ Terra Minoika (p213)

➜ Cretan Villa Hotel (p217)

➜ Villa Olga (p193)

➜ Petra Nova Villas (p205)

➜ Big Blue (p219)

Road Distances (km)

	Ierapetra	Agios Nikolaos	Elounda	Sitia
Agios Nikolaos	36			
Elounda	45	10		
Sitia	62	73	70	
Kato Zakros	98	106	116	36

NORTHERN COAST

Agios Nikolaos
Αγιος Νικόλαος
POP 11,421

Tumbling down the hillside to the shores of the glittering bay of Mirabello, Agios Nikolaos (*ah*-yee-os nih-*ko*-laos), Lasithi's capital, caters to an international cast of visitors and welcomes them with typical *filoxenia* (hospitality). Its streets are a colourful blend of bars, traditional tavernas and upscale clothes shops, counterbalanced with fish markets and earthy *kafeneia* (coffee houses). By night it really comes into its own when the harbour is illuminated by the lights of effervescent bars, and the adjoining bottle-green lagoon of Voulismeni Lake is even more beguiling.

Cosmetically, like many Cretan towns, Agios Nikolaos' architecture may lack the neoclassical grace of the Dodecanese and the sugar cube simplicity of the Cyclades, but it's stylish nonetheless, teeming with chic boutiques hawking jewellery, sea sponges and the usual offering of carved olive wood artefacts and busts of Achilles.

Stroll the harbour front alongside a young crowd of Greek fashionistas, park yourself at a cafe and listen to the buzz of conversation, or head to one of a handful of neighbouring beaches. And for all the glitz there's a surprising amount of affordable accommodation, while tavernas and restaurants offer both great-value Cretan specialities and wider Mediterranean-influenced cuisine. There's also free wi-fi in the harbour area and its surrounds.

The bus station is located just under a kilometre to the northwest of Voulismeni Lake. Most banks, travel agencies and shops are on Koundourou and the parallel pedestrian street 28 Oktovriou.

◉ Sights

Archaeological Museum   MUSEUM
(✉28410 24943; Paleologou Konstantinou 74; 📶) Due to the economic crisis at the time of writing, this museum was closed until 2016 for refurbishment and expansion. When open, the extensive collection is the second-most significant Minoan collection in existence, and includes clay coffins, ceramic musical instruments and gold from the island of Mohlos. The highlight is the odd-looking Goddess of Myrtos, a clay jug from 2500 BC.

Folk Museum   MUSEUM
(✉28410 25093; Paleologou Konstantinou 4; admission €3; ⊙10am-2pm Tue-Sun) Next to the tourist office, this museum has a small, well-curated collection of traditional handicrafts and costumes.

Beaches
In town the beaches of sandy **Ammos** and pebbly **Kytroplatia** are small and overcrowded. Let your feet take you 1km north and south respectively to **Ammoudi** and **Almyros** beaches, for longer stretches of finer sand to call your own. Almyros is quieter than the other beaches around town, with fine sand and beautiful clear water. All have umbrellas and sun chairs for rent.

🏃 Activities

General   BOAT TRIPS
(✉28410 24376; www.sailcrete.com; Minos, Beach Hotel Bungalows; half-/full day incl food & drinks €900/1300; ⊙9am-6pm) Run by Captain Apostolos, the *General*, a handsome 44ft cat, takes you (and up to five others) to Spinalonga Island and beyond on half- and full-day cruises. Meet him in Agios Nikolaos or arrange to be picked up from Elounda harbour.

Creta Underwater Center   DIVING
(✉28410 22406; www.cretaunderwatercenter.com; Mirabello Hotel, Agios Nikolaos; dives from €50) Reef, wreck and night dives to a host of different locations. Four-day PADI open-water courses also available.

Creta Semi-Submarine   BOAT TRIPS
(✉28410 24822, 6936051186; www.semi-submarine.gr; adult/child €15/10) The *Nautilus* has a submerged viewing cabin that is popular with youngsters and adults.

Pelagos   DIVING
(✉28410 24376; www.divecrete.com; Minos Beach Art Hotel; dives from €50, night dives €70) Offers dives and PADI courses.

Nostos Tours   BOAT TRIPS
(✉28410 22819; 30 Rousou Koundourou; trips to Spinalonga without/with barbecue €15/25, fishing trips €50) Runs boat trips to Spinalonga including a swim at Kolokytha. Also offers trips to Spinalonga Island including a barbecue, and fishing trips with food, including anything you catch.

Lasithi Highlights

① Wander among the fascinating ruins on **Spinalonga Island** (p201), as well as the settlements of its tragic leper colony.

② Ascend 630m to witness the finest wall paintings in Crete, at the mountain-bound **Church of Panagia Kera** (p198), one of Crete's most important churches.

③ Brave the creepy, forbidding darkness as you venture into Dikteon Cave, Zeus' mythic birthplace high up on the **Lasithi Plateau** (p202).

Paximada

Dragonada

Gianysada

Sea of Crete

Cape
Sideros

Itanos

Vaï ⊙   Vaï
Beach

**Moni
Toplou**
⑤

Kouremenos
Beach

Palekastro

Hiona
Beach

✈ **Sitia**

Petras

Agia Fotia

Roussolakkos

Skopi

Mohlos

Langada

Maronia

Mitato

Hohlakies Hohlakies Gorge

Azokeramos

Praisos

Katsidoni

Zakros

Kato Zakros
⑥

LASITHI

Mt Orno
(1238m)

Kato
Kria

Voila

Mt Tragistalos
▲ (515m)

Mt Thriptis
(1476m)

Handras

Ziros

Pefki

Aspros Potamos

Perivolakia

Xerokambos

Koutsouras

Makrygialos

Perivolakia
Gorge

Ambelos Beach

Mazidas Beach

Moni Kapsa

Agias Fotias

Goudouras

Koufonisi

*Mediterranean
Sea*

④ Explore the ruins at
Gournia (p204) for a deeper
insight into its Minoan
inhabitants.

⑤ Discover the chequered
history of **Moni Toplou**
(p209), more of a fortress
than a temple, and a beacon of
Greek resistance and bravery.

⑥ Explore the Valley of the
Dead at **Kato Zakros** (p213),
following it through wildflower
paths, under the watchful eyes
of eagles.

Agios Nikolaos

Martinbike Crete
CYCLING

(☑ 28410 26622; www.martinbike.com; Hotel Sunlight, Elounda Rd, Agia Gallini; day trip from €65; ☺ Apr-Nov) Celebrating 20 years' operating in Crete, this excellent cycling tour specialist is based at Hotel Sunlight, halfway between Agios Nikolaos and Elounda. It runs one- and five-day trips in the surrounding areas, taking you through olive groves, sweeping mountain vistas and more on sturdy Scott bikes with skilled guides.

👉 Tours

Travel agencies offer bus tours to Crete's top attractions and the boats along the harbour advertise their various excursions.

Little Train Tours
TRAIN

(☑ 28140 25420; www.littletraintours.gr; Akti Themistokleous; adult/child ½hr ride €9/3, 3½hr trip €20/14) Youngsters love these trips that vary from a half-hour ride round town to a 3½-hour trip that takes in an olive farm and a visit to the village of Kritsa. Tours start from the eastern harbour front.

✱ Festivals & Events

Lato Cultural Festival
MUSIC, DANCE

(☺ Jul & Aug) In July and August Agios Nikolaos hosts the Lato Cultural Festival, with concerts by local and international musicians, folk dancing, *mantinadhes* (rhyming couplets) contests, theatre and art exhibitions. Ask at the tourist office for details.

Marine Week
WATER SPORTS

(☺ Jun) Held during the last week of June in even-numbered years, this celebration has swimming, windsurfing and boat races.

🛏 Sleeping

Hotel Doxa
HOTEL €

(☑ 28410 24214; www.doxahotel.gr; Idomeneos 7; s/d/tr incl breakfast €45/50/65; ❋ 🛜) This shadowy, bijou hotel down a side street has smart but cramped rooms with chocolate-brown quilts, marble floors, flat-screen TV, and immaculate en suite bathroom. Great breakfast. There is a lift, and Ammos beach and car parking are just a short stroll away.

Pension Mary
PENSION €

(☑ 28410 23760; Evans 13; s/d/tr €15/35/45; ❋) Expect simple white-walled rooms with fridge and pine furniture at this old-fashioned pension in a narrow street just up from Kytroplatia beach. Rooms have bathrooms, and there's a communal kitchen and a pleasant shaded area out back where you can spend time reading or eating. Best of all, you can hear the sea as you go to sleep!

Pergola Hotel
HOTEL €

(☑ 28410 28152; Sarolidi 20; s/d/apt incl breakfast €35/40/60; ❋ 🛜) Run by charming management, this basic pension has really cosy rooms with waffled bedspreads, TV, spotless en suite, and balconies with great views of the bay. If you're a family or two couples, keep an eye out for the recently added apartment with widescreen views and top spec en suite. There's also fresh bread, honey and boiled eggs for breakfast.

Delta
HOTEL €

(☑ 28410 28893; www.agiosnikalaos-hotels.gr; Tselepi 22; r €50; ❋) Opposite Kytroplatia beach and behind a taverna, these bright, clean rooms are run by the owners of the Hotel Creta. There's a minimum two-night stay.

★ Villa Olga
APARTMENT €€

(☑ 28410 25913; www.villa-olga.gr; Anapafseos 18, Ellinika; s €45, apt €80-95; ❋ 🛜 ❄) These delicious self-catering studios and apartments (two to six persons) enjoy serene views of the Bay of Mirabello from their rising terraces set in lush gardens scattered with urns and shaded by olive trees. The interiors are traditional chic with tiled floors and tasteful bed linen and furniture. There's a small swimming pool.

Villa Olga is reached by following the waterfront road, Akti Koundourou, northeast from the centre of Agios Nikolaos. At a junction above Ammoudi beach take the right-hand branch towards Elounda for about 500m and look out for the Villa Olga sign on the left.

Du Lac Hotel
HOTEL €€

(☑ 28410 22711; www.dulachotel.gr; 28 Oktovriou 17; s/d/studio with lake view €40/55/70; ❋ 🛜) Slick and modern, this delightful central hotel is the businessman's choice with fresh studios and apartments enjoying wood-effect walls, laminate floors, and balconies with fine views over Voulismeni Lake. Studio kitchenettes are modern and well equipped, while apartments also have baths. Downstairs there's a pleasant restaurant. Expect excellent value off season.

Lato Hotel
HOTEL €€

(☑ 28410 24581; www.lato-hotel.com.gr; Ammoudi; s/d €55/70; 🅿 ❋ 🛜 ❄) Popular with travellers for its cleanliness, buffet breakfast,

THREE PERFECT DAYS

Day One

From Agios Nikolaos it's a short drive along the Kritsa road to the **Church of the Panagia Kera** (p198), where there's a feast of fabulous 13th-century frescoes. Then drop back 2000 years at the nearby Hellenistic-Dorian site of **Lato** (p198). Head back to **Kritsa** (p197), weave your way past the needlework sellers and wander the old town. At day's end, reflect on the astonishing island history and culture while dining at one of Agios Nikolaos' archetypal Cretan restaurants such as **Pelagos** (p195).

Day Two

A reading of the romantic novel *The Island* will lead you to the compelling island of **Spinalonga** (p201), the one-time leper colony where the novel and its television series are set. You can get here by boat from Agios Nikolaos, Elounda or Plaka. Before you go, a visit to Agios Nikolaos' delightful **Folk Museum** (p189) conjures up a sense of time and place regarding the older Crete portrayed in the book. Finish the day at Elounda's **Arodamos** (p200) restaurant for Cretan cuisine.

Day Three

Start the day early. From Sitia head for **Moni Toplou** (p209), one of Crete's outstanding monasteries. Continue to Palekastro and on to **Kato Zakros** (p211) for some Minoan magic at the remains of an ancient palace. Take a stroll into the awesome **Valley of the Dead** (p213), and then drive back through rugged mountains to Sitia for a gourmet evening at traditional **Zorba's Tavern** (p207).

pool and friendly owners. Rooms are cosy with fridge and spotless en suite, but try for a quieter room at the back with a sea view. Catch the Elounda bus from Agios Nikolaos and ask to get off at the hotel. The beach is about 300m away.

The same management runs the charming Karavostassi (The Stone House) Apartments in an old carob warehouse on an isolated cove about 8km east from the Lato.

Pension Mylos   PENSION €€
(☑ 6945992661, 28410 23783; www.pensionmyl os.com; 24 Sarolidi; s/d/tr €45/55/65; ❋ ☎ ⛊) From the faded sign outside you might not guess, but within lie gorgeously welcoming rooms with bedside lamps, shiny en suites, seaward balconies and great attention to detail like orthopedic mattresses and linen sheets. The welcoming owner delivers her tagline of 'home from home'. Fridge, TV and coffee-making service, too. A few minutes' walk up from the harbour. There's limited parking on the street.

Hotel Creta   APARTMENT €€
(☑ 28410 28893; www.agiosnikaloas-hotels.gr/creta; Sarolidi 22; s/d/tr €50/60/70; ❋ @ ☎) Bland but good-value studios with kitchenette, balcony and fine views of the glittering bay beyond. Just a few minutes' walk up from the harbour, the location is ideal for the town centre, yet in a quiet location. There's a lift and limited parking in the surrounding streets.

Minos Beach Art Hotel   BOUTIQUE HOTEL €€€
(☑ 28410 22345; www.minosbeach.com; Akti Ilia Sotirchou; r incl breakfast from €280; ℙ ❋ ☎ ⛱) In a superb location just out of town, this classy resort is a veritable art gallery, with sculptures from leading Greek and foreign artists adorning the grounds right down to the beach. The low-rise design and cool style maintain the hotel's status as one of the island's finest. Follow the waterfront road, Akti Koundourou, northeast from the centre of Agios Nikolaos for about 1km. The hotel is signposted 'Minos Beach Hotel' on the seaward side of the road.

✗ Eating

For earthier, tastier food, head around the harbour to Kytroplatia beach where the locals eat.

Sarri's   GREEK €
(Kyprou 15; mains €10; ☺ lunch & dinner) Shaded by the branches of a eucalyptus tree, with its check-cloth tables and sun-beaten ambience, Sarri's evokes old Greece. Get stuck in to shrimp *saganaki,* souvlaki, calamari, pizza or a mezedhes platter with wine for

€9. The garden terrace is ideal for breakfast, lunch or dinner. To find it reach the top of the hill and walk down 20m.

Faros
GREEK €

(Kytroplatia beach; mains €10; ⊙ noon-late) Right by the sea, this aromatic, family-run taverna exudes atmosphere, with meat and fish aglow on the brazier out front. There's outdoor seating beneath a sheltered canopy, or a homey setting within the restaurant. The food is no less than superb with huge salads, mouthwatering calamari, *kleftiko* (slow oven-baked lamb or goat) and *stifadho* (meat cooked with onions in a tomato puree)... maybe free baklava and *raki,* too. *Filoxenia* (hospitality) in extremis!

Katzarolakia Ble
GREEK €

(Akti Koundourou; mains €8; ⊙ lunch & dinner; 🕾) Enjoying great views of the harbour, this effervescent restaurant, with its modern decor of exposed stone, turquoise walls and white-wood floors, offers a contemporary take on Greek cuisine. Tzatziki, halloumi, souvlaki, octopus and many more. Not surprisingly it's packed out with young Greeks and deservedly so. Take the lift up to the top floor.

Itanos
CRETAN €

(📋 28410 25340; Kyprou 1; mains €9; ⊙ noon-midnight; 🕾🕾) Earthy Itanos has terrific Cretan homestyle cooking dished up by Chef Kostas. Select from trays of fresh *mayirefta* (casseroles and oven-baked dishes) such as goat with artichokes, tasty meatballs, moussaka, a wealth of vegie dishes and *kleftiko* (slow oven-cooked lamb) to die for. From outside it might not look much but there's magic brewing in that kitchen.

Embassy
GREEK €

(www.cretaembassy.com; Kondylaki; mains €7; ⊙ noon-late) Hung with ornate mirrors and Venetian masks overlooking gypsy-chic tables, this traditional restaurant is welcoming. Lamb *kleftiko,* veal with lemon, oven-baked pies and calamari with mouthwatering olives.

Palazzo Cafe Bar
CAFE €

(Kytroplatia beach; mains €4; ⊙ 8am-late; 🕾) This upscale cafe-bar with a sea-facing verandah exudes minimalist chic with faux marble walls and wood-topped tables. The menu covers salads, toasties, ice creams and sandwiches. There's storytelling and live music events in the evening.

Chrisofyllis
CRETAN €

(📋 28410 22705; Akti Pagalou; mezedhes €4-8; ⊙ 12.30pm-12.30am; 🕾) Well-priced food makes this *mezedhopoleio* a classic small-plate place with several varieties of ouzo to enhance things, as well as some Greek wines. Specials include cheese pies, fresh mussels, and chicken with saffron. Bookings advised.

★ Pelagos
MEDITERRANEAN €€

(📋 28410 25737; cnr Stratigou Koraka & Katehaki; mains €10; ⊙ lunch & dinner; 🕾) Neoclassical meets modern Greek in this breezy upscale restaurant, with faux-distressed walls hung with petal-glass lamps and icons, fresh orange and white tables, and a menu of salads, seafood, meat and pasta. Order the grilled prawns and try not to come back again! Exquisite. There's also a garden terrace.

Migomis
MEDITERRANEAN €€€

(📋 28410 24353; www.migomis.gr; Nikolaou Plastira 20; mains €12-38; ⊙ lunch & dinner Apr-Oct; 🕾) Commanding Olympian views of Voulismeni Lake, this tasteful eyrie sports candelabra, exposed stone walls, linen tablecloths and the soothing sounds of live piano on summer evenings. Cuisine spans Greek classics to Italian. Bookings advised.

🍸 Drinking & Entertainment

The waterfront cafe-bars lining Akti Koundourou above the harbour get going mid-morning and later morph into lively bars. There are also other options around town.

Bar Arudo
BAR

(Akti Koundourou; ⊙ 9.30am-late) This low-lit haunt buzzes with the conversation of earnest boho locals, offering a cocktail of cool tunes, a sea-facing outside terrace and a handsome wooden bar within.

Alexandros Roof Garden
BAR

(Kondylaki; ⊙ noon-late; 🕾) Classic sounds amid hanging plants, shrubs and funky decor.

Yianni's Rock Music Bar
BAR

(Akti Koundourou; ⊙ 10pm-5am) Haunting the wee hours since 1983, the town's oldest music bar flickers in candlelight on the waterfront, its walls peppered with old Brando and Stallone photos. Thundering rock music and plenty of atmosphere; a night owl's delight.

🛈 GETTING AROUND LASITHI

Roads between the main centres and larger resorts throughout Lasithi are good. Minor surfaced roads are adequate, but always watch out for potholes. Driving on unsurfaced roads is not advised unless with off-road vehicles and full insurance.

Most larger villages and resorts can be reached by bus from Agios Nikolaos, Sitia and Ierapetra. The best way of finding up-to-date information is from the bus stations themselves. Many villages only have early morning and midday services during school terms. Popular tourist destinations only have a summer service.

You can rent cars, bikes and scooters from main centres and from most resorts in summer.

Peripou Cafe CAFE
(28 Otkovriou 13; ☉9.30am-2am; 🛜) This arty bar with a verandah overlooking the lagoon has a bijou bookstore, plays indie tunes, sells toasties and has a boho charm from the moment you enter its wine-coloured facade.

Dioliko BAR
(Koundourou; ☉10pm-late) Contemporary stone interior with sport on the flat-screen TVs and a list of cocktails to work your way through in its sheltered booths. There's also breakfast, crêpes and coffee.

Ellinadiko CLUB
(25 Martiou; ☉10pm-late) This haunt popular with locals and visitors prides itself on being the only place in town to play *only* Greek music.

Cube Bar CLUB
(25 Martiou; ☉10pm-late) Hip hop and R&B at this funky late-night bar popular with a younger crowd.

🛍 Shopping

Aroma Coffee Shop FOOD & DRINK
(Plateia Venizelou 24) This aromatic shop has a selection of ground coffee, biscuits, sweets, nuts, wines and spirits, as well as beautiful handmade copper *briki* (coffee pots) for sale.

Zakros Souvenirs SOUVENIRS
(28 Oktovriou; ☉10am-10pm) Packed to the gills with classical statuary and repro icons.

Grab a bust of Hercules, ceramic pottery or puppets here.

Marieli CLOTHING
(28 Oktovriou 33; ☉10am-11pm) This quirky little boutique sells stylish ladies' tees, dresses, shoes and beachwear.

Kerazoza ARTS & CRAFTS
(Koundourou 42; ☉10am-10pm) Behind its turquoise exterior, this gem of a shop sells eye-catching necklaces, bracelets and rings, and masks and marionettes derived from ancient Greek theatre, along with some good-quality sculptures and ceramics.

Anna Karteri Bookshop BOOKS
(Koundourou 5 & Oktovriou; ☉10am-11pm) Well stocked with maps, guidebooks and thrillers in English and other languages. The shop has access from both streets.

🛈 Information

For more information visit www.lasithitravel.com and www.agiosnikolaos.com.

Byron Travel (Akti Koundourou 4; ☉8am-8.30pm) On the harbour, this excellent tour agency, run by Magdalene, books plane and boat tickets. It has reliable cars with fully comprehensive insurance from as little as €30 per day, and you can even drop off your ride at Iraklio airport.

General Hospital (☑ 28410 66000) OK for broken bones and x-rays, but for anything more serious you'll need to head to Iraklio. On the western side of town, at the top of the steep Paleologou Konstantinou.

Municipal Tourist Office (☑ 28410 22357; www.agiosnikolaos.gr; ☉8am-10pm Apr-Nov) Has helpful information and maps, changes money and assists with accommodation. Opposite the northern side of the Voulismeni Lake bridge.

National Bank of Greece (Nikolaou Plastira) Has a 24-hour exchange machine.

Post Office (28 Oktovriou 9; ☉7.30am-2pm Mon-Fri)

Tourist Police (☑ 28410 91408; Erythrou Stavrou 47; ☉7.30am-2.30pm Mon-Fri)

🛈 Getting There & Away

Buses leave Agios Nikolaos' **bus station** for Elounda (€1.70, 20 minutes, 16 daily), Ierapetra (€3.80, one hour, seven daily), Iraklio (€7.10, 1½ hours, 18 daily), Kritsa (€1.60, 15 minutes, 10 daily), Lasithi Plateau (Dikteon Cave; €6, three hours, two daily), Vaï (€14) and Sitia (€7.60, 1½ hours, seven daily). You can catch the Elounda bus at a stop opposite the tourist office. A local bus (every half hour) can also be boarded here for the main bus station.

Boats run regularly to Spinalonga Island throughout the morning and cost €15, returning mid-afternoon.

ℹ️ Getting Around

Typical **taxi** (☎ 28410 24100) charges include Elounda (€13), Plaka (€18), Kritsa (€13) and Lato (€15).

Car and motorcycle hire outlets can be found on 28 Oktovriou and the northern waterfront. **Club Cars** (☎ 28410 25868; www.clubcars.net; per day from €40) has cars for hire from about €40 per day.

Manolis Bikes (☎ 28410 24940; 25 Martiou 12; scooter/mountain bike per day from €20/12) has a huge range of scooters, motorcycles and quad bikes.

Kritsa   Κριτσά

POP 1296

Located beside the mouth of the dramatic Chauga Gorge, 11km from Agios Nikolaos, Kritsa (krit-*sah*) is achingly pretty. Its main draw is its authentic rural tempo and the paved, flag-festooned street of Kritzotopoula, beneath which walnut-brown octogenarians knit and hawk their wares of embroidered tablecloths and bed-runners.

At the heart of the main square, Plateia Melinas Merkouri (Melina Mercouri Sq), there's a handsome bust of Kritsotopoula, a local beauty and revered heroine of the 1820s. At the start of Kritzotopoula, which branches off right just uphill from the main square, is **Olive Wood** (Kritzotopoula; ⊙10am-9pm), a friendly little shop full of authentic handmade olive-wood spoons, bowls and candle-holders, as well as gypsy-chic hand-painted ceramics. Next door is the venerable shoemaker **Detorakis** (Kritzotopoula; ⊙9am-11pm), where you can buy a fine pair of Cretan sandals for adults (€25) and kids (€18). Look out too for **Philema** (Kritzotopoula; ⊙9am-11pm) which sells local olive oil and local wine.

After the comparative buzz of Agios Nikolaos, this diminutive village is a real slice of calm – despite the tour coaches piling into Kritsa from late morning until late afternoon.

🛏️ Sleeping

Rooms Argyro   PENSION €
(☎ 28410 51174; www.argyrorentrooms.gr; s/d/tr/f €30/40/50/70; ✳️) Situated on the left-hand side as you enter the village from the east, this delightfully clean place is run by a sweet lady and has stunning rooms with cool marble floors, spotless en suites, homey floral bedspreads, glass pendant lights and shabby-chic furniture. Many rooms have balconies, though the triple has the best mountain view.

🍴 Eating

Taverna Café Platanos   GREEK €
(Kritzotopoula; mains €6.50; ⊙10am-9pm) A taverna-*kafeneio* halfway along Kritzotopoula, Platanos has a pleasant setting under a giant 200-year-old plane tree and vine canopy. There's a tasty menu of grills, *stifadho* (lamb stew) and *mayirefta* (ready-cooked meals).

LASITHI KRITSA

KRITSOTOPOULA, THE CRETAN HERO

The rousing tale of the beautiful and heroic Cretan girl Kritsotopoula (child of Kritsa) tells the story of Rhodanthe (her real name), who lived in Kritsa in the early years of the 19th century during the Ottoman occupation of Crete. She was said to have had a beautiful singing voice, and it was her singing that one day caught the attention of a drunken Turkish officer who attempted to push his way into her house. Rhodanthe's mother resisted his attempts and was stabbed to death. The soldier then abducted Rhodanthe, but later that night while he slept Rhodanthe slit his throat, cut off her long hair, and took off for the mountains disguised as a man to join the Cretan freedom fighters.

In 1823, Rhodanthe distinguished herself in a fierce battle with the Turks near Ancient Lato. She was shot in the chest and died. Initial efforts to staunch the wounds revealed her sex and thereafter she became the revered Kritsotopoula, a classic symbol of Cretan resistance. As well as a bust in Kritsa's Plateia Melinas Merkouri (Melina Mercouri Sq), there is a bas-relief on local stone by the English sculptor Nigel Ratcliffe-Springall, sited in an enclosure on the way to Lato. It depicts the dying Kritsotopoula in the arms of her father, a local priest.

Saridakis Kafeneio
CAFE €

(Kritzotopoula; juice €3; ☺ 8am-midnight) An excellent little cafe, this place makes for a cool stop in the shade to grab some homemade honey and yoghurt or a fresh orange juice.

Cafe Bar Massaros
CAFE €

(Kritzotopoula; ☺ 7am-3am; @ 🛜) A pleasant cafe-bar just up from the main square with internet access (€1 per half hour) and wi-fi. It also serves toasties, crêpes, salads and pizza.

❶ Getting There & Away

There are hourly buses from Agios Nikolaos to Kritsa (€1.60, 15 minutes, 10 daily). A taxi from Agios Nikolaos costs €13.

Around Kritsa

Church of Panagia Kera

★ **Church of Panagia Kera** CHURCH

(🗗 28410 51806; admission €3; ☺ 8.30am-3pm Tue-Sun) The tiny triple-aisled Church of Panagia Kera, 1km northeast of Kritsa, contains the finest Byzantine frescoes in Crete. The oldest part of the church is the 13th-century central nave, but most of the frescoes date from the early to mid-14th century. The dome and nave are decorated with four gospel scenes: the Presentation, the Baptism, the Raising of Lazarus and the Entry into Jerusalem. On the western wall is a portrayal of the Crucifixion and grimly realistic depictions of the Punishment of the Damned.

The vault of the southern aisle recounts the life of the Virgin; the northern aisle is an elaborately worked-out fresco of the Second Coming. Nearby is an enticing depiction of Paradise next to the Virgin and the Patriarchs – Abraham, Isaac and Jacob. Judgement Day is portrayed on the western end, with the Archangel Michael trumpeting the Second Coming.

Ancient Lato
Λατώ

Ancient Lato ARCHAEOLOGICAL SITE

(admission €2; ☺ 8.30am-3pm Tue-Sun) Worth the wheeze for the rural serenity alone – the mountain a silvery sheen of wildflowers, the nearby peaks tipped with snow – the ancient city of Lato, 4km north of Kritsa, is one of Crete's few non-Minoan ancient sites. Lato (la-*to*) was founded in the 7th century BC

by the Dorians and at its height was one of the most powerful cities in Crete, until it was abandoned in 200 BC for its more convenient harbour, where Agios Nikolaos now stands.

The surviving ruins sprawl over the slopes of two acropolises in a lonely mountain setting, commanding stunning views down to the Bay of Mirabello. At a little elevation they begin to take form as you look down and imagine the bustling *agora* (market).

The **city gate** is the entrance to the site and leads to a long, stepped street. The wall on the left contains two towers, which were also residences. Follow the street to reach the *agora*, built around the 4th century BC, which contained a cistern and a rectangular sanctuary. Excavations of the temple have revealed a number of 6th century BC figurines. The circle of stones behind the cistern was a threshing floor.

The western side of the *agora* contains a **stoa** with stone benches. There are remains of a pebble mosaic nearby. A terrace above the southeastern corner of the *agora* contains the remains of a **rectangular temple**, probably built in the late 4th or early 3rd century BC. Between the two towers on the northern end of the *agora*, there are steps leading to the **prytaneion**, the administrative centre of the city-state. The centre of the prytaneion contained a hearth with a fire that burned day and night. On the eastern side of the prytaneion is a colonnaded court.

Below the prytaneion is a semicircular theatre that could seat about 350 people next to an **exedra** (stage), which has a bench around the walls.

Neachus, one of Alexander's generals, is said to have come from here. The city's name is derived from the goddess Leto, whose union with Zeus produced Artemis and Apollo, both of whom were worshipped here.

There are no buses to Lato. The road to the site is signposted to the right on the approach to Kritsa. It's a 30-minute road walk through pleasant wooded countryside.

Katharo Plateau & Kroustas

From Kritsa it is a 16km scenic climb up to the spectacular **Katharo Plateau**, which is cultivated by people from Kritsa, some of whom have summer homes here. Sitting at an altitude of 1200m, this beautiful wild-flower pleateau is often under deep snow in winter, and home to only 500 inhabitants. There are a couple of seasonal tavernas here.

Just 4.5km south of Kritsa is the village of **Kroustas**, where locals go for very traditional local cuisine. Popular **O Kroustas** (☺10am-10pm) has Cretan food, including a superb *lazania* (twisted handmade pasta, also called *stroufikta*) cooked in stock with *anthotiro* (a dry, white cheese) and rusks made in the wood oven.

Elounda   Ελούντα

POP 2185

This earthy little fishing village has grown in profile in recent years, thanks to the nearby uber-exclusive hotels enjoying an influx of A-list celebrities (think Ronaldo, Leonardo DiCaprio, U2 and Lady Gaga). The town itself lacks any of this style and glitz, though it seems happy enough about that. Locals will cheerfully take you fishing or to nearby Spinalonga Island, oblivious to the odd appearance of the Hollywood deities venturing from their gated Olympian haunts.

By night Elounda looks more inviting, the harbour aglitter with the lights of tavernas and bars. The pleasant but unremarkable town beach, to the north of the port, can get very crowded. On the southern side of Elounda an artificial causeway leads to the Kolokytha Peninsula.

★ Activities

Ferries go regularly to Spinalonga Island from Elounda. Numerous boats offer other trips (€10) around the area; they operate through a cooperative from the harbour quay.

Blue Dolphin Diving Centre   DIVING
(☑ 28410 41802; www.dive-bluedolphin.com; dives from €50, open-water course €390) The area around Elounda offers excellent diving. Try this PADI centre at the Aquila hotel.

Amazing Sailing in Crete   SAILING
(☑ 6944586475; www.amazingsailingincrete.com; Porta Elounda Resort, Elounda; 3hr sunset cruise/4hr half-day cruise/full-day cruise €650/750/1100) Visit hidden coves inaccessible by road and have lunch in a traditional fishing village. Drinks and fruit are included. Run by friendly Captain Yiannis.

🛏 Sleeping

Many hotels in and around Elounda are booked in advance by tour operators.

Delfinia Apartments   APARTMENT €
(☑ 28410 41641; www.pediaditis.gr; studio/apt €40/50; ❋ ❂ ❄ ❖) These delightful seaview rooms enjoy tasteful furnishings and well-equipped kitchenettes with sandwichmaker, fridge and microwave. So close to the waves they will lull you to sleep. The same family also run the nearby Milos Apartments, where there is a pool.

Hotel Aristea   HOTEL €
(☑ 28410 41300; www.aristeahotel.com; Main Sq; s/d incl breakfast €35/45; ❋ ❂) This elegantly faded dame close to the harbour, on the corner of the main square, has an authentic family feel and the lady owner is charming. Rooms are cosy with tangerine bedspreads, fridge, hairdryer, seaward balcony and spotless bathroom. Old-world charm.

Marin   APARTMENT €
(☑ 28410 41588; d/apt €40/55; Ⓟ ❂) Overlooking the town beach on the road to Plaka, these are simple whitewashed rooms and apartments with clean floors, tasteful furniture and basic kitchenettes. Each room also has a desk and balcony. The main draw is the cosy snack bar out front which has homemade food.

Kalypso Hotel   HOTEL €
(☑ 28410 41367; www.kalypsoelounda.gr; s/d €30/60; ❋ ❂) There are 16 bright, spotless rooms in this characterful, crenellated building next to the clock tower on the main square in the centre of the village. Rooms have sparkling bathrooms, large, comfy beds, desk and minimalist decor. There's an inviting restaurant downstairs with all the usual suspects on the menu.

Corali Studios   APARTMENT €€
(☑ 28410 41712; www.coralistudios.com; Akti Poseidonos; r €45-75; Ⓟ ❋ ❂ ❄) Set amid lush lawns with a shaded patio, and overlooking the nearby town beach, Corali has stucco-walled, fresh rooms with waffle quilts, balcony, large bathroom, and tasteful furniture. You'll find them a few hundred yards out of Elounda heading for Plakia. The same family run the **Portobello Apartments** (€65-75) next door.

Elounda Island Villas   APARTMENT €€
(☑ 28410 41274; www.eloundaisland.gr; d €85, 4-person apt €115; Ⓟ ❋ ❂) A secluded option on Kolokytha Island, reached along the

LASITHI ELOUNDA

narrow peninsula. The split-level apartments, with well-equipped kitchens, are set amid a pleasant garden and decorated with traditional furnishings. It's just under a kilometre's walk into town.

Eating

★ Arodamos
GREEK €

(☏28410 41122; Naksou 6; mains €4-9; ⊙11am-late; ☻) This hidden jewel sits two minutes' walk behind the square occupying a century-old cube house with Cycladic blue shutters and fronted by a garden of shady olive trees and palms. The menu is trad-Greek with meat cooked on the spit before your eyes; lamb chops, local sausage and *kondosouvli* (roasted liver wrapped in intestines).

Marilena
GREEK €

(mains €11; ⊙11am-11pm; ☷) One of the oldest and most traditional restaurants in town, Marilena enchants with check-cloth tables, Cretan handicrafts, musical instruments on the walls, and a lively atmosphere lit with good service and fine food. Try the *kleftiko* (slow oven-baked lamb). Romantic. It's on the road to Plaka.

Oceanis
CRETAN €

(☏28410 42246; mains €6.50-16; ⊙lunch & dinner) Adonis Bebelakis cooks for pleasure as well as profit, refrains from overcrowding his tables, and sources his local raw materials with care. The style is slow cooking, including such Cretan classics as oven-cooked lamb with garlic and sweet wine and Bebelakis family favourites such as *melidzanes tis mamas* (slices of aubergine baked with tomatoes, hard cheese and spearmint). Find it 500m out of town, on the road to Plaka.

Fresco Eatery
MEDITERRANEAN €

(mains €6; ⊙6am-late) On the corner of the main square beside the clocktower, this tasty joint has a lively alfresco area and dishes up huge fresh salads, pizza, pasta, *gyros* and burgers.

♟ Drinking & Nightlife

There are several cheerful bars and clubs in Elounda, though things are still fairly low key.

Haroupo Ergospacio Cafe Bar
BAR

(⊙noon-midnight) Easy tunes, cream shabby-chic furniture, a handsome stone and wood bar, as well as sofas and scattered wooden chests make this a tasteful waterfront spot

to gather by the lap of the waves and watch the sundown. Cocktails, juices and snacks.

Katafygio
BAR

(⊙9am-late) Looking a little faded now, Katafygio is known for its Cretan and Greek music nights and occasional belly-dancing sessions. Find it at the southern end of the Elounda waterfront, housed in a former carob-processing plant.

Alyggos Bar
BAR

Twenty-five years young, this popular tourist bar on the main square offers late-night disco, and by day, a cool, shadowy spot to watch the football. Wood ceiling, candelabra and a nice vibe.

Babel
BAR

(Akti Vritomartidos) Attractive decor and an upbeat tone make Babel a cool venue for drinks. It's just along from the prominent clock tower on the harbour.

⌂ Shopping

Trilogy
CRAFTS

(A Papandreou 9; ⊙10am-8pm) An attractive craft and gift shop that offers photocopying alongside its selection of books, stationery and artifacts.

❶ Information

The main square of Elounda is something of a large car park (parking per hour €1, six hours €3.50), but it overlooks an attractive fishing harbour still devoted to working boats. The post office and a couple of ATMs are located here.

Babel Internet Cafe (☏28410 42336; per hr €2) The Babel bar's other facility.

Municipal Tourist Office (☏28410 42464; ⊙8am-8pm Jun-Oct) Helps with accommodation and information, and changes money.

Olous Travel (☏28410 41324) Handles air and boat tickets and finds accommodation. It's overlooking the main square.

❶ Getting There & Around

Boats cross to Spinalonga Island every half-hour (return adult/child €10/5, 10 minutes).

There are 13 buses daily from Agios Nikolaos to Elounda (€1.70, 20 minutes). Buses stop at the main square, where there's a **taxi stand** (☏28410 41151). The fare is €13 to Agios Nikolaos and €7 to Plaka.

Cars, motorcycles and scooters can be hired at **Elounda Travel** (☏28410 41800; www.eloundatravel.gr), which has several offices in town including one on the main square. High season prices for cars range from €50 to €105 per day.

Kolokytha Peninsula
Χερσόνησος Κολοκύθα

Opposite Elounda is the Kolokytha Peninsula, reached by a low causeway. **Ancient Olous**, which was the port of Lato, stood on and around the original isthmus. Olous was a Minoan settlement that flourished from 3000 to 900 BC and was an important trade centre. It appears to have been destroyed by the Saracens in the 9th century AD.

Most of the ruins lie beneath the water on either side of the causeway and have made the area a popular place for snorkelling. Many birds nest here and pass through in spring and autumn. The remains of an early Christian mosaic, portraying dolphins, lies within an enclosure near the causeway.

Coming from Agios Nikolaos the causeway and peninsula are reached as you enter Elounda, by turning off the main road just beyond the prominent yellow signs of the Elounda Rent a Car offices and opposite Mam's House snack bar. It's a tight turn.

On the eastern side of the Kolokytha Peninsula, there's a sandy beach 1km from the causeway's end, reached by a narrow dirt track.

Plaka
Πλάκα

POP 94

Wind-blasted Plaka, 5km from Elounda, is a delightful bijou village of attractive boutiques, inviting restaurants and cafes, as well as some very cosy tavernas hugging the waterfront. Beyond the jetty, past the yellow nets and cobalt sea, is the skeletal ruins of Spinalonga Island, a former leper colony. Low-key Plaka is now internationally famous in the wake of the success of the novel and television series, *The Island (To Nisi)*.

Ask around the village or at one of the tavernas about boats to Spinalonga Island (about €10 return); they depart regularly with tour companies and on demand.

Petros Watersports (☑6944932760; www.spinalonga-windsurf.com; Marmin Bay Palace) rents kayaks by the hour (€15) and day, and offers ringo rides (€15), water skiing (€30) and wake-boarding.

🛏 Sleeping & Eating

★**Stella Mare Studios**   APARTMENT €
(☑28410 41814; studio/apt €45/55; ✳🛜) Just off the main road in the centre of the village, Stella has lush gardens spilling with flowers and comfy studios featuring wooden beds, check-cloth tables, lace curtains, kitchenette,

LASITHI KOLOKYTHA PENINSULA

WORTH A TRIP

SPINALONGA ISLAND

Tiny **Spinalonga Island** (Νήσος Σπιναλόγκα; admission €2; ☺9am-6pm) and its fortress lie in a picturesque setting just off the northern tip of the Kolokytha Peninsula and opposite the onshore village of Plaka. With the explosion of interest in Spinalonga in the wake of Victoria Hislop's romantic novel *The Island* (in Greek *To Nisi*), about the island's time as a leper colony, you're unlikely to feel lonely there. There's a reconstructed section of a street from the period featured in the novel, and although tour group leaders stir up a fine old babel, you can still enjoy a very pleasant stroll round the island, passing evocative ruins of churches, turrets and other buildings.

The Venetians built the formidable **fortress** (admission €3; ☺10am-6pm) in 1579 to protect the bays of Elounda and Mirabello. Spinalonga finally surrendered to Ottoman forces in 1715.

From 1903 until 1955, during the post-Ottoman era, the island was a colony where Greeks suffering from leprosy (Hansen's disease) were quarantined. The early days of the colony were allegedly squalid and miserable. However, in 1953, the arrival of the charismatic Athenian sufferer and law student, Epaminondas Remoundakis, heralded the introduction of decent living conditions and of a redemptive spirit on the island. The colony finally closed in 1973. It is this dramatic and touching story around which Hislop weaves her tale.

The island had previously featured in a short film, *Last Words*, made in 1968 by Werner Herzog.

There's a cafe and souvenir shops here. Regular excursion boats visit Spinalonga from Agios Nikolaos (from €15). Ferries also run from Elounda (€10) and Plaka (€10).

colourful art and balcony. The family apartments accommodate four and have superb views of the sea and Spinalonga Island.

★ **Taverna Giorgos** CRETAN €
(mains €8-16; ⊙11am-midnight; 🍴) Favoured by the cast of the hit TV series, *The Island* (whose photos are on the wall), this atmospheric wood-beamed hobbit hole is strung with eclectic nautical decorations and has a welcoming outdoor terrace fronting Spinalonga. A delicious menu of fired veal chops, steak, souvlakia, octopus, tzatziki and much more.

Captain Nikolas GREEK €
(mains €8; ⊙noon-midnight; 🍴) Named after a local sea captain, this attractive stone taverna on the waterfront excels in its execution of lobster, octopus and calamari. All complemented by amazing views of, you guessed it, the island of Spinalonga.

Ostria GREEK €€
(mains €10-50; ⊙noon-midnight) Aptly named Ostria (translated as 'south wind') sits on the sea, buffeted by wind and breeze, and has unblemished views of Spinalonga. Homemade food is cooked only in olive oil and there's a wide range of choice from mezedhes, octopus, sea urchin, clams, langoustine and mussels.

Milatos Μύλατος
POP 178

Milatos, the northern coast's easternmost beach, is a fairly low-key place in contrast to the heavily developed coastal strip between it and Iraklio. The village of Milatos itself is 2km inland from the pebbly beach and its straggle of tavernas and rooms.

There are two good fish tavernas, **Panorama** (📞28410 81213; ⊙10am-4pm) and **To Meltemi** (📞28410 81353; ⊙10am-4pm), located at either end of the beach.

The intriguing **Milatos Cave** is about 3km east of the village and is well signposted. It was here, in 1823, during Crete's famous bid for union with Greece, that an estimated 2500 local people hid in the cave as Turkish troops ravaged the area. The cave is located high on a cliff above a lonely gorge. The trapped Cretans held out for over two weeks before attempting an escape, only to be slaughtered or sold into slavery. There is a tiny church in the mouth of the cave. The cave is reached along a delightful walkway

above the gorge. Take a flashlight (torch) and be very careful of the sometimes slippery surfaces underfoot.

LASITHI PLATEAU
ΟΡΟΠΕΔΙΟ ΛΑΣΙΘΙΟΥ

Nine hundred metres above sea level, in the domain of eagles, Lasithi Plateau rings with the trill of goat bells, is hemmed by the cloudy peaks of the rock-studded Dikti range, and is arrestingly beautiful, offering a glimpse of secluded, rural Crete at its most authentic. Think green fields interspersed with pear and apple orchards and almond trees, scattered with the skeletons of old windmills. Lasithi would have been a stunning sight in the days when it was dotted with some 20,000 metal windmills with white canvas sails. The original stone windmills were built by the Venetians in the 17th century. There are less than 5000 windmills standing today, most having been replaced by less-attractive but convenient mechanical pumps.

The Lasithi Plateau's rich soil has been cultivated since Minoan times. Following an uprising against Venetian rule in the 13th century, the Venetians expelled the inhabitants of Lasithi and destroyed their orchards. The plateau lay abandoned for 200 years until food shortages forced the Venetians to recolonise and cultivate the area and to build the irrigation trenches and wells that still service the region.

The main approaches to the plateau are from Iraklio, via the coast road east and then by turning south, just before Hersonisos. The best approach from Agios Nikolaos is via Neapoli. The plateau is a popular bike route, utilising the intersecting tracks across the central plain. The journey here via steep hairpin bends is a drama in itself, with barely any signage as you climb to Dikteon Cave (p204), the birthplace of the leader of the gods; a fitting denouement for the effort it takes to get here.

Expect some sudden and odd weather fronts; at the time of research in mid-April we were treated to a heavy fall of snow. There are plenty of cycling trails marked on the plateau. To ride here contact the excellent Martinbike Crete (p193) in Agios Nikolaos.

From Iraklio there are daily buses to Tzermiado (€6.50, two hours), Agios Georgios

(€6.90, two hours) and Psyhro (€6.50, 2¼ hours). There are also buses to the villages from Agios Nikolaos.

Tzermiado   Τζερμιάδο
POP 637

Tzermiado (dzer-mee-*ah*-do) is a likeable, down-to-earth farming town. It's the largest and most important town on the Lasithi Plateau and has a fair number of visitors from tour buses going to the Dikteon Cave. Its main hotels and eateries are remarkably well run and of good quality. A number of shops sell rugs and embroideries.

As you approach Tzermiado from the south, a sign on the right indicates the **Kronios Cave** (admission €4; ⊘ 8am-8pm Apr-Oct, 8.30am-3pm Nov-Mar), which is thought to have been used from the earliest human period as some form of shrine, and during the Minoan period as a grave site. A rough track of about 500m can be walked from the main road, to where a couple of hundred steps rise to the cave's narrow entrance. Taking a powerful torch is advised and you need to be surefooted on the uneven and occasionally muddy surfaces inside the cave.

There is only one main road running through town, plus a couple of ATMs and a post office on the main square.

🛏 Sleeping & Eating

Argoulias   HOTEL **€€**
(🖉 28440 22754; www.argoulias.gr; d incl breakfast €55-80; ※) An almost alpine style makes these apartments an outstanding choice. Built into the hillside above the main village and constructed of exposed local stone, they have sweeping views across the Lasithi Plateau to the mountains. The decor and furnishings are traditional and stylish, and there are open fires to keep things cosy in winter. The apartments are self-catering, although breakfast is delivered each morning. The owners also run an excellent restaurant across the road. Ask about use of bicycles. Look for signs to Argoulias on the entrance to Tzermiado coming from the east.

Taverna Kourites   GREEK **€**
(www.kourites.eu; mains €7.50-10.50; ⊘ 9am-10pm) On the outskirts of Tzermiado is well-run Kourites, a big taverna with a pleasant garden that offers local dishes including roast lamb and suckling pig, cooked in a wood-fired oven. They do vegetarian options also. There are clean and simple rooms above the taverna and in a nearby hotel (doubles €40, breakfast €5). Enquire about free use of bicycles.

Agios Georgios
Άγιος Γεώργιος
POP 541

Dusty, wind-blown and faintly ghostly, Agios Georgios (*agh*-ios ye-*or*-gios) is a tiny village on the southern side of the Lasithi Plateau and the most pleasant to stay in a fairly colourless bunch. If you have your own bicycle, you can base yourself here and explore the plateau at leisure.

◎ Sights

Folklore Museum   MUSEUM
(🖉 28440 31462; admission €3; ⊘ 10am-4pm Apr-Oct) The village boasts a Folklore Museum housed in the original home belonging to the Katsapakis family. Exhibits are spread over five rooms and include some intriguing personal photos of writer Nikos Kazantzakis.

🛏 Sleeping & Eating

Hotel Maria   HOTEL **€€**
(🖉 28440 31774; d/tr/q incl breakfast €60/80/100) These pleasantly quirky rooms on the northern side of the village are in a building fronted by a leafy garden. The traditional mountain beds are rather narrow and are on stone bases. Local furnishings and woven wall hangings add to the cheerful atmosphere.

Taverna Rea   GREEK **€**
(mains €7-8; ⊘ 9am-10pm) A cheerful little restaurant with an orange-and-stone interior hung with Cretan artefacts. Don't be surprised if the charming owner cossets you with extra dishes. The souvlaki is excellent, as are the pork and lamb chops cooked on the range. Upstairs are four rooms (€30) with twin beds and bathroom.

Psyhro   Ψυχρό
POP 133

Psyhro (psi-*hro*) is the closest village to the Dikteon Cave, has one main street, a sword-waving memorial statue, a few tavernas, and plenty of souvenir shops. Buses to Psyhro stop at the northern end of town, from where it's about a kilometre's walk uphill to the cave. The bus is known to divert to the cave car park if lots of passengers are going there, but don't bank on it.

Eating

Stavros
CRETAN €

(grills €7-9; ☺9am-10pm) Long-established Stavros, flanked by geranium pots and propped up by old timers, is eye-catching, with alfresco seating and a menu spanning salads, pasta, souvlaki and locally sourced veg. It's located on the main road.

Petros Taverna
GREEK €

(mains €6-8.50; ☺9am-5pm) Hearty Greek fare is what you'll find at this longstanding restaurant at the foot of the steps to the cave. Ask here about walks in the area, including the long hike up to the summit of Mt Dikti.

Dikteon Cave
Δικταίον Αντρον

Dikteon Cave
CAVE

(Cave of Psyhro; ☎28410 22462, 28440 31316; http://odysseus.culture.gr; admission €4; ☺8am-8pm Apr-Oct, 8.30am-3pm Nov-Mar) Eight hundred metres up a winding, sheer path just outside the village of Psyhro, the Dikteon Cave is as mysterious and forbidding as Greek myth itself. Here, according to legend, Rhea hid her newborn Zeus from Cronus, his offspring-gobbling father. Corkscrewing into the slick, wet dark, the vertiginous staircase passes through overhanging stalactites formed over millennia, resembling squashed, bulbous heads. Home to long-eared bats, the cavern is effectively lit with eerie red and green lights.

As you descend like Orpheus into the Underworld, we challenge your imagination not to go into overdrive. Lower down in the bowels of the cave it gets more dramatic still. In the back on the left is the smaller chamber where legend has it that Zeus was born. There is a larger hall on the right, which has small stone basins filled with water that Zeus allegedly drank from in one section, and a spectacular stalagmite that came to be known as the Mantle of Zeus in the other.

The cave covers 2200 sq m and was excavated in 1900 by the British archaeologist David Hogarth, who found numerous votives indicating it was a place of cult worship. These finds are housed in the Archaeological Museum in Iraklio. Earlier still, Sir Arthur Evans, who discovered Knossos, visited here in 1894.

The cave was used for cult worship from the Middle Minoan period until the 1st century AD. Stone tablets inscribed with Linear A script were found here, along with religious bronze and clay figurines.

It is a breathless 15-minute walk up to the cave entrance. You can take the fairly rough but shaded track on the right with views over the plateau or the less interesting, unshaded paved trail on the left of the car park. Given the altitude there's often rain, and both paths can be dangerously slippy on the descent.

NORTHEASTERN COAST

Gournia
Γουρνιά

★ Gournia
ARCHAEOLOGICAL SITE

(admission €3; ☺8.30am-3pm Tue-Sun) The compelling Late Minoan site of Gournia (pronounced goor-nyah) lies just off the coast road, 19km southeast of Agios Nikolaos. The ruins, which date from 1550 to 1450 BC, are made up of a town overlooked by a palace. Gournia's palace was far less ostentatious than the ones at Knossos and Phaestos, as it was the residence of an overlord rather than a king. The town is a network of streets and stairways flanked by houses with walls up to 2m high. Domestic, agricultural and trade implements found on the site indicate that Gournia was a thriving little community. Sitia and Ierapetra buses from Agios Nikolaos can drop you at the site (30 minutes).

South of the palace is a large rectangular court, which was connected to a network of paved stone streets. Nearby is a large stone slab used for sacrificing bulls. The room to the west has a stone *kernos* (large earthen dish) ringed with 32 depressions and was probably used for cult activity. North of the palace was a Shrine of the Minoan Snake Goddess, which proved to be a rich trove of objects from the Postpalatial period. Notice the storage rooms, workrooms and dwellings to the north and east of the site.

Mohlos
Μόχλος

POP 121

Worth the vertiginous switchback drive 5km down the mountain from the Sitia–Agios Nikolaos highway, little Mohlos (*moh*-los) is an authentic fishing village packed with

CRETAN MYTHS

Some of the key stories in the panoply of Greek *mythos* (myths) emanate from Crete.

Zeus & Cronus

Before Zeus formed the pantheon of the gods, the earth was in the hands of his father Cronus and his monster titans. When Cronus learned he was destined to be overthrown by one of his sons, he ate each of them – including Hades and Poseidon – upon their birth. When Zeus was born in the Dikteon Cave on Crete's Lasithi Plateau, his mother Rhea deceptively wrapped a stone in swaddling clothes and gave it to Cronus who promptly swallowed it. Zeus grew up, overthrew Cronus, freed his brothers and sisters from his father's belly, and imprisoned the titans in the underworld.

Theseus & the Minotaur

Seven Athenian sons and daughters were annually fed to the monstrous half-bull half-man imprisoned in the labyrinth of King Minos' palace in Knossos. Among them was Prince Theseus, who volunteered for the task, and through the intervention of Aphrodite was aided by Minos' daughter, Ariadne, who gave him a ball of thread to help him find his way out of the labyrinth. Theseus slayed the beast and escaped Crete, taking Ariadne with him, but forgot to change the sails from black to white, a sign to King Aegeus of Athens of his safe return. Broken-hearted Aegeus threw himself from the cliffs into the waves and the Aegean Sea was born.

Icarus & Daedalus

Master inventor Daedalus was called upon by Queen Parsiphae to design a contraption allowing her to couple with Poseidon's bull. The result and punishment of the gods was the hideous human-bull mutant she gave birth to, known as the Minotaur. Daedalus designed a maze strong enough to contain the monster, the famous 'labyrinth', but when Parsiphae's husband King Minos learnt of his master inventor's dark design with the Queen, he sent his soldiers after him. Ever the quick thinker, Daedalus fashions some wings from wax and seagull feathers for his son Icarus and himself, warning the boy not to fly too near the sun as they escape Crete. Icarus didn't listen, the wax melted and the boy plunged to his death as Daedalus flies on.

LASITHI MOHLOS

earthy tavernas, cheery locals, and a small pebble and grey-sand beach. On windy days its rollers hammer against the coast with the wrath of Poseidon. In antiquity, it was joined to the small island that is now 200m offshore, and from the period 3000 to 2000 BC was a thriving Early Minoan community. Excavations still continue sporadically on both Mohlos Island and at Mohlos village.

Accommodation varies from basic in town, to thoroughly luxurious a few hundred yards out of it. There's a minimarket and some gift shops, and the centre has wi-fi connection.

When swimming, beware of strong currents further out in the channel between the island and the mainland shore.

🛏 Sleeping

Hotel Sofia HOTEL €
(☏ 28430 94554; sofia-mochlos@hotmail.com; r €35-45; ❄) Right by the sea, this down-to-earth taverna has small rooms upstairs with

wine-coloured bedspreads, antique armoire, fridge, bathroom and some with balconies. You pay a little extra for a sea view. The owners also have spacious apartments (€40 to €55) 200m east of the harbour, where longer stays are preferred.

Kyma Apartments STUDIO €
(☏ 28430 94177; soik@in.gr; studio/apt €35/50; ❄) These well-kept, self-catering studios on the western side of Mohlos are a reasonable deal. The family room has three beds. Ask at the supermarket in the village.

★ Petra Nova Villas VILLA €€
(☏ 6984365277, 28430 94080; www.petranovavillas.gr; Mochlou St; apt €95-125; P ❄ 🛜 👪) These stone villas blend seamlessly into the hillside and are just a few minutes' walk up the road from the waterfront. One- or two-bedroom options, all with private parking, boutique-style interiors, satellite TV and balconies. Contact Elaine for more info.

Mohlos Mare
APARTMENT €€

(☑ 28430 94005; www.mochlos-mare.com; studio & apt €50-80; P ❄ 🛜 🍴) Sugar-white exteriors exploding with coral-pink bougainvillea, these house-proud apartments are just out of town. Decent kitchenettes, well-sized rooms and unbroken sea views from balconies at a slight elevation. There's also a communal outdoor kitchen and barbecue. One of the four apartments has two bedrooms and caters for up to six.

✖ Eating

To Bogazi
GREEK €

(☑ 28430 94200; mezedhes €2-7, mains €7; ⊙ 10am-late) With widescreen views of the turquoise sea just yards away, eat outside on a lovely terrace or upstairs in the wood-beamed interior warmed by a log burner. Serves grilled food, salads, rabbit in wine, octopus, goat cutlet and mezedhes.

Cafe Dimitris
GREEK €

(mains €7; ⊙ 10am-late; 🛜) This super-fresh, blue-and-white waterfront cafe sports a marlin skull on the wall, colourful art and a zesty menu of omelettes and mezedhes, salads and crêpes.

★ Ta Kochilia
GREEK €€

(☑ 28430 94432; mains €7; ⊙ lunch & dinner; 🛜) Famed for its sea-urchin salad, which is available only in high summer, this pretty waterfront taverna, painted Cycladic white and blue, has a menu rich with pasta and traditional Cretan dishes like spinach pies, lamb with artichokes in lemon sauce, and oven-baked feta with tomatoes, peppers, oregano and olive oil.

❶ Getting There & Away

There is no public transport to Mohlos. Buses between Sitia and Agios Nikolaos will drop you off at the Mohlos turn-off. From here, you'll need to hitch or walk the 6km to the village, steeply down and steeply back.

Sitia
Σητεία

POP 9348

Enjoying an average 300 days' sunshine, Sitia (si-*tee*-a) is an attractive seaside town built ampitheatrically on the side of a hill, with a big open harbour backed by a wide promenade lined with tavernas and cafes. It's a friendly place where tourism is fairly low-key and the farming of wine and olives are the mainstays of the economy.

A sandy beach skirts a wide bay to the east of town. Sitia mainly attracts French and Greek tourists, but at the height of the season the town retains its relaxed atmosphere. Sitia makes a good transit point for ferries to the Dodecanese islands.

History

Archaeological excavations indicate that there were neolithic settlements around Sitia and an important Minoan settlement at nearby Petras. The original settlement was destroyed and eventually abandoned after an earthquake in 1700 BC.

In the Graeco-Roman era there was a town called Iteia in or around modern Sitia, although its exact site has not yet been located. In Byzantine times Sitia became a bishopric, which was then eliminated by the Saracens in the 9th century. Under the Venetians, Sitia became the most important port in eastern Crete and their name for the port, La Sitia, is said to have given the Lasithi area its name.

The town was hit by a disastrous earthquake in 1508 – a blow from which it never really recovered – and the Turkish blockade of Sitia in 1648 marked its death knell. The remaining inhabitants fled and the town was destroyed. It was not until the late 19th century, when the Turks decided to make Sitia an administrative centre, that the town gradually came back to life.

Crete's most famous poet, Vitsentzos Kornaros, writer of the epic poem the 'Erotokritos', was born in Sitia in 1614.

◉ Sights

Sitia Archaeological Museum
MUSEUM

(☑ 28430 23917; Piskokefalou; admission €2; ⊙ 8.30am-3pm Tue-Sun) This museum houses an important collection of local finds spanning neolithic to Roman times, with emphasis on the Minoan civilisation. One of the most significant exhibits is the *Palekastro Kouros* – a figure pieced together from elements of hippopotamus tusks and gold. Finds from Zakros Palace include a winepress, bronze saw, jars, cult objects and pots that are clearly scorched from the great fire that destroyed the palace. English and Greek labelling.

Folklore Museum
MUSEUM

(☑ 28430 28300; Kapetan Sifinos 28; admission €2; ⊙ 10am-1pm Mon-Fri) This museum displays a collection of local weaving and other exhibits of folk life.

Petras   ANCIENT SITE

About 2km southeast of town on a low hill overlooking the sea are the remains of this Minoan palace and of later buildings. The site is always accessible. There is limited parking.

Kazarma   FORT

(Neas Ionias; ⊙8.30am-3pm) **FREE** Strategically perched atop a hill above town, this structure is locally called *kazarma* (from the Venetian *casa di arma*) and was built as a garrison by the Venetians. These are the only remains of the fortifications that once protected the town. The site is now used as an open-air venue.

✺ Festivals & Events

Kornaria Festival   PERFORMING ARTS

(⊙mid-Jul–Aug) This festival runs from mid-July to the end of August, with concerts, folk dancing and theatre productions staged in the Kazarma and other venues. Posters around town announce the events, some of which are free.

🛏 Sleeping

El Greco Hotel   HOTEL €

(☑28430 23133; www.elgreco-sitia.gr; G Arkadiou; r incl breakfast €40-55; ❋ 🛜) Smart and impeccably clean rooms with tiled floors, choice furniture, TV, fridge and balcony with sea views. Buffet breakfast in an attractive wood-beamed lobby.

Hotel Arhontiko   HOTEL €

(☑28430 28172; Kondylaki 16; d/studio €30/35) A quiet location uphill from the port enhances the charm of this guesthouse in a neoclassical building. There's great period style, and everything is spotlessly maintained. A little garden out front is shaded by jasmine and orange trees.

Hotel Krystal   HOTEL €

(☑28430 22284; www.ekaterinidis-hotels.com; Kapetan Sifinos 17; s/d/tr incl breakfast €35/50/60; ❋ 🛜) Krystal is clean with functional rooms varying in size with bathroom, tiled floors, desks and dark-wood furniture. There's a nice eating area for breakfast.

Sitia Bay Hotel   HOTEL €€

(☑28430 24800; www.sitiabay.com; s/d €105/120; P ❋ 🛜 ⚒) Modern hotel with friendly service of the highest order. Most of the comfortable and tasteful one- and two-room apartments have sea views, and there's a pool, hydrospa, minigym and sauna. Breakfast is €6.

Hotel Flisvos   HOTEL €€

(☑28430 27135; www.flisvos-sitia.com; Karamanli 4; s/d incl breakfast €45/70; P ❋ 🛜) Comfortable rooms at this modern waterfront hotel enjoy safety deposit boxes, clean bathrooms, balcony, TV and large beds. Opt for a sea view. There's also a lift.

Itanos Hotel   HOTEL €€

(☑28430 22900; www.itanoshotel.com; Karamanli 4; r incl breakfast €45-70; ❋ @) This businesslike seafront hotel is very clean and has large rooms with balcony, fridge, bathroom and fresh cream walls and flat-screen TV. There's also a lift, a cafe downstairs and an open-air restaurant.

🍴 Eating & Drinking

★Zorba's Tavern   TAVERNA €

(Plateia Iroön Polytehniou; mains €8; ⊙noon-late) Gregarious owner Zorba, with his sailor's roll, sea captain's cap and bushy moustache, looks as if he's stepped from a traditional Greek painting. And traditional is what this place excels in: think bouzouki music, blue tables and chairs, and the rich aromas of home-cooked food. Succulent lamb chops, zingy salads and many more. Your taste buds will be jumping!

Oinodeion   GREEK €

(El Venizelou 157; mains €6-9; ⊙lunch & dinner; 🛜) Traditional Greek fare in a bijou interior hung with cooking utensils and old black-and-white photos on the walls. *Saganaki* (fried cheese), souvlaki, octopus and shrimp salad with a fine view of the sea from the outdoor terrace. Atmospheric.

LASITHI SITIA

Sitia

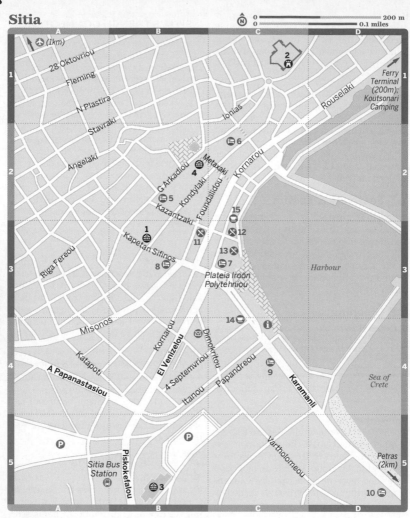

Balcony

FUSION €€

(☏28430 25084; www.balcony-restaurant.com; Foundalidou 19; mains €13-20; ☺lunch & dinner; ☎) The most stylish dining in Sitia is on the 1st floor of a purple and cream neoclassical building where owner-chef Tonya Karandinou rules supreme with a sense of theatre. Cretan-based cuisine, with Mexican and Asian influences, ranges from grilled squid to tender goat. Fine Greek wines complement it all.

Nouvelle Boutique

CAFE

(El Venizelou 161; ☺9am-late) This lively bar packs in a young crowd with funky sounds, stone-walled interior, a huge bar and flat-screen TVs with sport on all day. There's a patio outside by the water and cocktails and snacks all day. Look out for karaoke and live music nights.

Kafe

CAFE

(Karamanli; ☺9am-late) With its quirky art and easy tunes, this is a welcome slice of boho charm. Fruit salads, club sandwiches, fresh juices and coffee make Kafe a great pitstop for breakfast or an afternoon pick-me-up (snacks €5).

Sitia

◎ Sights
1	Folklore Museum	B3
2	Kazarma	C1
3	Sitia Archaeological Museum	B5
4	Venetian Building	B2

⊜ Sleeping
5	El Greco Hotel	B2
6	Hotel Arhontiko	C2
7	Hotel Flisvos	C3
8	Hotel Krystal	B3
9	Itanos Hotel	C4
10	Sitia Bay Hotel	D5

⊗ Eating
11	Balcony	B3
12	Oinodeion	C3
13	Zorba's Tavern	C3

◉ Drinking & Nightlife
14	Kafe	C4
15	Nouvelle Boutique	C2

❶ Information

The town's main square is Plateia Iroön Polytehniou – recognisable by its palm trees and statue of a dying soldier. There are lots of ATMs and places to change money around town. See www.sitia.gr for more information.

Java Internet Cafe (☑ 28430 22263; Kornarou 113; per hr €2; ⊙ 9am-late)

National Bank of Greece (A Papanastasiou & Katapoti) Has a 24-hour exchange machine.

Post Office (Dimokritou; ⊙ 7.30am-3pm) Heading inland, it's the first left off El Venizelou.

Tourist Office (☑ 28430 28300; Karamanli; ⊙ 9.30am-2.30pm & 5-8.30pm Mon-Fri, 9.30am-2pm Sat) Winter opening hours may be uncertain. On the promenade.

Tourist Police (☑ 28430 24200; Therisou 31) At the main police station. Head west out of town on Therisou to get here.

Tzortzakis Travel (☑ 29211; www.tzortzakis-travel.com; 17 M Alexandrou St; ⊙ 9am-9pm) This helpful travel agency books rooms, flights and boats as well as organising car hire.

❶ Getting There & Away

AIR

Sitia's airport (p262) has an expanded international-size runway, with summer flights to Amsterdam and Lyon.

Astra Airlines (www.astra-airlines.gr) has five weekly flights to Athens (€68, one hour).

Olympic Air (www.olympicair.com) has daily flights to Kassos (€57, 20 minutes) and then on to Karpathos (€63, one hour) and Rhodes (€63, two hours).

BOAT

Ferries dock about 600m north of Plateia Iroön Polytehniou. **Aegeon Pelagos Sea Lines** (EP; ☑ Hania 28210 24000) has two ferries a week from Sitia to Iraklio (€11, three hours), Milos (€25, 11½ hours), Piraeus (€41, 17 hours), Santorini (€26, 7½ hours) and Rhodes (€27, nine hours 20 minutes). There are four ferries a week to Kassos (€11, 2½ hours) and Karpathos (€18, four hours). Several of these departures are in the early hours of the morning.

BUS

From Sitia's **bus station** (☑ 28430 22272) there are six buses per day to Ierapetra (€8, 1½ hours), seven buses to Iraklio (€14, three hours) via Agios Nikolaos (€8, 1½ hours), four to Vaï (€3, one hour), and two to Kato Zakros (€8, one hour) via Palekastro (€5, 45 minutes) and Zakros (€8, one hour). The buses to Vaï and Kato Zakros only run between May and October.

❶ Getting Around

The airport (signposted) is 1.5km out of town. There is no airport bus; a taxi costs about €6.

Car- and motorcycle-hire outlets are mostly found on Papandreou and Itanou. Try **Club Cars** (☑ 28430 25104; Papandreou 4; per day from €35).

Moni Toplou   Μονή Τοπλού

★ **Moni Toplou**   MONASTERY
(☑ 28430 61226; admission €3; ⊙ 10am-5pm Apr-Oct, Fri only Nov-Mar) The imposing Moni Toplou, 18km east of Sitia, looks more like a fortress than a monastery – a necessity imposed by the dangers it faced at the time of its construction. It is one of the most historically significant and progressive monasteries in Crete. The middle of the 15th century was marked by piracy, banditry and constant rebellions. The monks defended themselves with all the means at their disposal, including a heavy gate, cannons (the name Toplou is Turkish for 'with a cannon') and small holes for pouring boiling oil onto the heads of their attackers. Nevertheless, it was sacked by pirates in 1498, looted by the Knights of Malta in 1530, pillaged by the Turks in 1646 and captured by the Turks in 1821.

Moni Toplou had always been active in the cause of Cretan independence. Under the Turkish occupation, a secret school operated in the monastery, and its reputation for hiding rebels led to severe reprisals. During WWII, Abbot Silingakis was executed after sheltering resistance leaders who operated an underground radio transmitter.

The monastery's star attraction is undoubtedly the icon *Lord Thou Art Great* by celebrated Cretan artist Ioannis Kornaros. Each of the 61 scenes painted on the icon is beautifully worked out and inspired by a phrase from the Orthodox prayer that begins, 'Lord, thou art great'.

A **museum** tells the monastery's history and has a collection of icons, engravings and books, as well as weapons and military souvenirs from the resistance.

The monastery is a 3km walk from the Sitia–Palekastro road. Buses can drop you off at the junction. A taxi from Sitia costs about €22.

EASTERN COAST

Vaï   Βάï

Vaï beach, 24km northeast of Sitia, is a tiny inlet of turquoise sea lapping soft sand backdropped by a forest of palm trees. Out in the tiny bay perches a small island. You may have to manually shut your jaw as it's that gorgeously pretty, all the more so for the incongruous presence of *Phoenix theophrastii* palms (the word Vaï is a local word for palm fronds). One explanation for their existence here is that they sprouted from date pits spread by either Egyptian soldiers, Roman legionaries, Phoenicians or feasting pirates.

In July and August, you'll need to arrive early to appreciate both palms and beach. The place is packed and the beach is covered in sun chairs and umbrellas (€6), while jet skis prattle and posture offshore.

At the southern end of the beach, stone steps lead up to a gazebo lookout. Follow your nose about a kilometre beyond here and a rocky path descends eventually to a less crammed beach, or head over the hill to the north of Vaï beach for a series of clothes-optional coves.

Restaurant-Caféteria Vai (mains €10; ⊘ 9am-late) is a delightfully chic beachside taverna with Cretan cheeses, dolmadhes, salads, calamari, swordfish and bream. What a spot to eat fresh fish!

There are buses to Vaï from Sitia (€3, one hour, five daily) from May to October. There is a car park where buses stop, and a few hundred metres further is a beachside car park (€3).

Itanos   Ίτανος

About 3km north of Vaï is the ancient Minoan site of Itanos. It may appear fairly forlorn today, but this was once an important site. Inhabited from about 1500 BC, Itanos was clearly prosperous by the 7th century BC since it was an important trading post for exports to the Near and Middle East. It was at odds with local rivals such as Praisos and later with Ierapetra (then known as Ieraptyna). Poke around and you will find remains of two early Christian basilicas and a Hellenistic wall. The basilica ruin, on high ground towards the sea, is littered with toppled columns. Look for one stone base marked with circular motifs. You can swim from coves nearby, or follow the road from Vaï beach and at the first crossroads head right (north) for about 2.5km.

Palekastro   Παλαίκαστρο

POP 953

Palekastro (pah-leh-kas-tro) is an unpretentious farming village underpinned with low-key tourism. It lies in a rocky landscape interspersed with fields and is within easy distance of a beach at Kouremenos as well as the beaches of Moni Toplou and Vaï. The village has most services and facilities. If you want to explore widely your own transport is more or less essential.

About 1km each of town, towards Hiona Beach, is the archaeological site of Roussolakkos, where archaeologists believe a major Minoan palace is buried. This is where the *Palekastro Kouros* (ivory figurine) – now residing in the Archaeological Museum (p206) in Sitia – was found.

◎ Sights & Activities

Folk Museum of Palekastro   MUSEUM
(admission €2; ⊘ 10am-1pm & 5-8pm Mon-Sat mid-Jun–mid-Oct) Tucked away in a back street and signposted from the main road, the well-presented Folk Museum of Palekastro is housed in a traditional manor house with displays in the old stables and bakery.

Hiona Beach   BEACH
Hiona Beach, 2km east of Palekastro, is a quiet choice to the east, with some great fish tavernas.

Kouremenos
BEACH

Kouremenos, north of Palekastro, is a pebble beach with good shallow-water swimming and excellent windsurfing.

Freak Mountain Bike Centre
WINDSURFING

(☏6979253861; www.freak-mountainbike.com; ☺10am-6pm Jun-Oct) On the edge of Palekastro village keep an eye out for Freak Mountain Bike Centre in a stone cube building. Run by Jan De Vriendt, it rents bikes and offers great guided four-day programs around eastern Crete. You can hire boards from its other branch, **Freak Windsurf** (☏28430 61116, 6979254967; www.freak-surf.com), at Kouremenos beach.

🛏 Sleeping

Hotel Hellas
HOTEL €

(☏28430 61240; www.palaikastro.com/hotelhellas; s/d €25/40; ❊🛈) Clean and sunny rooms in these town-centre digs, with cool tile floors, balcony, TV, desk and large bathroom. There's also a great restaurant downstairs.

Hiona Holiday Hotel
HOTEL €€

(☏28430 29623; s/d incl breakfast €50/65; P ❊) The plain facade of this hotel belies its comfy rooms and decent facilities. There's a well-stocked bar and pleasant public areas. It's a few minutes' walk down the hill from the centre of the village.

Esperides
APARTMENT €€

(☏28430 61433, 6945255243; isabel-t@otenet.gr; apt €85-105; P ❊ ✵) In a good location, just inland from Kouremenos Bay, these lovely buildings have traditional furnishings and all modern self-catering facilities.

Grandes Apartments
APARTMENT €€

(☏28430 61496; www.grandes.gr; q studio €85; P ❊) Located behind Kouremenos beach, these self-catering options are surrounded by a flower-filled garden and trees. They are well equipped and decorated with style, and there's a nearby beachfront taverna run by the owners.

✕ Eating

To Finistrini
MEZEDHES €

(mezedhes/mains €4/7; ☺10am-late) About 200m along the Vaï road, this neat little *ouzerie*-cum-*mezedhopoleio* dishes up tasty mezedhes that go down well with a shot or 10 of *raki*. It also sells myriad grilled dishes, souvlaki, chicken fillet, pasta and *mousakas*. Eat inside or outside.

Mythos
GREEK €

(mains €5; ☺10am-midnight) Attractively finished in colourful murals, this friendly taverna on the main street cooks only with olive oil and has some lovely dishes like chicken with lemon sauce, red mullet and tasty mezedhes with plenty of vegie options. Romantic by night.

❶ Information

The main street forks at the village centre beside a big church with attendant palm trees. The **tourist office** (☏28430 61546; ☺9am-5pm Mon-Fri May-Oct) has information on rooms and transport. There's an ATM next door and further on a postal agent, a bank with ATM, and the useful **Argo Bookshop**, which has internet access (€1 per half hour) and can also do photocopying.

❶ Getting There & Away

There are five buses per day from Sitia that stop at Palekastro on the way to Vaï. There are also two buses daily from Sitia to Palekastro (€1.70, 45 minutes) that continue to Kato Zakros (€2.80, one hour). The bus stop is in the centre of town.

Zakros & Kato Zakros
Ζάκρος & Κάτω Ζάκρος

POP 640 & 22

The village eyrie of Zakros (*zah*-kros), 45km southeast of Sitia, is at best a prelude to compelling Kato Zakros, 7km away on the coast. However, the village has a few decent tavernas and a minimart, and also an excellent Natural History Museum. Zakros is the starting point for the trail through the Zakros Gorge, known as the **Valley of the Dead**, which takes its name from the ancient burial sites in the numerous caves dotting the canyon walls.

The setting of **Kato Zakros** (*kah*-to *zah*-kros) is simply awesome. A long winding road snakes downhill from Zakros through rugged terrain. Halfway down it takes a big loop to the left and reveals a vast curtain wall of mountains ahead; the highest, Traóstalos (515m) and Lakómata (378m), dominate the skyline and the red jaws of the Valley of the Dead breach the foreground cliffs. On the low ground close to a string of pretty tavernas and a pebbly beach pounded by cobalt surf is the remarkable 17th century BC ruins of the Minoan Zakros Palace. Add to all of this its isolated tranquillity and sense of peace and you have the perfect recipe for escapism. But there's one more gift the gods added: every August a fully waxed moon seemingly rises like a glowing mothership from the ocean – nature's little trick on the eye.

◉ Sights

Zakros Natural History Museum   MUSEUM
(Zakros Village; admission €2; ⊙10am-1pm & 5-8pm Mon-Sat mid-Jun–mid-Oct) A short distance past the village square en route to Kato Zakros, this great little museum is dedicated to the flora and fauna found in the Valley of the Dead, with stuffed animals, rocks and fossils.

Zakros Palace   ARCHAEOLOGICAL SITE
(☑28410 22462; Kato Zakros; adult/child €3/free; ⊙8.30am-3pm) Although Zakros Palace was the last Minoan palace to have been discovered (1962), the excavations proved remarkably fruitful. The exquisite rock-crystal vase and stone bull's head, now in Heraklion Archaeological Museum, were found at Zakros, along with a treasure trove of Minoan antiquities. Ancient Zakros, the smallest of Crete's four palatial complexes, was a major port in Minoan times, trading with Egypt, Syria, Anatolia and Cyprus. Some parts of the palace complex are submerged.

If you enter the palace complex on the southern side you will first come to the **workshops** for the palace. The **King's Apartment** and **Queen's Apartment** are to the right of the entrance. Next to the King's Apartment is the **Cistern Hall**, which once had a cistern in the centre surrounded by a colonnaded balustrade. Seven steps descended to the floor of the cistern, which may have been a swimming pool, an aquarium or a pool for a sacred boat. Near-

by, the **Central Court** was the focal point of the whole palace. Notice the altar base in the northwestern corner of the court; there was also a **well** in the southeast corner of the court at the bottom of eight steps. When the site was excavated the well contained the preserved remains of olives that may have been offered to the deities.

Adjacent to the central court is the **Hall of Ceremonies** in which two rhytons (ceremonial drinking vessels) were found. To the south is the **Banquet Hall**, so named for the quantity of wine vases found there. To the north of the central court is the kitchen. The column bases probably supported the dining room above. To the northwest of the central court is another light well and to the left of the banquet hall is the **Lustral Basin**, which once contained a magnificent marble amphora. The Lustral Basin served as a washroom for those entering the nearby **Central Shrine**. You can still see a ledge and a niche in the southern wall for the ceremonial idols.

Below the Lustral Basin is the **Treasury**, which yielded nearly a hundred jars and rhytons. Next to the treasury is the **Archive Room**, which once contained Linear A record tablets. Close to the northwest corner of the North East Court is the **bathroom** with a cesspit.

⌂ Sleeping

Zakros is but a footnote to Kato Zakros and you should head to the latter for a spectrum of accommodation from simple rooms to downright beautiful digs. Rooms in Kato Zakros fill up fast in high season, so it is best to book.

Zakros Palace

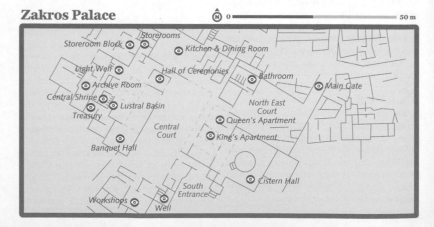

TREKKING THE VALLEY OF THE DEAD

Trekking in **Zakros Gorge** (Kato Zakros) is now fully marked with well-organised trails established by Elias and Stella Pagianidis, trekking experts and conservationists who have painstakingly marked out all the trails within the gorge and are more than helpful giving advice to walkers.

Head to Entrance A and park for longer walks – it takes 1½ to two hours from here to Kato Zakros, the end of the 2.5km gorge. Entrance B, just after Zakros, is an easier route, taking just 45 minutes. The stretch between A and B is the most beautiful. A taxi from Zakros to Entrance A costs about €12, and to Entrance B, €10. The round-trip walk from Zakros takes four hours. We recommend you do the trip outside of winter, because there is still water in the gorge as late as April. Maps are available from Stella's Traditional Apartments.

There's also a new route marked to **Pelekita Cave** in Karoumbi, 3km from Kato Zakros. With magnificent views of the sea 100m below, this 300m-long cave also has signs of neolithic habitation within its stalactite- and stalagmite-rich interior. To explore it bring decent trainers and a flashlight (torch).

Katerina Apartments APARTMENT €
(☎28430 26893; www.katozakros.cretefamily-hotels.com; Kato Zakros; apt €50-60) Located high up on the hillside overlooking Kato Zakros, with turquoise surf and an ancient ruined palace far below, the four excellent stone-built studios and maisonettes here can sleep up to four and, clearly, enjoy a superb setting.

Athena & Coral Rooms PENSION €
(☎6974656617, 28431 10710; www.kato-zakros.gr; r €60; ❄) Above the beach just behind the Akrogiali Taverna, these stone-effect rooms have fridge, TV, bathroom and cheerful orange bedspreads. Simple and romantic, they are just yards away from the lulling waves. The sea view from the communal sun terrace is magic.

★Terra Minoika VILLAS €€
(☎28430 23739; www.stelapts.com; Kato Zakros; villa €120; P❄ᯤ) Set high on the hillside overlooking the surf below, these stone cube houses are breathtaking; imagine wood-beamed ceilings, widescreen views from balconies, chic rustic furniture, urns mounted on walls, and stone floors. Incurably romantic, every villa is individual and has a fully equipped kitchenette.

There's a terrific gym guests are welcome to use. Owner Elias Pagianidis is an ex Mr Greece bodybuilder, and the driving force behind marking the walking trails in the Valley of the Dead; he and his wife Stella are experts on trekking and local ecology.

The owners also run Stella's Traditional Apartments.

Stella's Traditional Apartments APARTMENT €€
(☎28430 23739; www.stelapts.com; Kato Zakros; studio €60-90; P❄ᯤ) Close to the wooded mouth of Zakros Gorge, these charming self-contained studios are in a lovely garden setting and decorated with distinctive wooden furniture and other artifacts made by joint owner Elias Pagianidis. There are hammocks under the trees, barbecues and an external kitchen with an honesty system for supplies. Elias and his wife Stella have excellent knowledge and experience of hiking trails in the area.

Kato Zakros Palace APARTMENT €€
(☎28430 29550; www.katozakros-apts.gr; Kato Zakros; r/studio €60/70; P❄ᯤ) Above Kato Zakros beach and beside the approach road, these immaculate studios are white interiored and well equipped with safety deposit boxes, spotless bathroom, kitchenettes, satellite TV, mosquito screens, and hairdryers. Free laundry facilities.

Eating

Akrogiali Taverna CRETAN €
(☎28430 26893; Kato Zakros; mains €8; ⏲8am-midnight; ᯤ) Decked in blue and white, this pretty seafront taverna is packed to the gills with lobster, swordfish and souvlaki. The squid portions are huge and the salads are full of vim.

Kato Zakros Bay GREEK €€
(mains €7; ⏲8am-midnight; ᯤ✎) With its stone floors, open range and tables topped with Cretan rugs, this is an atmospheric spot for dinner. Local vegetables are grown next

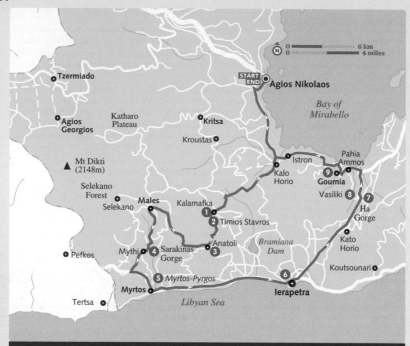

Driving Tour
Mountain Meander

START/FINISH AGIOS NIKOLAOS
LENGTH 55KM; ONE DAY

A network of winding roads links tiny villages on the southeastern edge of the Dikteon Mountains within a landscape of rocky pinnacles and escarpments clothed in dense woodland and scrub.

The route from Agios Nikolaos takes you south on the E75 Sitia road. After 5.3km, turn right following signs to Kalo Horio but remain on the road marked for the village of **1 Kalamafka**. From there the road climbs steadily into the mountains. Take time here to climb the steep steps, over 220 of them, to the cave chapel of **2 Timios Stavros** on the summit of the rocky pinnacle of Kastelos for spectacular views.

Continue south from Kalamafka for a stroll around the village of **3 Anatoli** where a slow decline has been stemmed and where original shopfronts are being preserved and old houses renovated as second homes.

Northwest from Anatoli you pass through wild and rocky countryside until the great valley of Sarakinas opens out. Follow the road south through the valley to Mythi where signs direct you to the **4 Sarakinas Gorge**, if you fancy stretching your legs even for a short stroll. Further south you reach the coast at Myrtos. Just east of Myrtos is the ruin of **5 Myrtos-Pyrgos**, a Minoan hilltop villa reached by a path.

Continue east from here along the coast road to **6 Ierapetra**, through less-than-scenic plastic-greenhouse country. Stop for a short exploration of Ierapetra's pleasant seafront and town centre and then continue north alongside the escarpment of the Thripti Mountains, where views of the dramatic gash of the **7 Ha Gorge** dominate the last few kilometres. Turn left after about 10km to visit the small Minoan ruin of **8 Vasiliki**. Reach the E75 at Pahia Ammos, where a left turn leads back towards Agios Nikolaos past the splendid Minoan site of **9 Gournia** (p204).

door, and occasionally the owner plays live music. A menu of mussels, dolmadhes, and other Greek staples including rabbit *stifadho* (stew cooked with tomatoes and red wine).

ℹ Getting There & Away

There are buses to Zakros from Sitia via Palekastro (€4.50, one hour, two daily). From June to August, the buses continue to Kato Zakros (€5.20, one hour 20 minutes). Buses to Kato Zakros only run between May and October.

Friendly driver Yiannis from **Sitia Taxi** (Yiannis Soldatos; ☑ 6995900900; www.sitiataxi.com) can pick you up in Sitia and bring you here to trek Kato Zakros. He drops you in Zakros and waits for you by the sea in Kato Zakros before taking you back to Sitia. It costs €60.

Xerokambos   Ξερόκαμπος

POP 56

Xerokambos (kse-*ro*-kam-bos) is a quiet resort and farming settlement on the far southeastern flank of Crete. Its isolation means that tourism is pretty much low-key, even at its busiest in July and August. The attractions for visitors are two of eastern Crete's most pristine and beautiful beaches, which are backdropped by mountains and have unbelievably clear water. There are a few scattered tavernas and some studio accommodation. The town, which flourished here in the Hellenistic period, had commercial relations with Rhodes and Karpathos.

There are no buses to Xerokambos. From Zakros there's a signposted turn-off to the resort via 8km of winding surfaced road. The continuation to Ziros is through some very wild country and some very wild bends.

SOUTHERN COAST

Ierapetra   Ιεράπετρα

POP 12,355

On approach Ierapetra (yeh-*rah*-pet-rah) cannot be accused of being the best looker in Crete, but on closer inspection this sea-facing town backed by snowcapped mountains is vibrant, with tasteful shops, tavernas and stylish coffee shops. Locals are friendly and there's plenty to do, from diving to boat trips to the nearby sandy island of Gaïdouronisi (also known as Hrysi).

Ierapetra is the commercial centre of southeastern Crete's substantial greenhouse-based agri-industry and the countryside surrounding it is crammed full of greenhouses interspersed with storage depots and other buildings.

Historically the town was an important city for the Dorians and the last major outpost to fall to the Romans, who made it a major port of call in their conquest of Egypt. The city languished under the Venetians, who built the fortress at the western end of the harbour. Even Napoleon is said to have stopped off on his progress towards Egypt.

There's a rich archaeological collection to be explored, a Venetian fort at the harbour, and the odd remnant of a Turkish quarter. The town beach and surrounding beaches are reasonable, the nightlife lively and the overall ambience Cretan.

Every Saturday there is a street **market** on Psilinaki from 7am to 2pm.

◉ Sights

The main beach is near the harbour, while a second beach stretches east from the bottom of Patriarhou Metaxaki. Both have coarse, grey sand, but the main beach offers better shade.

Ierapetra
Archaeological Museum   MUSEUM
(☑ 28420 28721; Adrianou 2; admission €2; ⊙8.30am-3pm Tue-Sun) Ierapetra's small but worthwhile archaeological collection is located in a former school of the Ottoman period. A highlight among a collection of headless classical statuary is an intact statue of the goddess Persephone that dates from the 2nd century AD. Another splendid piece is a big *larnax* (clay coffin), dated around 1300 BC, that is decorated with 12 painted panels showing hunting scenes, an octopus and a chariot procession.

Kales Fortress   FORTRESS
(⊙8.30am-3pm Tue-Sun) **FREE** South along the waterfront is the medieval fortress, built in the early years of Venetian rule and strengthened by Francesco Morosini in 1626. Climb to the upper walls (watch your footing) for grand views to the eastern mountains.

Old Quarter   NEIGHBOURHOOD
Inland from the fortress is the labyrinthine old quarter, where you will see a **Turkish fountain**, the restored **mosque** with its

minaret, and the old churches of **Agios Ioannis** and **Agios Georgios**.

Napoleon's House · NOTABLE BUILDING

This is where the man himself is said to have stayed incognito with a local family when his ship anchored in Crete for one night in 1798 on the way to Egypt. He apparently left a note revealing his identity. To find the building, go down the alleyway to the right of Babis Taverna. The two-storeyed corner building, in exposed stone, has wooden shutters and the number 9 on its door. There is no entry.

Festivals & Events

Kyrvia Festival · CULTURAL

(⊙Jul & Aug) This annual festival runs from July to August and features a program of cultural activities including singing and dancing nights by local folk and popular groups, special concerts by famous artists, film screenings, theatre performances and much singing and dancing in the streets of the old town.

Activities

Excursion boats (about €20, 30 minutes) to Gaïdouronisi (p218) leave from Ierapetra's port in the morning and return in the afternoon.

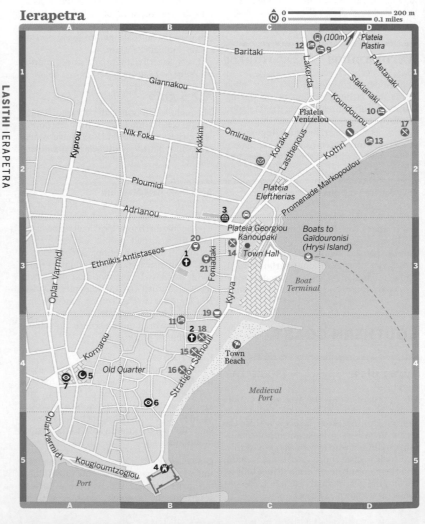

Ierapetra

Ierapetra Diving Centre DIVING

([phone] 6944531242 28420 26703; www.ierapetra
divingcentre.com; Ierapetra Port, Old Town; dives
from €55, open-water course €550; [clock] 8am-2pm
& 5pm-10pm) Run by Lefteris, this PADI-
certified outfit offers cave and wreck dives
and open-water courses.

🛏 Sleeping

★ Cretan Villa Hotel HOTEL €

([phone] 28420 28522; www.cretan-villa.com; Lakerda
16; d/tr €50/70; [icons]) Hidden in the centre
of town behind a thick wooden door leading into a vine-shaded courtyard, this is a
restful, friendly space with beautiful rooms
boasting stained glass windows, fine furniture, large bathrooms, wood-beamed ceilings and satellite TV. The management are
especially helpful. It's only a few minutes'
walk from the bus station.

Coral Hotel HOTEL €

([phone] 28420 27755; Katzonovatsi 12; s/d €30/40)
Just behind the seafront in the old town,
this small hotel has clean, white rooms with
wooden furniture, crisp linen and fresh
bathrooms, though they are a tad cramped.

Koutsounari Camping CAMPGROUND €

([phone] 28420 61213; www.camping-koutsounari.gr;
camp sites per adult/child/tent €6.50/3.50/4.50,
cabin/studio €18/30; [P][icon]) About 7km east
of Ierapetra at Koutsounari, Koutsounari
Camping has a pool, restaurant, snack bar
and minimarket. As well as sites there are
wooden cabins and studios. Ierapetra–Sitia
buses pass the campground.

Akrolithos Apartments APARTMENT €€

([phone] 28420 28522; www.ierapetra-apartments.net;
Lakerda 16; apt €70; [icons]) These recently refurbished apartments have stunning interiors with original fireplaces, well-equipped
kitchenettes, loads of space and a great central location. You may not want to leave they
are so cosy.

El Greco BOUTIQUE HOTEL €€

([phone] 28420 28471; www.elgreco-ierapetra.gr; Mi-
hali Kothri 42; s/d/ste incl breakfast €85/95/145;
[icons]) Twenty contemporary rooms with
olive-green accents, glass pendant lights,
balconies, wicker furniture, satellite flat-
screen TV, and cavernous bathrooms with
rain-showers. The views of the nearby sea
are widescreen. There's also a tempting cafe-
bar and restaurant on the ground floor. The
suite has a jacuzzi on its balcony if you're
feeling indulgent.

Astron Hotel BUSINESS HOTEL €€

([phone] 28420 25114; www.hotelastron.com.gr; Kothri 56; s/d/tr incl breakfast €75/85/100; [icons])
Sixty-six stylish rooms with brown and
mushroom-grey colour schemes, low lights,
modish furniture, satellite flat-screen TV,
fridge, balcony, and plenty of space. The As-
tron is in a good position at the eastern end
of the promenade, with the sea a few steps
away. An excellent breakfast buffet is served
in the art deco–accented lobby.

🍴 Eating

★ Napoleon GREEK €

([phone] 28420 22410; Stratigou Samouil 26; mains €6;
[clock] noon-midnight; [icons]) This capacious traditional Cretan place has a covered area by
the sea flanked by palm trees and an attractive restaurant. Expect tasty dolmadhes,
snails, spinach pies, calamari and inkfish
risotto.

LASITHI IERAPETRA

Ierapetra

I Kalitexnes
GREEK, ARABIC €

(📋 28430 28547; Kyprou 26; mains €5-9; ☉ lunch & dinner Mon-Sat; 🛜) A quirky little place tucked in a side street, Kalitexnes has classic dishes prepared using organic ingredients. There are also spicier dishes such as falafel and kebabs introduced by the Egyptian owner.

Taverna Gorgona
GREEK €

(Stratigou Samouil; mains €8; ☉ noon-late) Look out for the faded mural of the mermaid on its facade, then follow the delicious aromas of grilled sea bream, souvlaki and calamari to this traditional restaurant with fetching views of the sea.

Ariston Cafe
CAFE €

(snacks €4; ☉ 7am-late) This is a handy breakfast or lunch stop for coffees and sandwiches from the freshly presented deli, as well as cakes, cheese pies and omelettes. It's opposite the town hall.

Chocolicious
SWEETS €

(Stratigou Samouil; ☉ 7.30am-late) Carb heaven for sweet-toothed travellers. True to its name this cafe and tasty chocolaterie alchemises homemade chocolate infused with varieties of milk, nuts and fruit. It also dishes up waffles, chocolate cakes, cookies and apple pies.

Pizzeria Ristorante Siciliana
PIZZA €€

(Promenade Markopoulou 1; mains €5-15; ☉ noon-late) This peach-interiored pizzeria overlooks the big blue with a choice of classic Greek starters followed by wood-fired pizzas as well as grilled meat dishes, crêpes and local wines.

🍸 Drinking & Nightlife

Kyrva is Ierapetra's main nightlife strip. You'll find more nightclubs around the corner on Foniadaki.

Ntoukiani
BAR

(Ethnikis Antistaseos 19; ☉ 8pm-late; 🛜) Ntoukiani specialises in *raki* and has a boho feel, with rosé-hued interior spattered with antique Campari posters.

Island Cafe
CAFE

(Stratigou Samouil; snacks €4; ☉ 8am-late) With its mint-blue and white interior, modern tunes and mixed crowd of young students and old boys flicking worry beads, this is a good spot for breakfast, coffee, ice cream and fresh juices.

Privilege
CLUB

(☉ 10pm-late) Caters to locals with non-stop Greek club music.

Parados
BAR

(☉ 10pm-late; 🛜) This diminutive jazz cafe is peppered with Ella Fitzgerald and Ray Charles pictures with a soundtrack to match. There's a library upstairs and live music on Saturday evening. A peaceful spot to grab an iced coffee and chill.

❶ Information

There are ATMs around the main square. See www.ierapetra.gr for more info.

Ierapetra Express (📋 28420 28673; express@ ier.forthnet.gr; Kothri 2; ☉ 9am-9pm) Central tourist office with friendly service and good information.

Post Office (Koraka 25; ☉ 7.30am-2pm)

Street Café (Promenade Markopoulou 73; ☉ 10am-10pm; 🛜) There's wi-fi access for customers at this trendy and popular bar-cafe.

❶ Getting There & Away

The **bus station** (📋 28420 28237; www.ktelherlas.gr; Lasthenous) is inland at the eastern side of town. There are nine buses per day to Iraklio (€11, 2½ hours) via Agios Nikolaos (€3.80, one hour) and Gournia (€2.10, 40 minutes), seven to Sitia (€6.30, 1½ hours) via Koutsounari (for camp sites; €1.60), and seven to Myrtos (€2.20, 30 minutes).

Taxis (📋 28420 26600) can take you anywhere for a fixed fare. Fares are posted outside the town hall **taxi stand**, for destinations including Iraklio (€110), Agios Nikolaos (€45), Sitia (€75) and Myrtos (€20). There is another rank at Plateia Venizelou.

Auto Tours (📋 28420 22571; Plateia Plastira; per day from €25; ☉ 9am-8pm) is reliable for car hire.

Around Ierapetra

Gaïdouronisi (Hrysi Island)
Γαϊδουρονῆσι (Χρυσή)

Just off the coast of Ierapetra, you will find greater tranquillity at Gaïdouronisi – marketed in Ierapetra as Hrysi or Hrissi (Golden Island) – where there are good sandy beaches, a taverna, and a stand of Lebanon cedars, the only one in Europe. It can get very crowded when the tour boats are in, but you can generally still find a quiet spot.

In summer, **excursion boats** for Gaïdouronisi leave from Ierapetra's quay every morning and return in the afternoon. Most travel agents around the quay sell tickets (about €20).

East of Ierapetra

About 13km east is the lovely beach of **Agia Fotia**. Much of this coastline has been enveloped by plastic-covered greenhouses and haphazard tourism development, but there are still appealing places.

A new stretch of road bypasses **Koutsouras**, but turn off the main road for **Taverna Robinson** (☑28430 51026; www. robinsontaverna.gr; mezedhes €5-7.50; ⊗3pm-late), housed in an attractively renovated Venetian-style building. The pink interior is hung with an installation of light bulbs while the menu is packed with local cheeses along with fresh fish and meat cooked on the grill.

The fine white sandy beach at the eastern end of **Makrygialos**, 24km from Ierapetra, is one of the best on the southeastern coast. It gets very busy in summer, but the beachside promenade is a cheerful place and there are plenty of cafes and eating places.

Just above Makrygialos on the road to Pefki is **Aspros Potamos** (☑28430 51694; www.asprospotamos.com; d/tr/q €50/65/75). Here the 300-year-old stone cottages have been lovingly restored by owner Aleka Halkia as guesthouses. Lit by oil lamps and candles, using only renewable energy, Potamos is fiercely ecofriendly. You'll find no electrical sockets whatsoever. The stone floors, traditional furnishings and winter fireplaces add to the traditional ambience. It's the perfect spot for nature buffs and walkers, since you're close to the 2km-long Pefki Gorge.

Myrtos   Μύρτος
POP 441

Little known Myrtos (*myr*-tos), 14km west of Ierapetra, is fringed by an apron of dark sand and bright-blue water, and offers a slow boho pulse, with a few wind-battered, sun-bleached boutiques and guesthouses, plus a cluster of tavernas on its languid seafront. In short, it's a traveller's jewel, the perfect antidote to noise and haste.

◉ Sights & Activities

Myrtos' Museum   MUSEUM
(☑28420 51065) **FREE** Myrtos' small museum houses the private collection of a former teacher who sparked the archaeological digs in the area after finding Minoan artefacts on field trips with students. The collection includes Vasiliki pottery from the nearby Minoan sites of **Fournou-Korifi** and **Pyrgos** as well as an impressive model of the Fournou-Korifi site exactly as it was found, with all the pots and items in situ.

Paradise Scuba Diving Centre   DIVING
(☑28420 51554; www.paradisedivingmirtos.com; dives from €75, open-water course €500; ⊗10am-8pm) Run by Nikos, Paradise can take you cave and wreck diving. It's located on the waterfront.

⌨ Sleeping

★Big Blue   APARTMENT €
(☑28420 51094; www.big-blue.gr; studio €30-40, apt €50-80; P☀☎♿) Modern amenities meet trad-Greece in these exquisite seafacing studios with white walls hung with fine art. Balconies boast expansive views and awnings, and thanks to its elevation, the views are jawdropping. Apartment 'Blue Eye' has a stunning pop art display of *mati* (evil eye); in fact, every room is different. Out front there is a fragrant garden for sundowners.

Villa Mertiza   APARTMENT €€
(☑28420 51208, 6932735224; www.mertiza.com; studio/apt €55/€65; ☀☎) Owned by a friendly Dutch guy, these are tastefully finished studios and apartments with self-catering facilities, Moroccan wallhangings and walls peppered with stunning photography. Rooms enjoy fresh bathrooms, flat-screen TV and generous dimensions. There's also a book exchange. The owner also has some lovely villas (€110) a little further out, and other accommodation options.

✗ Eating

★Thalassa Taverna   GREEK €
(mains €8-12; ⊗10am-midnight; ☎) This powder-blue, hole-in-the-wall waterfront restaurant has an interior festooned with coral and shells, and a few tables outside to tuck into mussels, calamari, cuttlefish, shrimps, octopus... Enough seafood to keep a shoal of mermaids quiet.

Platanos
CRETAN €

(mains €5-12; ⊙11am-late; 🛜) Beneath a giant plane tree, Platanos is a focus of village social life and has live music on many summer evenings. Reliable Cretan staples such as rabbit *stifadho* (stew cooked with onions in a tomato purée), aubergine salad, meatballs and baklava.

Taverna Myrtos
GREEK €

(Main St; mains €7-12; ⊙6.30am-midnight; 🛜✏️) Attached to Myrtos Hotel, this high-ceilinged joint is redolent with homemade food: souvlaki, swordfish, red mullet and veal cutlet. It's unpretentiously old school and popular with locals.

❶ Information

There is no post office or bank. Internet access is available at **Prima Travel** (✏️ 28420 51035; www.sunbudget.net; per hr €3.50), which can also advise on a range of services and activities around the area.

❶ Getting There & Away

There are seven buses daily from Ierapetra to Myrtos (€2.20, 20 minutes).

Understand Crete

Crete Today

Being a large, often self-contained island with an independent history, Crete can sometimes seem a world away from mainland Greece. But as the nation struggles with its economy and its relationship with the EU, Crete also has to face the governmental shortfalls and the recession that are impacting people all over Greece. Other challenges are Crete's natural environment and its position abutting the Middle East and Africa, from where many migrants flee north.

Best on Film

Zorba the Greek (1964) Boasting three Academy Awards, this is still the quintessential Crete-filmed movie, based on the excellent novel of the same name.

Night Ambush (1957) Gripping retelling of the kidnapping of Nazi General Heinrich Kreipe by British forces in 1944.

El Greco (2007) Greek-made biopic tells the life story of the Cretan-born Renaissance painter.

Two Faces of January (2014) Intrigue ensues at the ruins of Knossos and on Cretan back roads.

Best in Print

Freedom or Death (Nikos Kazantzakis, 1950) Powerful account of the 1889 Cretan rebellion against the Turks.

The Cretan Runner (George Psychoundakis, 1955) Cretan resistance in WWII, as told by a local shepherd turned messenger.

Dark Labyrinth (Lawrence Durrell, 1958) Philosophical tale of a group of English travellers determined to find and explore a dangerous labyrinth.

The Island (Victoria Hislop, 2005) Bestselling beach read weaving romance and tragedy, set on Spinalonga Island.

Crete & the Fiscal Crisis

As with anywhere in Greece, Crete has not been immune to the country's severe debt crisis. Between 2010 and 2012, the 'troika' (European Commission, European Central Bank and International Monetary Fund) approved two bailout loan packages totalling €240 billion (not all of which was disbursed) to prevent Greece from defaulting on its debt (equal to 150% of its GDP). The deals required the government to impose strict austerity measures (public spending and pension cuts, reduction of red tape, crack-downs on tax evasion and across-the-board tax increases) as well as to raise billions through the privatisation of state-controlled assets.

The country has fallen into a depression: GDP shrunk by about 20% during five years. By 2014 unemployment climbed to 28%, with youth unemployment at a staggering 60%. In early 2015 the ECB cut off emergency aid (already totalling €130 billion), the banks closed briefly and capital controls were imposed, and remain in effect as of the time of writing (July 2015).

Throughout these machinations, tumultuous social and political repercussions have rocked Greece. These include mass protests and widespread strikes. Disillusionment with the long-ruling PASOK and New Democracy parties ultimately yielded parliamentary elections in January 2015, which saw Alexis Tsipras of the leftist anti-austerity party Syriza become prime minister. As Greece teeters on the brink of default, talks with the troika remain embattled as a third loan package and debt restructuring are being negotiated. The possibility remains that Greece could exit the eurozone.

The reality of lost jobs, capital controls, cut wages and pensions, unpayable taxes, and disappearing social services has been exacerbated by the disillusioning uncertainty that accompanies each of these political and economic manoeuvres. Yet it is possible that for its part,

Crete itself may weather whatever storms are coming better than elsewhere in the country. Crete's relative abundance of natural resources and geographical isolation from the more urbanised mainland shield it to a degree from problems. The retention of strong family ties and traditions means that informal societal safety structures remain in place. But how long can people's ingenuity and savings hold out?

Tourism in Crete

As in Greece overall, locals breathed a collective sigh of relief when tourism grew by 15% in 2014. As a key engine of the Cretan economy, tourism generates some 40% of its output and accounts for at least one in five jobs. Though welcome, the uptick does not mean that Crete is out of the woods, especially since visitors are sometimes lured by lower prices.

Environmental Awareness

A growing number of locals are becoming increasingly sensitive to the long-term dangers of environmental degradation, and are tapping into the potential of sustainable ecotravel. The lack of prior planning and regulation is most evident in the tourist zones along the highly developed northern coast. In response, local environmental groups, students and expats have banded together to successfully prevent several large-scale developments. Whether the country's fiscal crisis and the need to raise revenue leads to environmental initiatives going by the wayside, is anybody's guess for now.

Border Issues

The EU is concerned about Greece's role in illegal or refugee migration. European border policing mission Frontex (http://frontex.europa.eu) began operations on the Greece–Turkey border and at sea in 2010. The flow of migrants leaving North Africa increased due to the Arab Spring revolts in 2011, and people fleeing Afghanistan, Pakistan and Syria in 2014 and 2015 caused an overall 149% increase from 2014 to 2015.

Traffickers' vessels packed with migrants in inhumane conditions have in recent years been found both washed up on Cretan shores and off the island. Many of the vessels are bound for Italy, but according to Amnesty International more than 2500 people of the estimated 150,000 who tried to make the crossing in 2014 went missing or drowned. Communities in the south of Crete, like Ierapetra or Paleohora, end up in a tough situation: trying to shelter the stranded migrants temporarily, but unable to support them long-term, and the migrants' fates are uncertain. Some, deemed political refugees, are given a temporary permit to remain in Greece, others are sent for deportation.

It is clear that the issue, which has become a major political one across the country and Europe as a whole, will continue to be a challenge for Crete.

POPULATION: **623,000**

AREA: **8336 SQ KM**

GDP: **€10.955 BILLION**

GDP PER CAPITA: **€19,500**

ANNUAL NUMBER OF VISITORS: **3.5 MILLION**

NUMBER OF OLIVE TREES: **30 MILLION**

if Crete were 100 people

58 would live in rural areas
42 would live in the six largest cities

belief systems
(% of population)

95
Greek Orthodox

3
Muslim

1
Roman Catholic

1
Other

population per sq km

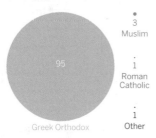

GREECE   ENGLAND   CRETE

≈ 75 people

History

Crete's colourful history goes back 5000 years and is evident across the island, from ancient palaces and Roman cities to spectacular Byzantine churches, Venetian fortresses and Ottoman buildings. Crete's prominent place in world history dates back to the illustrious Minoans, who were lording over lavish palaces at a time when other Europeans were huddled in primitive huts. Ever since, Crete's strategic location in the middle of the Mediterranean has involved it in a parade of momentous world events.

Myth & the Minoans

Top Minoan Sites

Knossos (Iraklio)

Phaestos (Iraklio)

Zakros (Lasithi)

Malia (Iraklio)

Crete's early history is largely shrouded in myth, making it all the more fascinating. It is clear from both legends and physical remains, however, that it was home to Europe's first advanced civilisation: the Minoans.

This enigmatic culture emerged in the Bronze Age, pre-dating the great Mycenaean civilisation on the Greek mainland. Minoan society interacted with, and was inspired by, two great Middle Eastern civilisations: the Mesopotamians and the Egyptians. Immigrants arriving from Anatolia around 3000 BC brought with them the skills necessary for making bronze, a technological quantum leap that enabled the emerging Minoans to flourish almost uninterrupted for over one-and-a-half millennia.

While many aspects of the less-evidenced neolithic life endured during the Early Minoan period, the advent of bronze allowed the Minoans to build better boats and thus expand their trade in the Near East. Pottery and goldsmithing became more sophisticated, foreshadowing the subsequent great achievements of Minoan art, and the island prospered from trade.

The chronology of the Minoan age is debated. But most archaeologists generally split the Minoan period into three phases: Protopalatial (3400–2100 BC), Neopalatial (2100–1450 BC) and Postpalatial (1450–1200 BC). These periods roughly correspond, with some overlap, to the older divisions of Early Minoan (some parts also called Prepalatial), Middle Minoan and Late Minoan; the terms are used interchangeably throughout.

TIMELINE	6500 BC	3000 BC	2000 BC
	Crete's earliest-known inhabitants are hunter-gathers. Neolithic people live in caves or wooden houses, worship female fertility goddesses, farm, raise livestock and make primitive pottery.	Bronze-making North African or Levantine immigrants arrive, and the Bronze Age begins. Society changes, with these early Cretans beginning to trade. Pottery and jewellery making develops.	Minoan civilisation reaches its peak: architectural advances lead to the first palaces in Knossos, Phaestos, Malia and Zakros, while pottery making improves and Crete's first script emerges.

CRETE IN ANCIENT GREEK MYTH

Crete has a prominent place in Ancient Greek mythology as the place where Rhea gave birth to Zeus and hid him from his child-gobbling father, and where Zeus' own son, Minos, had his legendary reign. Icarus and Daedalus launched their ill-fated flight in Crete, while Theseus made the voyage from Athens to Crete to slay the Minotaur in the famous labyrinth. For more about Cretan myths, see the boxed text on p205.

The Minoan civilisation reached its peak during the Protopalatial period, also called the Old Palace or Middle Minoan period. Around 2000 BC, the large palace complexes of Knossos, Phaestos, Malia and Zakros were built, marking a sharp break with neolithic village life.

During this period, Crete was probably governed by local rulers, with power and wealth concentrated at Knossos. Society was organised along hierarchical lines, with a large population of slaves, and great architectural advances were made. The first Cretan script also emerged during this period. At first highly pictorial, the writing gradually changed from the representations of natural objects to more abstract figures that resembled Egyptian hieroglyphics.

In 1700 BC the palaces were suddenly destroyed by what most archaeologists believe was an earthquake. But soon after came the Minoan golden age, and the rebuilding of the palaces at Knossos, Phaestos, Malia and Zakros; their new and more complex design was remarkably advanced. There were multiple storeys, sumptuous royal apartments, grand reception halls, storerooms, workshops, living quarters for staff, and an advanced drainage system. The design later gave rise to the myth of the Cretan labyrinth and the Minotaur.

During the Neopalatial period, the Minoan state developed into a powerful *thalassocracy* (state known for prosperous maritime trade), purportedly ruled by King Minos, with the capital at Knossos. Trade with the eastern Mediterranean, Asia Minor and Egypt boomed, helped by Minoan colonies in the Aegean. Minoan pottery, textiles and agricultural produce such as olive oil and livestock subsequently found ready markets throughout the Aegean, Egypt, Syria and possibly Sicily.

Minoan civilisation came to an abrupt and mysterious halt around 1450 BC after the palaces (except for Knossos) and numerous smaller settlements were smashed to bits. Scientific evidence suggests the Minoans were weakened by a massive tsunami and ash fallout from a cataclysmic volcano that erupted on nearby Santorini. But there is much debate about both the timing and explanation for the ultimate demise of the Minoans. Some argue it was caused by a second, powerful earthquake

Minoan civilisation may have been destroyed by a tsunami. Minoan artefacts mixed with pebbles, shells and marine life have been found at sites 7m above sea level, and dated to 1450 BC, when Santorini's volcano erupted, sending a 23m-high wave spanning 15km into Crete's northern coast.

1700 BC	1450 BC	1400 BC	1100 BC
The Minoan palaces are destroyed, probably by an earthquake. However, they are rebuilt bigger and better, with multiple storeys, storerooms, workshops, living quarters and advanced drainage systems.	Minoan culture comes to an abrupt and unexplained halt. The palaces (except Knossos) are destroyed by what some archaeologists believe was a massive tsunami following a volcanic eruption on Santorini.	The Mycenaeans colonise Crete. Weapons manufacture flourishes; fine arts fall into decline. Greek gods replace worship of the Mother Goddess.	The Dorians overrun the Mycenaean cities and become Crete's new masters; they reorganise the political system. A rudimentary democracy replaces monarchical government.

CRETE'S FIRST SEAFARERS

During excavations carried out in 2008 and 2009 near Plakias and Preveli, archaeologists were astonished to discover chiselled stone tools dating back at least 130,000 years. The tools came as the first evidence that humankind had engaged in sea travel so long ago. (The earliest known sea voyage previous to the Crete finds was a mere 60,000 years ago.)

The idea that the first Cretans arrived by boat much earlier than anyone had ever thought has revolutionary implications for the entire anthropological conventional wisdom, which had it that the first humans migrated to Europe from Africa by land alone. Since experts believe the Cretan tools may in fact date back up to 700,000 years, it's clear that there are more revelations ahead. The digging continues.

a century later. Other archaeologists blame the invading Mycenaeans. Whether the Mycenaeans caused the society's fall or merely profited from a separate catastrophe, it is clear that their presence on the island closely coincided with the destruction of the palaces and of Minoan civilisation.

The Rise & Fall of the Mycenaeans

The Mycenaean civilisation, which reached its peak between 1500 and 1200 BC, was the first great civilisation on the Greek mainland. Named after the ancient city of Mycenae, it is also known as the Achaean civilisation after the Indo-European branch of migrants who had settled on mainland Greece.

Unlike Minoan society, where the lack of city walls seems to indicate relative peace under some form of central authority, Mycenaean civilisation was characterised by independent city-states, the most powerful of them all being Mycenae, ruled by kings who inhabited palaces enclosed within massive walls on easily defensible hill tops.

The Mycenaeans wrote in what is known as 'Linear B' script. Clay tablets inscribed with the script found at the Palace of Knossos provides evidence of Mycenaean occupation of the island. Their colonisation of Crete lasted from 1400 to 1100 BC. Knossos probably retained its position as capital of the island, but its rulers were subject to the mainland Mycenaeans. The Minoan Cretans either left the island or hid in its interior, while the Mycenaeans founded new cities such as Lappa (Argyroupoli).

The economy of the island stayed more or less the same, still based upon the export of local products, but the fine arts fell into decline. Only the manufacture of weapons flourished, reflecting the new militaristic spirit that the Mycenaeans brought to Crete. The Mycenaeans also

800 BC	431–386 BC	67 BC	27 BC
Local agriculture and animal husbandry become sufficiently productive to trigger renewed maritime trading.	While Greece is embroiled in the Peloponnesian War, Crete also sees internal strife: Knossos against Lyttos, Phaestos against Gortyna, Kydonia against Apollonia, and Itanos against Ierapitna.	The Romans finally conquer Crete after invading two years earlier at Kydonia. Gortyna becomes the capital and most powerful city. The 'Pax Romana' ends internal wars.	Crete is united with eastern Libya to form the Roman province of Creta et Cyrenaica, reorganising population centres and ushering in a new era of prosperity.

replaced worship of the Mother Goddess with new Greek gods such as Zeus, Hera and Athena.

Mycenaean influence stretched far and wide, but was eventually weakened by internal strife; they were no match for the warlike Dorians.

Classical Crete

Despite fierce resistance, Dorians conquered Crete around 1100 BC, and many inhabitants fled to Asia Minor. Those who remained, known as Eteo-Cretans or 'true Cretans', retreated to the hills and thus preserved their culture.

The Dorians heralded a traumatic break with the past. The next 400 years are often referred to as Greece's 'dark age', though they brought iron with them and developed a new style of pottery, decorated with striking geometrical designs. The Dorians worshipped male gods instead of fertility goddesses and adopted the Mycenaean gods of Poseidon, Zeus and Apollo, paving the way for the later Greek religious pantheon.

The Dorians reorganised Crete's political system and divided society into three classes: free citizens who owned property and enjoyed political liberty (including land-holding peasants); merchants and seamen; and slaves. The monarchical system was replaced by a rudimentary democracy. Free citizens elected a ruling committee that was guided by a council of elders and answered to an assembly of free citizens. Unlike in Minoan times, women were subordinate.

By about 800 BC, local agriculture and animal husbandry had become sufficiently productive to trigger renewed maritime trading. As new Greek colonies were established throughout the Mediterranean basin, Crete took on a prominent role in regional trade.

Greece's various city-states started to become more unified by the development of a Greek alphabet, the verses of Homer and the founding of the Olympic Games. The establishment of central sanctuaries, such as Delphi, began to give Cretans a sense of national identity as Greeks.

Rethymno, Polyrrinia, Falasarna, Gortyna and Lato were built according to the new defensive style of Dorian city-states, with a fortified acropolis at the highest point, above an *agora* (market), a bustling commercial quarter, and beyond it residential areas.

As the rest of Greece entered its golden age from the 6th to 4th centuries BC, Crete remained a backwater. Constant warfare between large commercial centres and smaller traditional communities left the island increasingly impoverished. Although Crete did not participate in the Persian Wars or the Peloponnesian Wars, economic circumstances forced many Cretans to sign up as mercenaries in foreign armies or to turn to piracy.

HISTORY CLASSICAL CRETE

The 6th century BC *Laws of Gortyna*, discovered in the late 19th century AD at Gortyna, reveals the societal structure of Dorian Crete. Inscribed on 12 large stone tablets, the laws cover civil and criminal matters, with clear distinctions drawn between the classes of free citizens and between citizens and slaves.

AD 63	250	395	727
Christianity is established after St Paul visits Crete and leaves his disciple, Titus, to convert the island. St Titus becomes Crete's first bishop.	The first Christian martyrs, the so-called Agii Deka (Ten Saints) are killed in the village of the same name, as Roman officials begin major Christian persecutions.	The Roman Empire splits and Crete is ruled by Byzantium. Crete becomes a self-governing province; Gortyna is its administrative and religious centre. Trade flourishes; many churches are built.	Cretan supporters of icon worship revolt after iconoclast Emperor Leo III bans them. The uprising is smashed and a fierce wave of retribution is unleashed.

During this time, Crete's role as the birthplace of Greek culture drew the attention of philosophers such as Plato and Aristotle, who wrote extensively about Crete's political institutions. Knossos, Gortyna, Lyttos and Kydonia (Hania) continued to vie for supremacy, causing ongoing turmoil. Egypt, Rhodes and Sparta got involved in the Cretan squabbles and piracy flourished.

The Roman Empire

In order to turn the Mediterranean into a 'Roman lake', the Roman Empire needed to curtail piracy and control shipping routes. As the most strategic island in the central Mediterranean, Crete had been on Rome's to-do list since the 3rd century BC. But it wasn't until the third Mithridatic War (73–63 BC) that it was able to intervene, playing the piracy card. When Mark Antony's father, Marcus Antonius, unsuccessfully attacked, the Cretans sent envoys to Rome, but they were rebuffed. An army of 26,000 men was hastily established to defend the island. Roman consul Metellus launched the decisive invasion in 69 BC near Kydonia (Hania), and within two years had taken Crete, despite valiant local resistance.

Roman rule and reorganisation brought a new era of peace to Crete, and land and towns were given as favours to various Roman allies. In 27 BC, Crete was united with eastern Libya to form the Roman province of Creta et Cyrenaica. By this time, the Romans had spent decades building up their new possession, with Gortyna becoming the capital and most powerful city under Roman rule (circa 67 BC). Roman amphitheatres, temples and public baths livened things up, and the population increased. Knossos fell into disuse, but Kydonia (Hania) in the west became an important centre. Roman towns were linked by roads, bridges and aqueducts, parts of which are still visible in places. Under the Romans, the Cretans continued to worship Zeus in the Dikteon and Ideon Caves, and also incorporated Roman and Egyptian deities into their rituals.

At Gortyna, the remnants of the 6th century AD Basilica of Agios Titus attest to this disciple of St Paul. St Titus' relics, recovered in 1966 from Venice, where they had been taken for safekeeping during the Ottoman period, are today found in the cathedral named after him in Iraklio.

Christianity Comes to Crete

In AD 63, Christianity was brought to Crete by St Paul himself. His disciple, St Titus (who died in AD 107 at the age of 94), remained to convert the island and became its first bishop. Although the early years of Cretan Christianity seem to have been quiet, the 3rd century brought large-scale persecution, as elsewhere in the Roman Empire. The first Christian martyrs, the so-called *Agii Deka* (Ten Saints), were killed in the eponymous village in 250.

In 324, Emperor Constantine I (also known as Constantine the Great), a Christian convert, transferred the capital of the empire from Rome to Byzantium, which was renamed Constantinople (now İstanbul). By the

824	960	1204	1363
Arab Saracens conquer Crete and establish a fortress called Chandax in Iraklio to store their pirated treasure. The island sinks into a century-and-a-half gloom and cultural life dwindles.	Byzantine General Nikiforos Fokas launches the 'Expedition to Crete', liberating the island. Coastal defences are fortified, and Chandax becomes capital and archdiocese seat.	After Crusaders sack Constantinople, Boniface of Montferrat sells Crete to Venice. Venice rapidly colonises Crete, importing settlers and building towns and defences in Rethymno, Hania, Iraklio and elsewhere.	Venice quells a joint uprising by Crete's Venetian leaders and Greeks in the Revolt of St Titus, though fighting continues for several years against Greek nobles like the Kallergis clan.

end of the 4th century, the Roman Empire was formally divided into western and eastern sections; Crete, along with the rest of Greece, was in the eastern half, also known as the Byzantine Empire.

Although the doctrinal differences that would later separate Catholicism from Orthodox Christianity were centuries from realisation, the division of the empire geographically also expedited divergences in practice, custom and allegiances that would come to define the Orthodox Church, presided over by the patriarch in Constantinople.

In the early Byzantine Empire, Crete was a self-governing province, with Gortyna as its administrative and religious centre. Piracy decreased and trade flourished, leaving the island wealthy enough to build many churches.

Crete's attachment to the worship of icons provoked a revolt in 727 when Emperor Leo III banned their worship as part of the iconoclastic movement. This broke out in different periods of the 8th and 9th centuries and had complex theological, economic and political roots, but was partly influenced by questions provoked by the rise of Islam. The uprising was smashed and the Byzantine emperor unleashed a fierce wave of retribution against Crete's iconophiles. However, the policy became officially overturned for good by decree of Empress Theodora in 843, an event still celebrated as the 'Triumph of Orthodoxy' on the first Sunday of Lent.

Cretan author Nikos Psilakis' 2008 book *Byzantine Churches and Monasteries of Crete* is a very useful and well-illustrated portable guide to hundreds of Crete's spiritual sites.

Between Pirates & the Pope

The peaceful period of Byzantine rule came to an end around 824 with the arrival of Arabs from Spain, who gradually conquered Crete and used it as a base for attacks across the Aegean. The Arabs established a fortress called Chandax in what is now Iraklio, essentially to store their pirated treasure. As the island's criminal reputation grew, its economy dwindled and its cultural life ground to a halt. There are few records for this period, considered Crete's 'dark age'. While some of the population seems to have been forcibly converted to Islam, this would not outlive the occupation.

Byzantine armies sought to rescue Crete several times, in 842 and again in 911 and 949, but were not successful until Nikiforos Fokas launched the legendary Expedition to Crete in 960. After a bitter siege of Chandax, Crete was liberated in 961, and the Byzantines quickly started fortifying the Cretan coast and consolidating their power. Chandax emerged as the new capital of the theme (a Byzantine term for province) of Crete, and was the seat of the restored Cretan archdiocese. The church undertook efforts to bring errant sheep back to the Christian flock.

1453	1541	1587	1645
Constantinople falls to the Turks. Byzantine scholars and intellectuals flee to Crete, sparking a renaissance of Byzantine art. The 'Cretan School' of icon painting emerges.	Dominikos Theotokopoulos, later known as 'El Greco', is born in Candia; his subsequent creations in Italy and Spain are marked by both 'Cretan School' influence and bold personal innovation.	Vitsentzos Kornaros of Sitia writes the *Erotokritos,* a voluminous verse epic that becomes Crete's greatest literary achievement – and remains one of the most important works of all Greek literature.	A huge Turkish force lands in Hania, establishing the Turks' first foothold on the island. After Rethymno is defeated, they secure the western part of the island.

The following two-and-a-half centuries were relatively peaceful, save for a short-lived revolt by the governor, Karykes, in 1092. A few years later, it was brought, with southern Greece and the Peloponnese, under the control of the Byzantine navy's main commander.

This happy existence was shattered by the perfidious Fourth Crusade of 1204, which saw Venetian-bankrolled Western crusaders opt to attack Christian Constantinople rather than the 'infidels' down in Egypt. While Crete was originally granted to Crusade-leader Boniface of Montferrat, he soon sold it to the Venetians. However, the latter's Genoese archrivals seized it first, and it took until 1212 for Venice to establish control. Their colonial rule would last until 1669. Today, Venice's former influence is evident throughout Crete's major towns, in former mansions and massive fortresses that guarded the port towns and harbours.

Venice colonised Crete with noble and military families, many of whom settled in Iraklio (Candia). About 10,000 settlers came during the 13th century alone, to be rewarded with the island's best and most fertile land. Formerly landowners, the Cretans now worked as serfs for their Venetian masters. Cretan peasants were ruthlessly exploited, and taxes were oppressive. Further, the all-powerful influence of the papacy meant that Venetian rulers sought to impose Catholicism over Orthodoxy. Unsurprisingly, revolts were frequent.

Iraklio's Museum of Christian Art has an important collection of icons from artists including the great Michael Damaskinos, who introduced a distinctive painting style to Cretan art in the 16th century.

Sophistication & Spirit

Over time, the wealth and stability that the Venetian empire could provide for Crete would pay cultural dividends; an environment developed in which the cosmopolitan ideas and goods that came with a maritime trade power combined with local creative talent and tradition. While Western Europe, the Balkans and Byzantium were being decimated by civil wars, dynastic disputes and Islamic invasions, Crete was usually a tranquil isle in the sun (despite occasional revolts) where thinkers could take refuge and where first-rate educations were available, generally through the Church. Venetian Crete was also known for its cultural intellectual centres, such as the Accademia degli Stravaganti in Candia (Iraklio), where rhetoricians sparred and philosophers pored over ancient texts.

This cultural flowering was greatly expedited by two factors: the renewed Western curiosity in ancient Greek and Latin thought, and the fall of Constantinople in 1453. After the captures of Trebizond, and Mystras in the Peloponnese a few years later, Crete became the last major remaining bastion of Hellenism, and Byzantine scholars and intellectuals relocated to the island. They brought their manuscripts, icons and experience, and established schools, libraries and printing presses.

Venetian Vintage

Harbour fortresses, Iraklio, Rethymno and Hania
·········
Morosini (Lion) Fountain, Iraklio
·········
Spinalonga Island, near Elounda
·········
Moni Arkadiou, south of Rethymno
·········
Frangokastello, southern coast

1669	1770	1821	1828
Iraklio (Candia) finally falls to the Turks, 24 years after the capture of the rest of the island. Ottoman rule sees the construction of mosques and heavy taxation of Christians.	Under Ioannis Daskalogiannis, 2000 Sfakiots revolt in Sfakia, but are defeated. Daskalogiannis is skinned alive in Iraklio.	The Greek War of Independence is declared. The insurgency spreads to Crete but Turkish-Egyptian forces outnumber the rebellion. Continued resistance provokes massacres of Cretans.	In one of the bloodiest battles in the War of Independence, 385 rebels make a heroic last stand at Frangokastello. About 800 Turks are killed along with the rebels.

REBELLION & A SHORT-LIVED REPUBLIC

Some interesting twists in Crete's many revolts against the Venetian government indicate a complex and interesting reality. One example is the August 1363 Revolt of St Titus, which saw oppressed Cretans join forces with Venetian settlers exasperated at a new tax. Despite attempts at an amicable settlement, top officials proved deaf and the call to arms was raised. Aside from the commercial grievances that motivated rebels, the events showed that after only a couple of generations living in Crete, the settlers seemed to view their Greek neighbours as fellow countrymen (rather than those in far-off Venice).

The rebellion quickly resulted in the overthrow of the local government and the pronunciation of equality for Greeks and Orthodoxy. The island's patron saint, Titus, became the official emblem for this, the new 'Commune of Crete'. Venetian diplomats dissuaded other great powers, particularly the Genoese, from aiding the rebels, though, and by spring 1364 a Venetian military force had retaken Candia. After the leaders of the uprising were executed, the Venetian overlords celebrated. But it was not the end by any means.

Indeed, most fighters had already escaped into Crete's rugged mountains, where Greek noble families such as the Kallergis clan in the west sought to overthrow Latin rule completely, and reunite with Byzantium. This was all too much for the Venetian doge, who convinced the Pope to declare a crusade against the Kallergis. But all of western Crete joined the rebellion, under the banner of a battle for the salvation of Orthodoxy: it would take the Venetians almost five years to restore order.

Although Venice kept ultimate control, these rebellions were not in vain, as they forced the colonisers to make concessions. And so, by the 15th century, Cretans of both Greek and Italian background had made a sort of truce – one that allowed a remarkable and unique cultural flowering that would help shape the Italian Renaissance.

The cross-pollination between Byzantine traditions and the flourishing Italian Renaissance is particularly famous for its 'Cretan School' of icon painting, which became most highly developed in the 16th and 17th centuries, combining Byzantine and Venetian elements. Already, from the 13th to the early 16th centuries, churches around Crete had been adorned with frescoes – many of which can still be seen today. The 14th century's greatest icon painter was Ioannis Pagomenos, while the world's best-known such artist is Dominikos Theotokopoulos (1541–1614), who studied in Italy before moving to Spain, where he became known as El Greco ('The Greek').

At the same time, Crete enjoyed a tremendous literary flowering, in which the traditional Cretan folk verse style influenced – and was influenced by – poetic and musical trends popular in France, Italy and Constantinople. Indeed, the island's literary masterpiece, the epic *Erotokritos*,

1830-40	1866	1877–78	1883
Crete is given to Egypt. The Turks defeat Egypt in Syria and reclaim Crete. Repeated violations spark more uprisings and demands for Crete's union with Greece.	About 2000 Turkish soldiers attack Moni Arkadiou, where over 900 rebels and their families shelter. Refusing to surrender, the Cretans light a store of gunpowder, killing all but one.	The Russo-Turkish War prompts another Cretan uprising, but despite gains the Treaty of Berlin rejects union with Greece. Crete becomes a semi-autonomous, discontented Ottoman province.	Greece's most famous writer, Nikos Kazantzakis, is born in Iraklio. He becomes famous for works like *Zorba the Greek* and *The Last Temptation of Christ* in the mid-20th century.

was penned in Greek by the Venetian-descended Vitsentzos Kornaros of Sitia in the late 16th century. A vernacular epic of more than 10,000 lines, it has a verse structure based on traditional Cretan songs (*mantinadhes,* traditional Cretan rhyming couplets), but its subjects of courtly love and bravery resemble 15th-century French predecessors, themselves influenced by earlier Byzantine Greek epics.

Resistance & the Tourkokratia

By the 17th century, the expanding Ottoman Empire was finally able to take on Venice on the high seas, with Cyprus and Crete the two most strategic Venetian possessions sought by the sultans. Following a two-month Turkish siege, Hania fell to the Turks in 1645, followed soon by Rethymno. However, Candia's massive walls kept the besieging Ottomans out until 1669. Only the fortresses of Gramvousa, Spinalonga and Souda remained in Venetian hands, the latter two until 1715. Thus began the *Tourkokratia* (Turkish rule).

Cretans who managed to escape the Turks took to the mountains, where they could enjoy freedom and attack the Turks, especially in the rugged, southwestern Sfakia region. In 1770, Sfakiot leader Ioannis Daskalogiannis led 2000 fighters into battle, after Russia promised assistance. However, help never came, and the Turks publicly skinned Daskalogiannis alive in Iraklio.

The 1821 Greek War of Independence fuelled another fruitless uprising, and the Ottomans massacred Cretan civilians and priests, who they identified as ideological agitators behind Greek nationalism. Nevertheless, the Cretan resistance, combined with the Peloponnesian and mainland Greek insurrections, forced the sultan to ask Egypt's rulers to attack the Christians, which they did with gusto, massacring many thousands across the Aegean. Crete's rebels fought furiously, but lost to the numerically superior Turkish-Egyptian forces.

In 1830, Greece became independent, but Crete was given to Egypt. The Turks and the Egyptians then went to war in Syria, and the Egyptians were defeated, so in 1840 Crete reverted to Ottoman rule. Meanwhile, *Enosis i Thanatos* (Union or Death) became a slogan for continuing rebellions in western Crete.

The Turks and Egyptians brought more massacres to the Cretans, whose struggle attained international notoriety in 1866 when 900 resolute rebels and their families holed up in Moni Arkadiou ignited their entire gunpowder stock, killing themselves and 2000 besieging Turkish soldiers. The event shocked the world, fuelling sympathy for the heroic Cretans. Yet Great Britain and France maintained a pro-Turkish stance, and prevented Greece from aiding the Cretan rebels.

Imagine sitting on the beach and seeing phantom warriors marching into the sea. The *drosoulites* – the ghosts of 385 Cretan fighters killed by the Turks, during a heroic last stand at Frangokastello on the south coast in 1828 – are said to appear each year in May.

1898	1900	1905	1908
Turks slaughter hundreds of Christian civilians, 17 British soldiers and the British consul in Iraklio. Britain orders the Turks out; Crete is placed under international administration, with Hania as capital.	Arthur Evans begins excavations at Knossos, quickly unearthing the palace and stunning the archaeological world with the discovery of the advanced Minoan civilisation.	A revolutionary assembly in Theriso declares unity with Greece. Eleftherios Venizelos sets up a rival government to administer the island. The Great Powers appoint a new governor of Crete.	The Cretan assembly declares unity with Greece, but Cretan deputies are not allowed to sit in the Greek parliament until 1912.

Freedom & Union

Even the Great Powers (France, Britain, Italy, Austria-Hungary, and Russia) could not stop the wave of revolutionary nationalism sweeping southeastern Europe. The 1877 Russo-Turkish War, which liberated Bulgaria and almost toppled the Ottoman government, encouraged both Cretan rebels and the Greek government. Despite significant gains by the Cretan rebels, the controversial Treaty of Berlin in 1878 rejected the idea of Enosis (Unification); instead, Crete gained semi-autonomous status, with Greek becoming the official language, though they were still under Turkish rule.

Following parliamentary infighting in 1889, another rebellion against Turkish rule prompted another Turkish crackdown. In Sfakia, Manousos Koundouros' secret fraternity, which sought to secure autonomy and eventual unification, besieged the Turkish garrison at Vamos, leading to violent reprisals and eventual intervention by the Great Powers, who forced a new constitution on the Ottomans.

When violence erupted again in 1896, the Greek government sent troops, declaring unification with Crete. However, the Great Powers blockaded the coast, preventing both Turks and Greeks from reinforcing their positions, and Greece withdrew. The unpopular Prince George, son of King George of Greece, was appointed as high commissioner of Crete by the Great Powers.

Violent outrage soon accomplished what decades of high international diplomacy hadn't: the expulsion of the Turks. In 1898 a group of Turks stormed through Iraklio slaughtering hundreds of Christian civilians – along with 17 British soldiers and the British consul. The main leaders were found and hanged, and a British squadron of ships arrived. Ottoman rule over Crete was finally over.

The charismatic Eleftherios Venizelos, a young politician from Hania and Prince George's minister of justice, broke with the regent, who refused to consider Enosis. Venizelos convened a revolutionary assembly in the village of Theriso near Hania, in 1905, raising the Greek flag and declaring unity with Greece.

Venizelos' upstart government was given teeth by armed support from local Cretans. The Great Powers asked King George to appoint a new governor. In 1908 the Cretan assembly declared unity with Greece, but even with Venizelos now prime minister, the Greek government refused to allow Cretan deputies into parliament, fearing it would antagonise both Turkey and the Great Powers. Not until the First Balkan War (1912) did Cretans finally enter parliament in Athens. The 1913 Treaty of Bucharest formally recognised Crete as part of the Greek state.

Intrepid and dedicated shoppers will occasionally still find (especially in village shops) late-19th-century flags emblazoned with the famous *Enosis i Thanatos* (Union or Death) slogan under which Cretan rebels fought against the Turks.

1913	1921	1941	1944
Turkey, angered by the parliamentary move, seeks revenge but is defeated in the Balkan Wars by Greece, Bulgaria, Serbia and Montenegro. The post-war Bucharest Treaty officially unites Greece with Crete.	Eight years after the 1913 Bucharest Treaty united Crete with Greece, the Greek–Turkish population exchange sees 30,000 Cretan Muslims replaced by Anatolian Greeks. Ottoman structures languish.	Germany invades Greece. Allied troops arrive to defend Crete. Germany launches an airborne invasion to capture the airport at Maleme, in the famous Battle of Crete. Allied soldiers are evacuated from Hora Sfakion.	The Cretan Resistance kidnaps German commander General Kreipe and, aided by the Allies, sends him to Egypt, sparking fierce German reprisals. Cities are bombed, villages annihilated and civilians shot.

After the disastrous Greek invasion of Smyrna, the 1923 Treaty of Lausanne mandated a population exchange between Greece and Turkey. Crete's Muslim population of 30,000 people was swapped for incoming Greek refugees from Anatolia.

WWII & the Battle of Crete

As in innumerable conflicts of yore, Crete's strategic geographical position made it highly enticing to foreign invaders in WWII. Hitler sought to dominate the Mediterranean and have a base from which to challenge British Egypt and forces in the eastern Mediterranean. On 6 April 1941, mainland Greece was rapidly overrun from the north, as the Royalist Yugoslav government was defeated, and Greek leader Emmanouil Tsouderos (1882–1956) set up a government in exile in his native Crete.

With all available Greek troops fighting the Italians in Albania, Greece asked Britain to help defend Crete. Churchill obliged, as he recognised the strategic significance of the island and was determined to block Germany's advance through southeastern Europe. More than 30,000 British, Australian and New Zealand troops poured into the last remaining part of free Greece, two-thirds of them having first been evacuated from mainland Greece.

From the start, the defenders were faced with difficult challenges. Commitments in the Middle East were already draining military resources. There were few fighter planes, and military preparation was hampered by six changes of command in the first six months of 1941. Crete's difficult terrain also meant the only viable ports were on the exposed northern coast, while inadequate roads precluded resupplying from the more protected southern ports.

After a week-long aerial bombardment, Hitler launched the world's first full-bore paratrooper invasion on 20 May 1941, starting what became known as the Battle of Crete, one of the war's most deeply pitched battles. Aiming to capture the airport at Maleme 17km west of Hania, thousands of German paratroopers floated down over Hania, Rethymno and Iraklio.

Cretan civilians of all ages grabbed rifles, sickles and whatever they could find to join the soldiers in defending the island. German casualties were appalling, but they managed to rally and capture the Maleme airfield by the second day and, despite the valiant and fierce defence, the Allies and Cretans lost the brutal battle after about 10 days.

After the Battle of Crete, the Cretans risked German reprisals by hiding thousands of Allied soldiers and helping them escape across the Libyan Sea. Allied undercover agents coordinated the guerrilla warfare waged by Cretan fighters, known as *andartes*. Allied soldiers and Cretans alike were under constant threat from the Nazis while they lived in caves,

Distinguished British archaeologist John Pendlebury, who took over Sir Arthur Evans' work at Knossos, was executed by the Germans in 1941 while fighting with the Cretan Resistance. He is buried at the Allied war cemetery in Souda.

1946–49	1951	1955	1960s–'70s
Greek civil war breaks out between communists and right-wing royalists. Crete is largely spared the bloodshed and bitterness that engulfs Greece.	Greece joins NATO, together with Turkey. Both become key Western allies during the cold war. Military bases, used still (in 2011, against Libya's Colonel Gaddafi), are established at Souda Bay.	*The Cretan Runner*, George Psychoundakis' memoir of being a dispatch runner during the German occupation, is published.	The arrival of foreign tourists launches one of the island's major modern industries.

WAR MEMORIALS

The Battle of Crete had a monumental impact on the outcome of WWII, and the massive casualties on all sides make it a significant war memorial pilgrimage. Every May, war veterans from Great Britain, Australia, New Zealand and Greece attend commemoration celebrations held throughout Crete. Major anniversaries include a re-enactment of the airborne invasion at Maleme.

More than 1500 Allied soldiers are buried at the Souda Bay War Cemetery near Hania. War monuments overlook the cliffs at Moni Preveli and mark Stravromenos on the north coast, as well as Hora Sfakion, the southern port from where Allied troops were evacuated.

Ironically, one of the caretakers of the German war cemetery at Maleme, where 4500 soldiers are buried, was the late George Psychoundakis (1920–2006), the former shepherd boy whose memoir of being a resistance dispatch runner during the German occupation was published as *The Cretan Runner* (1955).

sheltered in monasteries such as Preveli, trekked across peaks or unloaded cargo on the southern coast. Among them was celebrated author Patrick Leigh Fermor (1915–2011), who lived in the mountains for two years with the Cretan Resistance and was involved in the daring kidnapping of German commander General Kreipe in 1944.

German troops responded with fierce reprisals against the civilian population. Cities were bombed, villages burnt down, and men, women and children lined up and shot. When the Germans finally surrendered in 1945 they insisted on surrendering to the British, fearing that the Cretans would inflict upon them some of the same punishment they had suffered for four years.

Greek Civil War & Reconstruction

Although the German occupation of Greece had ended, the strife was hardly over. The postwar scenario of a capitalist West trying to contain a communist East would play out violently in Greece, where the mainland resistance had been dominated by communists. When WWII ended, the communists boycotted the 1946 election that saw King George II reinstated, with the backing of Winston Churchill and other Western leaders. Fortunately for Crete, the island was largely spared the bloodshed of the Greek Civil War (1946–49). When all was said and done, Greece was in the Western camp and joined NATO in 1951. Souda Bay air and sea base is the most important NATO base in Crete, and it was heavily used in the 2011 air campaign against Libya's Colonel Gaddafi.

For Crete as for Greece, the major challenge following the wars was reconstruction and the need to rebuild a shattered economy, while adjusting to a rapidly modernising world. In Crete, rural traditions play

1967–74	1981	2002	2008–09
Army colonels stage a coup and impose martial law across Greece. The junta is toppled seven years later following the Turkish invasion of northern Cyprus.	Greece becomes the 10th member of the EEC (now EU), giving Cretan farmers new access to EU funds. The islanders strongly back the first PASOK socialist government, led by Andreas Papandreou.	Greece becomes a full member of the European Monetary Union and the drachma is replaced by the euro. Prices jump across the country.	Excavations near Plakias and Preveli unearth chiselled stone tools dating back at least 130,000 years.

a strong social role, yet changes came in the 1960s and '70s with the arrival of foreign tourists who launched one of the island's major modern industries.

The Junta & Modern Crete

In 1967, four Greek army colonels staged a coup, establishing a military junta that imposed martial law, abolished all political parties, banned trade unions, imposed censorship, and imprisoned, tortured and exiled thousands of citizens. In Crete, resentment intensified when the colonels muscled through major tourist development projects rife with favouritism. When the junta was toppled there was a resurgence of support for left-wing causes and a new democratic constitution. A 1975 referendum officially deposed the king, Konstantinos II, ending the last vestiges of Greek royalism, and previously exiled politician George Papandreou returned to Greece. A towering figure in modern Greek history, Papandreou founded the socialist PASOK party, winning elections in 1981.

Greece joined the EU (then known as the EEC) in 1981, and Cretan farmers have garnered EU agricultural subsidies, while the island's infrastructure has been modernised thanks to EU support. Tourism boomed with direct charter flights to Crete, almost tripling tourist arrivals between 1981 and 1991, and tourism numbers doubled again with the advent of package tourism and budget airlines during the next decade.

The major challenge affecting all Greece, however, has been the country's recent financial woes and the government's controversial austerity measures. Crete's relative abundance of natural resources and geographical isolation from the more urbanised mainland shield it to a degree from some problems, such as violent protests, but the island cannot be shielded from pension cuts, bank instability and unemployment.

The branches given to athletes during the 2004 Athens Olympic Games were cut from a 3250-year-old olive tree – one of the world's oldest – which grows near Kavousi in northeast Crete.

2009	2011–12	2009–15	2015
Eurozone countries approve a US$146 billion (€110 billion) rescue package for the country's economic crisis in exchange for implementing austerity policies. It's the first in a series of bailouts.	Tens of thousands march on parliament in Athens to oppose government austerity policies. Nevertheless, a second, €130-billion bailout is approved.	Disillusionment with ruling parties New Democracy and PASOK rises. Left-wing Syriza comes to power in 2015, while fringe parties like neo-Nazi Golden Dawn find support.	The new government deals with Greece's budget deficit and austerity measures; despite a referendum opposing austerity, a third 'troika' bailout package is under negotiation.

The Cretan Way of Life

Cretans are a very distinctive clan of Greeks, with their own spirited music and dances, remarkable cuisine and traditions. Proud, patriotic and fierce yet famously hospitable, Cretans maintain a rich connection to their culture. They will often identify themselves as Cretans before they say they are Greek, and even within different parts of Crete people maintain strong regional identities. Explore beyond major tourist centres and you'll meet Cretans speaking local dialects, creating regional delicacies, and merging the old world with the new.

Lifestyle & State of Mind

Centuries of battling foreign occupiers have left Cretans with a fiercely independent streak, residual mistrust of authority and little respect for the state. Personal freedom, regional pride, and democratic rights are sacrosanct and there is a strong aversion to the Big Brother approach of highly regulated Western nations. National laws are routinely ignored. Guns, for example, are strictly regulated in Greece, yet the evidence suggests that Cretans are stashing an astounding arsenal. Several smoking bans (the last one introduced in 2010) have been widely flaunted. When it comes to road rules, many visitors are surprised to learn that they even exist. Despite hefty fines, wearing a seatbelt is treated as an optional inconvenience; creative and inconsiderate parking is the norm; dangerous overtaking is rife; and you may well see people riding motorbikes helmet-less as they chat on their mobile phones.

These days, though, the resilience of Cretan culture and traditions is being tested by globalisation, market forces and social change. The Cretan lifestyle has changed dramatically in the past 30 years. As Cretan society has become increasingly urbanised, living standards have improved significantly; Cretans are conspicuously wealthier and the towns have more sophisticated restaurants, bars and clubs. In the shift from living a largely poor, agrarian existence to becoming increasingly urban dwellers, Cretans are also delicately balancing cultural and religious mores. The younger generation is highly educated, and most speak English and often German as well. They are also living in a wealthier and much more high-tech society than their parents and grandparents.

As with most households in Greece, Cretans have felt the impact of higher living costs since the introduction of the euro and the more recent economic crisis and austerity measures. Eating out has become much more expensive, although there are still many reasonably priced tavernas, particularly in the villages. Still, Cretans have a work-to-live attitude and pride themselves on their capacity to enjoy life. They enjoy a rich social life, and you'll often see them dressed up and going out en masse for their *volta* (evening walk) and filling tavernas and cafes, with family or their *parea* (group of friends). Cretan society is also deeply influenced by the Greek Orthodox Church and its rituals and celebrations.

Harvard anthropologist Michael Herzfeld makes interesting observations of Cretans in *The Poetics of Manhood: Contest and Manhood in a Cretan Village*, while his *A Place in History* looks at life in and around Rethymno, including issues such as the Cretan vendetta.

Unlike many Western cultures where people avoid eye contact with strangers, Cretans are unashamed about staring and blatantly observing and commenting on the comings and goings of people around them. Few subjects are off limits, from your private life and why you don't have children to how much money you earn or how much you paid for your house or shoes. And they are likely to tell you of their woes and ailments rather than engage in polite small talk.

Family Life

Cretan society is still relatively conservative and it is uncommon for Greeks to move out of home until they are married, apart from leaving temporarily to study or work. While this is slowly changing among professionals, lack of economic opportunities and low wages are also keeping young people at home.

Parents strive to provide homes for their children when they get married, with many families building apartments for each child above their own homes. Construction is often done in a haphazard fashion depending on cash flow, which accounts for the large number of unfinished houses you encounter throughout the island.

Extended families often play an important role in daily life, with parents preferring to entrust their offspring to the grandparents rather than hiring outside help.

Cretans who moved away to other parts of Greece or overseas maintain strong cultural and family links and return regularly to their ancestral land. Even the most remote mountain villages are bustling with family reunions and homecomings during national and religious holidays, and Cretan weddings and baptisms are huge affairs.

> Cretans turn their heads downward to indicate yes (*nai*) and upward to signal no (*ohi*). The latter is often accompanied by an upward eye roll and a tongue click.

> Greece has compulsory nine-month military service for all males aged 19 to 45 years. Women are accepted into the Greek army, though they are not obliged to join and rarely do.

City vs Countryside

Generational and rural/city divides are other features of modern Crete. In rural areas you will see shepherds with their flocks and men congregating in the *kafeneia* (coffee shops) after their afternoon siesta. Mountain villages are repositories of traditional culture and you'll find that many older women and many men are still clad in black *vraka* (baggy trousers) and leather boots.

In general terms, the major population centres of the north attract companies, industry and universities, whereas agriculture accounts for the bulk of economic activity in the less-populated interior and south. The mountainous southwest has some of the more traditional villages on the island. But even pastoral life has changed. While people still live off the land – and provide for their families in the cities – subsistence farming has mostly given way to commercial production. Well-to-do

TRIGGER-HAPPY

Cretans have a reputation for their fierce fighting ability (they have battled with invaders for centuries, after all) and for having Greece's most notable gun culture. Estimates have indicated that one in two Cretans owns a gun, while others suggest there could be over one million weapons on Crete – more than the island's population.

At Cretan weddings and celebrations, volleys of gunshots occasionally punctuate events. Some musicians refuse to play in certain areas unless they get an assurance that there won't be any guns. At one time, acclaimed composer Mikis Theodorakis led a campaign trying to change the island's gun culture. But, today, road signs riddled with bullet holes are the first inkling that you are entering the mountain country that was historically a stronghold for Crete's resistance fighters, particularly around Sfakia in Hania and Mylopotamos province in Rethymno. Sfakiots are aware of their reputation, though, and you'll find T-shirts in their souvenir shops with images of the bullet-riddled signs.

KOMBOLOÏ

You see men stroking, fiddling and masterfully playing with them everywhere: the de-stressing worry beads called *komboloï*, an amalgam of the words *kombos* (knot) and *leo* (to say). Although they look like prayer beads, *komboloïa* (plural) have no religious purpose and are only used for fun and relaxation – there just seems to be something soothing about flicking and flipping those beads. Some people also use them to help them stop smoking.

Komboloïa were traditionally made from amber, but coral, handmade beads, semi-precious stones and synthetic resin are also widely used. No exact number is prescribed but most *komboloïa* have between 19 and 23 beads strung in a loop. There's a fixed bead that is held between the fingers, a shield that separates the two sides of the loop, and a tassel.

The vast majority of what you see in souvenir shops is plastic but there are also rare and old *komboloïa* that can be worth thousands of euros and are considered highly collectable.

farmers drive pick-up trucks and shepherds can often be seen tending to their flocks while chatting away on their mobile phones. In the fields, foreign workers are also a major part of accomplishing the grunt work.

No matter where you are, though, you'll find that a pride and connection to food and local produce, from mountain herbs and honey to regional dishes and cheeses made uniquely in each village, are vital to Cretan daily life.

Hospitality & Tourism

The Cretan people have a well-justified reputation for hospitality and for treating strangers as honoured guests. They pride themselves on their *filotimo* (dignity and sense of honour) and *filoxenia* (hospitality, welcome, shelter). If you wander into mountain villages you may well be invited into someone's home for a coffee or even a meal. In a cafe or taverna it is customary for people to treat another group of friends or strangers to a round of drinks (however, be mindful that it is not the done thing to treat them straight back – in theory, you will do the honours another time).

Surprisingly, this hospitality and generosity diminish in the public sphere, where customer service is not a widely lauded concept. The notion of the greater good can play second fiddle to personal interests, and there is little sense of collective responsibility in relation to issues such as the environment, though that is starting to change with the younger generation.

Crete takes in more than three-and-a-half-million visitors annually, which has an impact on both the environment and the economy: the majority of tourists come on package trips and are sequestered in northern-coast all-inclusive hotels. The over-development of much of northern-coast Crete has left hotel owners susceptible to larger trends in the travel world, whereas smaller places elsewhere on the island experience less volatile swings as the economy waxes and wanes. New EU grants have been given to promote green tourism and to restore historic buildings and traditional settlements, and there is a growing awareness that sustainable, ecofriendly tourism will pay dividends as the tastes of foreign visitors change.

Cretans often deal with the seasonal invasion of foreign tourists by largely operating in a different space-time continuum to their guests. They will often tell you a particular place is 'only for tourists', and that's normally their hint to you to avoid it. From April to around October,

Despite the country's fiscal downturn, Crete remains one of Greece's most popular holiday destinations, welcoming some three-and-a-half-million tourists every year. Crete has 22% of the total number of hotels in Greece and 28% of the hotel beds. Some 20% of all charter flights to Greece go to Iraklio.

many Cretans live in the hurly-burly of the coastal resorts and beaches – running shops, pensions or tavernas – and then return to their life in the cities, or in the hills for the autumn olive and grape harvests.

While many tourists eat early in the evening (by Greek standards, at least) in restaurants along a harbour or beach, Cretans drive out to village tavernas or frequent known local favourites, for a dinner that begins as late as 10pm. Nightlife goes equally late.

Multiculturalism

After the exodus of Crete's Turkish community in the population exchange of 1923, the island became essentially homogeneous and its population virtually all Greek Orthodox. In recent years, though, Crete has become an increasingly multicultural society as migrants from the Balkans and Eastern Europe, especially Albania, Bulgaria and Russia, are filling labour shortages in agriculture, construction and tourism. The total foreign population is now about 10%.

Economic migrants are a relatively new phenomenon for Crete which, like most of Greece, is struggling to come to terms with the new reality and concepts of multiculturalism. While there are tensions and mistrust, immigrants appear to have fared better in Crete than in many other parts of Greece.

A small group of English, German and northern European expats have also settled and bought property on Crete, though they live on the more affluent fringes, and there are some foreigners married to Cretans.

Religion

The Orthodox faith is the official and prevailing religion of Crete and a key element of Greek identity, ethnicity and culture. While the younger generation isn't necessarily devout, nor does it attend church regularly, most observe the rituals and consider the faith integral to their identity. Between 94% and 97% of the Cretan population belongs at least nominally to the Greek Orthodox Church.

The Orthodox religion held Cretan culture together during the many centuries of foreign occupation and repression, despite numerous efforts by the Venetians and Turks to turn locals towards Catholicism and Islam, respectively. Under Ottoman rule, religion was the most important criterion in defining a Greek.

Despite growing secularism, the Church still exerts significant social, political and economic influence. Religious affiliation appeared on national identity cards until recently. The year is centred on the saints' days and festivals of the church calendar. Name days (celebrating your namesake saint) are more important than birthdays, and baptisms are an important rite. Most people are named after a saint, as are boats,

For a useful but by no means exhaustive list of books about Crete, with reviews, visit www.hellenicbookservice.com.

The New Testament was written beginning around AD 50 in Koine Greek, which was the day-to-day language in the eastern part of the Roman Empire at the time.

ROADSIDE SHRINES

Buzzing around Crete's winding country roads, you'll see them everywhere: dollhouse-sized chapels on metal pedestals by the roadside. Called *kandylakia,* they come in all shapes and sizes, some simple, some elaborate, some weathered, some shiny and new. A votive candle may flicker behind tiny dust-encrusted windows, faintly illuminating the picture of a saint. They are especially prevalent on hairpin turns, blind curves and the edges of precipitous slopes. Many will have been put there by the families of those who died in an accident on this very spot, but some are also set up in gratitude by those who miraculously survived such accidents or to honour a particular saint. As you're driving, recognize these symbols of both tragedy and happy endings as a reflection of those things important to Cretans: family, faith and tradition.

suburbs and train stations. If you're invited to a name-day celebration, it's a good idea to bring a present, but don't be surprised if it won't be opened until you've left; any meal or offering of food, sweets or drink is usually paid for by the celebrant.

There are hundreds of tiny churches dotted around the countryside, predominantly built by individual families, dedicated to particular saints. Regrettably, many small churches and chapels are kept locked nowadays, but it's usually easy enough to locate the caretakers to see if they will open them for you.

Women in Society

The role of women in Cretan society has been complex and shifting since Greek women first gained universal suffrage in 1952. While traditional gender roles are prevalent in rural areas and among the older generation, the situation is much more relaxed for younger women in cities and large towns. Entrenched attitudes towards the 'proper role' for women are changing fast, as more women are educated and entering the workforce. Still, although some 40% of Greek women are in the workforce, they struggle mightily when it comes to even finding the career ladder or earning the same as their male counterparts. Though the numbers have slowly increased, women still hold only 23% of seats in Parliament. There are few public programs to help them balance careers and motherhood.

Paradoxically, despite the machismo, Cretan society is essentially matriarchal. Men love to give the impression that they rule the roost and take a front seat in public life, but it's often the women who run the show, both at home and in family businesses.

In villages, men and women still tend to occupy different spheres. When not tending livestock or olive trees, Cretan men can usually be found in a *kafeneio* (coffee house) playing *tavli* (Greek backgammon), gossiping and drinking coffee or *raki*. Although exceptions are made for foreign women, the *kafeneio* is a stronghold of male chauvinism and is generally off limits to Cretan women.

The older generation of Cretan women is house-proud and, especially in villages, spends time cultivating culinary skills. Most men rarely participate in domestic duties (or certainly don't own up to it). While rare these days, in villages you still might find women sewing, crocheting or embroidering in their free hours. Young Cretan women and city women are more likely to be found in cafes or operating businesses than behind looms.

The most common name for women in Crete is Maria. The most common names for men are Yannis (John), Giorgos (George) and Manolis.

Minoan Art & Culture

The Minoans' palaces were lavishly decorated with art, and the surviving paintings, sculptures, mosaics, pottery and jewellery housed today at archaeological sites and museums across Crete demonstrate the Minoans' extraordinary artistry. Minoan painting is virtually the only form of Greek painting to have survived through the ages; large-scale sculptures having disappeared in natural disasters like the great tsunami that swept over from Thira (Santorini) in 1450 BC. Minoan art inspired the invading Mycenaeans and its influence spread to Santorini and beyond.

Minoan Society

Mystery shrouds the Minoans: we don't even know what they called themselves, 'Minoan' being the term given by archaeologist Sir Arthur Evans, in honour of the mythical King Minos. They are thought to have been possibly related to the pre-Greek, Pelasgian people of western Anatolia and the Greek mainland, and to have spoken a unique language unrelated to the Indo-European ones.

Evidence uncovered in the island's grand palaces indicates they were a peaceful, sophisticated, well-organised and prosperous civilisation with robust international trade, splendid architecture and art, and seemingly equal status for men and women. The Minoans had highly developed agriculture, extensive irrigation systems and advanced hydraulic sewerage systems. The accounts and records left behind suggest that their society was organised as an efficient and bureaucratic commercial enterprise.

Although the evidence for a matriarchal society is scant, women apparently enjoyed a great degree of freedom and autonomy. Minoan art shows women participating in games, hunting and all public and religious festivals. They also served as priestesses, administrators and participated in trade.

Pottery

Minotaur: Sir Arthur Evans and the Archaeology of the Minoan Myth by Joseph Alexander MacGillivray is a fascinating portrait of the British archaeologist who revealed the Palace of Knossos to the world, and a study in relative archaeology.

Pottery techniques advanced in the Early Minoan years. Spirals and curvilinear motifs in white were painted on dark vases and several distinct styles emerged. Pyrgos pottery was characterised by black, grey or brown colours, while the later Vasiliki pottery (made near Ierapetra) was polychromatic. In the Middle to Late Minoan period, the style shifted to a dark-on-light colour technique.

Highly advanced levels of artisanship developed in the workshops of the first palaces at Knossos and Phaestos. Kamares pottery, named after the cave where the pottery was first found, was colourful, elegant and beautifully crafted and decorated with geometric, floral, plant and animal motifs. Human forms were rarely depicted. During the entire Middle Minoan period, Kamares vases were used for barter and were exported to Cyprus, Egypt and the Levant.

With the invention of the potter's wheel, cups, spouted jars and *pithoi* (large Minoan storage jars) could be produced quickly and there was a new crispness to the designs. The most striking were the 'eggshell' vases with their extremely thin walls.

In the late Neopalatial era, marine and floral themes in darker colours reigned. After 1500 BC, vases sprouted three handles and were frequently shaped as animal heads, such as the bull's-head stone *rhyton* (libation vessel) in the Heraklion Archaeological Museum. The decline of Minoan culture saw the lively pottery designs of previous centuries degenerate into dull rigidity.

Jewellery & Sculpture

Jewellery making and sculpture in various media reached an exceptional degree of artisanship in the Protopalatial period. The exquisite bee pendant found at Malia displays extraordinary delicacy and imagination. Another Minoan masterpiece is a 15th-century-BC gold signet ring found in a tomb at Isopata, near Knossos, which shows women in an ecstatic ritual dance in a meadow with lilies, while a goddess descends from the sky.

KING MINOS & DAEDALUS

Minos, the legendary ruler of Crete, was the son of Zeus and Europa and attained the Cretan throne, aided by Poseidon. Homer describes him and his land in the 'Odyssey': 'Out on the dark blue sea there lies a rich and lovely land called Crete that is densely populated and boasts 90 cities... One of the 90 cities is called Knossos and there for nine years, King Minos ruled and enjoyed the friendship of the mighty.'

Whatever his character might have been, his fate was ultimately interwoven with an Athenian master craftsman named Daedalus, who, having fled from Athens for murdering his nephew (for being more inventive), sought sanctuary in Crete. Minos was quick to utilise his skills, commissioning the inventor to design the legendary Palace of Knossos. It is said that Daedalus' statues were so lifelike that they had to be chained down to stop them moving. However, the inventor's talents were sometimes used to dark ends, as when Minos' Queen Pasiphae, who had fallen in love with the white bull of Poseidon, urged Daedalus to make a hollow wooden bull that she might satisfy her inflamed desire with it. Meanwhile, with Knossos as his base, Minos gained control over the whole Aegean basin, colonising many of the islands and ridding the seas of pirates. Again his naval success was often attributed to the ingeniousness of Daedalus, whose successes included designing the prow of the modern boat.

Then, as with many great partnerships, the relationship soured when the infamous half-bull, half-human Minotaur was birthed by Queen Pasiphae as a punishment from the gods. Daedalus was called upon to create a prison strong enough to contain the monster, which possessed the strength of an army. The inventor's answer was to construct the labyrinth, an endless maze of tunnels, where the creature was fed with seven boys and seven girls from Athens every year.

When Daedalus and his son Icarus left Crete without permission, Minos was enraged. In their escape the inventor lost his son, who famously flew too near the sun, his waxened feathers melting. Minos pursued him to the city of Kamikos, baiting the inventor with a challenge: a reward to anyone who could pass a thread through a shell. Overtaken by hubris, Daedalus solved the problem, but it was Minos who came to a nasty end not the wily inventor, who was under the protection of King Kokalios. After Minos threatened a war if the legendary father of flight did not turn up, the Sicilian king tricked the Cretan into bathing with his daughters – who promptly killed him with a device Daedalus had designed, a pipe that poured boiling water over his head. After his death, the Cretan king became a dread judge in Hades' realm, the Underworld.

As to whether King Minos actually existed and reigned, however, is open to debate. The Homeric reference *enneaoros* used to describe Minos could mean 'for nine years' or 'from the age of nine years'. Was Minos able to create an empire in nine short years, or was he a long-reigning monarch who started his kingly career as a boy?

Minoan sculptors created fine miniatures, including idols in faience (quartz-glazed earthenware), gold, ivory, bronze and stone. One of the most outstanding examples is the bare-breasted serpent goddess with raised arms wielding writhing snakes above an elaborately carved skirt. Another incredible piece is the small rock-crystal *rhyton* from the Palace of Zakros. All of the above are displayed at the Heraklion Archaeological Museum.

The art of seal-stone carving also advanced in the palace workshops. Using semi-precious stones and clay, artisans made miniature masterpieces that sometimes contained hieroglyphic letters. Goats, lions, griffins, and dance scenes were rendered in minute detail. Arthur Evans spent much of his first trip to Crete collecting these seals.

In the Postpalatial period, the production of jewellery and seal-stones was replaced by the production of weaponry, reflecting the influence of the warlike Mycenaeans.

The Famous Frescoes

Minoan frescoes are renowned for their vibrant colours and the vivid naturalism in which they portray landscapes rich with animals and birds, marine scenes teeming with fish and octopuses, and banquets, games and rituals. Although fresco painting probably existed before 1700 BC, all remnants vanished in the cataclysm that destroyed Minoan palaces around that time. Knossos yielded the richest trove of frescoes from the Neopalatial period, most of which are on display in the Heraklion Archaeological Museum.

For photos and descriptions of more than 50 Minoan sites around Crete, see archaeology buff Ian Swindle's comprehensive website at www.minoan crete.com.

Only fragments of the frescoes survive but they have been very carefully (and controversially) restored, and the technique of using plant and mineral dyes has kept the colours relatively fresh. Minoan fresco painters borrowed heavily from certain Egyptian conventions but the figures are far less rigid than most Egyptian wall paintings.

The Knossos frescoes suggest Minoan women were white-skinned with elaborately coiffured glossy black locks. Proud, graceful and uninhibited, these women had hourglass figures and were dressed in stylish gowns that exposed shapely breasts. The bronze-skinned men were tall, with tiny waists, narrow hips, broad shoulders and muscular thighs and biceps; the children were slim and lithe.

Many of the frescoes show action scenes, from boxing and wrestling to solemn processions, saffron gathering to bull-leaping.

Religious Symbols

The Minoans were not given to building colossal temples or religious statuary. Caves and mountain-peak sanctuaries appear to have been used for cult or religious activity, and were probably only visited once a year for a particular ritual (like the many tiny chapels you see dotted around Greece). Tables and jars found around these sites suggest agricultural

---

NO BULL

The bull was a potent symbol in Minoan times, featuring prominently in Minoan art. The peculiar Minoan sport of bull-leaping, where acrobatic thrill-seekers seize the charging bull's horns and leap over its back, is depicted in several frescoes, pottery and sculptures. Scantily clad men and women are shown participating in the sport, which may have had religious significance. One of the most stunning examples is the Middle Minoan bull-leaping fresco found at the Palace of Knossos, which shows a man leaping over the back of a bull with a female figure on each side. Another prized bull is the carved stone *rhyton* (libation vessel) in the shape of a bull's head, with rock-crystal eyes and gilded wooden horns.

DECIPHERING THE MYSTERIES OF LINEAR B

The methodical decipherment of the Linear B script, achieved by English architect and part-time linguist Michael Ventris in 1952, provided the first tangible evidence that the Greek language had a recorded history longer than any scholar had previously believed. The language was an archaic form of Greek some 500 years older than the Ionic Greek used by Homer.

Linear B was written on clay tablets that lay undisturbed for centuries until they were unearthed at Knossos. Further tablets were unearthed later on the mainland at Mycenae, Tiryns and Pylos in the Peloponnese and at Thebes in Boeotia in central Greece.

The clay tablets, found to be mainly inventories and records of commercial transactions, consist of about 90 different signs, and date from the 14th to the 13th centuries BC. Little of the social and political life of these times can be deduced from the tablets, although there is enough to give a glimpse of a fairly complex and well-organised commercial structure.

Importantly, what is clear is that the language is undeniably Greek, thus giving the modern-day Greek language the second-longest recorded written history, after Chinese. Read Andrew Robinson's biography, *The Man Who Deciphered Linear B,* to learn more about the fascinating life and great genius of Michael Ventris.

produce was left as an offering. Minoan spiritual life was organised around the worship of a Mother Goddess. Often represented with snakes or lions, the Mother Goddess was both healer and the deity-in-chief, while the male gods were clearly subordinate.

The double-axe symbol that appears in frescoes and on the palace walls at Knossos was a sacred symbol for the Minoans. Other religious symbols that frequently appear in Minoan art include the mythical griffin and figures with a human body and an animal head. The Minoans appear to have worshipped the dead and believed in some form of afterlife, while evidence uncovered in Anemospilia suggests that human sacrifice may also have taken place.

> The Minoans knew how to enjoy themselves – playing board games, boxing, wrestling and performing bold acrobatic feats including the sport of bull-leaping, while Minoan dancing was famous throughout Ancient Greece.

Writing & Language

In Crete, Minoan painting is virtually the only form of Greek painting to have survived; large-scale sculptures having disappeared in natural disasters like the great tsunami that swept over from Thira (Santorini) in 1450 BC. Minoan art inspired the invading Mycenaeans and its influence spread to Santorini and beyond. At the same time their inscrutable written hieroglyph system, Linear A, provides another indication of a culture that was very advanced. The Cretan hieroglyphic was the system of writing used in the Protopalatial period that later evolved into Linear A and B scripts. The most significant example of this writing is on the inscrutable 3600-year-old terracotta tablet known as the Phaestos Disk, which has been the object of much speculation since it was discovered at Phaestos in 1908. The disk, about 16cm in diameter, consists of an Early Minoan pictographic script made up of 242 'words' written in a continuous spiral from the outside of the disk to the centre (or the other way round). The repetition of sequences of words or sentences has led to speculation it may be a prayer. It has never been deciphered.

As far as the spoken language of the Minoans goes, this too remains unclear. While Mycenaean-era Linear B records something that is definitely an archaic form of Greek, Linear A may well be a script for something completely different. Scholars have speculated that it may have had connections with pre-Greek Mesopotamian tongues, but unless more samples are found, it will remain a mystery.

The Arts

Crete is a powerhouse for music, dance and the visual arts, going back millennia. From priceless Minoan sculptures to homegrown mountain musicians playing the *lyra* in tavernas, this massive island has developed its own ways of living, loving, lamenting and showing it all to the world through the arts. Prepare to browse museums, read local lit while you sunbathe, seek out frescoed chapels, or dance in the streets – this is Crete!

Music

The oldest surviving folk songs in Greece, dating from the 17th century, were found at Mt Athos and were revealed to be *rizitika* (patriotic songs) from western Crete.

Cretan music is the most dynamic and enduring form of traditional music in Greece today, and on the island it remains the most popular music, staving off mainstream Greek and Western pop. You'll hear it accompanying weddings, holidays, harvesting and any other celebration. Crete's thriving local music scene generates successive generations of folk musicians who perform regularly and produce new recordings of traditional songs, as well as contemporary styles based on Cretan tradition. You'll also find Cretan music on the world-music scene as a genre in its own right.

Instruments & Musical Styles

Cretan music has been influenced by many musical traditions over the centuries and resembles eastern modal music. The lead instrument is the *lyra,* a three-stringed instrument similar to a violin that is played resting on the knee. It is often accompanied by the eight-stringed *laouto* (lute), which keeps the rhythm for the *lyra*. Other traditional instruments include the *mandolino* (mandolin), the *askomandoura* (bagpipe), the *habioli* (wooden flute) and the *daoulaki* (drum). The bouzouki, so associated with Greek music, is not part of traditional Cretan music.

One of Crete's favourite forms of musical expression is the *mantinadha* (a style of traditional Cretan rhyming couplets), which expresses the timeless concerns of love, death and the vagaries of fate. Thousands of *mantinadhes* helped forge a sense of national identity during the long centuries of occupation. *Mantinadhes* rely on the decapentasyllabic (15-syllable) count of Byzantine vernacular literature, which goes back at least to the 12th century. The best 'rhymers' at Cretan festivals would tailor their songs to the people present and try to outdo each other in skill and composition. These days, young Cretans continue the tradition, and *mantinadhes* are still part of the modern courtship ritual, albeit often via mobile-phone messages. The best-known piece of Cretan Renaissance literature, the 17th-century *Erotokritos* by Vitsentzos Kornaros, consists of language and rhyme consistent with *mantinadhes*, and continues to inspire Crete's musicians today.

One of the oldest pieces of written music ever found is from 408 BC. The music was sung by a choir in performances of the ancient Greek tragedy *Orestes* by Euripides.

Another popular form of music is *rizitika* (patriotic songs), which are centuries-old songs from western Crete, especially the Lefka Ori (White Mountains) region. They are thought to have derived from the songs of the border guards of the Byzantine Empire, though their roots may be even older. Many of the *rizitika* deal with historical or heroic themes. One of the most popular is the song of Daskalogiannis, the Sfakiot hero who led the rebellion against the Turks in 1770; it has 1034 verses. The period of German occupation in WWII also produced a fertile crop of *rizitika*.

Prominent Musicians

Traditional folk music was shunned by the Greek bourgeoisie during the period after independence, when they looked to Europe – and classical music and opera – rather than their eastern or 'peasant' roots. However, a new wave of *entehni mousiki* (artistic music) that emerged in Athens in the 1960s drew on urban folk instruments such as the bouzouki and created popular hits from the works of Greek poets.

Acclaimed composer Yiannis Markopoulos (from Ierapetra) upped the ante by introducing rural folk music into the mainstream. He's best known internationally for his composition for the TV series *Who Pays the Ferryman?* Markopoulos was also responsible for bringing the icon of Cretan music, the late Nikos Xylouris, to the fore. The latter's career was tragically cut short in 1980 when he died of a brain tumour at the age of 43. With his superb voice and talent on the *lyra,* he remains the biggest-selling and most revered Cretan musician. During the junta years, Xylouris' music became a leading voice of the resistance. He came from a great musical family in Anogia, a village that has spawned many musicians and which has a good museum today.

Xylouris, Thanasis Skordalos and Kostas Mountakis are considered the great masters of Cretan music, and most current musicians follow one of their styles. The most prominent Cretan musician today is the legendary Psarantonis (Antonis Xylouris, brother of Nikos); he's known for his unique style of playing music and is instantly recognisable from his wild beard and mane of hair. Psarantonis still performs – everywhere from the smallest Cretan village to the clubs of Athens and the international festival circuit. In addition to the Xylouris family from Anogia, another famous musician from the village is Loudovikos Ton Anogion.

An intriguing figure of Crete's music scene is Ross Daly (of Irish descent), a master of the *lyra* and the creator of a high-calibre world-music workshop in Houdetsi.

Greeks have been playing music for thousands of years. In fact, archaeologists have found ancient Greek vases decorated with depictions of an instrument very much resembling the *lyra.*

THE ARTS MUSIC

CRETAN MUSIC TOP 10

The following provides an introduction to Cretan music past and present.

➡ **Tis Kritis Ta Politima (2009)** A good overall introduction to Cretan music.

➡ **Dimotiki Anthologia-Nikos Xylouris (1976)** This album shot Crete's legendary musical son, Nikos Xylouris, to stardom.

➡ **Ta Oraiotera Tragoudia Tou (1974)** Fine anthology paying tribute to postwar master, Kostas Mountakis, known as 'the teacher'.

➡ **Thanasis Skordalos (2006)** Part of *To Elliniko Tragoudi* series with the greats of Greek music; Skordalos is one of Crete's *lyra* legends.

➡ **Anastorimata (1982)** Landmark album heralding Psarantonis' unique musical style; also features *mantinadhes* by Vasilis Stavrakakis.

➡ **Beyond the Horizon (2002)** Ross Daly's album presents his orchestration of traditional Cretan music.

➡ **Embolo (2004)** Double-disc set featuring Yiannis and Giorgos Xylouris, two of the greats of Cretan music.

➡ **Xatheri (2003)** Stellar collaboration featuring Crete's top vocalist Vasilis Stavrakakis, Giorgos Xylouris on lute, Nikos Xylouris and others playing Cretan classics with a fresh sound.

➡ **Palaïna Seferia (1997)** Excellent self-titled first album of contemporary Cretan ensemble led by Zacharias Spyridakis, a student of *lyra* master Mountakis.

➡ **Haïnides (1991)** Self-titled first album of popular Cretan band.

The excellent sextet Haïnides is one of the more popular acts to emerge from Crete in recent years, playing their own brand of music and giving memorable live performances around Greece. Other leading figures include Mitsos and Vasilis Stavrakakis and contemporary musicians such as the band Palaïna, Nikos Zoidakis, Stelios Petrakis from Sitia, Papa Stefanis Nikas and Yiannis Haroulis. Other names to watch include Australian-born Sifis Tsourdalakis and Belgian-born Mihalis Tzouganakis.

Popular artists of Cretan origin playing mainstream Greek music include the talented Manos Pirovolakis with his rock-*lyra* sound. One of Greece's most famous international performers, Nana Mouskouri, was born in Hania, though her family moved to Athens when she was three years of age.

Dance

Dancing has been part of social life in Crete since the dawn of Hellenism. Some folk dances derive from the ritual dances performed in ancient Greek temples. Dancers are also depicted on ancient Greek vases and Homer lauded the ability of Cretan dancers.

Cretan dances are dynamic, fast and warlike, and many of them are danced by groups of men. Dances for women are traditionally related to wedding or courtship, and are more delicate and graceful. Like most Greek dances they are normally performed in a circle; in ancient times, dancers formed a circle to seal themselves off from evil influences. In times of occupation, dancing became an act of defiance and a way to keep fit under the noses of the enemy.

The most popular Cretan dances are the graceful and slow *syrtos* and the *pentozali*. The latter was originally danced by armed warriors and has a slow version and a faster one that builds into a frenzy, with the leader doing kicks, variations and fancy moves while the others follow with more mild steps. Another popular dance is the *sousta,* a bouncy courtship dance with small precise steps that is performed by couples. The *maleviziotiko* (also known as *kastrino* or *pidikto*) is a fast, triumphant dance.

Dancing well is a matter of great personal pride, and most dancers will take their turn at the front to demonstrate their prowess. Be aware that cutting in on somebody's dance is absolutely bad form, as families have usually paid for the dance (this is how Cretan musicians often make their living).

The best place to see Cretan dancing is at festivals, weddings and baptisms. Folkloric shows are also put on for tourists in many areas. Although these are more contrived, they can still be a decent show.

Fine Arts

The artistry of the Minoans ranks with the best in human history. During a brief artistic renaissance on the island that lasted from the 8th to 7th centuries BC, a group of sculptors called the Daedalids perfected a new technique of making sculptures in hammered bronze, working in a style that combined Eastern and Greek aesthetics. Their influence spread to mainland Greece. Cretan culture went into decline at the end of the 7th century BC, though there was a brief revival under the Romans, a period notable for richly decorated mosaic floors and marble sculptures. Then came the paintings and frescoes that culminated in the renowned Cretan School of painting.

Byzantine Art

Greek painting came into its own during the Byzantine period, which lasted roughly from the 4th century BC until the fall of Constantinople in 1453. Much Byzantine art was destroyed in popular rebellions during the 13th and 14th centuries. In the 11th century, émigrés from Constantinople

---

Top Films Shot in Crete

Zorba the Greek (1964)

Two Faces of January (2014)

The Inbetweeners Movie (2011)

He Who Must Die (1956)

El Greco (2007)

The *syrtaki* dance, immortalised by Anthony Quinn in the final scene of *Zorba the Greek,* was in fact a dance he improvised, as he had injured his leg the day before the shoot and could not perform the steps and leaps originally planned. The scripted energetic dance became a slow shuffle that he falsely claimed was traditional.

EL GRECO THE CRETAN

One of the geniuses of the Renaissance, El Greco ('The Greek' in Spanish), was a Cretan named Dominikos Theotokopoulos. He was born in the Cretan capital of Candia (present-day Iraklio) in 1541, during a time of great artistic activity, following the arrival of painters fleeing Ottoman-held Constantinople. These painters had a formative influence upon the young El Greco, giving him grounding in the traditions of late-Byzantine fresco painting.

El Greco went to Venice in his early twenties, joining the studio of Titian, but he came into his own as a painter after he moved to Spain in 1577, where his highly emotional style struck a chord with the Spanish. He lived in Toledo until his death in 1614. Many of his famous works, such as *The Burial of Count Orgaz* (1586), are in Toledo but his paintings are in museums around the world. *View of Mt Sinai and the Monastery of St Catherine* (1570), painted in Venice, hangs in Iraklio's Historical Museum of Crete (p149), next to the tiny *Baptism of Christ*. You can see *Concert of Angels* (1608) at the National Gallery in Athens.

A marble bust of the painter stands in Iraklio's Plateia El Greco, and there are streets, tavernas and hotels named after him throughout the island. A small museum dedicated to El Greco has been established in the village of Fodele, in a house he allegedly spent time in as a child. The 2007 biopic *El Greco* was partly shot in Iraklio.

THE ARTS FINE ARTS

brought portable icons to Crete, but the only surviving example from this period is the icon of the Virgin at Mesopantitissa, now in Venice.

From the 13th to the early 16th centuries, churches around Crete were decorated with frescoes on a dark-blue background, with a bust of Christ in the dome, the four Gospel writers in the corners, and the Virgin and Child in the apse. They also feature scenes from the life of Christ and figures of saints. Many fine frescoes can still be seen today, albeit moodily faded. The great icon painter of the 14th century was Ioannis Pagomenos, who worked in western Crete. Examples of his frescoes can be found in the churches of Agios Nikolaos in Maza, where he's also buried, and in Agios Georgios in Sfakia.

The Cretan School

With the fall of Constantinople in 1453, Crete became the centre of Greek art as many Byzantine artists fled to the island. At the same time, the Italian Renaissance was in full bloom and many Cretan artists studied in Italy. The result was the 'Cretan School' of icon painting that combined technical brilliance and dramatic richness. Artists drew inspiration from both Western and Byzantine styles. In Iraklio alone there were more than 200 painters working from the mid-16th to mid-17th centuries.

The most famous and internationally successful of these artists was El Greco, who was heavily influenced by the great Iraklio-born Michael Damaskinos (1530–91). Damaskinos' long sojourn in Venice introduced him to new techniques of rendering perspective. The centrepieces of the collection of the Museum of Christian Art in Iraklio are six Damaskinos icons. The third star in the trio of Cretan top artists is Theophanes Strelitza (aka Theophanes the Cretan), who was a prominent mural painter of the day, though all of his frescoes are in mainland Greece.

Contemporary Arts

The fine arts have a relatively low profile in Crete today. Though contemporary artists and artisans work and exhibit on the island, many live and work in Athens and abroad. Rethymno's Museum of Contemporary Art is one of the island's leading galleries for local artists, as are municipal art galleries around Crete. Private galleries and art boutiques can be found in Hania and Iraklio.

The first complete English prose translation of Crete's 10,000-line epic *Erotokritos* by Vitsentzos Kornaros was published by Byzantina Australiensia in 2004, with a scholarly introduction and notes.

Famous Novels Set in Crete

Zorba the Greek, *Nikos Kazantzakis (1946)*

Dark Labyrinth, *Lawrence Durrell (1958)*

The Colossus of Maroussi, *Henry Miller (1941)*

The Island, *Victoria Hislop (2005)*

NIKOS KAZANTZAKIS

Crete's most famous contemporary writer is Nikos Kazantzakis. Born in 1883 in Iraklio, the then Turkish-dominated capital, Kazantzakis spent his early childhood in the ferment of revolution and change. In 1897 the revolution against Turkish rule forced him to leave Crete for studies in Naxos, Athens and later Paris. It wasn't until he was 31 that he turned his hand to writing, by translating philosophical books into Greek. He travelled throughout Europe, thus laying the groundwork for travelogues in his later literary career.

Kazantzakis was a complex writer and his early work was heavily influenced by philosophical and spiritual thought, including the philosophies of Nietzsche. His relationship with religion was equally complex – his official stance was that of a nonbeliever, yet he studied and wrote about religion and religious figures.

Kazantzakis' self-professed greatest work is *The Odyssey: A Modern Sequel* (1938), an opus of 33,333 iambic verses, and a modern-day epic loosely based on the trials and travels of ancient hero Odysseus (Ulysses). It was only much later in his career, though, when Kazantzakis turned to novel writing, that his star shone brightest. Works such as *Christ Recrucified* (1948), *Kapetan Mihalis* (1950; now known as *Freedom and Death*) and *The Life and Adventures of Alexis Zorbas* (1946; later renamed *Zorba the Greek*) made him internationally known. Zorba gave rise to the image of the ultimate, free-spirited Greek male, immortalised by Anthony Quinn in the 1964 movie.

Kazantzakis died of leukemia in Germany on 26 October 1957, while travelling. Despite resistance from the Orthodox Church, he was given a religious funeral and buried in the Martinengo Bastion of Iraklio. There is a museum honouring him in Myrtia (p166).

Literature
Literary Lions

Greece's best-known and most widely read author since Homer is Nikos Kazantzakis (1883–1957), born in Crete amid the last spasms of the island's struggle for independence from the Turks. His novels, all of which have been translated into English, are full of drama and larger-than-life characters such as the magnificent title character in *Zorba the Greek* (1946) and the tortured Captain Michalis in *Freedom and Death* (1950), two of his finest works. Along with Zorba, *The Last Temptation* (1953) was also made into a film. *Zorba the Greek* takes place in Crete and provides a fascinating glimpse into the harsher side of Cretan culture. Kazantzakis had a chequered, and at times troubled, literary career, clashing frequently with the Orthodox Church for his professed atheism.

Kazantzakis may be Crete's most famous writer, but it was Odysseus Elytis (1911–96) who won the Nobel Prize in Literature in 1979. One of his main works is *Axion Esti – It is Worthy* (1959), a complicated poem that deals with existentialist questions and the identity of the main character's country and people. It was set to music by Mikis Theodorakis and to this day is one of the best-known poems and songs in Greece.

A noted contemporary of Elytis was Rethymno-born Pandelis Prevelakis (1909–86). He was primarily known as a poet, but also wrote plays and novels. His best-known work is *The Tale of a Town*, a nostalgic look at his home town in the early 20th century.

Nikos Kazantzakis modelled his Zorba character on a real person, Yorgos Zorbas, a workman from Macedonia, whom he first met in 1915. Kazantzakis hired him two years later to help him set up a lignite mine in the Peloponnese, to help meet the demand for coal during WWI.

Contemporary Writers

Contemporary Cretan writers include Rhea Galanaki (b 1947), whose prize-winning *The Life of Ismail Ferik Pasha* (1989) has been translated into six languages; it's a story about the clash of Christianity and Ottoman Islam in Crete. Ioanna Karystiani (b 1952), who wrote the screenplay for *Brides* (2004), received the Greek National Award for Literature for her novel *Mikra Anglia* (*Little England,* published in English as *The Jasmine Isle,* 2006), also made into a film, which describes the lives of a sailor's family on the island of Andros. Other Cretan writers include Minas Dimakis, Manolis Pratikakis, Yiorgis Manoussakis and Victoria Theodorou.

Nature & Wildlife

Crete is an island of geographical contrasts to say the least; you can swim in Vaï's palm-fringed bay and ski in the Lefka Ori (White Mountains) all in the same day. As you pass through its myriad caves, gorges, plateaux, and up and down its stickleback mountains and vast coastline, it feels like many countries rolled into one. It's no surprise, then, that Crete has a dizzying biodiversity of flora and fauna, from monk seals to golden eagles.

Animals

While Crete is known for its large population of sheep and goats, the island is also home to some endemic fauna, including hares, rabbits and weasels and its own subspecies of badger. You are unlikely to catch sight of the big-eared Cretan spiny mouse, but you never know. The island also has a large population of bats, insects, snails and invertebrates. Other local species include the tiny Cretan tree frog and the Cretan marsh frog.

The southern coastline, with its steep underwater cliffs, is home to the Mediterranean Sea's most significant population of sperm whales, who gather, feed and possibly mate in the area year-round. It's also abundant with squid, on which the whales feed. Keep your eyes open while on boat trips. Groups of striped dolphins, Risso's dolphins and Cuvier's beaked whales frequent waters off the southern coast. Bottlenose dolphins are often spotted in the shallow waters off Paleohora between Gavdos Island and its tiny neighbouring islet of Gavdopoula.

The Cretan Sperm Whale Project, run by the Pelagos Cetacean Research Institute (www.pelagosinstitute.gr), monitors the whale population.

With an area of 8335 sq km, Crete is the largest island in the Greek archipelago. It's 250km long, about 60km at its widest point and 12km at its narrowest.

Bird Life

Crete flies high in the bird world. It lies on the main Africa–Europe migratory routes and well over 400 species have been recorded on the island, including both resident and migratory species. Along the coast you'll find birds of passage such as egrets and herons during spring and autumn migrations.

The mountains host a wealth of interesting birds. Look for blue rock thrushes, buzzards and the huge griffon vulture. Other birds in the mountains include alpine swifts, stonechats, blackbirds and Sardinian warblers. The fields around Malia host tawny and red-throated pipits, stone-curlews, fan-tailed warblers and short-toed larks. On the hillsides below Moni Preveli you may find subalpine and Ruppell's warblers. The

Samaria Gorge is the only national park in Crete and is soon to be a Unesco protected biosphere reserve.

EXOTIC ANIMALS OF CRETE

Although you might not spot them, Crete is home to a variety of exotic animals, among them the European rattlesnake (non-venomous), dice snake, cat snake and whip snake. There are also three kinds of scorpion. Arachnophobics should stop reading now, for there are also black widow and araneus spiders in Crete, though instances of people being bitten are few. Finally, about 30 different types of shark are found in the Mediterranean, some of which are seen in waters around the island.

ENDANGERED SPECIES

Crete's most famous animal is the *agrimi* or *kri-kri,* a distinctive wild goat with large horns often depicted in Minoan art. Only a few survive in the wild, in and around Samaria Gorge and on the islands of Agioi Theodoroi off Hania and Dia off Iraklio.

You may spot a lammergeier (bearded vulture) – one of the rarest raptors in Europe, with a wingspan of nearly 3m – in Samaria Gorge or hovering above the Lasithi Plateau. A few golden eagles and Bonelli's eagles are also recorded in these areas and elsewhere, including the Kato Zakros area. Much good work has been carried out by various organisations in rehabilitating raptors such as bearded vultures and eagles and releasing them into the more remote areas of the Lefka Ori (White Mountains) and other ranges.

Crete is battling to protect its population of loggerhead turtles, which have been nesting on island shores since the days of the dinosaurs. The island also has a small population of the rare and endangered Mediterranean monk seal, breeding in caves on the south coast.

Hard-core bird-watchers should come equipped with *A Birdwatching Guide to Crete* by Stephanie Coghlan, or for a comprehensive reference on Greece's bird life, try *The Birds of Greece* by Christopher Helm.

Akrotiri Peninsula is good for birdwatching – around the monasteries of Agias Triadas and Gouvernetou you'll find collared and pied flycatchers, wrynecks, tawny pipits, black-eared wheatears, blue rock thrushes, stonechats, chukars and northern wheatears. Migrating species, including avocets and marsh sandpipers, can be spotted in wetland areas such as Elafonisi.

Plants

Crete blooms in every sense of the word. An estimated total of about 1750 plant species, of which around 170 are endemic, are said to make Crete their home. Crete's gorges are mini-botanical gardens and their isolation has helped preserve many species.

Along the coast, sea daffodils flower in August and September. In April and May knapweeds are in flower on the western coast and the purple or violet petals of stocks provide pretty splashes of colour on sandy beaches. At the same time of year in eastern Crete, especially around Sitia, watch for crimson poppies on the borders of the beach. At the edge of sandy beaches not yet lined with a strip of hotels you'll find delicate pink bindweeds and jujube trees that flower from May to June and bear fruit in September and October. In the same habitat is the tamarisk tree, which flowers in spring.

The Flowers of Greece and the Aegean by William Taylor and Anthony Huxley is the most comprehensive field guide to flowers in Greece and Crete.

If you come in summer, you won't be deprived of colour, since milky white and magenta oleanders bloom from June through to August.

On the hillsides look for cistus and brooms in early summer, and yellow chrysanthemums in the fields from March to May. The rare endemic blue flowers of *Anchusa caespitosa,* a type of Bugloss, are only found in the high peaks of the Lefka Ori (White Mountains).

Survival Guide

Directory A–Z

Accommodation

There is a full range of accommodation available in Crete, suiting every taste and budget. By law, a notice must be displayed in every room, stating the category of the room and the price charged in each season. It's difficult to generalise accommodation prices, as rates depend entirely on season and location.

Outside the cities – and especially along the coasts – most properties close down from November to March or April. Booking ahead is usually necessary only for summer months.

➡ Prices include community tax and VAT (value added tax).

➡ A 10% surcharge may be added for stays of fewer than three nights, but this is not mandatory.

➡ Mandatory charge of 20% is levied for an additional bed (often waived if for a child).

➡ July and August accommodation owners charge maximum price.

➡ Spring (April to June) and autumn (September and October) prices can drop by 20%.

➡ Prices drop even further in winter (November to March).

Location

The location of your stay is one of the most vital decisions when planning a holiday to Crete. The island has unique regions and many resort towns, each with its own character, and driving times between places can sometimes be long.

Broadly speaking, if you're after sandy beaches and crowded resorts, look on the northern coast. For a quiet rural retreat, head for the hills or the remote villages and beaches along the southern shoreline. The Iraklio region is home to the island's most developed resorts – Malia and Hersonisos – with a 24-hour party culture. Rethymno has some quieter getaways, plus Crete's longest sandy beach; it's a good base if you want to immerse yourself in the island's culture. Hania, in the west, is a ravishing town and has beach resorts to the west; it is ideal if you're looking for a wide range of outdoor pursuits, from diving to mountain climbing. Lasithi in the east is the island's quietest area and the exclusive resorts of Elounda and Agios Nikolaos are the strongholds of Crete's high-end tourism.

Hotels

Crete has some of the best resort hotels in Greece, including elite spa-hotels, but standards vary dramatically. Some midrange hotels are little better than domatia (rooms, usually in a private home). There's a smattering of boutique-style hotels, especially in Hania and Rethymno, in superbly restored Venetian mansions or historic buildings.

Hotels in Greece are divided into six categories: deluxe, A, B, C, D and E. Hotels are categorised according to the size of the rooms, whether or not they have a bar, and the ratio of bathrooms to beds, rather than standards of cleanliness, comfort of beds and friendliness of staff – all elements that may be of greater relevance to guests. We, therefore, don't quote them in our reviews.

Pensions are a basic form of hotel, usually with fewer services, but sometimes more cosy.

All-Inclusive Resorts

Almost 80% of visitors to Crete arrive on the island on a package holiday, often only available through tour operators. All-inclusive resorts are especially prevalent along the northern coast, east of Iraklio and west of Hania.

Studios & Apartments

To slow down and get to know Crete better, renting a studio or apartment for a week or more can be ideal, especially for budget-minded travellers, self-caterers, families and small groups. Facilities include a kitchenette or full kitchen, cable or satellite TV, air-conditioning and heating units and, occasionally, washing machine. High-season rates typically range from €35 to €60 for a studio and €50 to €90 for an apartment for four people.

Domatia

Domatia (literally 'rooms') are the Greek equivalent of the British B&B, minus the breakfast. Most are only open April to October.

In former times, domatia comprised little more than spare rooms in the family home. Nowadays most are purpose-built appendages to the family home, and may be studios or small apartments. Domatia remain a popular option for budget travellers and are often more appealing (and sometimes better equipped) than generic midrange hotels. Expect to pay from €20 to €60 for a double, depending on whether bathrooms are shared or private, the season and the length of your stay.

Agrotourism

Agrotourism is booming in Crete. Traditional guesthouses, villas and apartments in tranquil villages away from the coastal hubbub are sometimes attached to organic farms, allowing you to participate in seasonal activities, such as sheep shearing, *raki* distilling, olive harvesting, grape crushing or cheesemaking. Some owners also give cooking courses. Budget between €70 and €100 for a traditional cottage.

Camping

Crete's dozen or so campgrounds are privately run and range from sun-baked dirt patches to tree-shaded, resort-style grounds with pools, shops, tavernas and wi-fi. Some also rent caravans, tents and bungalows. The core season runs from May to October, although a few remain open year-round. The **Panhellenic Camping Association** (www.panhellenic-camping-union.gr) publishes information about its member sites, their facilities and opening months on its website.

If you're camping in the height of summer, bring a silver fly sheet to reflect the heat off your tent (the dark tents that are all the rage in colder countries become sweat lodges). Between May and mid-September the weather is warm enough to sleep out under the stars with a light cover. It's a good idea to have a foam pad to lie on and a waterproof cover for your sleeping bag.

➡ Camping fees are highest from mid-June through to the end of August.

➡ Campgrounds charge €5 to €7 per adult and €3 to €4 for children aged four to 12. There's no charge for children under four.

➡ Tent sites cost from €4 per night for small tents, and from €5 per night for large tents.

➡ You can often rent tents for around €5 to €10.

➡ Caravan sites start at around €6; car costs are typically €4 to €5.

➡ Free (wild) camping is illegal and the police are increasingly cracking down on scofflaws.

Hostels

Crete does not have any Hostelling International–affiliated hostels, but there are independent contenders in Rethymno and Plakias, which are well-run and sociable places, with dorm beds, basic facilities and inexpensive food. Dorm beds cost around €10; discounts are usually available for longer stays.

Mountain Refuges

Crete has seven mountain shelters run by the regional **mountaineering clubs** (p36): four in the Lefka Ori (White Mountains), two around Mt Psiloritis and one on Mt Dikti. Nonmembers pay around €15 per bunk bed. Facilities vary and may include basic cooking facilities, wood-burning stoves and water from a spring or a rainwater tank. Get in touch with the regional club before hitting the trail. For an overview of shelters, check www.crete.tournet.gr/en/crete-activities/936-mountain-shelters.

Customs Regulations

There are no longer duty restrictions within the EU. Upon entering the country from outside the EU, customs inspection is usually cursory for foreign tourists and a verbal declaration is generally all that is required. Random searches are still occasionally made for drugs.

Climate

Crete (Iraklio)

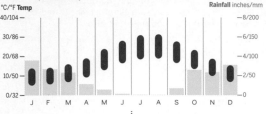

Import regulations for medicines are strict; if you are taking medication, make sure you get a statement from your doctor before you leave home. It is illegal, for instance, to take codeine into Greece without an accompanying doctor's certificate.

It's strictly forbidden to export antiquities (anything more than 100 years old) without an export permit. This crime is second only to drug smuggling in the penalties imposed. It is an offence to remove even the smallest article from an archaeological site. The place to apply for an export permit is the Antique Dealers and Private Collections section of the **Athens Archaeological Service** (http://nam.culture.gr; Polygnotou 13, Plaka, Athens) website.

If you happen to be carrying more than €10,000 in cash, you must declare it.

Duty-free allowances (for adults) are:

➜ 200 cigarettes or 50 cigars or 250g of tobacco

➜ 1L spirits

➜ 2L wine

➜ other goods up to the value of €430 (€150 for under 15 years)

Discount Cards

Discounts and free admission are widely available for seniors, children and students, often without using a discount card, just your ID.

Camping Card International (www.campingcardinternational.com) Up to 25% savings on camping fees and third-party liability insurance while in the campground.

European Youth Card (www.europeanyouthcard.org) Available for anyone up to the age of 30 (you don't have to be a resident of Europe); provides discounts of up to 20% at sights, shops and for some transport.

International Student Identity Card (www.isic.org) Entitles the holder to half-price admission to museums and ancient sites, and discounts at some budget hotels and hostels. Available online or from travel agencies in Athens (none in Crete) or in your home country. Applicants require documents proving their student status, a passport photo and the fee.

Electricity

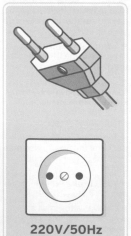

220V/50Hz

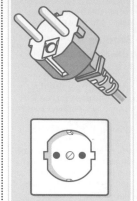

220V/50Hz

Food

The following price ranges refer to the average cost of a main course and are inclusive of tax and service charges.

€ less than €10

€€ €10–20

€€€ more than €20

Gay & Lesbian Travellers

The church still plays a prominent role in shaping Cretans' views, so homosexuality is generally frowned upon by many locals – especially outside major cities. It pays to be discreet.

➜ Although homosexuality is legal over the age of 17, Crete does not really have much of a gay, let alone lesbian, scene. There is no overtly gay nightlife and public displays of affection are frowned upon outside the cities.

➜ Hersonisos has the gay-owned and -oriented guesthouse **Villa Ralfa** (www.villaralfa.com). Many venues in Iraklio are quietly gay-friendly, as are relaxed

EMBASSIES & CONSULATES

The UK is the only country with a consulate in Crete (in Iraklio). Other countries are represented by their embassies in Athens.

COUNTRY	TELEPHONE	WEBSITE
Australia	☑ 210 870 4000	www.greece.embassy.gov.au
Canada	☑ 210 727 3400	www.greece.gc.ca
France	☑ 210 339 1000	www.ambafrance-gr.org
Germany	☑ 210 728 5111	www.athen.diplo.de
Ireland	☑ 210 723 2771	www.embassyofireland.gr
Netherlands	☑ 210 725 4900	www.dutchembassy.gr
Turkey	☑ 210 726 3000	embassy.athens@mfa.gov.tr
UK	☑ 28102 24012 (Iraklio)	www.ukingreece.fco.gov.uk/en
USA	☑ 210 721 2951	http://athens.usembassy.gov

resorts such as Paleohora and most nude beaches.

➡ *The Spartacus International Gay Guide* (www.spartacusworld.com/en), published by Bruno Gmünder (Berlin), is widely regarded as the leading authority on gay travel.

➡ The website www.gaygreece.gr has some information on cruising areas as well as gay-friendly bars and clubs.

➡ Popular international smartphone apps are also in use.

Health

Crete is a generally healthy place – the main risks are likely to be sunburn, foot blisters, insect bites, minor stomach problems and hangovers.

Before You Go

➡ Bring your medications in original, clearly labelled containers.

➡ Get a signed and dated letter from your doctor describing your medical conditions and medications, including generic names. In Greece it is illegal to import codeine-based medication without a doctor's certificate.

➡ No vaccinations are required for travel to Crete but the World Health Organization (WHO) recommends that all travellers be covered for diphtheria, tetanus, measles, mumps, rubella and polio.

Availability & Cost of Health Care

➡ If you need an ambulance call ☑ 166.

➡ For minor illnesses, pharmacies provide valuable advice, sell medication (often available only on prescription in the US and other European countries) and advise on whether to see a doctor.

➡ Medical training is of a high standard in Greece, but the health service is chronically underfunded. Public hospitals are often overcrowded, hygiene can be a problem and relatives are expected to provide food for the patient. That said, Iraklio, Hania and Rethymno have modern hospitals.

➡ Condoms are widely available (in kiosks, supermarkets and pharmacies) but emergency contraception may not be.

Environmental Hazards

➡ Dangerous snakes include the adder and the less common viper and coral snakes. To minimise the possibilities of being bitten, always wear boots, socks and long trousers when walking through undergrowth where snakes may be present.

➡ Mosquitoes can be an annoying problem, though there is no danger of contracting malaria. The electric mosquito-repellent devices are usually sufficient to keep the insects at bay at night. Choose accommodation that has fly screen on the windows wherever possible.

➡ The Asian tiger mosquito (*Aedes albopictus*) may be encountered in mountainous areas, can be a voracious daytime biter, and is known to carry several viruses, including Eastern equine encephalitis, which can affect the central nervous system and cause severe complications and death. Use protective sprays or lotion if you suspect you are being bitten during the day.

Insurance

If you're an EU citizen, a European Health Insurance Card (EHIC; formerly the E111) covers you for most medical care but not emergency repatriation home or non-emergencies. It is available from health centres, and post offices in the UK.

Citizens from other countries should find out if there is a reciprocal arrangement for free medical care between their country and Greece. If you do need health insurance, make sure you get a policy that covers you for the worst possible scenario, such as an accident requiring an emergency flight home. Find out in advance if your insurance plan will make payments directly to providers or reimburse you later for overseas health expenditures.

Water

➡ Tap water is chlorinated and safe to drink in most of Crete.

➡ Bottled water is widely available.

Insurance

➡ Comprehensive travel insurance to cover theft, loss and medical problems is highly recommended.

➡ Some policies specifically exclude dangerous activities such as diving, motorcycling and even trekking; read the fine print.

➡ Check that the policy covers ambulances or an emergency flight home.

➡ Find out if your insurance plan makes payments directly to providers or reimburses you later.

➡ Paying for airline tickets or car hire with a credit card sometimes provides limited travel insurance – ask your credit-card company what it covers.

➡ Worldwide travel insurance is available at www.lonelyplanet.com/travel-insurance. You can buy, extend and claim online anytime – even if you're already on the road.

Internet Access

➡ Most cafes and bars in towns and cities have free wi-fi. Many hotels also offer wi-fi access, though hot spots are often in the lobby rather than in your room.

➡ Many hotels have an internet corner for guests, often at no charge. These are identified in reviews with the internet icon @.

➡ There's free municipal wi-fi in parts of Hania, Paleohora, Rethymno, Iraklio and Agios Nikolaos.

Legal Matters

➡ Carry your passport with you at all times in case you're stopped by the police and questioned. Greek citizens are presumed to have identification on them at all times and the police expect much the same from foreign visitors.

➡ Greek drug laws are the strictest in Europe. Greek courts make no distinction between possession and pushing. Possession of even a small amount of marijuana is likely to land you in jail.

➡ If you're arrested insist on an interpreter (διερμηνέας; *the*-lo dhi-ermi-*nea*) and/or a lawyer (δικηγόρος; *the*-lo dhi-ki-*go*-ro).

Maps

If you're planning on doing extensive driving or hiking around Crete, a good map is essential. They are widely available in bookshops and tourist shops and cost around €8. Car-hire agencies and hotels often distribute free maps but these are not always accurate.

Anavasi (www.anavasi.gr) Publishes excellent road and hiking maps, including three separate road maps covering Hania, Rethymno and Iraklio, and Lasithi at a scale of 1:100,000 and the comprehensive *Crete Atlas* at a scale of 1:50,000. Walking maps cover the Lefka Ori (Sfakia and Pahnes), Samaria/Sougia, Mt Psiloritis and Zakros-Vaï at a scale of 1:25,000.

Terrain (www.terrainmaps.gr) Tops for hiking maps, with good labelled distances. Offers western Crete, central Crete and eastern Crete maps at 1:100,000. Some maps are available as a smartphone app.

Harms (www.harms-ic-verlag.de) German publisher has 1:100,000 *Kreta Touristikkarte* maps covering the east (*Der Osten*) and west (*Der Westen*) of Crete.

Michelin (www.michelin.com) Single-sheet map of the entire island at 1:140,000.

Petrakis Editions (☑2810 282630) Iraklio-based trekker Giorgos Petrakis produces trekking and road maps for each of the four prefectures at a scale of 1:100,000.

Money

Currency in Crete is the euro (€), with seven notes (five, 10, 20, 50, 100, 200 and 500) and eight coins (one- and two- euro coins and one-, two-, five-, 10-, 20- and 50-cent coins).

PRACTICALITIES

➡ **Weights & measures** Greece uses the metric system for weights and measures.

➡ **Newspapers** Greek current affairs available in the daily English-language edition of *Kathimerini* (www.ekathimerini.com), published as part of the *International New York Times*.

➡ **DVDs** Be aware that Greece is region code 2 when you buy DVDs to watch back home.

ATMs

➡ The easiest, quickest and usually cheapest way to obtain cash is by using your debit (bank) card at an ATM linked to international networks such as Cirrus, Plus, Star and Maestro.

➡ There are ATMs in almost every town large enough to support a bank, and in tourist areas. In rural areas, only larger towns have ATMs, so plan ahead, especially in the southwest. It pays to have a back-up.

Cash

➡ Cash is king in Crete, so always carry some with you and plan to pay cash almost everywhere. It's also a good idea to set aside a small amount of euros as an emergency stash.

➡ Shopkeepers and small-business owners have a perennial problem with having any small change. If buying small items it is easier to tender coins or small-denomination notes.

Credit Cards

➡ Big resorts and hotels accept credit cards, but family-owned properties rarely do. Ask. Likewise, upmarket shops and restaurants accept plastic but village tavernas and small shops almost never do.

➡ The main credit cards – MasterCard and Visa – are widely accepted. American Express and Diners Club are common in tourist areas only.

Moneychangers

➡ Banks will exchange major currencies in cash or travellers cheques. Your passport is required to change travellers cheques, not always for cash.

➡ Post offices can exchange banknotes – not travellers cheques – and charge less commission than banks.

STANDARD OPENING HOURS

BUSINESS	OPENING HOURS
Banks	8am-2.30pm Mon-Thu, to 2pm Fri
Bars	8pm-late
Cafes	9am-midnight
Post offices	7.30am-2pm Mon-Fri (rural); 7.30am-8pm Mon-Fri, 7.30am-2pm Sat (urban)
Restaurants	11am-3pm & 7pm-1am
Shops	9am-2pm Mon-Sat, 5.30-8.30pm or 9pm Tue, Thu & Fri, all day in summer in resort areas
Supermarkets	8am-9pm Mon-Fri, to 6pm Sat

➡ Travel agencies and hotels often change money and travellers cheques at bank rates, but commission charges are higher.

➡ Automated foreign-exchange machines are sometimes available in major tourist areas. They take all the major European currencies, Australian and US dollars and Japanese yen, and are useful in an emergency, although they charge a hefty commission.

Travellers Cheques

The main reason to carry travellers cheques rather than cash is the protection they offer against theft. They are, however, becoming obsolete as more and more travellers opt to withdraw cash at ATMs as they go.

American Express, Visa and Thomas Cook cheques are available in euros and are all widely accepted and have efficient replacement policies.

Opening Hours

➡ Museum and archaeological site opening hours depend on budgeting, ie if there's enough cash to hire afternoon staff. It's always good to check ahead, especially for afternoon visits. Most sites are closed on Monday.

➡ *Periptera* (kiosks) open from early morning until late at night and sell everything from bus tickets and cigarettes to condoms.

➡ We give high-season hours for sights and attractions; hours are generally reduced in winter.

Photography

➡ Crete is a photographer's dream. A good general resource is Lonely Planet's *Guide to Travel Photography*.

➡ Never photograph a military installation or anything else signed as forbidding photography.

➡ Flash photography is never allowed inside churches, and it's taboo to photograph the main altar, icons, or during services.

➡ People generally don't seem to mind being photographed in the context of an overall scene, but if you want a close-up shot, ask first. Same goes for video.

Postal Services

Tahydromia (post offices) are easily identifiable by the yellow signs outside. Normal postboxes are also yellow, with red boxes for express mail.

➡ To mail abroad, use yellow post boxes labelled *exoteriko*.

➡ Some tourist shops sell stamps, but with a 10% markup.

➡ Don't wrap a parcel before sending it: post office staff may wish to inspect it.

Public Holidays

Most banks, shops, post offices, public services, most museums and ancient sites close on public holidays. Greek national public holidays observed in Crete:

New Year's Day 1 January

Epiphany 6 January

First Sunday in Lent February

Greek Independence Day 25 March

Good Friday March/April

(Orthodox) Easter Sunday 1 May 2016, 16 April 2017, 8 April 2018, 28 April 2019

May Day (Protomagia) 1 May

Whit Monday (Agiou Pnevmatos) 50 days after Easter Sunday

Feast of the Assumption 15 August

Ohi Day 28 October

Christmas Day 25 December

St Stephen's Day 26 December

Safe Travel

Crete is generally a safe, friendly and hospitable place and crime rates are much lower here than in other parts of southern Europe. Thefts, especially, are more likely to be committed by other tourists than locals. Still, as with anywhere, it pays to follow a few simple precautions to lower your risk of getting ripped off.

➡ Keep track of your possessions on public transport, in markets and other crowded areas. Do not leave luggage unattended in cars.

➡ Lock your rental car and hotel rooms. If the latter doesn't lock properly,

including windows, ask for your valuables to be locked in the hotel safe.

➡ Avoid dark streets and parks at night, particularly in the major cities.

Tourist Police

If you need to report a theft or loss of passport, try to go to the tourist police in your area first, and then they will act as interpreters between you and the regular police.

Smoking

Several smoking bans have been instituted – and flaunted – over the years, but in September 2010 the government's latest attempt went into effect. It's the toughest yet, prohibiting tobacco advertising as well as smoking in all enclosed public spaces, including cafes, restaurants, nightclubs, offices, businesses and transport stations. At the time of writing, this law was again widely ignored, both by smokers and local police.

Telephone Services

The Greek telephone service is maintained by the public corporation OTE (pronounced o-teh; Organismos Tilepikoinonion Ellados). Public telephones are ubiquitous but sometimes out of order, a result of the decline in demand with the proliferation of mobile phones. The phones are easy to operate, take phonecards, not coins, and can be used for local, long-distance and international calls. The 'i' at the top left of the push-button dialing panel brings up the operating instructions in English.

All phone numbers have 10 digits. Landline numbers start with '2', mobile numbers start with '6'.

Mobile Phones

➡ Mobile (cell) phones operate on GSM900/1800.

➡ Check with your service provider about roaming charges – charges for calls to a mobile phone from a landline or another mobile can be exorbitant.

➡ If you have an unlocked multiband phone, getting a prepaid SIM card with a local number might work out cheaper than using your own network. Cards are available from Greece's three mobile phone service providers – Vodafone, Cosmote and Wind. These automatically revert to global roaming when you leave Greece. Top up cards are sold at supermarkets, kiosks and newsagents. All offer 3G connectivity.

➡ Cosmote tends to have the best coverage in remote areas.

➡ Use of a mobile phone while driving is prohibited, unless using a headset.

Phone Codes

Calling Crete from abroad Dial your country's international access code, then ☑30 (Greece's country code) followed by the 10-digit local number.

Calling internationally from Crete Dial ☑00 (the international access code), the country code, and the local number.

Reverse-charge (collect) calls Dial the operator (domestic ☑129; international ☑139) to get the number in the country you wish to call.

Phonecards

➡ Public phones take OTE phonecards (*telekarta*), not coins. These cards are sold at kiosks, corner shops and tourist shops. A local call costs around €0.30 for three minutes.

➡ Don't remove your card before you are told to do so or you could wipe out the remaining credit.

➡ You can also buy a range of prepaid international

calling cards (hronokarta) with good rates. This involves dialling an access code, then punching in your card number. Cards come with instructions in Greek and English.

Time

Clocks in Greece are set to Eastern Europe Time (GMT/UTC plus two hours). Daylight-saving time starts on the last Sunday in March and ends on the last Sunday in October.

Tipping

Restaurants Normally included in the bill and a tip is not expected, but it is customary to round up the bill or add about 10% if the service was good.

Bartenders Round to nearest euro.

Taxi drivers Round up the fare.

Hotel porters or stewards on ferries Small gratuity between €1 (per bag) and €3.

Toilets

➥ One peculiarity of the Greek plumbing system is that it can't handle toilet paper, as the pipes are too narrow and back up easily. Toilet paper, tampons etc should all be placed in the small bin provided.

➥ Very occasionally outside the big towns you might come across squat toilets in older houses, kafeneia (coffee houses) and public toilets.

➥ Public toilets are rare, except at airports and bus and train stations. Cafes are the best option, but you are expected to buy something for the privilege.

Tourist Information

Municipal tourist offices are a mixed bag. Some are helpful, while others are staffed by not very knowledgeable or enthusiastic folks. Expect limited opening hours outside high season and only a smattering of free maps and brochures. Travel agencies often fill the void.

Travellers with Disabilities

If mobility is a problem, visiting Crete will present serious challenges. Most hotels, ferries, museums and sites are not wheelchair accessible, and narrow streets, steep curbs and parked cars make getting around difficult. Newly built hotels are required to be more accessible to people with disabilities by having lifts and rooms with extra-wide doors and spacious bathrooms. People who have visual or hearing impairments are rarely catered to. Assume nothing.

Eria Resort (☑28210 62790; www.eria-resort.gr) in Maleme in western Crete is one of the few in Greece designed for travellers with disabilities. It caters for special needs and equipment and offers medical support and excursions and activities.

Find English-language tips on www.disabled.gr and www.greecetravel.com/handicapped.

Visas

Greece is a Schengen Agreement nation and governed by those rules.

➥ **EU & Schengen countries** No visa required.

➥ **Australia, Canada, Israel, Japan, New Zealand & USA** No visa required for tourist visits of up to 90 days. For longer stays, contact your nearest Greek embassy or consulate and begin your application well in advance. Applications for a Schengen Visa must be filed with the embassy or consulate of the country that is your primary destination.

➥ **Other countries** Check with a Greek embassy or consulate.

Volunteering

Crete for Life (www.creteforlife. com) Recuperative holiday camp for disadvantaged kids near Ierapetra.

Global Volunteers (www. globalvolunteers.org) Teach conversational English to children in Gazi, west of Iraklio.

Sea Turtle Protection Society of Greece (www.archelon.gr) Includes monitoring programs.

Women Travellers

➥ Crete is remarkably safe for women to explore, even for solo travellers. Going alone to cafes and restaurants is perfectly acceptable. This does not mean you should be lulled into complacency; bag-snatching and sexual harassment do occur.

➥ On beaches and in bars and nightclubs, solo women are likely to attract attention from men. Kamaki, the Greek word for men on the hunt for foreign women, translates as 'fishing trident'.

➥ If you don't want company, most men will respect a firm 'no, thank you'. If you feel threatened, protesting loudly will often make the offender slink away or spur others to come to your defence.

Transport

GETTING THERE & AWAY

Flights, tours and rail tickets can be booked online at www.lonelyplanet.com/bookings.

Entering the Country

Entering Crete is usually a very straightforward procedure. If arriving from any of the Schengen countries (ie EU member states plus Iceland, Norway and Switzerland), passports are rarely given more than a cursory glance, but customs and police may be interested in what you are carrying. EU citizens may also enter Greece on a national identity card. Visitors from outside the EU may require a visa (p261). This must be checked with consular authorities before you arrive.

Air

Most travellers arrive in Crete by air, usually with a change in Athens. Between May and October, charter and low-cost airlines like easyJet and Ryanair operate direct flights to Crete, mostly from UK, German and Scandinavian airports. Ryanair also offers cheap domestic flights between Crete and Athens.

Airports & Airlines

Hania Airport Ioannis Daskalogiannis (☑28210 83800; www.chaniaairport.com) Hania's airport is 14km east of town on the Akrotiri Peninsula, and is served year-round from Athens and seasonally from throughout Europe.

Nikos Kazantzakis International Airport (HER; ☑general 28103 97800, info 28103 97136; www.heraklion-airport.info) About 5km east of Iraklio (Crete). Has a bank, ATM, duty-free shop and cafe-bar.

Sitia Airport (☑28430 24666) Flights to Athens, Iraklio, Kassos, Karpathos and Rhodes. Summer flights to Amsterdam and Lyon.

DOMESTIC CARRIERS

The safety records of Aegean and Olympic airlines are exemplary.

Aegean Airlines (www.aegeanair.com) Services from Iraklio and Hania to Athens and Thessaloniki, Rhodes, with numerous onward connections throughout Europe as well as to Cairo, İstanbul, Tel Aviv, New York and Toronto. Direct flights from London-Heathrow, Milan, Paris, Marseille and Rome. Seasonal flights to Iraklio include Vienna, Prague, Moscow, Frankfurt, Amsterdam and Nantes. Partially merged with the other domestic carrier, Olympic Air.

Olympic Air (www.olympicair.com) Connects Iraklio and Hania with Athens, Sitia with Rhodes, and operates other domestic routes.

CLIMATE CHANGE & TRAVEL

Every form of transport that relies on carbon-based fuel generates CO_2, the main cause of human-induced climate change. Modern travel is dependent on aeroplanes, which might use less fuel per kilometre per person than most cars but travel much greater distances. The altitude at which aircraft emit gases (including CO_2) and particles also contributes to their climate change impact. Many websites offer 'carbon calculators' that allow people to estimate the carbon emissions generated by their journey and, for those who wish to do so, to offset the impact of the greenhouse gases emitted with contributions to portfolios of climate-friendly initiatives throughout the world. Lonely Planet offsets the carbon footprint of all staff and author travel.

SUSTAINABLE TRAVEL BY TRAIN

The trip from London to Iraklio by air generates 0.55 metric tons of emission. If you're driving, it's about the same or more, depending on your vehicle. However, travelling by train, you can cut that number down dramatically to just 0.05 metric tons.

Of course, travelling to Crete by train is not quick. Depending on where you start, budget two or three days. Coming from London would see you catching the Eurostar to Paris and then a train to Milan in Italy. From there, a coastal train takes you to Bari where there's an overnight boat to Patra on the Peloponnese. Or train from Paris to Venice, then boat to Patra. From Patra, a bus takes you to Athens' port at Piraeus where you catch the Crete-bound ferry. See www.raileurope.com for more routes and tickets.

It's also possible to travel by train all the way to Athens from London/Paris via Munich, Zagreb, Belgrade and Thessaloniki, or via Budapest, Sofia and Thessaloniki. The excellent website www.seat61.com has comprehensive details.

Sky Express (www.sky express.gr) Greek destinations from Iraklio include Athens, Mytilini (Lesvos), Rhodes, Kos, Samos, Chios, Karpathos and Volos. From Sitia flights serve Iraklio, Alexandroupolis and Preveza. Strict baggage allowances.

Astra Airlines (www.astra -airlines.gr) Airline connecting Iraklio, Hania and Sitia with Thessaloniki. Connects Sitia with Athens.

Tickets

EasyJet and Ryanair offer some of the cheapest tickets between Greece and the rest of Europe and cover a huge range of destinations. If you're coming from outside Europe, consider a cheap flight to a European hub and then an onward ticket with a budget airline. Some airlines also offer cheap deals to students. If you're planning to travel between June and September, it's wise to book ahead.

Land

Bus

KTEL (www.e-ktel.com) Offers buses (via ferries) from Hania to Thessaloniki, Ioannina and Patra.

Car & Motorcycle

When bringing your own vehicle to Greece, you need a valid driving licence, your car registration certificate and proof of insurance. Foreign cars must display a nationality sticker unless they have official Euro-plates. You should also carry a warning (hazard) triangle, fire extinguisher and first-aid kit.

From most European countries, travelling to Crete by car takes several days and thus only makes sense for longer stays. The fastest way is to hop on a ferry from Italy. There are overnight ferries to Patra at the northwestern tip of the Peloponnese from Ancona (21 hours), Bari (14½ hours), Brindisi (14½ hours) and Venice (31 hours). See www.greekferries.gr for schedules and prices. From here it's about a 200km drive south to Piraeus (near Athens), where you can catch another ferry to Iraklio, Sitia or Hania.

It is still possible to drive to Greece via Slovenia, Croatia, Bulgaria and the Former Yugoslav Republic of Macedonia, but the savings are not huge and are far outweighed by the distance involved and the necessity of crossing five borders.

Train

You can reach Athens from London/Paris on a fascinating rail route via Munich, Zagreb, Belgrade and Thessaloniki, or via Budapest, Sofia and Thessaloniki. Or train to the western coast of Italy (there are connections throughout most of Europe) to Bari, Brinidisi, Ancona or Venice, and then take a ferry to Patra in the Peloponnese, bus to Athens' port at Piraeus and ferry from there to Crete.

Eurail (www.eurail.com) Greece is part of the Eurail network. Eurail passes can only be bought by residents of non-European countries and are supposed to be purchased before arriving in Europe, but they can also be bought in Europe if your passport proves that you've been here for less than six months. The Attica Pass includes four domestic ferry trips in Greece and two international ferry trips between Greece and Italy. See the website for full details of passes and prices.

Inter-Rail Pass (www.interrail net.com) Greece is also part of the Inter-Rail Pass system, available to those who have resided in Europe for six months or more.

OSE (Organismos Sidirodromon Ellados; www.trainose.gr) The Greek railways organisation OSE has been seriously affected by the country's financial problems. The situation is variable, so check ahead.

Sea

Services are considerably curtailed from November to April.

➜ **Iraklio & Hania** Crete is well served by ferry, with at least one daily departure from the port at Piraeus (near Athens) to Iraklio and Hania year-round and three

Ferries to Crete

or four per day in summer. Faster catamarans connect Iraklio to Santorini, Mykonos and other Cycladic Islands. Ferries sail east from Iraklio to Rhodes via Agios Nikolaos, Sitia, Kasos, Karpathos and Halki.

➡ **Kissamos (Kastelli)** This small western port is connected with Kythira, Antikythira and Gythio (in the Peloponnese) and Piraeus (by a very slow route).

➡ **Sitia** Two slow ferries a week from Sitia in the east serve Iraklio, Milos, Piraeus, Santorini and Rhodes. Four ferries a week connect Sitia and Kasos and Karpathos.

Tickets

Timetables change from season to season, and ferries are subject to delays and cancellations at short notice due to bad weather, strikes or mechanical problems. Check www.openseas.gr for schedules.

➡ During high season, or if you're bringing a car, book

well in advance, especially for overnight and high-speed catamaran services.

➡ Tickets are best purchased online either from the ferry company directly or through a booking engine such as www.greekferries.gr and www.ferries.gr.

➡ If a service is cancelled, you can transfer your ticket to the next available service with that company.

➡ Prices are determined by the distance and the class, which ranges from deck class to double-berth outside cabins.

➡ Children, students and seniors usually qualify for discounts ranging from 10% to 50%. Children under the age of five often travel free.

Yacht

Although yachting is a popular way to explore the Greek islands, Crete is a long way from other islands and does not have a huge yachting industry. The sailing season

lasts from April until October; however, between July and September the *meltemi* winds can ground you regularly.

Tours

Another way to visit Greece by sea is to join one of the many cruises or package tours and holidays that come to Crete.

GETTING AROUND

Air

Sky Express (www.skyexpress. gr) Occasional flights between Sitia and Iraklio.

Bicycle

Cycling is becoming more common in Crete, but the often-hilly terrain means you need strong leg muscles and endurance. You can hire bikes in most tourist areas. Prices range from €10 to

HIGH-SEASON FERRY ROUTES TO/FROM CRETE

For current routes and timetables, consult the ferry company's website or go to www.gtp.gr, www.openseas.gr, www.ferries.gr and www.greekferries.gr. The latter two also have a ticket booking function.

ROUTE	COMPANY	FARE (€)	DURATION (HR)	FREQUENCY
Hania-Piraeus	Anek	42	8½	1 daily
Iraklio-Halki	Aegeon Pelagos (Anek)	21	11¾	1 weekly
Iraklio-Ios	Hellenic Seaways	66	4	1 daily
Iraklio-Ios	Sea Jets	62.70	3½	1 daily
Iraklio-Karpathos	Aegeon Pelagos (Anek)	18	7½	1 weekly
Iraklio-Kasos	Aegeon Pelagos (Anek)	19	5¾	1 weekly
Iraklio-Milos	Aegeon Pelagos (Anek)	22	7½	2 weekly
Iraklio-Mykonos	Hellenic Seaways	81	4¾	1 daily
Iraklio-Mykonos	Sea Jets	82.70	5½	1 daily
Iraklio-Naxos	Sea Jets	69.70	5	1 daily
Iraklio-Paros	Hellenic Seaways	71	4	1 daily
Iraklio-Piraeus	Minoan	43	6½-7½	1-2 daily
Iraklio-Piraeus	Anek-Superfast	36	6½-9½	1-2 daily
Iraklio-Rhodes	Aegeon Pelagos (Anek)	28	14	1 weekly
Iraklio-Santorini (Thira)	Anek	15	4¼	2 weekly
Iraklio-Santorini (Thira)	Sea Jets	59.70	2	1 daily
Iraklio-Santorini (Thira)	Hellenic Seaways	63	2	1 daily
Iraklio-Sitia	Aegeon Pelagos (Anek)	15	3	1 weekly
Kissamos-Antikythira	Lane	10	2	4 weekly
Kissamos-Gythio	Lane	25	5	4 weekly
Kissamos-Kythira	Lane	17	4	4 weekly
Kissamos-Piraeus	Lane	24	12	2 weekly
Sitia-Iraklio	Aegeon Pelagos (Anek)	11	3	2 weekly
Sitia-Karpathos	Aegeon Pelagos (Anek)	18	4¼	4 weekly
Sitia-Kassos	Aegeon Pelagos (Anek)	11	2½	4 weekly
Sitia-Milos	Aegeon Pelagos (Anek)	25	11½	2 weekly
Sitia-Piraeus	Aegeon Pelagos (Anek)	41	17	2 weekly
Sitia-Rhodes	Aegeon Pelagos (Anek)	27	9½	2 weekly
Sitia-Santorini (Thira)	Aegeon Pelagos (Anek)	26	7½	2 weekly

€20 per day. Bicycles are carried free on ferries.

For more details, as well as information on mountain-biking tours, see www.cycling.gr.

Boat

Boats link the towns along Crete's southwestern coast in the Sfakia region of Hania. Some of the villages are only accessible by sea. Some boats are passenger-only, others carry cars.

Anendyk (www.anendyk.gr) In summer there are daily Anendyk boats between Paleohora, Sougia, Agia Roumeli, Loutro and Hora Sfakion, in both directions. Boats to Gavdos Island leave from Hora Sfakion and Paleo-hora, sometimes stopping in Sougia, Agia Roumeli or Loutro en route. Schedules change seasonally; always check ahead.

Tourist Boats Run excursions to offshore islands and nearby beaches, including Ierapetra to Gaïdouronisi (Hrysi) Island, Agios Nikolaos to Spinalonga Island, Kissamos to the Gramvousa Peninsula (Balos beach), and Paleohora to Elafonisi.

FERRY COMPANIES

Anek Lines (www.anek.gr) To/from Piraeus; one weekly ferry to the Cyclades operated by affiliated Aegeon Pelagos company.

Hellenic Seaways (www.hellenicseaways.gr) High-speed services to the Cyclades.

LANE Lines (www.lane.gr) Long-haul ferries to/from Piraeus from Kissamos.

Minoan Lines (www.minoan.gr) High-speed luxury ferries to/from Piraeus.

Sea Jets (www.seajets.gr) High-speed catamarans to/from the Cyclades.

Taxi Boats Taxi boats operate in several southern coastal towns. These are essentially small speedboats that transport people to places that are difficult to get to by land. Some owners charge a set price for each person, and others charge a flat rate for the boat.

Bus

Buses are the only form of public transport in Crete, but a fairly extensive network makes it relatively easy to travel around the island. Fares are government-regulated and quite reasonable by European standards.

For schedules, which change monthly, and prices, check www.bus-service-crete-ktel.com for western Crete and www.ktelherlas.gr for central and eastern Crete.

There's hourly service along the main northern coastal road and less-frequent buses to the inland villages and towns on the south coast. Buses also go to major tourist attractions, including Knossos, Phaestos, Moni Arkadiou, Moni Preveli, Omalos (for Samaria Gorge) and Hora Sfakion. In summer only there are once-daily buses to famous beaches such as Elafonisi.

Larger towns usually have a central, covered bus station with waiting rooms, toilets and a snack bar. In small towns and villages the 'bus station' may be no more than a stop outside a *kafeneio* (coffee house) or taverna, which often doubles as a ticket office. If not, or if it's closed, you can buy your ticket on the bus.

Car & Motorcycle

Having your own wheels is a great way to explore Crete if you can brave the roads and drivers.

➡ Hire car and motorcycle companies abound.

➡ In remote areas (particularly the south) you'll still find unpaved roads that are only suitable for 4WDs. Take care on narrow and windy mountain roads.

➡ Crete is a large island and the distances, erratic drivers and rough roads can make hard work for motorcyclists.

➡ Beyond the main highways roads are generally badly signposted. When signs exist, they are usually marked in Greek and English (the English phonetic sign follows a few metres after the Greek) except in remote areas. Beware: spelling of place names can vary wildly from names on maps.

➡ Invest in a good map; even the best don't cover all side roads.

Automobile Associations

The Greek automobile association **ELPA** (☑10400; www.elpa.gr) offers reciprocal services to members of national automobile associations with a valid membership card.

Driving Licences

➡ Drivers with an EU driving licence can use it to drive in Crete.

➡ If your driving licence is from outside the EU, you technically need to obtain an International Driving Permit (IDP) before you leave home; check with your local automobile association. In practice, many car-hire companies will accept licences from Europe and North America, but the police may not.

➡ Motorcycle hire requires a licence that shows proficiency to ride the category of bike you wish to rent; this applies to everything from 50cc up.

Fuel & Spare Parts

Fuel is widely available in Crete, but service stations may be closed on Sunday and public holidays. Self-service pumps are not the norm in Greece, nor are credit-card pumps, and out-of-the-way stations don't take plastic at all, so it is always advisable to keep the tank topped up.

Spare parts can be tricky to find, especially if you are in the more remote parts of the island. For a referral to the nearest dealer ask at a service station or call ELPA on ☑10400.

Hire

CAR

Crete has cheaper car hire than many islands due to the level of competition.

➡ All the major international companies have branches at airports and in the towns, but you usually get a better deal if you hire from a local company and negotiate.

➡ By Greek law, rental cars have to be replaced every six years, so most vehicles you rent will be relatively new.

➡ The minimum driving age in Greece is 18 years, but most car hire firms require you to be at least 21, or 23 for larger vehicles.

➡ Rates for car hire vary quite considerably by model, pick-up date and location, but you should be able to get an economy-size vehicle from about €35 per day, plus insurance and taxes. Expect surcharges for additional drivers and one-way hire.

➡ Child or infant safety seats may be hired for about €5 per day and should be reserved at the time of booking.

➡ Most hire cars are manual, so book ahead if you need an automatic car as they are rare and usually more expensive.

➡ Always check what the insurance includes; there are often rough roads or dangerous routes that you can only tackle by renting a 4WD.

➡ Even with a credit card, many hire companies will require a deposit (€120 per day or up).

MOTORCYCLE

➡ Mopeds, motorcycles and scooters are available for hire wherever there are tourists to rent them. Most machines are newish and in good condition. Nonetheless, check the brakes at the earliest opportunity.

➡ You must produce a licence that shows proficiency to ride the category of bike you wish to rent; this applies to everything from 50cc up. British citizens must obtain a Category A licence from the Driver & Vehicle Licensing Agency (www.dft.gov.uk/dvla) in the UK (in most other EU countries separate licences are automatically issued).

➡ Rates start from about €15 per day for a moped or 50cc motorcycle, to €30 per day for a 250cc motorcycle. Out of season these prices drop considerably.

➡ Most motorcycle hire companies include third-party insurance in the price, but it's wise to check this. This insurance will not include medical expenses.

➡ Helmets are compulsory and rental agencies are obliged to offer one as part of the hire deal.

Insurance

Third-party liability insurance is compulsory for all vehicles in Greece, including cars brought in from abroad. When hiring a vehicle, make sure your contract includes adequate liability insurance. Car hire agencies almost never include insurance that covers damage to the vehicle itself, called Collision Damage Waiver (CDW) or Loss Damage Waiver (LDW). It's optional, but driving without it is not recommended. Some credit-card companies cover CDW/LDW for a certain period if you charge the entire rental to your card. Always confirm with your card issuer ahead of time what coverage it provides in Greece.

Road Hazards

The main danger of driving in Crete lies in the local driving culture and rough roads. Road rules are routinely ignored and there is barely any police presence.

➡ Cretan drivers are generally erratic. Expect to be tailgated, honked at and aggressively and illegally overtaken if you move too slowly. Overtaking on bends and ignoring double lines and stop signs is prevalent.

➡ Slower drivers are expected to straddle the narrow service lane and let the traffic pass.

➡ Try to avoid night driving; drink-driving laws are barely

enforced so roads are dangerous.

➡ Road surfaces change unexpectedly when a section of road has succumbed to subsidence or weathering.

➡ In the mountains, expect to stop for herds of sheep or goats on the road.

➡ Many falling rock zones are not signposted, nor hemmed with tarps; keep eyes open for loose rocks on the road.

Road Rules

➡ In Greece, as throughout Continental Europe, you drive on the right and overtake on the left.

➡ On roads, hard shoulders are used for driving, especially when being overtaken. Move over if someone wants to pass you or if you're being tailgated.

➡ Outside built-up areas, traffic on a main road has right of way at intersections. In towns, vehicles coming from the right have right of way. This includes roundabouts – even if you're in the roundabout, you must give way to drivers coming onto the roundabout to your right.

➡ Seat belts must be worn in front seats, and in back seats if the car is fitted with them.

➡ Children under 12 years of age are not allowed in the front seat.

➡ It is compulsory to carry a first-aid kit, fire extinguisher and warning (hazard) triangle, and it is forbidden to carry cans of petrol.

➡ Helmets are compulsory for motorcyclists if the motorcycle is 50cc or more. Police will book you if you're caught without a helmet.

➡ Outside residential areas the speed limit is 120km/h on highways, 90km/h on other roads and 50km/h in built-up areas. The speed limit for motorcycles up to 100cc is 70km/h, and for larger motorcycles, 90km/h. Drivers exceeding the speed limit by 20% are liable to receive a fine of €60; exceeding it by 40% costs €150.

➡ Traffic fines are not paid on the spot – you will be told where to pay.

➡ A blood-alcohol content of 0.05% can incur a fine of €150, and over 0.08% is a criminal offence.

➡ If you are involved in an accident and no one is hurt, the police will not be required to write a report, but it is advisable to go to a nearby police station and explain what happened. You may need a police report for insurance purposes. If an accident involves injury, a driver who does not stop and does not inform the police may face a prison sentence.

➡ Driving in the major cities and small towns is a nightmare of erratic one-way streets, double parking and irregularly enforced parking rules. Cars are not towed away but fines can be expensive.

➡ Designated parking for disabled drivers is a rarity.

Hitching

Hitching is never entirely safe, and we don't recommend it. Travellers who hitch should understand that they are taking a small but potentially serious risk. If you decide to hitch, remember that it's safer to travel in pairs and be sure to inform someone of your intended destination. In Crete you don't hitch with your thumb up as in northern Europe, but with an outstretched hand, palm down to the road.

Getting out of major cities tends to be hard work; hitching is much easier in remote areas. On country roads, it is not unknown for someone to stop and ask if you want a lift even if you haven't asked for one.

Local Transport

Bus

City buses operating around Iraklio, Rethymno and Hania service mostly the residential suburbs and thus are rarely useful for visitors. Tickets are normally bought at *periptera* (kiosks) or from the driver.

Taxi

Taxis are widely available except in remote villages, and are relatively cheap by European standards. Large towns have taxi stands that post a list of prices to outlying destinations, which removes anxiety about overcharging. Otherwise, in cities make sure the meter is used. Rural taxis often do not have meters, so you should always settle on a price before getting in.

Language

The Greek language is believed to be one of the oldest European languages, with an oral tradition of 4000 years and a written tradition of approximately 3000 years. Due to its centuries of influence, Greek constitutes the origin of a large part of the vocabulary of many Indo-European languages (including English), and many of the terms used in science.

Greek is the official language of Greece and co-official language of Cyprus, and is spoken by many emigrant communities throughout the world.

The Greek alphabet is explained on the next page, but if you read the blue pronunciation guides given with each phrase in this chapter as if they were English, you'll be understood. Note that dh is pronounced as 'th' in 'there'; gh is a softer, slightly throaty version of 'g'; and kh is a throaty sound like the 'ch' in the Scottish 'loch'. All Greek words of two or more syllables have an acute accent ('), which indicates where the stress falls. In our pronunciation guides, stressed syllables are in italics.

In Greek, all nouns, articles and adjectives are either masculine, feminine or neuter – in this chapter these forms are included where necessary, separated with a slash and indicated with 'm/f/n'.

BASICS

| Hello. | Γειά σας. | ya·sas (polite) |
| | Γειά σου. | ya·su (informal) |

WANT MORE?

For in-depth language information and handy phrases, check out Lonely Planet's *Greek Phrasebook*. You'll find it at **shop.lonelyplanet.com**, or you can buy Lonely Planet's iPhone phrasebooks at the Apple App Store.

Good morning.	Καλημέρα.	ka·li me·ra
Good evening.	Καλησπέρα.	ka·li spe·ra
Goodbye.	Αντίο.	an·di·o
Yes./No.	Ναι./Όχι.	ne/o·hi
Please.	Παρακαλώ.	pa·ra·ka·lo
Thank you.	Ευχαριστώ.	ef·ha·ri·sto
That's fine./ You're welcome.	Παρακαλώ.	pa·ra·ka·lo
Sorry.	Συγγνώμη.	sigh·no·mi

What's your name?
Πώς σας λένε;   pos sas le·ne

My name is ...
Με λένε ...   me le·ne ...

Do you speak English?
Μιλάτε αγγλικά;   mi·la·te an·gli·ka

I (don't) understand.
(Δεν) καταλαβαίνω.   (dhen) ka·ta·la·ve·no

ACCOMMODATION

campsite	χώρος για κάμπινγκ	kho·ros yia kam·ping
hotel	ξενοδοχείο	kse·no·dho·khi·o
youth hostel	γιουθ χόστελ	yuth kho·stel

a ... room	ένα ... δωμάτιο	e·na ... dho·ma·ti·o
single	μονόκλινο	mo·no·kli·no
double	δίκλινο	dhi·kli·no

How much is it ...?	Πόσο κάνει ...;	po·so ka·ni ...
per night	τη βραδιά	ti·vra·dhya
per person	το άτομο	to a·to·mo

air-con	έρκοντίσιον	er·kon·*di*·si·on
bathroom	μπάνιο	*ba*·nio
fan	ανεμιστήρας	a·ne·mi·*sti*·ras
TV	τηλεόραση	ti·le·o·ra·si
window	παράθυρο	pa·*ra*·thi·ro

DIRECTIONS

Where is ...?
Πού είναι ...; pu *i*·ne ...

What's the address?
Ποια είναι η διεύθυνση; pia *i*·ne i dhi·*ef*·thin·si

Can you show me (on the map)?
Μπορείς να μου δείξεις bo·*ris* na mu *dhik*·sis
(στο χάρτη); (sto *khar*·ti)

Turn left.
Στρίψτε αριστερά. strips·te a·ri·ste·*ra*

Turn right.
Στρίψτε δεξιά. strips·te dhe·*ksia*

at the next corner
στην επόμενη γωνία stin e·*po*·me·ni gho·*ni*·a

at the traffic lights
στα φώτα sta *fo*·ta

behind	πίσω	*pi*·so
in front of	μπροστά	bro·*sta*
far	μακριά	ma·kri·*a*
near (to)	κοντά	kon·*da*
next to	δίπλα	*dhi*·pla
opposite	απέναντι	a·*pe*·nan·di
straight ahead	ολο ευθεία.	o·lo ef·*thi*·a

EATING & DRINKING

a table for ...	Ενα τραπέζι για ...	e·na tra·*pe*·zi ya ...
(two) people	(δύο) άτομα	(*dhi*·o) a·to·ma
(eight) o'clock	στις (οχτώ)	stis (okh·*to*)

I don't eat ...	Δεν τρώγω ...	dhen tro·gho ...
fish	ψάρι	psa·ri
(red) meat	(κόκκινο) κρέας	(*ko*·ki·no) kre·as
peanuts	φυστίκια	fi·*sti*·kia
poultry	πουλερικά	pu·le·ri·*ka*

GREEK ALPHABET

The Greek alphabet has 24 letters, shown below in their upper- and lower-case forms. Be aware that some letters look like English letters but are pronounced very differently, such as **B**, which is pronounced v; and **P**, pronounced r. As in English, how letters are pronounced is also influenced by the way they are combined, for example the **ou** combination is pronounced u as in 'put', and **οι** is pronounced ee as in 'feet'.

Α α	a	as in 'father'		Ξ ξ	x	as in 'ox'
Β β	v	as in 'vine'		Ο ο	o	as in 'hot'
Γ γ	gh	a softer, throaty 'g', or		Π π	p	as in 'pup'
	y	as in 'yes'		Ρ ρ	r	as in 'road',
Δ δ	dh	as in 'there'				slightly trilled
Ε ε	e	as in 'egg'		Σ σ, ς	s	as in 'sand'
Ζ ζ	z	as in 'zoo'		Τ τ	t	as in 'tap'
Η η	i	as in 'feet'		Υ υ	i	as in 'feet'
Θ θ	th	as in 'throw'		Φ φ	f	as in 'find'
Ι ι	i	as in 'feet'		Χ χ	kh	as the 'ch' in the
Κ κ	k	as in 'kite'				Scottish 'loch', or
Λ λ	l	as in 'leg'			h	like a rough 'h'
Μ μ	m	as in 'man'		Ψ ψ	ps	as in 'lapse'
Ν ν	n	as in 'net'		Ω ω	o	as in 'hot'

Note that the letter **Σ** has two forms for the lower case – **σ** and **ς**. The second one is used at the end of words. The Greek question mark is represented with the English equivalent of a semicolon (;).

What would you recommend?
Τι θα συνιστούσες;   ti tha si·ni·*stu*·ses

What's in that dish?
Τι περιέχει αυτό το   ti pe·ri·e·hi af·*to* to
φαγητό;   fa·ghi·*to*

That was delicious.
Ηταν νοστιμότατο!   *i*·tan no·sti·*mo*·ta·to

Cheers!
Εις υγείαν!   is i·*yi*·an

Please bring the bill.
Το λογαριασμό,   to lo·ghar·ya·*zmo*
παρακαλώ.   pa·ra·ka·*lo*

Key Words

appetisers	ορεκτικά	o·rek·ti·*ka*
bar	μπαρ	bar
beef	βοδινό	vo·dhi·*no*
beer	μπύρα	*bi*·ra
bottle	μπουκάλι	bu·*ka*·li
bowl	μπωλ	bol
bread	ψωμί	pso·*mi*
breakfast	πρόγευμα	*pro*·yev·ma
cafe	καφετέρια	ka·fe·*te*·ri·a
cheese	τυρί	ti·*ri*
chicken	κοτόπουλο	ko·*to*·pu·lo
coffee	καφές	ka·*fes*
cold	κρυωμένος	kri·o·*me*·nos
cream	κρέμα	*kre*·ma
delicatessen	ντελικατέσεν	de·li·ka·*te*·sen
desserts	επιδόρπια	e·pi·*dhor*·pi·a
dinner	δείπνο	*dhip*·no
egg	αυγό	av·*gho*
fish	ψάρι	*psa*·ri
food	φαγητό	fa·yi·*to*
fork	πιρούνι	pi·*ru*·ni
fruit	φρούτα	*fru*·ta
glass	ποτήρι	po·*ti*·ri
grocery store	οπωροπωλείο	o·po·ro·po·*li*·o
herb	βότανο	*vo*·ta·no
high chair	καρέκλα	ka·*re*·kla
	για μωρά	yia mo·*ra*
hot	ζεστός	ze·*stos*
juice	χυμός	hi·*mos*
knife	μαχαίρι	ma·*he*·ri
lamb	αρνί	ar·*ni*
lunch	μεσημεριανό	me·si·me·ria·no
	φαγητό	fa·yi·*to*
main courses	κύρια φαγητά	*ki*·ri·a fa·yi·*ta*
market	αγορά	a·*gho*·ra

KEY PATTERNS

To get by in Greek, mix and match these simple patterns with words of your choice:

When's (the next bus)?
Πότε είναι   *po*·te *i*·ne
(το επόμενο   (to e·*po*·me·no
λεωφορείο);   le·o·fo·*ri*·o)

Where's (the station)?
Πού είναι (ο σταθμός);   pu *i*·ne (o stath·*mos*)

I'm looking for (Ampfilohos).
Ψάχνω για   *psakh*·no yia
(το Αμφίλοχος).   (to am·*fi*·lo·khos)

Do you have (a local map)?
Εχετε οδικό   e·he·te o·dhi·*ko*
(τοπικό χάρτη);   (to·pi·*ko* khar·ti)

Is there a (lift)?
Υπάρχει (ασανσέρ);   i·*par*·hi (a·san·*ser*)

Can I (try it on)?
Μπορώ να   bo·*ro* na
(το προβάρω);   (to pro·*va*·ro)

I have (a reservation).
Εχω (κλείσει   e·kho (*kli*·si
δωμάτιο).   dho·*ma*·ti·o)

I'd like (to hire a car).
Θα ήθελα (να   tha *i*·the·la (na
ενοικιάσω ένα   e·ni·ki·a·so e·na
αυτοκίνητο).   af·to·*ki*·ni·to)

menu	μενού	me·*nu*
milk	γάλα	*gha*·la
nut	καρύδι	ka·*ri*·dhi
oil	λάδι	*la*·dhi
pepper	πιπέρι	pi·*pe*·ri
plate	πιάτο	*pia*·to
pork	χοιρινό	hi·ri·*no*
restaurant	εστιατόριο	e·sti·a·*to*·ri·o
salt	αλάτι	a·*la*·ti
soft drink	αναψυκτικό	a·nap·sik·ti·*ko*
spoon	κουτάλι	ku·*ta*·li
sugar	ζάχαρη	za·kha·ri
tea	τσάι	*tsa*·i
vegetable	λαχανικά	la·kha·ni·*ka*
vegetarian	χορτοφάγος	khor·to·*fa*·ghos
vinegar	ξύδι	*ksi*·dhi
water	νερό	ne·*ro*
(red) wine	(κόκκινο) κρασί	(*ko*·ki·no) kra·*si*
(white) wine	(άσπρο) κρασί	(*a*·spro) kra·*si*
with/without	με/χωρίς	me/kho·ris

EMERGENCIES

Help!	Βοήθεια!	vo·i·thya
Go away!	Φύγε!	fi·ye
I'm lost	Εχω χαθεί.	e·kho kha·thi
There's been an accident.	Εγινε ατύχημα.	ey·i·ne a·ti·hi·ma

Call ...!	Φωνάξτε ...!	fo·nak·ste ...
a doctor	ένα γιατρό	e·na yi·a·tro
the police	την αστυνομία	tin a·sti·no·mi·a

I'm ill.
Είμαι άρρωστος.   i·me a·ro·stos
It hurts here.
Πονάει εδώ.   po·na·i e·dho
I'm allergic to (antibiotics).
Είμαι αλλεργικός/   i·me a·ler·yi·kos/
αλλεργική   a·ler·yi·ki
(στα αντιβιωτικά)   (sta an·di·vi·o·ti·ka) (m/f)

NUMBERS

1	ένας/μία	e·nas/ mi·a (m/f)
	ένα	e·na (n)
2	δύο	dhi·o
3	τρεις	tris (m&f)
	τρία	tri·a (n)
4	τέσσερεις	te·se·ris (m&f)
	τέσσερα	te·se·ra (n)
5	πέντε	pen·de
6	έξη	e·xi
7	επτά	ep·ta
8	οχτώ	oh·to
9	εννέα	e·ne·a
10	δέκα	dhe·ka
20	είκοσι	ik·o·si
30	τριάντα	tri·an·da
40	σαράντα	sa·ran·da
50	πενήντα	pe·nin·da
60	εξήντα	ek·sin·da
70	εβδομήντα	ev·dho·min·da
80	ογδόντα	ogh·dhon·da
90	ενενήντα	e·ne·nin·da
100	εκατό	e·ka·to
1000	χίλιοι/χίλιες	hi·li·i/hi·li·ez (m/f)
	χίλια	hi·li·a (n)

SHOPPING & SERVICES

I'd like to buy ...
Θέλω ν' αγοράσω ...   the·lo na·gho·ra·so ...
I'm just looking.
Απλώς κοιτάζω.   ap·los ki·ta·zo
May I see it?
Μπορώ να το δω;   bo·ro na to dho
I don't like it.
Δεν μου αρέσει.   dhen mu a·re·si
How much is it?
Πόσο κάνει;   po·so ka·ni
It's too expensive.
Είναι πολύ ακριβό.   i·ne po·li a·kri·vo
Can you lower the price?
Μπορείς να κατεβάσεις   bo·ris na ka·te·va·sis
την τιμή;   tin ti·mi

ATM	αυτόματη μηχανή χρημάτων	af·to·ma·ti mi·kha·ni khri·ma·ton
bank	τράπεζα	tra·pe·za
credit card	πιστωτική κάρτα	pi·sto·ti·ki kar·ta
internet cafe	καφενείο διαδικτύου	ka·fe·ni·o dhi·a·dhik·ti·u
mobile phone	κινητό	ki·ni·to
post office	ταχυδρομείο	ta·hi·dhro·mi·o
toilet	τουαλέτα	tu·a·le·ta
tourist office	τουριστικό γραφείο	tu·ri·sti·ko ghra·fi·o

TIME & DATES

What time is it?	Τι ώρα είναι;	ti o·ra i·ne
It's (2 o'clock).	είναι (δύο η ώρα).	i·ne (dhi·o i o·ra)
It's half past (10).	(Δέκα) και μισή.	(dhe·ka) ke mi·si

today	σήμερα	si·me·ra
tomorrow	αύριο	av·ri·o
yesterday	χθες	hthes
morning	πρωί	pro·i
(this) afternoon	(αυτό το) απόγευμα	(af·to to) a·po·yev·ma
evening	βράδυ	vra·dhi

Monday	Δευτέρα	dhef·te·ra
Tuesday	Τρίτη	tri·ti
Wednesday	Τετάρτη	te·tar·ti
Thursday	Πέμπτη	pemp·ti
Friday	Παρασκευή	pa·ras·ke·vi
Saturday	Σάββατο	sa·va·to
Sunday	Κυριακή	ky·ri·a·ki

January	Ιανουάριος	ia·nu·ar·i·os
February	Φεβρουάριος	fev·ru·ar·i·os
March	Μάρτιος	mar·ti·os
April	Απρίλιος	a·pri·li·os
May	Μάιος	mai·os
June	Ιούνιος	i·u·ni·os
July	Ιούλιος	i·u·li·os
August	Αύγουστος	av·ghus·tos
September	Σεπτέμβριος	sep·tem·vri·os
October	Οκτώβριος	ok·to·vri·os
November	Νοέμβριος	no·em·vri·os
December	Δεκέμβριος	dhe·kem·vri·os

Signs

ΕΙΣΟΔΟΣ	Entry
ΕΞΟΔΟΣ	Exit
ΠΛΗΡΟΦΟΡΙΕΣ	Information
ΑΝΟΙΧΤΟ	Open
ΚΛΕΙΣΤΟ	Closed
ΑΠΑΓΟΡΕΥΕΤΑΙ	Prohibited
ΑΣΤΥΝΟΜΙΑ	Police
ΑΣΤΥΝΟΜΙΚΟΣ ΣΤΑΘΜΟΣ	Police Station
ΓΥΝΑΙΚΩΝ	Toilets (Women)
ΑΝΔΡΩΝ	Toilets (Men)

cancelled	ακυρώθηκε	a·ki·ro·thi·ke
delayed	καθυστέρησε	ka·thi·ste·ri·se
platform	πλατφόρμα	plat·for·ma
ticket office	εκδοτήριο εισιτηρίων	ek·dho·ti·ri·o i·si·ti·ri·on
timetable	δρομολόγιο	dhro·mo·lo·gio
train station	σταθμός τρένου	stath·mos tre·nu

TRANSPORT

Public Transport

boat	πλοίο	pli·o
city bus	αστικό	a·sti·ko
intercity bus	λεωφορείο	le·o·fo·ri·o
plane	αεροπλάνο	ae·ro·pla·no
train	τραίνο	tre·no

Where do I buy a ticket?
Πού αγοράζω εισιτήριο; pu a·gho·ra·zo i·si·ti·ri·o

I want to go to ...
Θέλω να πάω στο/στη ... the·lo na pao sto/sti...

What time does it leave?
Τι ώρα φεύγει; ti o·ra fev·yi

Does it stop at (Iraklio)?
Σταματάει στο sta·ma·ta·i sto
(Ηράκλειο); (i·ra·kli·o)

I'd like to get off at (Iraklio).
Θα ήθελα να κατεβώ tha i·the·la na ka·te·vo
στο (Ηράκλειο). sto (i·ra·kli·o)

I'd like (a) ...	Θα ήθελα (ένα) ...	tha i·the·la (e·na) ...
1st class	πρώτη θέση	pro·ti the·si
2nd class	δεύτερη θέση	def·te·ri the·si
one-way ticket	απλό εισιτήριο	a·plo i·si·ti·ri·o
return ticket	εισιτήριο με επιστροφή	i·si·ti·ri·o me e·pi·stro·fi

Driving & Cycling

I'd like to hire a ...	Θα ήθελα να νοικιάσω ...	tha i·the·la na ni·ki·a·so ...
car	ένα αυτοκίνητο	e·na af·ti·ki·ni·to
4WD	ένα τέσσερα επί τέσσερα	e·na tes·se·ra e·pi tes·se·ra
jeep	ένα τζιπ	e·na tzip
motorbike	μια μοτοσυκλέττα	mya mo·to·si·klet·ta
bicycle	ένα ποδήλατο	e·na po·dhi·la·to

Do I need a helmet?
Χρειάζομαι κράνος; khri·a·zo·me kra·nos

Is this the road to ...?
Αυτός είναι ο af·tos i·ne o
δρόμος για ... dhro·mos ya ...

Can I park here?
Μπορώ να παρκάρω bo·ro na par·ka·ro
εδώ; e·dho

The car/motorbike has broken down (at ...).
Το αυτοκίνητο/ to af·to·ki·ni·to/
η μοτοσυκλέττα i mo·to·si·klet·ta
χάλασε στο ... kha·la·se sto ...

I have a flat tyre.
Έπαθα λάστιχο. e·pa·tha la·sti·cho

I've run out of petrol.
Έμεινα από βενζίνη. e·mi·na a·po ven·zi·ni

GLOSSARY

For culinary terms, see Eat & Drink Like a Local (p41).

Achaean civilisation – see *Mycenaean civilisation*

acropolis – highest point of an ancient city

agia (f), agios (m), agii (pl) – saint(s)

agora – commercial area of an ancient city; shopping precinct in modern Greece

agrimi – endemic Cretan animal with large horns similar to a wild goat; also known as the *kri-kri*

amphora – large two-handled vase in which wine or oil was kept

basilica – early Christian church

bouzouki – stringed lute-like instrument associated with *rembetika* music

Byzantine Empire – characterised by the merging of Hellenistic culture and Christianity and named after Byzantium, the city on the Bosphorus that became the capital of the Roman Empire in AD 324; when the Roman Empire was formally divided in AD 395, Rome went into decline and the eastern capital, renamed Constantinople after Emperor Constantine I, flourished; the Byzantine Empire (324 BC–AD 1453) dissolved after the fall of Constantinople to the Turks in 1453

capital – top of a column

Classical period – era in which the Greek city-states reached the height of their wealth and power after the defeat of the Persians in the 5th century BC; the Classical period (480–323 BC) ended with the decline of the city-states as a result of the Peloponnesian Wars, and the expansionist aspirations of Philip II, King of Macedon (r 359–336 BC) and his son, Alexander the Great (r 336–323 BC)

Corinthian – order of Greek architecture recognisable by columns with bell-shaped capitals with sculpted elaborate ornaments based on acanthus leaves; see also *Doric* and *Ionic*

dark age (1200–800 BC) – period in which Greece was under Dorian rule

domatio (s), domatia (pl) – room, often in a private home; a cheap form of accommodation

Dorians – Hellenic warriors who invaded Greece around 1200 BC, demolishing the city-states and destroying the *Mycenaean civilisation*; heralded Greece's *dark age*, when the artistic and cultural advancements of the Mycenaean and *Minoan* civilisations were abandoned; the Dorians later developed into land-holding aristocrats, encouraging the resurgence of independent city-states led by wealthy aristocrats

Doric – order of Greek architecture characterised by a column that has no base, a fluted shaft and a relatively plain capital, when compared with the flourishes evident on *Ionic* and *Corinthian* capitals

Ellada or Ellas – see *Hellas*

ELPA – Elliniki Leschi Aftokinitou kai Periigiseon; Greek motoring and touring club

ELTA – Ellinika Tahydromia; Greek post office organisation

EOS – Ellinikos Orivatikos Syllogos; the association of Greek Mountaineering Clubs

EOT – Ellinikos Organismos Tourismou; main tourist office (has offices in most major towns), known abroad as *GNTO* (Greek National Tourist Organisation)

estiatorio – restaurant serving ready-made food as well as à la carte

Geometric period – the period (1200–800 BC) characterised by pottery decorated with geometric designs; sometimes referred to as Greece's *dark age*

GNTO – Greek National Tourist Organisation; see also *EOT*

Hellas – the Greek name for Greece; also known as Ellada or Ellas

Hellenistic period – prosperous, influential period (323–146 BC)

of Greek civilisation ushered in by Alexander the Great's empire-building and lasting until the Roman sacking of Corinth

hora – main town, usually on an island

Ionic – order of Greek architecture characterised by a column with truncated flutes and capitals with ornaments resembling scrolls; see also *Doric* and *Corinthian*

kastro – walled-in town; also describes a fortress or castle

Koine – Greek language used in pre-Byzantine times; the language of the church liturgy

kouros – male statue of the Archaic period, characterised by a stiff body posture and enigmatic smile

kri-kri – endemic Cretan animal with large horns similar to a wild goat; also known as the *agrimi*

KTEL – Kino Tamio Eispraxeon Leoforion; national bus cooperative, which runs all long-distance bus services

leoforos – avenue

libation – in ancient Greece, wine or food that was offered to the gods

Linear A – Minoan script; so far undeciphered

Linear B – Mycenaean script; has been deciphered

lyra – small violin-like instrument or lyre, played on the knee; common in Cretan and Pontian music

mantinadha (s), mandinadhes (pl) – a style of traditional Cretan rhyming couplets

megaron – central room or quarters of a Mycenaean palace

meltemi – dry northerly wind that blows throughout much of Greece in the summer

mezedhopoleio – restaurant specialising in *mezedhes*

Minoan civilisation – Bronze Age (3000–1200 BC) culture of Crete named after the mythical King Minos, and characterised by pottery and metalwork of great beauty and artisanship; it had three periods: Protopalatial (3400–2100 BC), Neopalatial (2100–1580 BC) and Postpalatial (1580–1200 BC)

mitata – round stone shepherd's huts

moni – monastery or convent

Mycenaean civilisation – first great civilisation (1900–1100 BC) of the Greek mainland, characterised by powerful independent city-states ruled by kings; also known as the *Achaean civilisation*

New Democracy – Nea Dimodratia; conservative political party

necropolis – literally 'city of the dead'; ancient cemetery

nisi – island

nymphaeum – in ancient Greece, building containing a fountain and often dedicated to nymphs

odeion – ancient Greek indoor theatre

odos – street

OTE – Organismos Tilepikoinonion Ellados; Greece's major telephone carrier

ouzerie – place that serves ouzo and light snacks

Panagia – Mother of God or Virgin Mary; name frequently used for churches

paralia – waterfront

pediment – triangular section, often filled with sculpture above the columns, found at the front and back of a classical Greek temple

periptero (s), periptera (pl) – street kiosk

peristyle – columns surrounding a building, usually a temple or courtyard

pithos (s), pithoi (pl) – large Minoan storage jar or urn

plateia – square

propylon (s), propylaia (pl) – elaborately built main entrance to an ancient city or sanctuary; a propylon had one gateway and a propylaia more than one

prytaneion – the administrative centre of the city-state

rembetika – blues songs, commonly associated with the underworld of the 1920s

rhyton – another name for a *libation* vessel

rizitika – traditional, patriotic songs of western Crete

stoa – long colonnaded building, usually in an *agora*; used as a meeting place and shelter in ancient Greece

taverna – the most common type of traditional restaurant that serves food and wine

tholos – Mycenaean tomb shaped like a beehive

Behind the Scenes

SEND US YOUR FEEDBACK

We love to hear from travellers – your comments keep us on our toes and help make our books better. Our well-travelled team reads every word on what you loved or loathed about this book. Although we cannot reply individually to postal submissions, we always guarantee that your feedback goes straight to the appropriate authors, in time for the next edition. Each person who sends us information is thanked in the next edition – the most useful submissions are rewarded with a selection of digital PDF chapters.

Visit **lonelyplanet.com/contact** to submit your updates and suggestions or to ask for help. Our award-winning website also features inspirational travel stories, news and discussions.

Note: We may edit, reproduce and incorporate your comments in Lonely Planet products such as guidebooks, websites and digital products, so let us know if you don't want your comments reproduced or your name acknowledged. For a copy of our privacy policy visit lonelyplanet.com/privacy.

OUR READERS

Many thanks to the travellers who used the last edition and wrote to us with helpful hints, useful advice and interesting anecdotes:

Alexander Roc, Barbara Santos, Clare Hannah, Diana Loch, Elena Carati, Giles Moon, Heather Lyons, Jacquelien Meijer, Keren Lupu, Marcel du Chatinier, Marcos Charalambous, Margaret Chappell, Marianne Skovsted, Morten Ziersen, Paul Barker, Paul Finn, Paul Ormrod, Peter Golda, Regine Haensel, Robin Smit, Robin van Beek, Roy Milani, Seraphim Schuchter, Takashi Kishi

AUTHOR THANKS

Alexis Averbuck

Boundless gratitude to Alexandra Stamopoulou for her always-inspiring tips and overall INSPIRATION. She travels with me everywhere. Ryan Ver Berkmoes was, yet again, a peachy road companion. Thank you to Ramona for an insider's take on Gavdos. Big cheer for Team Crete: Brana, Korina, Kate and Richard, who made this project a joy. And *efharisto poli* to all of the people who welcomed me so warmly around Crete – you are the reason I really love the place!

Kate Armstrong

A special Cretan *efharisto* to Brana for the unexpected opportunity to visit this gem. To all those in Iraklion who extended so much of the Cretan *filoxenia*, especially Fondas, Manolis, Gunnar, Noi and Lefteris and Antonis of Roadside Travel Bookshop. To my wonderful Grecophile fellow authors, Alexis (coordinator extraordinaire), Richard and Korina. To Di Miller in London for her kindness. And finally, to Chris, who constantly rearranges his life around me.

Korina Miller

An enormous thank you to Kirk and my mum and dad for minding the fort while I was away and making it possible for me to take on this project. Thank you to my fabulous daughters, Monique and Simone, for letting me work and also encouraging me to take breaks. Thank you to Brana at Lonely Planet for her support and to my coauthors for their insights and camaraderie. A warm *efharisto* to all of the people I met on the road – both locals and travellers – who shared their stories, knowledge and enthusiasm for Greece. And thanks to Bing the loyal coonhound for keeping me company while I burned the midnight oil.

Richard Waters

Special thanks to Magdalena at Byron, and all of the folk in Lasithi who aided my way.

THIS BOOK

This 6th edition of Lonely Planet's *Crete* guidebook was researched and written by Alexis Averbuck, Kate Armstrong, Korina Miller and Richard Waters. The previous edition was written by Andrea Schulte-Peevers, Chris Deliso and Des Hannigan. This guidebook was produced by the following:

Destination Editor
Branislava Vladisavljevic

Coordinating Editor
Gabrielle Innes

Product Editors Carolyn Boicos, Kate Mathews

Senior Cartographer
Valentina Kremenchutskaya

Book Designer Wibowo Rusli

Assisting Editors Jodie Martire, Anne Mulvaney

Cover Researcher Naomi Parker

Thanks to Andi Jones, Karyn Noble, Gabrielle Stefanos, Gina Tsarouhas, Tony Wheeler, Amanda Williamson, Sofia Zournatzidi

ACKNOWLEDGMENTS

Climate map data adapted from Peel MC, Finlayson BL & McMahon TA (2007) 'Updated World Map of the Köppen-Geiger Climate Classification', Hydrology and Earth System Sciences, 11, 1633¬44.

Illustration pp158–9 by Javier Martinez Zarracina.

Cover photograph: Moni Preveli, Rethymno, Markus Lange/Corbis.

BEHIND THE SCENES

Index

Map Legend

Sights

- Beach
- Bird Sanctuary
- Buddhist
- Castle/Palace
- Christian
- Confucian
- Hindu
- Islamic
- Jain
- Jewish
- Monument
- Museum/Gallery/Historic Building
- Ruin
- Shinto
- Sikh
- Taoist
- Winery/Vineyard
- Zoo/Wildlife Sanctuary
- Other Sight

Activities, Courses & Tours

- Bodysurfing
- Diving
- Canoeing/Kayaking
- Course/Tour
- Sento Hot Baths/Onsen
- Skiing
- Snorkelling
- Surfing
- Swimming/Pool
- Walking
- Windsurfing
- Other Activity

Sleeping

- Sleeping
- Camping

Eating

- Eating

Drinking & Nightlife

- Drinking & Nightlife
- Cafe

Entertainment

- Entertainment

Shopping

- Shopping

Information

- Bank
- Embassy/Consulate
- Hospital/Medical
- Internet
- Police
- Post Office
- Telephone
- Toilet
- Tourist Information
- Other Information

Geographic

- Beach
- Gate
- Hut/Shelter
- Lighthouse
- Lookout
- Mountain/Volcano
- Oasis
- Park
- Pass
- Picnic Area
- Waterfall

Population

- Capital (National)
- Capital (State/Province)
- City/Large Town
- Town/Village

Transport

- Airport
- Border crossing
- Bus
- Cable car/Funicular
- Cycling
- Ferry
- Metro station
- Monorail
- Parking
- Petrol station
- S-Bahn/S-train/Subway station
- Taxi
- T-bane/Tunnelbana station
- Train station/Railway
- Tram
- Tube station
- U-Bahn/Underground station
- Other Transport

Note: Not all symbols displayed above appear on the maps in this book

Routes

- Tollway
- Freeway
- Primary
- Secondary
- Tertiary
- Lane
- Unsealed road
- Road under construction
- Plaza/Mall
- Steps
- Tunnel
- Pedestrian overpass
- Walking Tour
- Walking Tour detour
- Path/Walking Trail

Boundaries

- International
- State/Province
- Disputed
- Regional/Suburb
- Marine Park
- Cliff
- Wall

Hydrography

- River, Creek
- Intermittent River
- Canal
- Water
- Dry/Salt/Intermittent Lake
- Reef

Areas

- Airport/Runway
- Beach/Desert
- Cemetery (Christian)
- Cemetery (Other)
- Glacier
- Mudflat
- Park/Forest
- Sight (Building)
- Sportsground
- Swamp/Mangrove

OUR STORY

A beat-up old car, a few dollars in the pocket and a sense of adventure. In 1972 that's all Tony and Maureen Wheeler needed for the trip of a lifetime – across Europe and Asia overland to Australia. It took several months, and at the end – broke but inspired – they sat at their kitchen table writing and stapling together their first travel guide, *Across Asia on the Cheap*. Within a week they'd sold 1500 copies. Lonely Planet was born. Today, Lonely Planet has offices in Franklin, London, Melbourne, Oakland, Beijing and Delhi, with more than 600 staff and writers. We share Tony's belief that 'a great guidebook should do three things: inform, educate and amuse'.

OUR WRITERS

Alexis Averbuck

Coordinating Author; Hania Alexis lives in Hydra, Greece, and makes any excuse she can to travel the isolated back roads of her adopted land. While she is committed to dispelling the stereotype that Greece is simply a string of sandy beaches, she admits that Crete's pink sands blow her mind. A lover of local cuisine, Alexis enjoys sampling the amazing food of Crete, and exploring villages in search of delectable treats. She was overjoyed to cover Hania again; it's one of her favourite cities in Greece. Alexis also wrote the Plan Your Trip section (excluding Outdoor Activities and Travel with Children), Best of Crete, Crete Today, History, The Cretan Way of Life, The Arts, and the Survival Guide section. A travel writer for two decades, Alexis has lived in Antarctica for a year, crossed the Pacific by sailboat and written books on her journeys through Asia and the Americas. She's also a painter – visit www.alexisaverbuck.com.

Kate Armstrong

Iraklio Aeons ago, Kate visited Crete to hike the Samaria Gorge and visit Knossos full of post–Fine Arts 101 knowledge. Years later she returned for Lonely Planet to the land of *filoxenia*. In Iraklio, she gorged herself on sheep's-milk yoghurt and honey, manoeuvred her hire car down precipitous winding roads, hiked through magnificent gorges and chatted with the delightful souls of this special island. Not to mention discovered magic in the island's incredible 'piles of rock'. Follow her adventures at www.katearmstrongtravelwriter.com and @nomaditis.

Korina Miller

Rethymno Korina first ventured to Greece as a backpacking teenager, sleeping on ferry decks and hiking in the mountains. Since then, she's found herself drawn back to soak up the timelessness of the old towns and drink coffee with locals in seaside *kafeneia*. Korina grew up on Vancouver Island and has been exploring the globe independently since she was 16, visiting or living in 36 countries and picking up a degree in Communications and Canadian Studies and an MA in Migration Studies en route. Korina has written nearly 40 titles for Lonely Planet and also works as a children's writing coach.

Richard Waters

Lasithi Richard is an award-winning journalist who writes about Greece for the *Daily Telegraph*, the *Independent* and *Sunday Times Travel Magazine*. He lives with his family in the Cotswolds but his spiritual home is the islands of Greece, where he first went as a boy in 1974. Since then he has been over 20 times, and is most at home sitting in a *kafeneio* talking about myths, digging into freshly caught calamari, and island hopping. As ever his admiration goes out to the people of Greece, who despite unimaginably difficult times remain among the friendliest on the planet. Richard also wrote the Outdoor Activities, Travel with Children, Minoan Art & Culture and Nature & Wildlife chapters.

Published by Lonely Planet Publications Pty Ltd
ABN 36 005 607 983
6th edition – Feb 2016
ISBN 978 1 74220 755 1
© Lonely Planet 2016   Photographs © as indicated 2016
10 9 8 7 6 5 4 3 2 1
Printed in China